Discovery

An Introduction to Writing
Third Edition
Annotated Instructor's Edition

William J. Kelly
Bristol Community College

Deborah L. Lawton
Bristol Community College

PEARSON
Longman

New York   San Francisco   Boston
London   Toronto   Sydney   Tokyo   Singapore   Madrid
Mexico City   Munich   Paris   Cape Town   Hong Kong   Montreal

Dedication

To my brothers, Charles and Paul, with love.
—D. L. L.

To Flo and Leo for their love, support, and generosity in sharing
one of their treasures—their daughter, Michelle—with me.
—W. J. K.

VICE PRESIDENT AND EDITOR-IN-CHIEF: Joseph Terry
SENIOR ACQUISITIONS EDITOR: Steven Rigolosi
DEVELOPMENT MANAGER: Janet Lanphier
DEVELOPMENT EDITOR: Susan Messer
SENIOR MARKETING MANAGER: Melanie Craig
SENIOR SUPPLEMENTS EDITOR: Donna Campion
MEDIA SUPPLEMENTS EDITOR: Nancy Garcia
PRODUCTION MANAGER: Donna DeBenedictis
PROJECT COORDINATION, TEXT DESIGN, AND ELECTRONIC PAGE MAKEUP: Elm Street Publishing Services, Inc.
SENIOR COVER DESIGNER/MANAGER: Nancy Danahy
COVER ILLUSTRATION: Map art © 2003 Laszlo Kubinyi c/o theispot.com
PHOTO RESEARCHER: Photosearch, Inc.
MANUFACTURING MANAGER: Dennis J. Para
PRINTER AND BINDER: Webcrafters, Inc.
COVER PRINTER: Coral Graphic Services, Inc.

For permission to use copyrighted material, grateful acknowledgment is made to the copyright holders on p. 531, which is hereby made part of this copyright page.

Library of Congress Cataloging-in-Publication Data

Kelly, William J. (William Jude) 1953–
    Discovery: An Introduction to Writing / William J. Kelly, Deborah L. Lawton.—3rd ed.
        p. cm.
    Includes bibliographical references and index.
    ISBN 0-321-10379-3 (alk. paper)
        1. English language—Rhetoric. 2. English language—Grammar—Problems, exercises, etc.
        3. College readers. 4. Report writing. I.
Lawton, Deborah L. II. Title.

PE1408.K4735 2004
808'.042—dc21   2003046366

Please visit our Web site at http://www.ablongman.com/kelly

ISBN 0-321-10379-3 (Student Edition)
ISBN 0-321-10378-5 (Annotated Instructor's Edition)

1 2 3 4 5 6 7 8 9 10—WC—06 05 04 03

Detailed Contents

4 Revising: Refining Your Draft   61

5 Moving from Paragraph to Essay   96

Part Two Effective Sentences: Constructing Meaning   119

6 Subjects and Verbs   120

7 Sentence Fragments   140

Part Three   Verbs: Conveying Action and Time   213

Part Four   Sentence Elements: Striving for Precision   299

Part Five Consistency Workshop: Aiming for Correctness 377

Part Six   Discovering Connections through Reading   473

Appendix: Tips for ESL Writers   515

Preface

A blank page is a discovery waiting to be made. When you write on that page, you begin a journey through the world of ideas. Think of writing as a means of transportation, as a vehicle that can transport you and connect you to the rest of the world.

Writing unlocks your creativity and provides the opportunity for you to apply your reserves of knowledge on a variety of subjects. Writing also gives you the means to exchange information and react to what you learn from others. Most important, writing provides an avenue for you to learn about yourself, about the world, and about the people with whom you share it. *Discovery: An Introduction to Writing*, Third Edition, provides everything you will need to negotiate all the journeys on which writing can take you.

Three basic premises underlie *Discovery: An Introduction to Writing*, Third Edition:

1. **Confidence leads to competence.** You become a better writer by writing. The more comfortable you become with the writing process, the easier you will find it to practice, which will lead to improvement. Therefore, as it introduces the writing process, *Discovery* launches you on your journey by immediately involving you in stimulating writing activities.

2. **Good writing stems from a combination of sound critical thinking, creativity, and exchange with others.** Writing well requires that you be engaged by the subject and capable of analyzing it from a variety of perspectives. This edition of *Discovery* provides a wide variety of writing activities and assignments to stimulate your critical thinking, creative expression, and self-assessment. At the same time, it presents, in a clear and direct manner, the guidelines that govern written language. The text also emphasizes the value of collaboration, encouraging you to work with others in generating ideas, exchanging feedback, and revising your work.

3. **Good writing is a happy marriage of content and form.** You succeed as a writer when you communicate your good ideas in a form that is universally accepted and understood by all readers. For this reason, much of *Discovery* is devoted to basic sentence development and correct use of sentence elements.

Organization of the Text

Discovery's organization fosters cumulative skill development and allows for a flexible course design. Part One, "The Elements of Effective Writing," consists of five chapters that focus on the various stages of the writing process.

Chapter 1 introduces the writing process, emphasizing the importance of purpose in writing. Chapter 2 illustrates five prewriting techniques—freewriting, brainstorming, clustering, branching, and idea mapping—and also presents journal writing as a way to develop writing skills. Chapter 3 demonstrates how to transform raw ideas developed during prewriting into a clear topic sentence and effective supporting sentences. Chapter 4 illustrates how to assess and improve a first draft. It highlights the importance of revising for unity, coherence, and effective language and of seeking feedback from an objective reader. It also shows how to polish a draft through editing. Presented in order, the first four chapters provide stimulating, progressively sequenced, hands-on writing activities.

Chapter 5, new to this edition, provides a bridge from paragraph writing to essay writing, illustrating the various stages of the process, concluding with an annotated final-draft essay. Depending on the course focus, Chapter 5 could be presented midway through the semester or at the end as a preview of the next writing course.

The chapters in the next four parts of *Discovery* all piggyback on the lessons of Part One. All the areas of grammar and usage that challenge beginning writers are covered in these sections. Through clear explanations, examples, engaging exercises, activities, and writing assignments, these chapters each emphasize that effective writing is a *synthesis* of content and form.

The chapters in Part Two, "Effective Sentences: Constructing Meaning," explain how to write correct, effective sentences. Chapter 6 focuses on the basic architecture of a sentence, and Chapter 7 details ways to recognize and eliminate sentence fragments. Chapters 8 and 9 deal with subordination and coordination, and Chapter 10 shows how to recognize and eliminate two major sentence errors: comma splices and run-ons.

The chapters in Part Three, "Verbs: Conveying Action and Time," cover various aspects of verb use. Chapter 11 explores how to maintain agreement between subjects and verbs. Chapters 12 and 13 illustrate how to form the simple and perfect tenses of regular and irregular verbs. Chapters 14 and 15 focus on other aspects of verb use, such as voice, progressive tenses, and forms of *to be*.

Part Four, "Sentence Elements: Striving for Precision," covers the use of nouns, pronouns, and modifiers. Chapters 16 and 17 are newly configured in this edition. Chapter 16 now focuses solely on the use of nouns, while Chapter 17 now deals exclusively with pronouns, covering such areas as case, pronoun–antecedent agreement, and sexist language. Chapter 18 focuses on the various forms of adjectives, adverbs, and other modifiers, addressing usage problems such as double negatives and dangling modifiers.

Part Five, "Consistency Workshop: Aiming for Correctness," explains matters of mechanics. Chapters 19, 20, and 21 cover capitalization and punctuation, with Chapter 21 devoted solely to commas. Chapter 22 discusses spelling, and Chapter 23 illustrates correct use of parallelism.

Part Six, "Discovering Connections through Reading," is an anthology of fifteen professional and student readings, each followed by sets of questions designed to stimulate critical thinking and inspire additional writing. The introduction to this anthology focuses on active reading as a path to greater understanding, with a brief, annotated excerpt to illustrate the active reading process. Among the seven professional readings in this edition are Malcolm X's powerful "Education," Anna Quindlen's striking "Suicide Solution," and the first chapter of Sandra Cisneros's touching *The House on Mango Street*. The eight student readings are the products of assignments like those presented throughout *Discovery*.

In addition, a practical appendix, "Tips for ESL Writers," supplements the lessons in the text. This section is directed to non-native speakers of English, covering areas of grammar and usage that ESL students generally find confusing.

Features in the Text

Discovery's special features are designed to make the student's journey through the text both productive and pleasurable:

- The activities in each chapter are carefully laid out to provide for maximum learning. **Exercises** challenge students to demonstrate their understanding of the material presented and apply the principles, sometimes in conjunction with a classmate. **Challenge** sessions, many of which are also collaborative, call for critical thinking, drafting, or revising. Each chapter in Parts Two through Five also includes a **Chapter Quick Check** and a **Summary Exercise** covering all the concepts presented in the chapter in a single exercise.
- **Discovering Connections** are challenging writing activities, designed to stimulate interest, imagination, and critical thinking. They contain both verbal and visual cues to spark the creative associations that lead to thoughtful, effective writing. In Chapters 1 through 5, these assignments appear near the end of the chapter and are designed to stimulate prewriting that may later be developed into a finished piece. In Chapters 6 through 23, these assignments consist of two parts. The first part, at the beginning of each chapter, presents a quotation and a photo to consider and examine through prewriting. The second part, at the end of the chapter, provides more specific directions for writing, offers the opportunity for collaborative work, and ties in the material covered in each chapter. These features are unmatched in other basic writing texts.
- **Discovering Connections through Reading** assignments follow each of the readings in Part Six. These assignments call for written reaction to the ideas presented in or raised by the reading.

- Most exercises are **continuous discourse,** that is, in **paragraph form.** This method of presentation underscores one of the guiding principles of the text: The elements of grammar and usage are a part of writing, not a separate system of rules. Working through these paragraphs, on a wide variety of engaging subjects, deepens understanding about the structure of effective topic sentences and support.
- **Collaborative activities** are highlighted through the use of a **special icon.**
- The **attractive full-color design** provides visual stimulation and emphasis for key concepts.
- **Full-color charts** throughout the text offer graphic representations of key relationships among elements of the writing process, parts of speech, and sentence elements.
- **Chapter Recaps** provide **definitions of new terms** in the chapter as well as **visual summaries of key concepts.**
- **Engaging and realistic writing samples** model clear, effective writing as they illustrate all aspects of writing, grammar, and usage.
- **Extensive and comprehensive coverage** of the areas that most trouble student writers, including **sentence fragments, comma splices,** and **run-ons; subordination and coordination; subject–verb agreement; pronoun–antecedent agreement; modifiers; spelling, punctuation,** and **verb use.**
- An **anthology of seven professional and eight student readings** provides opportunities for critical thinking and active reading as well as for discussion and writing.
- **Each chapter in Parts Two through Five is self-contained,** allowing for maximum flexibility in course design and presentation of material.
- **Appendix: Tips for ESL Writers** presents additional **grammar and usage tips for ESL students.**

New in This Edition

From the time we started work on the first edition of *Discovery,* our goal has been the same: to create a text that is as **accessible, appealing, efficient,** and **practical** as possible. We have used *Discovery* with our classes, we have asked students for their reaction, and we have consulted colleagues, both here at Bristol Community College and across the nation, about changes they would propose to improve the text. As a result, *Discovery,* Third Edition, features a number of significant improvements:

- A **new chapter** devoted exclusively to **pronoun use,** including pronoun–antecedent agreement.
- A **new chapter, "Moving from Paragraph to Essay,"** that introduces the process of creating multi-paragraph writings, tracing an essay through each stage of the writing process.

- **New facsimile examples of all stages of the writing process,** plus **annotated papers, peer responses,** and **instructor's comments.**
- **Spotlight pieces** in Chapters 1 through 5 that feature student writing, modeling what students can achieve.
- **Photo prompts** added to writing assignments throughout the text, serving as additional cues for writing.
- **New chapter openings** featuring a **Question and Answer sequence,** encapsulating the focus of the chapter and framing the discussion to follow.
- **Writers' Cafés,** presented in brief, visually attractive, self-contained sections at the end of Parts One through Five, taking a deeper look at key facets of writing while responding to provocative questions.
- Numerous **new exercises and writing assignments** on high-interest subjects in every chapter, including **Chapter Quick Checks,** ten-sentence exercises covering all the concepts discussed in a chapter, which complement the existing **Summary Exercises.**
- **Five new readings,** four of them by student writers.

Supplement Package

A complete array of supplements is available to use with *Discovery: An Introduction to Writing,* Third Edition:

- The ***Annotated Instructor's Edition*** is a copy of the student text with all answers included on the page. 0-321-10378-5
- ***Instructor's Manual and Test Bank*** includes a wealth of teaching suggestions. Also included are a diagnostic test, tests for each chapter in Parts Two through Five, a comprehensive Mastery Test, and more. Ask your Longman sales representative for ISBN 0-321-10377-7.
- The **Companion Website,** written by Randall McClure of Marymount College, offers chapter objectives, online activities, links to useful writing- and grammar-related Web sites, and a message board. The Web site also offers students the opportunity to e-mail completed assignments to their instructors or classmates to facilitate online and collaborative learning. Visit *Discovery Online* at **http://www.ablongman.com/kelly.**

The Longman Basic Skills Package

In addition to the book-specific supplements discussed above, many other skills-based supplements are available for both instructors and students. All of these supplements are available either free or at greatly reduced prices.

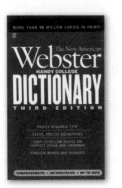

For Additional Reading and Reference

The Dictionary Deal. Two dictionaries can be shrinkwrapped with this text at a nominal fee. *The New American Webster Handy College Dictionary* is a paperback reference text with more than 100,000 entries. *Merriam Webster's Collegiate Dictionary,* Tenth Edition, is a hardback reference with a citation file of more than 14.5 million examples of English words drawn from actual use. For more information on how to shrinkwrap a dictionary with your text, please contact your Longman sales representative.

Penguin Quality Paperback Titles. A series of Penguin paperbacks is available at a significant discount when shrinkwrapped with this text. Some titles available are Toni Morrison's *Beloved,* Julia Alvarez's *How the Garcia Girls Lost Their Accents,* Mark Twain's *Huckleberry Finn,* Frederick Douglass's *Narrative of the Life of Frederick Douglass,* Harriet Beecher Stowe's *Uncle Tom's Cabin,* Dr. Martin Luther King, Jr.'s *Why We Can't Wait,* and plays by Shakespeare, Miller, and Albee. For a complete list of titles or more information, please contact your Longman sales consultant.

Penguin Academics: *Twenty-Five Great Essays, Fifty Great Essays, and One Hundred Great Essays,* edited by Robert DiYanni. These alphabetically organized essay collections are published as part of the "Penguin Academics" series of low-cost, high-quality offerings intended for use in introductory college courses. All essays were selected for their teachability, both as models for writing and for their usefulness as springboards for student writing. For more information on how to shrinkwrap one of these anthologies with your text, please contact your Longman sales consultant.

100 Things to Write About. This 100-page book contains 100 individual assignments for writing on a variety of topics and in a wide range of formats, from expressive to analytical. Ask your Longman sales representative for a sample copy. 0-673-98239-4

***Newsweek* Alliance.** Instructors may choose to shrinkwrap a 12-week subscription to *Newsweek* with any Longman text. The price of the subscription is 59 cents per issue (a total of $7.08 for the subscription). Available with the subscription is a free "Interactive Guide to *Newsweek*"—a workbook for students who are using the text. In addition, *Newsweek* provides a wide variety of instructor supplements free to teachers, including maps, Skills Builders, and weekly quizzes. For more information on the *Newsweek* program, please contact your Longman sales representative.

Electronic and Online Offerings

The Writer's ToolKit Plus. This CD-ROM offers a wealth of tutorial, exercise, and reference material for writers. It is compatible with either a PC or Macintosh platform and is flexible enough to be used either occasionally for practice or regularly in class lab sessions. For information on how

xix

to bundle this CD-ROM free with your text, please contact your Longman sales representative.

The Longman Writer's Warehouse. This innovative and exciting online supplement is the perfect companion to any developmental writing course. Created by developmental English instructors especially for developing writers, the Writer's Warehouse covers every stage of the writing process. It also includes journaling capabilities, multimedia activities, diagnostic tests, an interactive handbook, and a complete instructor's manual. The Writer's Warehouse requires no space on your school's server; rather, students complete and store their work on the Longman server and are able to access it, revise it, and continue working at any time. For more details about how to shrinkwrap a free subscription to The Writer's Warehouse with this text, please consult your Longman sales representative. For a free guided tour of the site, visit **http://longmanwriterswarehouse.com.**

For Instructors

Electronic Test Bank for Writing. This electronic test bank features more than 5,000 questions in all areas of writing, from grammar to paragraphing, through essay writing, research, and documentation. With this easy-to-use CD-ROM, instructors simply choose questions from the electronic test bank and then print out the completed test for distribution. CD-ROM: 0-321-08117-X; Print version: 0-321-08486-1

Competency Profile Test Bank, Second Edition. This series of 60 objective tests covers ten general areas of English competency, including fragments, comma splices and run-ons, pronouns, commas, and capitalization. Each test is available in remedial, standard, and advanced versions. Available as reproducible sheets or in computerized versions. Free to instructors. 0-321-02224-6

Diagnostic and Editing Tests and Exercises, Sixth Edition. This collection of diagnostic tests helps instructors assess students' competence in Standard Written English for purposes of placement or to gauge progress. Available as reproducible sheets or in computerized versions, and free to instructors. Paper: 0-321-19647-3; CD-ROM: 0-321-19645-7

ESL Worksheets, Third Edition. These reproducible worksheets provide ESL students with extra practice in areas they find the most troublesome. A diagnostic test and post-test are provided, along with answer keys and suggested topics for writing. Free to adopters. 0-321-07765-2

Longman Editing Exercises. These 54 pages of paragraph editing exercises give students extra practice using grammar skills in the context of longer passages. Free when packaged with any Longman title. 0-205-31792-8; Answer Key: 0-205-31797-9

80 Practices. A collection of reproducible, ten-item exercises that provide additional practices for specific grammatical usage problems, such as comma splices, capitalization, and pronouns. Includes an answer key, and is free to adopters. 0-673-53422-7

Teaching Online: Internet Research, Conversation, and Composition, **Second Edition.** Ideal for instructors who have never surfed the Net, this easy-to-follow guide offers basic definitions, numerous examples, and step-by-step information about finding and using Internet sources. Free to adopters. 0-321-01957-1

Using Portfolios. This supplement offers teachers a brief introduction to teaching with portfolios in composition courses. This essential guide addresses the pedagogical and evaluative use of portfolios, and offers practical suggestions for implementing a portfolio evaluation system in a writing class. 0-321-08412-8

The Longman Instructor's Planner. This all-in-one resource for instructors includes monthly and weekly planning sheets, to-do lists, student contact forms, attendance rosters, a gradebook, an address/phone book, and a mini-almanac. Ask your Longman sales representative for a free copy. 0-321-09247-3

For Students

Researching Online, **Fifth Edition.** A perfect companion for a new age, this indispensable new supplement helps students navigate the Internet. Adapted from *Teaching Online,* the instructor's Internet guide, *Researching Online* speaks directly to students, giving them detailed, step-by-step instructions for performing electronic searches. Available free when shrinkwrapped with this text. 0-321-09277-5

The Longman Writer's Journal. This journal for writers, free with any Longman English text, offers students a place to think, write, and react. For an examination copy, contact your Longman sales consultant. 0-321-08639-2

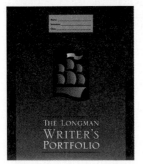

[NEW] The Longman Writer's Portfolio. This unique supplement provides students with a space to plan, think about, and present their work. The portfolio includes an assessing/organizing area (including a grammar diagnostic test, a spelling quiz, and project planning worksheets), a before-and-during-writing area (including peer review sheets, editing checklists, writing self-evaluations, and a personal editing profile), and an after-writing area (including a progress chart, a final table of contents, and a final assessment). Ask your Longman sales representative for ISBN 0-321-10765-9.

State-Specific Supplements

[FOR FLORIDA ADOPTIONS] *Thinking Through the Test,* **by D. J. Henry.** This special workbook, prepared specially for students in Florida, offers ample skill and practice exercises to help students prep for the Florida State Exit Exam. To shrinkwrap this workbook free with your textbook, please contact your Longman sales representative. Available in two versions: with answers and without answers. Also available: two laminated grids (one for reading, one for writing) that can serve as handy references for students preparing for the Florida State Exit Exam.

[FOR NEW YORK ADOPTIONS] *Preparing for the CUNY-ACT Reading and Writing Test*, **edited by Patricia Licklider.** This booklet, prepared by reading and writing faculty from across the CUNY system, is designed to help students prepare for the CUNY-ACT exit test. It includes test-taking tips, reading passages, typical exam questions, and sample writing prompts to help students become familiar with each portion of the test.

[FOR TEXAS ADOPTIONS] *The Longman TASP Study Guide,* **by Jeanette Harris.** Created specifically for students in Texas, this study guide includes straightforward explanations and numerous practice exercises to help students prepare for the reading and writing sections of the Texas Academic Skills Program Test. To shrinkwrap this workbook free with your textbook, please contact your Longman sales representative.

Acknowledgments

A number of people deserve thanks for their support as we completed this third edition of *Discovery*. We offer thanks first to John M. Lannon, University of Massachusetts, Dartmouth, and Robert Schwegler, University of Rhode Island, for their continuing encouragement, interest, and support, which mean so much to us.

We owe thanks to a number of people here at Bristol Community College. Our students continue to teach us so much, and for that we are grateful. We would also like to salute our colleagues, including Catherine Adamowicz, Deb Deroian, David Feeney, Tom Grady, Jeanne Grandchamp, Penny Hahn, Jerry LePage, Arthur Lothrup, Diana McGee, Linda Mulready, Joseph Murphy, Alan Powers, and Michael Vieira for their kind words and genuine interest in our work. Special thanks to Ruth Sullivan, associate director of the Learning Resources Center, for her assistance in locating the quotations used in the "Discovering Connections" writing assignments. Thanks also to Jack Warner, Commissioner of Higher Education for Rhode Island and Marge Condon, Director, Center for Teaching and Learning, University of Massachusetts, Dartmouth, for their support and friendship.

Paul F. Fletcher, professor emeritus of English and retired assistant dean for English, humanities, fine arts, and languages, deserves particular accolades. As our supervisor, Paul always led by example, emphasizing and valuing above all else excellence in teaching and compassion for students.

Of course, we are also indebted to the following talented professionals whose reviews helped to shape *Discovery:* Roberta Alexander, San Diego City College; Beverly Carpenter, Brookhaven College; Judith L. Carter, Amarillo

College; Marianne Dzik, Illinois Valley Community College; Patricia Hare, Brevard Community College; Frank Kelly, SUNY Farmingdale; Caren Kessler, Blue Ridge Community College; Paulette Longmore, Essex County College; Sharon Race, South Plains College; Nadine Roberts, Three Rivers Community College; Valerie Russell, Valencia Community College; and Ellen Yoffee, New Mexico Junior College.

In addition, we owe a great deal to a number of talented professionals at Longman for their outstanding contributions to this edition of *Discovery*. Senior Acquisitions Editor Steven Rigolosi has devoted much energy to ensure that *Discovery* is simply the best book in its field, and we are deeply grateful for his support as well as the keen insight and attention he has focused on every aspect of the text. We remain grateful to Senior Vice President and Publisher Joe Opiela for having provided the opportunity for us to develop *Discovery* in the first place. His intuition and leadership have inspired us and kept us on track. Susan Messer, Development Editor, deserves special thanks for her hard work in making sure our words say what we intended them to say. We couldn't have completed our work without her energy and enthusiasm. Donna DeBenedictis, Production Manager at Longman Publishers, and Sue Nodine, Project Editor for Elm Street Publishing Services, Inc., have done a terrific job transforming manuscript into text, and we offer them our special thanks for making our book—and us—look so good.

We are also indebted to our family and friends for making *Discovery* possible.

Debbie Lawton would like to thank Carlie, Barbara, and Michele for their friendship and support. Above all, she would like to thank her family for their love and encouragement. Her parents, Charles and Virginia Soucy, and her mother-in-law, Elizabeth McCleskey, have always been nearby to lend a helping hand or to give a pat on the back. She has learned much watching her children, Matthew and Amy, grow to adulthood. Her husband, Kevin, continues to be the spirit that guides her, both in her work and in her life, and to him she owes the greatest thanks.

Bill Kelly would like to acknowledge the love and support of his parents, the late Mary R. and the late Edward F. Kelly. They taught him and his brothers lessons that will remain forever. He is also grateful to his parents-in-law, Flo and Leo Nadeau, for their continued support of him and his work, and to his son-in-law, Timothy Matos. His children, Nicole Matos and Jacqueline Kelly, deserve far more thanks than anyone could possibly muster for the sheer joy they have provided in his life. But most of all, he offers his wife, Michelle Nadeau Kelly, thanks. For more than 31 years, she has provided unconditional love and her support for Bill and his work, and *thank you* falls far short in acknowledging all that she does, all that she means.

William J. Kelly
Deborah L. Lawton

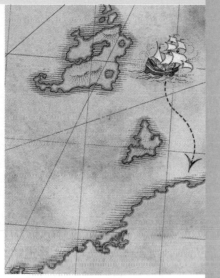

The Elements of Effective Writing

Chapter 1

Understanding the Writing Process

Getting Started... **Q:** I know I'm not a stupid person, but I sometimes feel stupid when I have to write anything more complicated than a short note or e-mail message. Why can writing seem so confusing and intimidating?

A: First, you are correct. You aren't stupid—far from it. Writing seems confusing and intimidating because it is a complex process that requires critical thinking and close attention to detail and to the needs of someone else, the reader. The good news is that if you can write a note or e-mail, you can also do the kind of writing that will be required of you in school and in your profession.

Overview: Seeing Writing as a Process of Discovery

Probably nobody would argue with this simple statement: Once you know how to do something well, it gets easier—in some cases, almost effortless. Maybe it's performing a move on the dance floor or on a skateboard. Maybe it's downloading information from the Internet or burning a CD. Or maybe it's completing an estimate of the amount of building materials needed for a construction project.

That task now seems simple and automatic, thanks to your experience and the confidence you've developed over time.

But in most cases, the task didn't always seem so easy. In the beginning, before you mastered it, that task probably felt anything but simple and automatic. "I'll never be able to do this," you told yourself then. Now, however, you probably wonder how you could *not* have understood how to do it.

A simple explanation exists for this change in attitude and ability: familiarity with the activity and practice. The more you worked at the task, the more skilled and comfortable you became with it. In other words, experience gave you the **confidence** to carry on until you developed **competence.**

That's exactly how it is with writing. At first, it can mystify, confuse, or overpower you, especially if you haven't done much writing. But with regular practice, you'll gain both confidence and competence. You'll discover that writing is not a product but a **process,** a series of stages called prewriting, composing, and revising. You'll also discover that a successful piece of writing doesn't result from a one-time attempt but rather from this series of efforts. And you'll discover the two main elements of effective writing: communicating your ideas clearly and directly to a *reader* and fulfilling an identifiable *purpose*.

Perhaps the most important lesson you'll learn is this: Writing is a journey of discovery. Through writing, you can explore your world and unleash your creativity. As you work through the writing process, you'll discover the significance of your ideas and the connections that exist between and among them. At the same time, you'll discover and master strategies that will enable you to present your ideas correctly in terms of usage, spelling, and punctuation.

Why should you care about any of this? This answer is simple. The stakes are so high. Solid writing skills are a primary requirement for success in both the classroom and the work world. Your instructors will grade you on the basis of the lab reports, essay answers, research papers, and critical, reflective, and analytical papers you produce. Your supervisors will assess your value as an employee on the basis of the letters, memos, reports, proposals, Web pages, legal briefs, and so on you write.

Maybe even more important, you should care because being able to write well offers such great rewards. Writing effectively in school or on the job earns you the respect of your instructors, colleagues, and supervisors. Most important of all, you gain greater self-respect as you begin to view a blank page as an invitation rather than a source of intimidation.

In this chapter, you will discover the basic elements of writing

- the three stages of the writing process—prewriting, composing, and revising

- the four interacting components of writing—writer, reader, message, and means

- the purposes of writing—to inform, to entertain, and to persuade

---

Understanding the Stages of the Writing Process

Flip through the channels on your television and you'll no doubt come upon some highlights from the previous day's sporting events. Watch the screen for a few minutes and you'll see some great plays—a player kicking a goal, smashing a homerun, hitting a straight drive, or making a jump shot. Each action appears to be a single fluid action.

But appearance often differs from reality. The truth is that each of these actions is not a single movement but a complex series of steps. The same is true for writing.

Prewriting is the first stage of the writing process. During this stage, you generate ideas and do preliminary planning. Think of prewriting as a warm-up exercise. After all, it's the rare athlete, musician, or artist who can perform at the top level without taking some time to stretch or practice. Before you develop a piece of writing, you need to examine a subject thoroughly and from different perspectives.

Any approach that enables you to examine a person, situation, idea, or concept more closely can be a good prewriting technique. Reading, talking, observing others, thinking, and so on are all great prewriting activities. Chapter 2, "Prewriting Developing Ideas," discusses and illustrates several specific prewriting techniques.

Composing is the second stage of the writing process. This stage, as you will see in Chapter 3, "Composing: Creating Topic Sentences and Supporting Sentences," involves selecting the most promising ideas you have generated during prewriting and then expressing them in sentences and organizing these sentences into paragraph form.

Revising is the third stage of the writing process. As Chapter 4, "Revising: Refining Your Draft," shows, a successful piece of writing evolves through versions, or **drafts.** During the revising stage, you first carefully examine or *reassess* the content of your writing. Next, you *redraft,* generating new material that fills the gaps you've identified. Finally, you *edit,* moving beyond concerns about content and instead concentrating on eliminating any remaining errors in form. This final step is particularly important because mistakes in form turn a reader's attention away from the good ideas you've developed. Overall, when you revise, you rework a piece of writing in order to develop a more effective, more polished draft.

This figure illustrates the writing process:

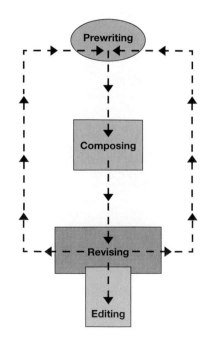

As this figure shows, when you write, you begin with prewriting, move to composing, and then advance to revising. Notice, however, the arrows in the illustration that flow back from revising to prewriting. The arrows then continue through composing, leading eventually to a polished draft. That's because the writing process is *recursive,* which means that you often repeat steps as you work your way through the process.

Exercise 1.1   **Understanding the Stages of the Writing Process**

1. In your own words, explain the purpose of prewriting.

   The purpose of prewriting is planning. It's a chance to warm up and consider a

   subject from different perspectives.

2. What do you do during the second stage of writing, composing?

   When you compose, you turn the promising ideas generated during prewriting into

   sentences and then organize them in paragraph form

3. How does revising differ from composing?

   Revising differs from composing because revising involves taking an already com-

   pleted writing and making it more effective. Composing involves transforming pre-

   writing material into a draft that will then be revised.

4. Why is editing such a crucial part of the revising stage of writing?

   Editing is vital because its focus is on errors in form, mistakes that distract the

   reader from the content of a piece of writing.

Exercise 1.2   **Considering the Impact of Writing**

How will being able to write well help you in your other classes?

Answers will vary, although most students will agree that writing well will help them

achieve better grades with any school tasks involving writing. Most will also indicate

that regardless of discipline, instructors will view good writing as a sign of intelligence

and clear thinking.

Challenge 1.1 **Examining Your Own Feelings about Writing**

1. How do you feel about writing? On the following lines, briefly explain your attitude about the act of writing and why you feel this way. What is easiest for you? What is most difficult?

Answers will vary. Some students may indicate that they like writing. Others,

however, will state that they are uncomfortable with writing, citing concerns with is-

sues of spelling, grammar, and punctuation, as well as doubts about being able to

express thoughts in writing or about having anything important to say.

2. Now compare your responses with a classmate's. What do the two of you have in common? In what ways do your attitudes differ? On a separate sheet of paper, briefly summarize these points.

Answers will vary.

Examining the Dynamics of Writing

Simply defined, writing is an act of communication. When you write, you commit words to paper so that someone else will understand your point. Writing differs from speaking and other means of communicating in a couple of ways. For one thing, writing is more *deliberate*—more fully and carefully thought out. For another, writing is more *precise*—more consciously crafted word by word to create just the right effect.

The act of writing involves four basic interacting components: (1) a **writer,** the person expressing ideas; (2) a **reader,** the audience; (3) a **message,** the writer's topic and supporting ideas about it; and (4) the **means** of expressing that message, written language. To understand how these four elements interact, take a look at the following figure:

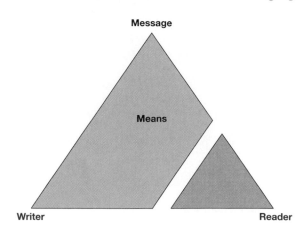

In this figure, the blue portion represents what you as the writer know and want to communicate. Notice that at this point, the portion of the figure to the right, representing your reader, is blank and separated from the rest of the figure. Your job as a writer is to use the *means*—written language—to communicate what you want the reader to know about your subject—your *message*. When you provide the right examples and details, you convey your message. In other words, you communicate, as this version of the figure, called the *communication triangle*, shows:

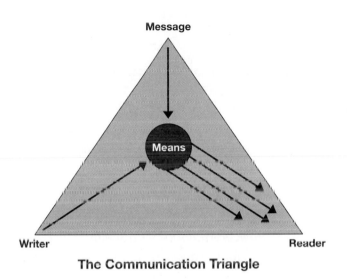

The Communication Triangle

Now, the reader is no longer separated from the other elements. As the arrows show, using the means to communicate the message completes the connection between you and your reader.

In fact, focusing on the reader is the key to success in writing. Writing that doesn't communicate its ideas to a reader is not effective. In some cases, you'll actually know who your reader is. Think about a paper for your sociology class or a memorandum about staffing needs at your place of employment. In the first case, the reader would be your sociology instructor, and in the second, it would be the supervisor in charge of hiring or scheduling workers.

But often you won't know exactly who your reader will be. In these cases, focus on the average reader. The average reader is like most of us. We all know a little about many subjects, but we lack detailed information about most of them. Think of yourself before you understood or learned what you know about your subject. That's what the average reader is like.

Exercise 1.3   **Recognizing the Dynamics of Writing**

1. What is the simplest definition of writing?

    Writing is an act of communication.

2. In what two ways does writing differ from speaking?

   Writing is more deliberate and more precise than speaking.

3. What are the four components that interact when you write?

   Writer, reader, message, and means

Exercise 1.4   **Considering Communication Situations**

1. List three situations in which you wouldn't necessarily know who your reader is.

   Answers will vary. Possible answers may include a letter of complaint, a note

   requesting information about a product, and a letter of application.

2. After examining the communication space triangle again, think of everything you understand about the topic *space exploration*. Make a list of ideas that expresses to an imaginary reader what you understand about this topic.

   Answers will vary.

Challenge 1.2   **Considering Your Own Attitudes about Writing and Speaking**

1. Speaking is less formal and deliberate than writing is. In what ways can this characteristic of speech sometimes be a disadvantage?

   Answers will vary, although some students will mention times when they spoke with-

   out fully considering their statements and the consequences that followed.

2. Working with a classmate, consider situations in which writing would make it easier to communicate a message than speaking would. Then, on a separate sheet of paper, list two of the situations you identified and explain why writing would be the better way to express your ideas.

   Answers will vary.

Recognizing the Purpose behind Your Writing

Whenever you write, consider the **purpose** or aim of your writing. The three primary purposes are to *inform,* to *entertain,* and to *persuade.* To inform means to supply information that explains or clarifies something. A paper discussing the use of wind "farms" as an alternative energy supply would inform. So would a writing on the increasing popularity of computer-generated animation in movies.

To entertain means to amuse, captivate, or arouse the reader's interest and emotions. A paper about a party at which everything that could go wrong did go wrong would entertain. So would a paper about encountering a bat flying through your bedroom.

To persuade means to sway a reader to consider the validity of a particular point of view. Sometimes also referred to as *argument,* this purpose frequently drives the writing you will face. College students often have to express and support a stand on some issue. Professionals often have to prepare grant proposals or pursue contracts for their companies. Private citizens often need to compose position pieces or letters to the editor about issues in their community.

A paper urging more people to register as organ donors would persuade. So would a writing asserting that the federal government should not institute mandatory DNA testing for all inmates.

Of course, you will discover a degree of overlap in the three purposes. The entertaining writing about the bat in your bedroom could also inform if it explained the proper method for removing a bat that enters a home. And the same paper could persuade if it asserts that bats are beneficial to humans and should be protected rather than killed.

Always take a moment to identify your primary and any secondary purpose. This way, you will be sure that your writing fulfills that purpose and meets the needs of your reader.

Exercise 1.5   Examining the Purposes in Writing

1. What are the three main purposes you fulfill when you write?

   to inform, to entertain, and to persuade

   _____

2. Why should you always consider purpose when you are creating a piece of writing?

   You should always consider purpose when writing so that you'll include the types of

   information and language dictated by that purpose.

Exercise 1.6   **Identifying the Purpose in a Piece of Writing**

1. Read the following paragraph:

> Too often, members of the media act irresponsibly when reporting on a news event, creating needless fear among the public. The media reaction to the near fatal mauling of a young boy by a shark off the coast of Florida in 2001 is a good example of this lack of responsibility. Once news of the horrific accident reached them, all the major news outlets rushed crews to the scene, leading to aggressive and sensationalized coverage. Because a few other attacks had already occurred in the U.S. and abroad, many reporters suggested that sharks now represented a huge risk to swimmers. They began to refer to 2001 as the "Year of the Shark Attack," even though statistics about shark attacks during this period did not indicate a dramatic increase. By overlooking or ignoring the statistics and focusing on the more lurid aspects of the incident, reporters needlessly terrified millions of beach goers. They also contributed to many misconceptions about sharks and shark attacks. The truth is that of the more than 350 species of sharks roaming the oceans, only a few are dangerous. Also, by feeding on injured or dying creatures, sharks perform a valuable service, helping to maintain balance in the ocean. In fact, many attacks on humans are actually cases of mistaken identity. Sharks prefer creatures such as sea lions or seals for their high fat content. Unfortunately, though, the facts often get lost when reporters focus on sensational details, and the public is misinformed and frightened as a result.

What is the primary purpose of this paragraph: to entertain, to inform, or to persuade? On the lines below, briefly explain your answer.

Most students will agree that the primary purpose in this writing is to persuade that

the media are often irresponsible when reporting events. It offers as support the be-

havior of news outlets following a shark attack. The coverage overemphasized the

risk of attack while failing to note that the frequency of shark attacks was actually

within the expected range.

2. What other purpose does the above paragraph fulfill? Use the lines below to explain.

Because it discusses statistics about sharks, most students will agree that this piece

also informs. And, because it discusses a compelling story in a compelling way,

some students will also feel that the piece entertains. The piece provides a good op-

portunity to discuss the overlapping nature of purpose in writing.

Exercise 1.7   **Developing Details Appropriate for the Purpose of a Writing**

1. Working with a classmate, choose one of the following subjects, and then list examples you might include for a writing that *entertains,* one that *informs,* and one that *persuades:* shopping on the Internet, home schooling, roller-blading.

   a. Purpose: to inform

   Answers will vary. If students choose shopping on the Internet, they might

   explain how to work through the process of buying online or the types of goods

   and services available through e-commerce.

   b. Purpose: to entertain

   Answers will vary. Students might relate an Internet shopping excursion gone

   bad or the fun of browsing through thousands of items from around the world.

   c. Purpose: to persuade

   Answers will vary. Students could assert the advantages of Internet shopping

   over traditional shopping or maintain that the risks involved in using a credit card

   online outweigh any benefit.

2. Which of the papers for which you've listed examples would you find easiest to write? Why? Which would you find hardest? Why?

   Answers will vary.

Challenge 1.3   **Developing Details to Fulfill the Purpose of Writing**

1. Working with a classmate, make a list on a separate sheet of paper about the effects of the increasing number of cellular phones.

2. How would you explain these reasons if the purpose of your paper were to entertain? Why would you present them this way?

   Answers will vary. Possible approaches relative to entertaining might involve writing

   about people talking while eating or using a public restroom, etc., or about incidents

   when cell phones went off at inappropriate times, for instance, during a funeral.

SPOTLIGHT PIECE

Considering the Process, Dynamics, and Purposes in a Piece of Writing

Here's a writing by student Ramon Laboy on the ways confidence can affect people. The annotations to the left of Ramon's essay offer some insight concerning the process, the dynamics, and purposes of writing. Read his essay and the annotations and then answer the questions that follow the piece.

Ramon is arguing that to be successful is to find a balance between confidence and arrogance. Because he is trying to convince his reader, his primary purpose is to persuade.

These were key prewriting ideas that Ramon developed and then revised for this paragraph.

These were also key prewriting ideas that Ramon developed and then revised.

By exploring this idea in full detail, Ramon meets the needs of his reader.

To Be, or Not to Be . . . Confident

Confidence is a feeling of self-assurance. It is vital to have confidence in life in order to be successful. But overconfidence is also a reason why some people fail or screw up. So you have to find a balance between confidence and caution.

For instance, a stock car racer starts in a race dead last, but still he is confident that he can win the race. He is confident that he is a better driver than the other racers. He doesn't drive dangerously, risking it all while putting himself and the other drivers in jeopardy. Even if he finishes last, he still comes back for another race. He never gives up because he is confident that his time will come.

On the other hand, a stockbroker spends all her life savings on one stock because she is confident that the stock is going to pay big time. Twelve hours later she is sitting on the edge of a 67th floor window, and she's about to jump because she was too confident about her big time stock that just hit rock bottom.

When it comes to confidence, you have to be cautious. If you take ridiculous risks or don't have all the facts, then you are really just acting on hope, not confidence.

Exercise 1.8   **Exploring the Reading**

1. In your view, which of the prewriting details identified in the annotations does Ramon do the best job revising? Why?

   Answers will vary. Students will be split, with many choosing the stockbroker

   example and many others choosing the stock car racer example.

2. As the annotations indicate, the primary purpose in Ramon's essay is to persuade. Now, working with a classmate, consider whether the writing fulfills any other purposes and explain your answer on the lines that follow.

   Most students will probably agree that the piece also entertains because it is enjoy-

   able to read. Some may also argue that because it gives readers some background,

   the essay also informs.

Understanding the Subject through Writing

In his essay, Ramon indicates that people need to find "a balance between confidence and caution." Now, on a separate sheet of paper, write a brief passage (50 to 100 words) in which you explain what you think is the best way to find this balance in your classes or in the workplace.

Discovering Connections 1.1

Look at the picture below. What does this illustration mean to you? What do you think when you see it? For example, does it remind you of

a door you've seen, perhaps one from some place in your childhood? Do you see it as a symbol of something awaiting you in the future, such as a success, a problem, or a life partner? Could it represent something hidden away—a talent or a secret—that is about to emerge?

For this assignment, focus on the picture, and discover what you think about it. Using the examples in this chapter to guide you, jot down what you think the average reader would need to know to understand your thoughts. Also, write down what your primary purpose would be if you were to write a paper about these thoughts. Save this work for later use.

Discovering Connections 1.2

Consider the topic *school.* For example, you might choose one aspect of your schooling generating ideas about your early years of school. For example, many people vividly remember their first day of school. Or you might prefer to think back to your middle school or high school years. Maybe you or a close friend became a star student or athlete. Maybe you had a problem dealing with cliques. Another possibility is to examine your time so far in college. What have you found easiest or hardest, and why? How will school help you meet your professional goal?

As you can see, this topic offers a number of avenues for exploration and discovery. Use a separate piece of paper to record your ideas. Think about what purpose you might fulfill in writing about the subject you've chosen. Save your work. You may want to develop this material into polished writing later.

UNDERSTANDING THE WRITING PROCESS

New terms in this chapter	Definitions
● the writing process	● the series of stages in writing, including prewriting, composing, and revising
● prewriting	● generating ideas to develop into a piece of writing
● composing	● selecting and then expressing in sentence and paragraph form some of your prewriting ideas
● revising	● creating new drafts through reexamining, improving, and polishing your initial version
● editing	● concentrating on eliminating remaining errors in form
● draft	● version of a paper
● writer	● the person expressing ideas through the written word
● reader	● the audience to whom a paper is directed
● message	● the topic and the supporting examples, details, and explanations that represent your understanding of the topic
● means	● the written language used to express ideas
● purpose	● the intent or aim of a paper

Steps to Writing Effectively

● Understand the stages of the writing process: **prewriting, composing,** and **revising.**

● Understand how the four elements of writing—**writer, reader, message,** and **means**—interact.

● Focus in particular on the **reader.**

● Recognize the **purpose** of any writing assignment:

  to *inform*—as in a paper explaining how a movie special effect is created
  to *entertain*—as in a paper recalling the first time you drove a car
  to *persuade*—as in a paper asserting that recycling should be mandatory throughout the United States

Chapter 2

Prewriting: Developing Ideas

Getting Started... **Q:** It's not that I don't want to write—it's that I don't know how to begin. What should I do?

A: Many, many activities—sports, art, music, dance, and so on—call for you to warm up before moving fully into action. When you write, you also need to warm up, and this warm-up is called prewriting. Once you decide which of the several prewriting techniques available best matches the way you work, getting started will seem a lot easier.

Overview: Understanding Prewriting

When you write, your discovery begins with *prewriting*, the first stage of the writing process. Whether the subject is one assigned in class or one that you'd like to explore on your own, prewriting is how you develop ideas about it.

A number of simple, informal activities—for example, talking (either with other people or alone into a recording device), doodling, and thinking—can serve as prewriting techniques. But prewriting also includes a number of more structured techniques, each of which enables people to generate ideas to be developed into a piece of writing. In this chapter, you'll discover the possibilities of each of these techniques. Then you can decide which technique, or combination of techniques, best suits your individual style.

> ***In this chapter, you will learn how to use the following prewriting techniques***
>
> - freewriting
> - brainstorming
> - clustering
> - branching
> - idea mapping
> - keeping a journal

Freewriting

One way to develop ideas for writing is **freewriting.** To freewrite, you write down all your ideas on a subject for a set period of time, usually ten minutes or so. The only rule in freewriting is not to let your pen or pencil leave the paper. Write down every idea that pops into your mind. Don't worry about expressing those ideas in complete sentences or about making errors. It's all right if the ideas don't immediately make sense or if you have drifted away from the subject. If while you are working you get stuck and can't think of anything else, write "I can't think" or make a rhyme for the word you just wrote until something comes to you. If you repeat yourself, it's OK. Just don't stop.

You can also do freewriting on a computer. Set the program to triple space so that you'll have room to write in additional material after. Then for ten minutes, simply type the ideas as they come to you. If you think seeing the words appear on the screen will distract you, darken it while you are working. When you are done, print out the material you have generated.

Here's what a freewriting on the subject of beauty might look like:

> Beauty – what is it really? Hard to say. Different kinds of beauty. In the eyes of the beholder, right? OK, what else, beauty of nature, like the outdoors, sunsets, mountains, the ocean. Physical beauty – everybody seems interested in that – all the stuff they sell to make people look better, special face creams, shampoos, makeup. Wonder if any of that stuff does anything special or is it just a scam? Lots of different fake schemes out there. Now there are scams on the Internet. People having surgery, implants, hair transplants, all to be more beautiful, all that money!!! All right, what else, what else? Harder subject than I first thought – stuck, can't think. All right, how about this – is beauty about being young, people not wanting to grow old? True beauty – not just the physical stuff, but inner things, your attitude, kindness, compassion, that's real beauty – why don't people pay more attention to this stuff instead of the face on a magazine cover?

As you can see, freewriting helps you generate plenty of ideas. Most of the ideas aren't expressed in correct sentences. At this point, that's not a problem. Converting the ideas into sentences will come later in the writing process.

Note also that the some of the ideas have been highlighted. Any time you prewrite, it's a great idea to identify and mark the ideas that you think have the most potential. Isolate them by highlighting, underlining, or circling them so that they stand out. That way you'll be ready to develop the ideas that make your point in the other stages of the writing process.

Exercise 2.1   **Considering Freewriting**

1. In your own words, explain freewriting.

   Freewriting is a method of prewriting during which you write down all your ideas on a

   subject for a set period of time, without worrying about mistakes and without stopping.

2. What advantage do you gain by highlighting, underlining, or circling some of the ideas you develop through freewriting?

   When you highlight, underline, or circle key ideas, you focus on the most promising

   material.

Exercise 2.2   **Analyzing a Freewriting Example**

Turn to the freewriting about beauty on page 16. Do you agree that the highlighted statements are the key ideas? Why?

Answers will vary. Students may say that this is a broad topic, and any of the ideas listed

could become key, depending on the writer's interests.

Exercise 2.3   **Trying Freewriting**

1. Now it's your turn to try freewriting. On a separate sheet of paper, freewrite for ten minutes on *beauty* or on either of the following subjects: *power* or *frustration*.

2. Highlight, underline, or circle the ideas in your freewriting that you want to explore further.

3. Choose the point that holds the most promise for development, and list it on your paper. Then add three additional details about this promising idea.

4. On the same piece of paper, answer the following questions:
   a. What did you like best about freewriting as a prewriting technique?
   b. What did you like least?

Challenge 2.1   **Evaluating Freewriting**

1. Now exchange your freewriting with a classmate. Put a ✓ next to the ideas that make you want to read more. Return the freewriting to the writer, and discuss the areas that seem most promising. Save your own freewriting for later use.

2. Will you use this prewriting strategy again? Explain your decision.

Answers will vary. Many students may like not having to worry about correctness or

completeness. Some won't like freewriting because of the lack of focus.

Brainstorming

Like freewriting, **brainstorming** also involves writing down ideas you generate on a subject. Brainstorming, however, is a more focused prewriting activity. You deliberately concentrate on one subject, and then list only those ideas that come to you that are directly related to the subject. You don't need to set a time limit, although some people feel more comfortable if they do.

Here's what a brainstorming on the subject of *fame* would look like:

> Fame - not always a good thing
> ✓ lose your privacy - can't even go out to a mall or restaurant
> ✓ people want to be around you just because of who you are
> ✓ some people want you to fail because they are jealous
> ✓ sometimes famous people develop a big head - like a diva - bad attitude
> ✓ can lose touch with the real world
> ✓ family and friends face attention they didn't ask for
> ✓ when all the fame is gone, how do you deal with the loss?

As you can see, you may generate fewer ideas with brainstorming than you do with freewriting, but the connections between the ideas will probably be more direct and obvious. You will probably still generate more ideas than you can use. When you brainstorm, you should isolate the best ideas you generate by highlighting, circling, or underlining them, as this example shows.

Exercise 2.4   **Defining Brainstorming**

1. In your own words, explain brainstorming.

Brainstorming means to pick a subject and list ideas that come to mind about it.

2. What are some characteristics of ideas generated during brainstorming?

The connections between them will likely be direct and obvious.

Exercise 2.5   **Analyzing a Brainstorming Example**

Review the brainstorming about fame on page 18, and then answer the questions below.

1. What points does the writer discover about fame?

   Experiencing fame isn't necessarily a good thing, leading to a loss of privacy,

   changes in attitude, problems for family and friends, and questions about the

   sincerity of others.

2. What part of the sample brainstorming do you think holds the most promise as a writing topic? Why?

   Answers will vary, although many students will choose the material about what hap-

   pens after fame passes or about losing touch with the real world.

Exercise 2.6   **Trying Brainstorming**

1. Now it's your turn to try brainstorming. On a separate sheet of paper, brainstorm on *fame* or on either of the following subjects: *television, my last birthday.*

2. Highlight, underline, or circle the ideas in your brainstorming that you think are worth developing further.

3. Choose the point that holds the most promise for development and list it on your paper. Then add three additional details about this promising idea.

4. On the same page, answer the following questions:
   a. What did you like best about brainstorming as a prewriting technique?
   b. What did you like least?

Challenge 2.2   **Evaluating Brainstorming**

1. Now exchange your brainstorming with a classmate. On your classmate's paper, place a ✓ next to the words or section that you find most interesting. Return it to the writer, and explain why the marked idea interests you. Save your own brainstorming for later use.

2. Will you use this prewriting strategy again? Explain your reasoning.

   Answers will vary. Some students will say they like the focus it provides, while others

   will dislike the technique because they will find it limiting.

Clustering

Another useful way to generate ideas is **clustering.** Clustering is a visual technique for developing ideas. With clustering, all the connections between ideas are graphically indicated. To begin, you write a general topic in the middle of the page and circle it. As related ideas pop into your mind, you write them down on the page around your topic and circle each of them. Draw lines to connect these related ideas to the topic. As the ideas you list lead to further new ideas and examples, write them down and circle them, too, again drawing lines to connect related ideas.

As you can see, clustering enables you to explore a subject in a variety of ways and from different perspectives. The result is a broad listing of ideas, with the connections between them emphasized. Remember to highlight, circle, or underline the strongest ideas, as in the cluster on credit cards, which you will develop more fully later in the writing process.

Exercise 2.7   **Defining Clustering**

1. In your own words, explain how to develop ideas using clustering.

   Write a topic in the middle of a page and circle it. As you think of related ideas, write

   them down and circle them, drawing lines to connect related ideas.

2. How does clustering differ from brainstorming and freewriting?

   Clustering is a visual technique that emphasizes the connections between ideas.

Exercise 2.8   **Analyzing a Clustering Example**

Look at the clustering about credit cards on page 20. Answer these questions.

1. What did the writer discover about the ways credit card companies operate?

   Credit card companies want you to buy more than you can afford and not pay off

   your balance. They encourage spending by extending credit limits.

2. In your opinion, what portion of the sample clustering offers the most promising writing ideas? Explain.

   Answers will vary. Many students will select the highlighted area or the material

   about spending more than budgeted.

Exercise7 2.9   **Trying Clustering**

1. Now it's your turn to try clustering. On a separate sheet of paper, create a clustering on *credit cards* or on either of the following topics: *ambition, high school gym class*.

2. Highlight, underline, or circle the ideas in your clustering that show potential for development.

3. Choose the point that holds the most promise for development and list it on your paper. Then add three additional details about this promising idea.

4. On the same page, answer the following questions:
   a. What did you like best about clustering as a prewriting technique?
   b. What did you like least?

Challenge 2.3   **Evaluating Clustering**

1. Now exchange your clustering with a classmate. Note the section of your partner's clustering that interests you most. Explain your choice to your partner as you return his or her paper. Save your own clustering for later use.

2. Will you use this prewriting technique again? Explain your reasoning.

   Answers will vary. Some students will like the flexibility that clustering provides.

   Others, however, will feel awkward working in a way that is different from the way

   they ordinarily work.

Branching

Another prewriting technique that emphasizes the connections between ideas is **branching.** To begin branching, write your topic on the left side of the paper. Then write the ideas that your topic inspires to the right of it, connecting them to the topic with lines. Those subcategories will bring to mind more related thoughts and details. Write these to the right again, letting the list branch out across the paper. Here's a branching on the subject of computers:

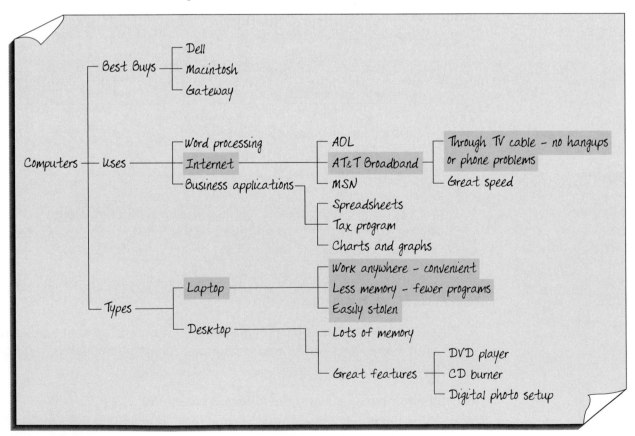

Branching allows one aspect of a subject to lead you to another aspect. As this method generates information for your writing, it also leads to a focused series of details and examples. In addition, branching often produces several distinctive groups of ideas. The most promising of these ideas are the ones that you should highlight, underline, or circle for use later on in the writing process as is done in the branching about computers.

Exercise 2.10   **Defining Branching**

1. In your own words, explain branching.

   Branching is a prewriting technique that involves writing a term on the left side of a

   paper and writing ideas that stem from it to the right. You continue branching off to

   the right as one idea leads to the next.

2. How does branching differ from clustering?

   Branching is more focused than clustering.

Exercise 2.11   **Analyzing a Branching Example**

Use the example of branching on the subject of computers on page 22 to answer these questions.

1. What are some of the differences between laptop and desktop computers?

   Differences include degree of convenience, amounts of memory, available features,

   and security from theft.

2. Choose one of the groups of ideas, and write it in the space below. Add another level of details, or branches, to the right.

   Answers will vary.

Exercise 2.12 **Trying Branching**

1. Now it's your turn to try branching. On a separate sheet of paper, create a branching on *computers* or on either of the following subjects: *a recent argument, advertisements.*

2. Highlight, underline, or circle the section or division of your branching that seems most interesting to you.

3. Choose the point that holds the most promise for development and list it on your paper. Then add three additional details about this promising idea.

4. On the same page, answer the following questions:
   a. What did you like best about branching as a prewriting technique?
   b. What did you like least?

Challenge 2.4 **Evaluating Branching**

COLLABORATION

1. Now exchange your branching with a classmate. On your classmate's paper, place a ✓ beside ideas about which you'd like to learn more. Return the paper and discuss your choices. Save your own branching for later use.

2. Will you use this prewriting technique again? Explain your reasoning.

   Answers will vary. Some students will like the focus this visual technique provides,

   while others will find this feature restrictive.

Idea Mapping

A wide-open prewriting activity that combines words and images such as doodles, symbols, sketches, icons, and so forth is **idea mapping.** You may find this technique to be a rich source of ideas. According to the theory underlying this technique, it stimulates different parts of your brain. The words flow from the parts of the brain responsible for logic and analysis. The sketches and doodles arise from the parts responsible for creativity.

To create an idea map, start anywhere on the page. Write or draw one idea after another, as your mind ranges freely from word to image and back again. You can emphasize ideas or images by underlining or circling them.

Look at this idea map on the subject of habits:

When you finish an idea map, you can translate the images into the words they represent to you. For example, look at the line of figures in the upper right of the map, followed by "BLEEP!!!" Translated into words, it might take this form: "People swear so much now—no matter where you are, at a restaurant, in line at the supermarket, people use language they can't even print in the paper. Terrible habit." And the image of the talking head in the figure above could be changed into words in this way: "Some people just monopolize conversation—they talk on and on, never noticing that other people want to talk." These written versions of the images can then serve as ideas for a piece of writing. Highlight, circle, or underline the parts, either words or images, that have the most potential. You can then develop them more fully later in the writing process.

Exercise 2.13   **Defining Idea Mapping**

1. How does idea mapping help you use different areas of your brain?

   The drawings stimulate the creative areas, and the words trigger the logical and

   language areas.

2. How can you use sketches, doodles, or icons to help you develop ideas for writing?

   You translate the images into words and then add these ideas to the others you've

   generated.

Exercise 2.14   **Analyzing an Idea Map**

1. Name three ideas about habits you find on the idea map on page 25.

   Answers will vary somewhat. The habits include people talking on and on, smoking,

   swearing, littering, and voicing annoying verbal tics.

2. What images or words on the idea map do you find most interesting? Why?

   Answers will vary.

Exercise 2.15   **Trying Idea Mapping**

1. Here's a way to help you discover ideas using different areas of your brain. Play a favorite piece of music. On a separate piece of paper, create an idea map of your thoughts and feelings as you listen. If you prefer, complete an idea map on one of the following subjects: *the environment, self-esteem.*

2. Highlight, underline, or circle the portions (words and images) of your idea map that you think you can develop further. Translate images into words.

3. Choose the point that holds the most promise for development and list it on your paper. Then add three additional details about this promising idea.

4. On the same page answer the following questions:
   a. What did you like best about idea mapping as a prewriting technique?
   b. What did you like least?

Challenge 2.5   **Evaluating Idea Mapping**

Now exchange your idea map with a classmate. On your classmate's paper, place a ✓ beside the portion that you'd most like to see developed. Return the paper to the writer and explain your choice. Save your own idea map for later use.

Keeping a Journal

For writing practice and a valuable source of topics, use **journal writing** in a notebook or a separate section of your class notebook. Your journal will be your idea book. Several times a week, in addition to whatever other writing you are doing, write in your journal. Keep track of ideas that impress you, topics you want to explore, and day-to-day experiences you want to examine more closely. For those occasions when you don't have a particular subject in mind, here is a list of possible topics that you could explore in your journal:

confidence	ignorance	the most exciting	superstition
security	disappointment	profession	relaxation
family	a first date	an influential	music
reading	graduation	person	movie
childhood	frustration	dreams	last party attended
accident	anticipation	a first love	habit
souvenir	pressure	deadlines	Friday the 13th
pride	hunger	fashion	future
happiness	a special	an important	time
depression	possession	relationship	power

Each time you write in your journal, spend at least ten to twenty minutes exploring your subject. Then look back at the material and decide which ideas you might be able to develop more fully. Highlight, underline, or circle them for future exploration and development.

Here is a journal entry on the subject of *freedom:*

> On holidays like the 4th of July, people talk about freedom. But are people really free? You can't just do anything you want when you want. Like speeding down the highway. You can get arrested and lose your license. How is that freedom? Maybe it's unrealistic to think we can have complete freedom. I guess we do need laws. But not so many. And we are free to do things here that people can't always do in other countries. Criticizing the government—in some other countries, you end up in jail, or dead. You have the freedom to travel anywhere in the country, too, even move anywhere if you have the money to live there. Money—now that's the way to be free. When you have enough money and you live here in the U.S.,

you have all kinds of freedom. We live in the land of the free, especially if you have plenty of cash.

Don't worry if your entries aren't as complete or correct as you'd like them to be. The purpose of your journal is not to create perfect writing, but to practice writing. The best way to improve as a writer is to practice. Journal entries are great opportunities to develop your skills as a writer. As with any other activity, writing becomes easier the more you do it. Writing regularly in your journal is one of the best ways to make writing seem as natural as talking and thinking.

Maintaining a Response Journal

Sometimes doing one thing accomplishes more than one aim. Maintaining a **response journal** is one of those situations. With this kind of journal, at least once a week you need to write in reaction to what you have covered in your various classes. Preparing the entries for your response journal gives you the opportunity to practice your writing. As a result, you develop a greater mastery of writing. In addition, because writing about something helps you gain a greater understanding of it, keeping a response journal will help you better understand what is going on in your classes.

Consider this entry in reaction to a sociology class:

> *Talked in class today about racism and sexism – students seemed afraid to be really honest about race relations. Everybody said they thought everyone was equal – I asked how come there's still so much racism out there in the news. Dr. Frank laughed, felt better. Girl who sits behind me, she has one black parent, one white – told us just yesterday someone in the bookstore said something about her under his breath. This other guy, walking home from the library one night, said some other guys started throwing rocks and yelling "gook" because he's from Cambodia. Room got real quiet. What's it mean? Dr. Frank asks. My answer – big trouble!!!!! After all the Civil Rights fights in the 1960s, there are still people who think they are superior to others based on appearance or gender. It's not over. We all need to treat each other with respect, as equals. That's what we are supposed to be about in the U.S.*

As you can see, this journal entry recounts what went on during a class discussion. But at the same time, it also explores the meaning of that experience. If you write a weekly journal entry for each of your courses, you very likely will feel more connected to what is going on in your classes. Even more important, you'll gain a greater understanding of the subject matter.

Exercise 2.16   **Defining a Journal's Purpose**

1. How does writing in a journal on a regular basis help you develop your skills as a writer?

   Journals offer a chance to practice writing until writing about ideas becomes as

   natural as thinking and talking about them. Regular writing helps students discover

   connections between writing and thinking.

2. What are the two advantages of maintaining a response journal?

   When you maintain a response journal, you improve your writing skills and you gain

   a greater understanding of the subject matter you are writing about.

Exercise 2.17   **Analyzing the Journal Entries**

1. Review the entry about *freedom* on pages 27–28. In your view, what is the most effective example or detail? Why do you feel this way?

   Answers will vary. Many students will focus on the material about money as it relates to

   freedom because money provides privileges beyond what average people experience.

2. Take another look at the entry concerning racism from the response journal on page 28. In your own words, explain the significance of what the writer learned from the class discussion on racism.

   Despite advances in the past 35 years, racism remains a serious problem, and it

   affects all communities.

Exercise 2.18   **Trying Journal Writing**

1. Now it's your turn to try journal writing. In your notebook, write a page on one of the following subjects: *sexism, dieting, learning a skill* (driving, dancing, computer operation, etc.).

2. Reread your entry, and highlight a section you'd like to explore in greater detail.

3. Look again at the part of your journal entry that you highlighted. Write this part on your notebook page, and add three more details about it.

4. On the same page of your notebook, answer the following questions:
   a. What did you like best about journal writing as a prewriting technique?
   b. What did you like least?

Challenge 2.6   **Analyzing Your Writing Rituals**

Think of the last time you did any extended writing outside the classroom and answer this question: When you write, what rituals do you follow?

For example, do you use a special pen or pencil or write on a special type of paper? Do you like music or television in the background or do you prefer silence? Do you change clothes? Where do you work—at a desk or table, on a bed, on the floor? Do you prefer a particular time of day? Write a journal entry about your writing rituals, and then share your entry with a classmate. See what rituals—if any—you have in common.

SPOTLIGHT PIECE:

Considering the Way Prewriting Ideas Are Developed

Here's a short essay by student Libelia Santos on how important getting an education has been for her. The annotations to the left of Libelia's essay offer some insight regarding how she effectively developed her prewriting material. Read her essay and the annotations, and then answer the questions that follow the piece.

The Answer I Was Looking For

Libelia indicates her focus—that getting an education is a necessity—to guide her reader.

I have learned a hard lesson in life that all people need to know. This lesson is that getting an education is one of the most important things in life. I did not always feel this way, but, believe me, I do now.

Here are the key prewriting ideas that Libelia developed to make her point about the need for education clear for her reader. Notice the additional details she supplied to make the ideas clear for her reader.

I came from Portugal when I was just about 10 years old. At first, it was very hard for me to adapt to life because I didn't know the language. After I was placed in a non-English class, it only took me a few months to learn the language. I did extremely well, and the following year I went to the fourth grade and continued with my classmates through eighth grade.

However, the day that I turned sixteen years old, my father told me that I had to quit school and go to work. I did exactly that. I really did not try to persuade my father to let me stay in school. I was already sixteen and in the eighth grade, and I just didn't fit in.

To make a long story short, I met my husband, married him, had seven children, and one miscarriage, but still no education. This was okay because my husband had a good job and supported all of us. I didn't have a lot, but I had what was necessary to live.

Suddenly one day my husband was diagnosed with multiple sclerosis. After he was diagnosed, he only worked for about a year and started to go downhill, and I went through hell and back trying to survive. Then one day I said to myself, I can't live like this anymore. First I took a test and became an American citizen and then I picked up the phone and registered for GED classes.

Libelia repeats her focus, emphasizing that education is the answer she has been seeking.

I passed my GED, and here I am in college taking courses. I love to learn, and I'm doing well. I work really hard, but now for the first time in a long time, I feel the hope that I had lost so long ago. I feel that I can accomplish something and get a good job, so I can take good care of my family. From my experiences, I now know that all people really need a good education.

COLLABORATION

Exercise 2.19   **Exploring the Reading**

1. In her first paragraph, as the annotations show, Libelia indicates the focus that grew out of the prewriting material. Working with a classmate, take another look at Libelia's introductory paragraph. Then, on the lines below, explain how the other sentences in that paragraph help to explain and support Libelia's focus.

   Answers will vary somewhat, but most students will note that the two additional sen-

   tences in the introduction emphasize that the lesson she has learned is an important

   lesson for everyone, regardless of stage or station in life.

2. Libelia uses her final paragraph to emphasize her focus again. In your view, what detail or sentence in this paragraph does the best job of demonstrating that what Libelia has said about education is true? Write your answer on the lines below.

   Answers will vary, although many students will make note of the sentence in which

   she explains that getting an education has given her hope once more.

Understanding the Subject through Writing

In her essay, Libelia makes it clear how important education is. If she is correct, why does it seem that so many students, especially in middle and high school, are uninterested and disruptive? On a separate sheet of paper, write a brief passage (50 to 100 words) in which you discuss why you think many of today's students reject what Libelia maintains is so important.

Discovering Connections 2.1

Take a look at this picture. No doubt you've seen this sign before. Does it remind you of an experience behind the wheel of a car or as a passen-

ger? Were you ever involved in or witness to an accident? What happened? Did you or a friend or family member go the wrong way on a one-way street or violate some other traffic law and get pulled over by the police? What occurred as a result? Focus on the details.

Or maybe the picture makes you think of what the words *one way* represent. Have you had an experience in your life when you were told you could go or do something one way only? What was it? How did you deal with it? Is there one way you have found to ensure success as a worker or student? What is it?

Use your favorite prewriting technique to explore your ideas about this picture. See what you can discover. Consider the purpose you might fulfill. Save your work for possible development into a polished writing later.

Discovering Connections 2.2

Using one of the prewriting techniques discussed in this chapter, explore the idea that many people juggle several roles in their lives. They are parents, employees, children, and students, to name only a few of these roles. When you think of who you are, what roles come to your mind? Which role is the most important or the most challenging at this point in your life? Why? Help readers understand who you are by writing about what you do in this most important role. Use a separate sheet of paper to record your ideas. Save your work. You may want to develop this material later.

RECAP PREWRITING: DEVELOPING IDEAS

New terms in this chapter	The Process
● **freewriting**	● Write everything that comes into your head for a ten-minute period without stopping to edit.
● **brainstorming**	● List specifically related ideas on a topic.
● **clustering**	● Draw a circle around a topic and then list and circle all ideas that come to mind, drawing lines to connect them.
● **branching**	● List the topic on the left and write the ideas that develop from the topic to the right, drawing lines to connect them.
● **idea mapping**	● Write words and doodle or draw pictures or symbols inspired by the topic.
● **journal writing**	● Several times a week, on a regular basis, write in a separate note-book on subjects that interest you.
● **response journal writing**	● Once a week, write your reaction to subjects covered in each of your classes.

Chapter 3

Composing: Creating Topic Sentences and Supporting Sentences

Getting Started... **Q:** I've developed some good ideas and I know what I want my focus to be. So what do I do now? How do I turn this focus and these ideas into a piece of writing that will make sense to somebody else?

A: By generating some solid ideas and identifying what you want to focus on, you've already laid the groundwork for an effective writing. Now you need to transform these ideas into units that communicate your meaning to a reader: complete sentences. In other words, you need to express your prewriting material in groups of words containing subjects and verbs and expressing complete thoughts. Once you do, you are on your way to creating an effective piece of writing.

Overview: Understanding Composing

The first step in writing, as Chapter 2, "Prewriting: Developing Ideas," shows, is identifying a subject and generating ideas about it. The second step is to *transform* your ideas, presenting them in a way that your reader can understand. In the writing process, this step is called *composing*. When you compose, you follow up on the exploration and discovery you've begun in prewriting. You examine the most promising ideas and the main point or focus you've identified in your prewriting material. Then, to make these ideas you have chosen understandable to others, you express them in complete sentence form. Finally, you organize these sentences into paragraphs. You do this by turning your main ideas into topic sentences and creating other sentences to explain or support your main idea.

In this chapter, you will learn how to create these two important paragraph elements

● topic sentences

● supporting sentences

Defining the Paragraph

A **paragraph** is a group of sentences that relate to one main idea or topic. Writers use paragraphs as units that organize and group their ideas. There is no ideal length for a paragraph. How many sentences you include in any one paragraph will always depend on what you are trying to say and why you are writing. In the kind of academic writing called for in this and other courses, however, paragraphs often run between five and ten sentences. One sentence states the main idea, and the other sentences support it.

The following figure shows how a paragraph is arranged:

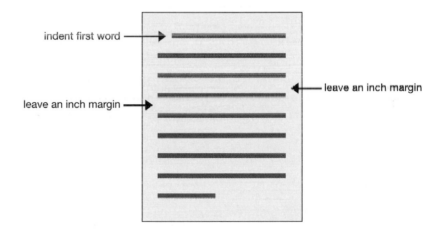

indent first word

leave an inch margin

leave an inch margin

As the illustration shows, you *indent* the first sentence, moving the first word in about one-half inch on the paper. This visual cue tells readers that they are about to encounter a new topic. The rest of the sentences in the paragraph flow from margin to margin, one following the other. After the last sentence in the paragraph, you leave the remainder of the line blank, and indent for the next new paragraph.

Consider this sample paragraph:

> *Rude and aggressive behavior seems to be all around us in today's world.* For example, many drivers treat streets and highways like they

are racetracks. They speed, cutting off other drivers and barely missing pedestrians. Yesterday I saw a car bounce up on the sidewalk to avoid a traffic jam and nearly hit an old woman. People waiting in line to shop are also often impolite and hostile. I've actually seen customers at the supermarket get into a shoving match. The big problem was that one of them had 13 items in the 12 items or less aisle. But the worst cases of offensive behavior are the ones that occur during youth sports games or matches. In some cases, parents or coaches become so infuriated during the games that they begin insulting and yelling at players and each other. Sometimes, there are even physical altercations. A couple of years ago, a parent actually beat a coach to death after a youth hockey game. Whether it's on the roads, in a shop or store, or in the grandstands, polite and respectful behavior is in short supply.

Like many paragraphs, this one opens with the **topic sentence,** the group of words that states the main idea. It answers the reader's unstated question: "What's the point?" The sentences that follow, known as the **body** of the paragraph, support or illustrate the topic sentence.

Also, when a paragraph, like this one on rude and aggressive behavior, stands as an entire document, it should include a **closing sentence.** This sentence brings the paragraph to an appropriate, logical close, reminding your reader of the significance of what you've just presented. With multi-paragraph writing, however, a closing sentence for each paragraph is often unnecessary. In these longer pieces, the meaning of one paragraph is generally expanded upon in the paragraph following it.

Exercise 3.1   **Defining the Process of Composing**

1. In your own words, explain the steps in the process of composing.

   First you decide which ideas you want to use from your prewriting. Next, you have

   to put those ideas into sentences. Then you need to arrange the sentences into a

   paragraph that has a topic sentence and supporting sentences.

2. What is the difference between the topic sentence and the sentences in the body of the paragraph?

   The topic sentence explains the main idea of the entire paragraph. The other sen-

   tences explain the topic sentence, providing additional examples and details.

Exercise 3.2   **Recognizing Topic Sentences**

1. The following passage contains two paragraphs run together. After reading the passage, put a paragraph symbol (¶) at the point where the second paragraph should begin and underline the two topic sentences.

<u>Professor Chen's U.S. history course was the most challenging class I took last semester.</u> First of all, there was too much material to cover. We had to learn all the major events in history from the Civil War to the present. Every week, I had to read fifty fact-filled pages in our textbook and pass a twenty-question true/false quiz. Also, I had to give a five-minute speech, using props, about an important historical leader I admired. (¶) <u>Math, on the other hand, was not as difficult for me as I thought it would be.</u> After every class I reviewed my notes on the lesson the instructor had explained that day. I didn't feel too rushed to learn everything at once, because we went step by step in class and never went to the next chapter until everyone had learned that one. We had tests every two weeks, so I had plenty of time to study.

2. On the following lines, briefly explain why you think the second paragraph should begin at that point.

The ¶ belongs after the fifth sentence. The first five sentences focus on history class,

but the final four deal with math class, indicating the need to begin a new paragraph.

Exercise 3.3   **Seeing the Connection between the Topic Sentence and the Body Sentences**

1. Here are two paragraphs with the topic sentences removed. Below each are three possible topic sentences. Read each paragraph, and circle the topic sentence that best fits each paragraph.

Verbal abuse affects children because it lowers their self-esteem. How can children who repeatedly hear their parents call them "worthless" or "stupid" think positively about themselves? In addition, physical abuse teaches children to respond to problems in life with violence. Many adult batterers report that they suffered physical abuse as children. Furthermore, people who were sexually abused as children often suffer from a wide variety of problems in adulthood. Statistics show that they experience higher than average rates of substance abuse, school difficulties, and marital problems.

a. Apathy about good parenting is a major problem here in the United States.

b. Childhood is the most important period in a person's life.

c. (Child abuse, no matter what type, affects its victims into adulthood.)

The grass in the back was matted and tangled, and the ground still oozed when you stepped on it. The flowers on the rhododendron bush next to the cellar door had fallen off, and the drain pipe had broken away from the gutter. In front of the house next to the stairs, the water had formed a pool several inches deep and four feet across. The stream running alongside the driveway had spilled over its banks, and the water was running rapidly. Several of the bushes and smaller trees next to the stream had been uprooted and were leaning into the water. In another hour or so, they'd be gone.

a. A lush lawn is an important feature when it is time to sell a home.

b. (The damage to our house and yard from two days of thunderstorms was unbelievable.)

c. Natural disasters cost insurance companies millions of dollars each year.

2. On the following lines, explain your choices.

Paragraph one ___Topic sentence c is the proper choice because the sentences in___

___the body all discuss types of child abuse.___

_____

Paragraph two ___Topic sentence b is the proper choice because the sentences in___

___the body all deal with the damage that occurred as a result of severe weather.___

_____

Focusing on a Topic

How do you decide what ideas to develop into topic sentences? Sometimes you already know what aspect of a subject will be your focus. When you don't, explore the general topic through the prewriting technique that works best for you. (See Chapter 2 to review prewriting techniques.)

For instance, imagine you have been asked to write about life in a big city. You like the topic because you have always lived in a city. You feel that life in a city has more to offer residents than life in the country, a small town, or the suburbs. To decide what aspect of life in the city you will focus on, you do some clustering. This is the result:

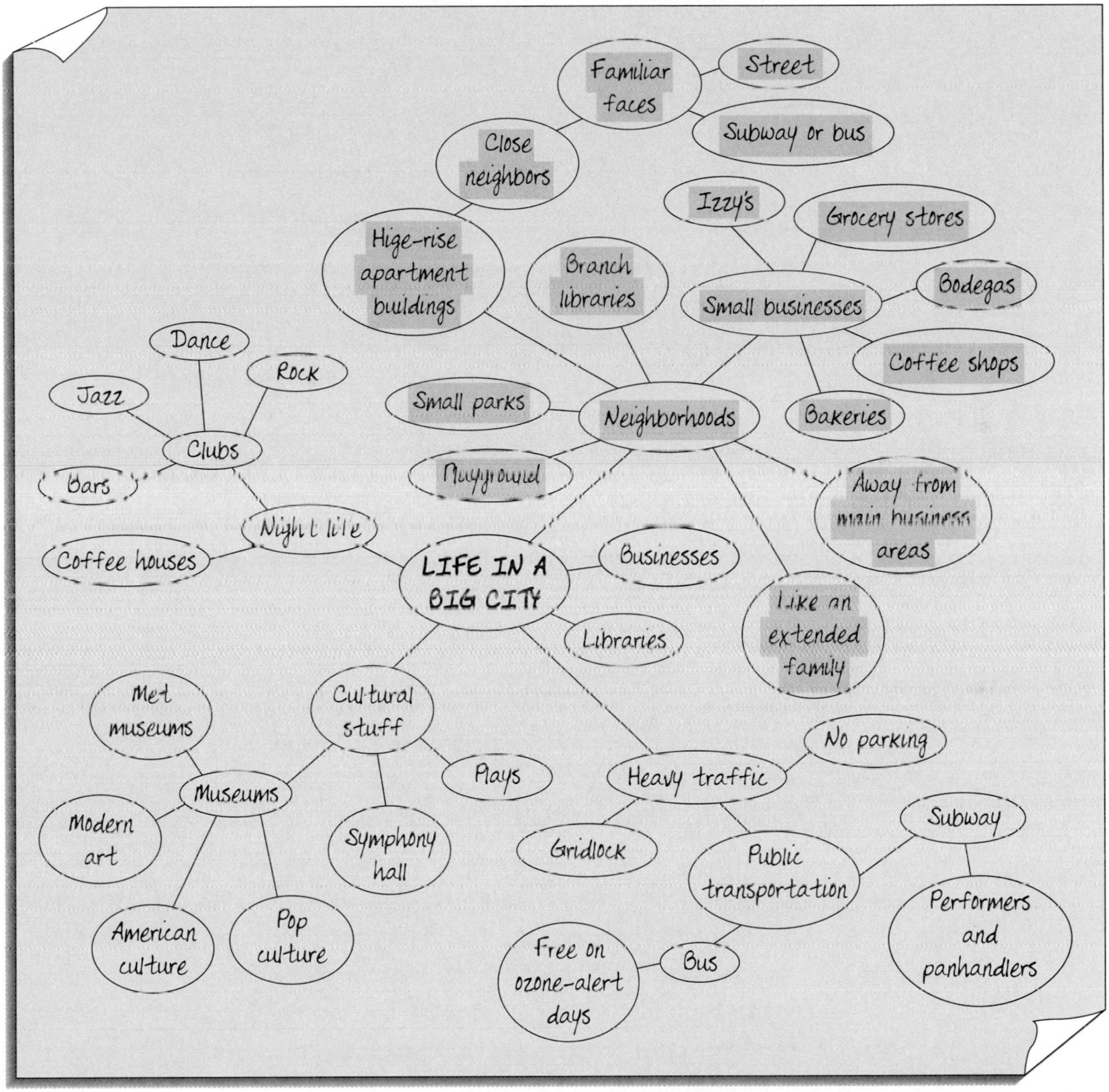

As the previous chapter indicates, once you have completed your prewriting, you need to identify the ideas that you would like to write about more. You can do this by highlighting, underlining, or circling them. In this case, several areas of the clustering feature good ideas. Overall, however, the material about neighborhoods offers this writer the most promise for development. Another writer might be more drawn to a different section of the cluster. Identify this material as the figure shows and you are all set for the next stage: identifying a specific focus and writing a topic sentence.

Exercise 3.4   **Understanding How to Focus on a Topic**

1. How do you turn a large, general subject into a smaller, focused topic you can cover well in a paragraph?

   You do some prewriting and then identify a solid focus and potential supporting ideas.

2. How can you identify ideas in a prewriting that you want to keep?

   You identify prewriting ideas to keep by highlighting, underlining, or circling them.

Exercise 3.5   **Selecting a Topic Focus**

1. Working with a classmate, take a look at the following prewriting on the subject *a special place*.

   > A special place?—special, don't know—room? can't seem to get started—how about the beach, the best, espec. in the winter, walk for a couple of miles, no other people, just seagulls—ok, what now, stuck, stuck, stuck!! help! being alone, same as lonely? no, big difference—back to the beach, love the smell, hair thick with moisture, take shoes off sometimes even in winter, sand always feels so damp, like to go there to think, totally relaxing, like taking a nap. Now what? relaxing, not lonely, by myself, private time, what else about the beach? Yes!! the little kids in the summer at the beach, little kids there are cool, just playing, making things with the sand, running along the edge of the water, makes me remember when I was a kid, no worries, no job, no school, just going to the beach and hating to leave

   Select a section or idea that you both feel holds promise. On a separate sheet of paper, develop at least five additional details about this aspect of the freewriting.

2. On the following lines, note which three of these new details you both think a reader would be most interested in and explain why.

   Answers will vary depending on the details selected.

Exercise 3.6   **Practicing Developing a Focus**

1. On a separate sheet of paper, prewrite on the subject *jealousy*, using the prewriting technique you prefer.

2. Highlight, circle, or underline the most promising ideas in this prewriting. Save this material for use for other exercises in this chapter. Or, if you prefer, perform these same steps on the prewriting you completed for Discovering Connections 2.1 or 2.2 in Chapter 2 (page 32), and use this material instead.

Challenge 3.1   **Offering a Classmate Help in Focusing a Topic**

COLLABORATION

Exchange the prewriting you worked on for Exercise 3.6 with a classmate. On the prewriting you receive, put an * in the margin next to one idea that sparks your interest. On the same paper, write one or two questions you have about this subject. Then return the paper to its owner.

Developing the Topic Sentence

Once you have decided which idea to develop into a topic sentence, you can begin working on the best way to express it. Typically, a topic sentence communicates two things: (1) the *topic* itself and (2) the writer's *attitude or reaction* to it. Look again at the topic sentence from the paragraph on page 35–36 about rude and aggressive behavior:

EXAMPLE

| topic | attitude or reaction |

Rude and aggressive behavior *seems to be all around us* in today's world.

As you can see, the topic is rude and aggressive behavior. The writer's attitude concerns the apparent inability to avoid such behavior.

When you develop a topic sentence, it's important that the sentence get right to the point, as the sample topic sentence does. Don't announce what you plan to do. Instead, concentrate on *expressing* what makes your point interesting or significant. Avoid beginning your topic sentence with words like "I am going to write about" or "This paragraph will cover."

If you were writing based on the big city clustering, your next task would be to express your attitude or reaction to the material on neighborhoods. You would try to answer the reader's question, "What's the point?"

One approach could be to explore people's misconceptions about what it's like to live in a big city. Many see big cities as cold, impersonal places where thousands—sometimes millions—of people live and work without ever getting to know each other.

But the clustering indicates something quite different. Specifically, a big city is actually a series of small neighborhoods, each with its own restaurants, shops, bakeries, and coffee shops. Apartment houses are close to each other, and they house hundreds of people who see each other every day on the streets, in the stores and diners, and on the subway or bus.

Here's a topic sentence that expresses this view:

```
  ┌────── topic ──────┐   ┌────── attitude or reaction ──────┐
```

EXAMPLE   **Living in a big city** *can seem like living in a small village.*

This topic sentence is effective because it answers the question "What's the point?" concerning living in the city. It therefore meets the needs of the reader.

Exercise 3.7   **Evaluating the Effectiveness of Topic Sentences**

1. On the lines that follow, explain what makes the following topic sentence effective:

   Answering essay questions successfully is a skill that can be learned.

   This topic sentence is effective because it contains both a topic—answering essay

   questions—and a clearly expressed attitude about taking such tests.

   _____

2. On the lines that follow, explain what makes the following topic sentence ineffective:

   I am going to write about ways you can successfully take an essay test.

   This topic sentence is ineffective because it is an announcement. It should be

   revised to eliminate the words that announce the writer's intent and to make the

   attitude or reaction about the topic clearer.

Exercise 3.8   **Identifying Topics and Writer Attitudes**

Read these possible topic sentences. In each sentence, circle the topic, then underline the writer's attitude or reaction to it. Study the example first.

EXAMPLE   (Children) *should* be (given pets) *only if they are able and willing to care*

for them.

1. The (minimum wage) should be raised.

2. The (new house) I bought needs a lot of minor repairs.

3. (Watching too much television) can harm children's imaginations.

4. (Voting in local elections) is a responsibility everyone should meet.

5. (Hollywood's view of senior citizens) reinforces negative stereotypes about them.

6. The (rise of white supremacist groups) is a frightening aspect of life in the United States.

7. The (ban on cigarette smoking) in most fast-food restaurants has made eating out more pleasant for millions of people.

8. (Knowing how to use a computer) is crucial for anyone looking for professional success.

Exercise 3.9   Identifying Elements of Topic Sentences

Choose a passage of five or six paragraphs from a section of one of your textbooks or a magazine article. Identify the topic sentences for three of the paragraphs, and write them on the lines that follow. Then circle the topic and underline the writer's attitude or reaction to it.

Topic Sentence 1   Answers will vary depending on the sentence chosen.

Topic Sentence 2   Answers will vary depending on the sentence chosen.

Topic Sentence 3   Answers will vary depending on the sentence chosen.

Exercise 3.10   Writing a Topic Sentence

COLLABORATION

Here are ten topics. Working with a classmate, write a possible topic sentence for each on the available lines.

1. The availability of new medications   means an improved quality of life for people with asthma.

2. Theme parks like Disney World   do a great job with crowd management.

3. NASCAR racing   is the most exciting sport I have ever witnessed.

4. Inexpensive cell phones ___have led to people having phone conversations in___ ___some pretty unusual places.___

5. Union members ___enjoy benefits like regular pay raises, pensions, and job___ ___security.___

6. The cost of going to a theater to see a movie ___is worthwhile due to the sound___ ___quality alone.___

7. Being able to create Web Pages ___makes you even more attractive to many___ ___employers.___

8. The introduction of hybrid gas and electric powered cars _____ ___has yet to have much effect on overall air quality.___

9. The popularity of reality television shows ___indicates the public's___ ___dissatisfaction with traditional sit-coms and dramas.___

10. Taking a volunteer position in your field ___is a great chance to___ ___|demonstrate your skills and abilities.___

Challenge 3.2   **Developing a Strong Topic Sentence**

For Exercise 3.6 (page 41), you identified some promising prewriting ideas. Using the discussion and examples on developing a strong topic sentence to guide you, write a topic sentence for this material.

Keeping Your Topic Sentence Clear and Specific

The secret to creating an effective topic sentence is to keep it clear and specific. For example, imagine you had chosen to write on another aspect of living in a big city: the opportunities for night life. You might write a topic sentence like this:

WEAK   Night life in the city can be fun.

This topic sentence is too vague, or general, to communicate your ideas clearly. It is also so broad in scope that you could fill many pages writing about it. In addition, it doesn't explain what you mean by "fun," and it does not name any "fun" activities.

Now look at this revised version:

> **STRONG** Night life in the city offers the opportunity to enjoy a wide variety of activities after dark, such as nightclubs, theaters, restaurants, and movies.

The revised topic sentence makes a strong, clear statement. It focuses specifically on the activities that make night life in the city attractive. In addition, it sets a direction for the supporting sentences that will follow.

Placing the Topic Sentence Effectively

Because the topic sentence presents the main idea of a paragraph, writers often place it first in the paragraph. That way, readers find out right away what the paragraph will be about and in what direction it is heading.

This is a good pattern to follow as you develop your writing skills. Occasionally, though, you'll find that the topic sentence fits better at the end or in the middle of the paragraph. As you become more experienced, you can try these other patterns. No matter where you place the topic sentence, always be sure that it clearly states the topic and your attitude toward it.

Exercise 3.11   **Considering Topic Sentence Placement**

1. Where is a topic sentence usually placed within a paragraph? Why?

   Generally, the topic sentence is placed at the beginning of a paragraph so readers

   will know right away what the paragraph will cover.

2. Here is a sample paragraph with the topic sentence listed after it:

   > About two minutes after the start of the race, I developed a mild ache in my side. I figured that I could keep going and the pain would go away. Ten minutes later the pain was worse. I found it harder and harder to breathe, but I refused to give into the pain. I had trained for two months, and I was determined to finish. Unfortunately, after another five minutes of struggling, I had to stop and walk the rest of the way.

   Topic sentence: *My first five-mile road race very quickly became a complete disaster.*

   Working with a classmate, consider three different placements for the topic sentence. First, insert the topic sentence at the beginning. Second, insert it in the middle. Finally, insert it at the end. Read the paragraph aloud with each placement. Then, on the lines below, explain where you think the topic sentence fits best and why.

Most students will agree that the topic sentence fits best at the beginning of the

paragraph because it prepares the reader for the rest of the story.

Exercise 3.12 **Identifying Effective Topic Sentences**

1. Here are several potential topic sentences. Label the strong topic sentences with an *S* and the weak ones with a *W.* Study the examples first.

EXAMPLES

<u>_W_</u> You can get a lot of free tourist information.

<u>_S_</u> When stress has you frazzled, try one of these techniques to relax and refresh yourself.

<u>S</u> a. I will never forget the confidence and encouragement that my high school math teacher gave me.

<u>W</u> b. Tabloid TV shows are a waste of time.

<u>S</u> c. Aggressive recycling programs are necessary in order for us to preserve precious natural resources.

<u>W</u> d. In-line skating is hard.

<u>W</u> e. Part-time jobs are important to college students.

<u>S</u> f. Joining a parent's council is a great way to help your child get a good education.

<u>W</u> g. Television game shows are boring.

<u>W</u> h. I don't enjoy dancing.

<u>S</u> i. The best thing about going back to school is feeling good about myself again.

<u>S</u> j. The Internet has provided the opportunity for people from all over the world to get in touch.

2. Working with a classmate, select two of the weak topic sentences you have identified above. On the lines that follow, rewrite them so that they are more effective.

Answers will vary depending on the weak topic sentence chosen. Here is a sample

response for sentence b: Because tabloid TV shows present the seamy side of life

rather than anything enlightening, educational, or entertaining, they are not worth

watching.

Writing Effective Topic Sentences

The following topic sentences are weak. Working with a classmate, improve and rewrite them on the lines that follow. Use the example to guide you.

Answers will vary. Sample responses are shown.

EXAMPLE   Mario's is a good restaurant.

Mario's serves the best, most authentic Italian food in town.

1. Virtual reality is a new computer technology.

   Computers can create a whole new experience of life for us, the world of virtual reality.

2. An appointment with the dentist is not fun.

   Taking a child to the dentist is not one of life's most pleasant experiences.

3. I'm going to write about an important lesson I learned as a child.

   When I cheated on a spelling test in fourth grade, I ended up learning a lesson

   about living.

4. The office where I work is an interesting place.

   If you want to see a diverse group of people work successfully together, come visit

   my office.

5. New technology is frustrating.

   Setting up my computerized personal organizer was unbelievably frustrating.

6. National Parks are great places.

National Parks like Yellowstone offer people the opportunity to experience the beauty

of animal and plant life in their truly natural settings.

7. Drivers face many hazards on the road.

The xenon headlights available on some new cars are so bright that other drivers

complain of being blinded.

8. Many states have some form of legalized gambling.

Advocates for gambling casinos fail to mention the increase in crime and personal

financial problems that often occur in surrounding areas when casinos are

established.

Challenge 3.3   **Analyzing and Revising Your Topic Sentence**

COLLABORATION

Exchange the topic sentence you wrote for Challenge 3.2 (page 44) with a classmate. Evaluate the draft topic sentence you receive to make sure it is clear and specific. If it is, mark it with a ✓. If not, circle the area that you feel needs to be adjusted, write a sentence explaining what it lacks, and return it to your reader.

Developing Supporting Ideas

Once you have developed a clear topic sentence, you need to develop the best possible supporting sentences. To do so, you reevaluate the ideas you highlighted in your prewriting, deciding which to use and which to save for possible use with another writing. Ultimately, you will select the best details and examples and then develop them to support your topic sentence.

Here again is the topic sentence that expresses the chosen focus about life in a big city:

EXAMPLE   **Living in a big city** can seem like living in a small village.

Look again at is the clustering on life in a big city on page 39, with the most promising ideas highlighted. A closer look at the highlighted section in the sample clustering shows that these ideas can be grouped into three general categories:

- **characteristics of buildings and public spaces:** *high-rise apartment houses, small parks, playground, branch library*
- **merchants and businesses in the neighborhood:** *bakeries, bodegas, grocery stores, local restaurants like Izzy's, coffee shops*
- **village-like characteristics:** *live close to neighbors, like an extended family, familiar faces on the street, in the shops, on the subway and bus*

Once you have grouped your ideas into categories, you can then decide which ideas to include as they are, which to combine with other ideas, and which to exclude because they won't offer sufficient support for the topic sentence.

Exercise 3.14   **Selecting Supporting Details**

1. What process should you follow to identify supporting ideas for your topic sentence?

   To identify supporting ideas for your topic sentence, you reevaluate the highlighted

   material in your initial prewriting.

2. What is the advantage putting potential supporting ideas you have developed into general categories or groups?

   Arranging promising prewriting details in general categories or groups makes it eas-

   ier to decide which ideas to keep, which to combine, and which to exclude.

Exercise 3.15   **Grouping Details into Categories**

1. Read this freewriting about *television*. Then on a separate sheet of paper, develop at least three categories and then list the bits of information in the appropriate groups. Cross out information that doesn't fit into any of the categories.

   Television - two sides, good and bad - good shows and great reruns - comedies - Seinfeld, Cheers, Friends, Raymond, Saturday Night Live, dramas - NYPD Blue, ER, Real World, Ally McBeal, always some game on - basketball, baseball, hockey - even classic games, watch too much now, put off stuff I should be doing like studying. How about innovations like satellite TV - 500 channels to pick from, built-in DVD player, TiVo system - records TV shows without tape. I hate losing the clicker, always gets stuck in the couch or under furniture. Public television - good science *shows, weekly political interviews, how much does it cost me in taxes? Too many fundraisers!! what about in the future? Will there be huge flat screen TVs. Maybe they'll broadcast in 3D. TV of the future will be total communications systems – computer, camera, telephone all in one*

2. Compare your categories and lists with a classmate. Together, choose the strongest category and, on the lines that follow, write a topic sentence for this material.

   Answers will vary depending on the material selected.

   _____

   _____

   _____

Challenge 3.4 **Developing Supporting Ideas for Your Paragraph**

COLLABORATION

Earlier in the chapter you did some prewriting for which you later created a topic sentence. You and a classmate then reevaluated this topic sentence for Challenge 3.3. Now, using the material above to guide you, arrange the most promising material from that original prewriting into groups of ideas with something in common.

Arranging Selected Details and Examples Effectively

After you group your ideas, you may want to subdivide the groups into smaller categories. You may also want to restate some of them or combine related ideas. In particular, you will want to think about the most logical order in which to present them so that your good ideas will come across clearly for your reader.

Here again is the information from the prewriting on life in the big city, arranged in categories.

- **characteristics of buildings and public spaces:** *high-rise apartment houses, small parks, playground, branch library*
- **merchants and businesses in the neighborhood:** *bakeries, bodegas, grocery stores, local restaurants like Izzy's, coffee shops*
- **village-like characteristics:** *live close to neighbors, like an extended family, familiar faces on the street, in the shops, on the subway and bus*

All three categories contain good information, but what would be the best order to present these ideas?

One approach would be to start with the businesses, to show that everything one needs is available in one small area. Next, you could move to the more general feature of the neighborhood and how these features bring people together, giving the place a small-village feeling. (For more on arranging information in a paragraph, see "Effective Organization" on pages 68–75 in Chapter 4 "Revising: Refining Your Draft.") Keep in mind that, at this point, you aren't locked into this plan. As you work through the rest of the writing process, you can always adjust the order if it will help you better communicate your ideas to your reader.

Exercise 3.16   **Observing the Importance of Order in a Paragraph**

1. Once you have grouped the details in your prewriting, what kinds of adjustments should you make?

   Once you have arranged your prewriting ideas in groups, you should consider

   subdividing the groups into smaller categories, restating some of the ideas,

   combining related ideas, and considering the most logical order for the material.

2. Why is it important to arrange your ideas in the most logical order?

   You should choose a logical order to present your information so that you will more

   effectively communicate your good ideas to your reader.

Exercise 3.17   **Identifying Strong Supporting Details**

1. Working with a classmate, look again at the three groups of information about life in the big city listed earlier. Decide which one you both think would be easiest to develop and, on the following lines, list it and explain your choice.

   Answers will vary somewhat. If students have lived in a neighborhood similar to the

   one suggested above—even if it was not in a big city—they may find the

   characteristics of the buildings and public spaces or the **merchants and**

   businesses in the neighborhood easiest to develop because they will be able to

   draw on their own backgrounds.

2. Choose one detail from the groups of information about life in the big city. On the lines that follow, turn this idea into a supporting sentence.

Answers will vary, depending upon the detail chosen. A representative sentence is

provided: Living so close to each other in high-rise apartment houses, most people

get to know their neighbors well.

<hr/>

Exercise 3.18   **Organizing Supporting Details**

1. Here is a brainstorming on the subject *nature*:

> camping trips every summer
> > swimming in Cosmo's Lake
> > day trips hiking
> pollution, ruining environment
> > that landfill outside of the city, ruining water
> > smell is awful
> > trash all over the city – really ugly mess
> my trip to the desert – so wide open and lonely
> > cactuses and weird rock formations
> > miles and miles of open road with no gas stations, etc. – scary
> rain forest – check notes from environment class!!
> > destruction of one species of plant or animal a day
> > reason for destruction – economic
> > land only good for one or two years of farming
> > affects weather in the rest of the world
> > what cures are we missing out on – herbs, etc.
> zoos
> > try to seem more natural
> > elephants and lions in Regional zoo given room to roam
> > new plains section

Working with a classmate, select one section of the brainstorming and, on a separate sheet of paper, copy it, adding at least five details or examples.

2. Group these ideas and set a preliminary order. Then on the same paper, explain why you both chose this order.

Challenge 3.5   **Grouping and Arranging Details for Your Paragraph**

1. For Challenge 3.4 (page 50) you established groups for the prewriting information you had identified as promising. Now, referring to the discussion and examples on arranging selected details and examples, write your supporting ideas in an effective order on a separate sheet of paper.

2. Exchange your listing with a classmate. On the sheet you receive, check the order. If you think the order is logical, put a ✓ on the page. If you have a suggestion for change, write it on the bottom of the page, explaining why your suggestion might work better, and return the list to your classmate.

Changing Writer-Centered Words into Reader-Centered Sentences

As you have seen, prewriting material isn't usually expressed in complete thoughts. This raw version of your first ideas is *writer centered*. It makes sense to you because they are your thoughts, but they won't make sense to anyone else unless you expand them and express them in a form that an independent reader can understand. In other words, you need to make your writing *reader centered* by explaining your ideas in detail and expressing them in *complete sentences*.

Think of making out a grocery list. When you write down an item like *peanut butter*, you probably don't include a brand name or size because you know exactly what you want to buy. Your list is *writer centered*.

However, if you were asking a friend to do your grocery shopping, you would need to provide more complete detail: *Please pick up a 16-ounce jar of Snazzle brand, crunchy, reduced-fat peanut butter*. Anyone who can understand written English could fulfill your request. The material is therefore *reader centered*. In other words, it makes sense to someone who lacks your specific background and knowledge about the subject you are discussing.

Consider this writer-centered detail from the clustering on life in the big city:

WRITER CENTERED   like an extended family

The idea does suggest something about living in a neighborhood within a big city. Right now, however, it doesn't explain why living there is like an extended family or what makes it seem that way to the writer. In short, it doesn't address the needs of the reader.

Look at how much more effective the point is in this reader-centered version that takes the needs of the reader into account:

READER CENTERED   The familiar faces on the streets, in the shops, and on the subway make the neighborhood seem like an extended family.

Exercise 3.19   **Defining Writer Centered and Reader Centered**

1. In your own words, explain the difference between writer-centered and reader-centered information.

   Writer-centered information is often brief and lacks detail. It is fully understood only

   by the writer. Reader-centered information is clear, detailed, and specific, easily

   understood by anyone.

2. How do you turn writer-centered details into reader-centered information?

   You turn writer-centered information into reader-centered information by adding all

   the details needed.

Exercise 3.20   **Making Your Writing Reader Centered**

1. Here are two details from another section of the clustering on life in a big city. On the lines provided, turn these writer-centered fragments into reader-centered sentences. (Answers will vary. Representative answers are shown.)

   a. night life   The dance clubs are open on Friday and Saturday night until 2 A.M.,

   and hundreds of people stay there dancing and socializing until closing.

   b. heavy traffic   By noontime, the downtown area has so much traffic that at

   several spots, cars, buses, and trucks don't even move for ten minutes at a time.

2. Exchange your sentences with a classmate. If you have a question about any of the sentences you receive, write it in the margin next to the sentence. Put a + beside sentences that already seem effectively reader centered.

Exercise 3.21   **Creating Reader-Centered Sentences**

1. Make a copy of a page of your notes from another class. Then exchange your notes with a classmate. On a separate sheet of paper, try to change your classmate's notes from writer-centered writing into reader-centered writing.

2. Give your reader-centered version of the notes to your classmate. When you get your own notes back, compare the version your classmate wrote with your original notes. Below your partner's version, list any details that were misunderstood or not fully explained. Rewrite one of these details so it explains what you meant.

Drafting a Complete Paragraph

If you have followed all the steps discussed so far, you have come a long way in your composing process. You have prewritten on a general topic and identified usable ideas. You have selected an important idea and developed it into a topic sentence. You have chosen supporting ideas, grouped them, and developed a plan for ordering them under your topic sentence. You also understand how to change your writer-centered prewriting into reader-centered sentences. Now you are ready to write a *first draft* of your paragraph.

The key here is relax. Your first draft doesn't have to be perfect. You will have the opportunity to *revise* it, to rework the less effective parts and polish it overall, as Chapter 4 will demonstrate. For now, concentrate on getting a reasonable version down on paper.

In fact, think in terms of creating *two* initial versions of your document: a rough draft and a first draft. The rough draft is the first complete version, and it is for your eyes only. Once this rough draft is complete, take a brief break and then scan it for any obviously awkward or unclear spots and any errors in form. Correct those, and you will have your first draft.

Whenever possible, use a computer to prepare your rough and first drafts. The various word-processing tools make it easier to eliminate problem spots as you work through the writing process. Always double or triple space your draft. If you can't use a computer, write on every other line. Either way, the additional spaces will give you room to make corrections by hand before you prepare your final draft.

Here's a first draft of a paragraph about life in the big city:

My Neighborhood: A Small Town
in the Middle of the Big City

Topic sentence

Supporting sentences

Living in a big city can seem like living in a small village. In my neighborhood, just about everything anybody could need is available within walking distance. There are several coffee shops, pizza places, bodegas, and small grocery stores. The area includes a small playground for children, its own branch library, and a small park with five benches and two picnic tables. The familiar faces on the streets, in the shops, and on the subway make the neighborhood seem like an extended family. The city recently increased the price of a weekly Public Transit Pass by 15 percent. Most residents live in really big apartment complexes. People get to know their neighbors and the shop owners and workers well. If you go into Izzy's, a small diner at the very center of the neighborhood, on a Friday or Saturday night, the tables and booths will be filled with people from the neighborhood. Many people spend a lot of time there. **On most days, it all seems so comfort-**

Closing sentence **able that I forget that my neighborhood is just a small part of an enormous city.**

As you can see, the paragraph begins with a strong topic sentence. The supporting ideas have been changed from their prewriting form into sentences. Some of the ideas have been adapted, and others have been combined. The supporting sentences are arranged somewhat according to the order shown on page 49. Also, this paragraph is intended to be a complete document, so it features a closing sentence that reemphasizes the point of the paragraph.

Certainly this first draft is not perfect. There is work still to be done, but that's all right. A first draft should never be your final draft. Instead, it should be a solid beginning, as this paragraph is.

Exercise 3.22   **Defining First Draft**

1. What is the final step in the process of composing?

   The final step in composing is to write a first draft—to write a clear paragraph with a

   topic sentence and supporting sentences.

   _____

   _____

2. Does your first draft have to be perfect? Explain.

   No, it does not have to be perfect because it will be revised.

   _____

   _____

   _____

Challenge 3.6   **Completing a First Draft Paragraph**

Using the paragraph on life in the big city to guide you, turn to the topic sentence and supporting ideas you developed for Challenge exercises in this chapter on page 53, and write a first draft paragraph on your chosen topic. Save this draft for later use.

SPOTLIGHT PIECE:

Considering a Complete First Draft Writing

Here's a short essay by student Rob Volpe about how his experiences growing up affected his view of himself and his choice of career. The annotations to the left of Rob's essay focus on several of Rob's topic sentences, illustrating the relationship between topic sentence and supporting sentences. Read his essay and the annotations and then answer the questions that follow the piece.

My Mission

Growing up, I was always teased for being poor and having the smallest house on the bus route. I would dread going to school, fearing the kids on the bus would make fun of me. I would even have trouble sleeping at night. I was always worried about what people thought of me. One year, for the first week of school, I even walked a quarter mile to my friend's house so I could take the bus there.

Topic sentence

Supporting sentences

This was a very tough time in my life, although it may seem like a little thing now. I can remember how lonely I felt. I knew I was different from everyone else in the upper middle class town in which I lived.

Topic sentence

It was not only my classmates but also the teachers who made things hard for me. Why didn't they stop the mockery? Sure, kids will be kids, but how can adults put up with seeing this? I even had a teacher tell me once when I was in the sixth grade, "Rob, you are nothing but a fuck up. You will never finish school. Maybe in prison you will have a chance."

Supporting sentences

Two years later, I read that teacher had been sentenced to prison for two years for cocaine dealing. After I read the headlines, I nearly died. I first thought to myself, "This guy is going to jail?" This was great. After what he told me, he must have felt pretty embarrassed. Wow!

Topic sentence

Next came a major turning point in my life. I decided I would send him a good luck card, because I knew he would need it. I thought, "Who should I listen to, negative people who just want to get in my head like those kids who made fun of me or that teacher, or to my head itself? I made up my mind then that I would become a teacher.

Supporting sentences

Every year of my life that has gone by, I feel stronger, no longer influenced by what others think. I can seriously say to myself now that I do not think I would have made it to high school, never mind become a college student, if this teacher had never been arrested. My reaction to what happened to him is why today I want to be a teacher.

Exercise 3.23 **Exploring the Reading**

1. Three of the paragraphs in Rob's essay are annotated. In your view, which of these paragraphs offers the best support for its topic sentence? On the lines that follow, explain your choice.

Answers will vary, although many students will select the second or third paragraph

because of the dramatic nature of the supporting information.

2. Working with a classmate, choose one of the other paragraphs and, on the lines below, explain the connection between the topic sentence and its supporting sentences.

Answers will vary, depending on which paragraph is chosen, but answers should

generally note that the supporting sentences illustrate the point made in the topic

sentence.

3. Here again are three of Rob's topic sentences. Working with a classmate, write the topic and the attitude or reaction for each on the lines that follow it.

a. This was a very tough time in my life although it may seem like a little thing now.

The topic is that it was a tough time and the attitude or reaction is how

surprising this reaction might seem.

b. It was not only my classmates but also the teachers who made things hard for me.

The topic is the behavior of the teachers and the attitude or reaction is how

difficult it made life for him.

c. Next came a major turning point in my life.

The topic is a turning point, and the attitude and reaction is that it had a major

impact on his life.

Understanding the Subject through Writing

In his essay, Rob explains how he was treated by one of his teachers and the way he responded when he discovered that this teacher was in serious legal trouble. On a separate sheet of paper, write a brief passage (50 to 100 words) in which you discuss Rob's reaction. Do you think you would have made the same choice? Why?

Discovering Connections 3.1

Look at the picture below. What story do you see in this illustration? Are you thinking of a great party you attended, or a deadly boring one? Are you thinking of the difficulty of finding the perfect gift for a special person in your life? Are you considering a special occasion in your own life—a birthday, a wedding, a graduation? Or perhaps you are considering an idea the package might represent: that we shouldn't judge what we see by its appearances. Flashy appearances can disguise a lack of substance. The opposite is true as well: What at first glance looks ordinary often turns out to be extraordinary.

For this assignment, explore and discover the possibilities of this photo. After you prewrite, apply the composing techniques introduced in this chapter to develop a first draft paragraph on your most workable idea. Also consider the purpose you might fulfill. Save all your work for later use.

Discovering Connections 3.2

For this assignment, focus on the topic *family*. The experiences, attitudes, and feelings that result from being part of a family provide rich subjects for writing. For example, is there one person in your family whose ideas and opinions shape the ideas and opinions of the rest of the family? Consider your own position in your family. Are you the youngest child, the oldest, or somewhere in the middle? Does this status make any difference in the way you are treated by family members? Think about your relationships with family members. Are you on bad terms with anyone? Why? Have you lost family members through death or divorce? Do you have friends that you consider family? Why?

Now that you've started thinking about family, you're ready to explore some aspect on paper. See what you can discover through prewriting. Then use the techniques introduced in this chapter to complete a first draft paragraph. Consider the purpose you might fulfill, too. Save your work. You may decide to revise it later.

RECAP COMPOSING: CREATING TOPIC SENTENCES AND SUPPORTING SENTENCES

New terms in this chapter	Definitions
● **paragraph**	● a group of sentences that relate to one main idea or topic
● **topic sentence**	● the sentence in a paragraph that states the main idea and the writer's attitude or reaction to it
● **body**	● sentences in a paragraph that support or explain the topic sentence
● **closing sentence**	● a sentence that brings a paragraph-length document to an appropriate, logical close, reemphasizing the significance of the paragraph

Steps to Developing an Effective Paragraph

7. Write a solid first draft, changing writer-centered words into reader-centered sentences.

6. Use a diagram to group and arrange the ideas for the paragraph.

5. From your prewriting, select the strongest supporting information and categorize it.

4. Make sure your topic sentence is specific and clear.

3. Name the topic and express your attitude or reaction toward it in a topic sentence.

2. Highlight, underline, or circle usable ideas and choose a topic.

1. Use the prewriting technique of your choice to generate ideas about a topic.

Chapter 4

Revising: Refining Your Draft

Getting Started... **Q:** OK, now I've completed my first draft. I've worked hard and made it as good as I could. So what do I gain by going back to work on it again?

A: Yes, you've worked hard, developing good ideas and an effective focus, and then you figured out the best way to express your ideas. You made your writing as good as you could—at that point. But whether you know it or not, doing so is tiring work. When you're fatigued you tend to overlook both weaknesses and possibilities for improvement. Let some time pass, and seek the response of an objective reader. You'll then see ways to make something good even better.

Overview: Understanding Revision

You may have heard from someone that you can complete an effective piece of work in just one draft. You may have thought so yourself.

It's simply not true.

Writing that's as good as it can be requires time, patience, and work. It must be reevaluated, reconsidered, and reworked. In other words, it must be *revised*. Revision is actually a three-step process. First, you **reassess** your writing, evaluating it and identifying what works and what doesn't. You do this by checking your writing for several things: (1) *unity*, or focus, (2) *coherence*, or smoothness and order, and (3) *effective language*. During reassessing, you should also enlist the aid of an objective reader.

Second, you **redraft.** This step involves rewriting to eliminate any problems with unity and coherence. It also involves **amplifying**—adding or clarifying details and examples, so that they communicate your meaning fully to your reader.

Finally, you **edit** your document. When you edit, you focus on eliminating any remaining errors in form. This step is vital because weaknesses in form distract a reader from the good ideas—the *content*—of a piece of writing. When you follow all these steps, the result is a greatly improved version of the initial draft.

This chapter explains how to improve, refine, and polish your first draft, making it clearer and more effective. You will learn that revising involves

- reassessing

- redrafting

- editing

Reassessing

Before you reassess your draft, put it aside for a day or so. You've worked hard, and you may feel that you have made your draft as good as it can be. If you allow a little time to pass, however, to create a distance, you will be able to look at your work with a fresher, more objective eye. When you are able to be objective, you're in a better position to check your draft for *unity, coherence,* and *effective language.*

Unity

If you want your reader to understand your ideas fully, you must make sure your writing is **unified.** In other words, all the examples and details must be directly related to your topic sentence. To give your writing unity, weed out any material that doesn't contribute directly to your main idea.

Look at this paragraph about witnessing an in-line skating accident and consider which material isn't directly connected to the topic sentence:

(1) Last week I saw an accident that demonstrates the importance of wearing wrist guards, elbow and kneepads, and a helmet when in-line skating. (2) I had just walked out of the cleaners when a young woman in-line skating without any safety equipment passed in front of the store. (3) I always have my dry cleaning done at this shop. (4) It has the best prices, and a classmate from middle school works there. (5) The skater looked back over her shoulder and didn't notice the orange cone in front of her. (6) Just beyond the cone, a segment of the sidewalk had been removed. (7) She skated past the cone, dropped into the trench, and immediately fell backward. (8) When I reached her, she was unconscious, with her right wrist bent out at a strange angle and the back of her head bleeding heavily. (9) While a clerk in the cleaners called the ambulance, a nurse who had been at the counter rushed out to take care of the skater. (10) The shortage of nurses in some areas of the United States is critical.

If you chose the third, fourth, and tenth sentences, you are correct. Although they are not *completely* unrelated, these sentences have nothing to do with the accident mentioned in the topic sentence and discussed in the body. Eliminate these three sentences, and the paragraph is unified.

Exercise 4.1   Defining Revision

1. On the following lines, briefly define and explain the three steps involved in revision.

   Revision involves three steps. The first step is reassessing, during which you evaluate

   your draft in terms of unity, coherence, and language. The second step is redrafting,

   during which you generate new information to address the gaps you've identified dur-

   ing reassessing. The third step is editing, during which you eliminate errors in form.

2. How do you make sure your writing is unified?

   To ensure that your writing is unified, you take out any information that is not directly

   related to your topic sentence.

Exercise 4.2   Analyzing Unity and Eliminating Unrelated Sentences

1. Underline the topic sentence in each of the following paragraphs. Then cross out any sentences that are not directly related to the topic.

   A. (1) <u>The number of people who read a daily newspaper is declining for several reasons.</u> (2) For one thing, many people don't have time. (3) Some people say they can't spare twenty minutes in their hectic days to sit down and read a paper. (4) ~~Stress from pressure at work can have serious health effects~~. (5) They tune into the news on their car radios as they drive to work, or they catch the highlights on TV as they get ready for bed at night. (6) ~~By adding a lot of color, *USA Today* has influenced the way newspapers look~~. (7) Also, some people prefer to watch news shows rather than read about news. (8) Finally, newspapers are printed only once a day, so the news in them may be a day or more old. (9) ~~Today's satellite TV systems are much more compact and much less expensive~~. (10) Television, however, can update the news any time during the day and can bring events as they are happening to our living rooms.

B. (1) <u>When I started school, I didn't always feel accepted by my classmates because of my hearing deficiencies.</u> (2) In first grade, for example, Timothy Julius, the boy who sat next to me, used to stick his fingers in his ears whenever he talked to me. (3) The teacher spoke with him about it several times, but he would still tease me whenever the teacher wasn't looking. (4) On many mornings, I ended up in tears. (5) ~~When Timothy was a sophomore in high school, he was arrested for breaking into a warehouse.~~ (6) ~~Now he is studying to be a minister.~~ (7) As a result of his teasing, I became more self-conscious and less confident. (8) For instance, I began to think that all the kids in class were staring at my hearing aids. (9) I finally started meeting with the school psychologist who worked with me to improve my self-image. (10) Thanks to her help, I began to feel more confident within a few months.

2. Working with a classmate, develop at least two additional sentences for each of these paragraphs, and write them on a separate sheet of paper.

Challenge 4.1   **Maintaining Unity in Your Writing**

1. Using the paragraphs in Exercise 4.1 as models, write a draft paragraph about your own reading habits or about one of your own experiences in school.

2. Exchange your draft paragraph with a classmate. Assess the paragraph you receive for unity. Put a ✓ next to any material you think may not be directly related to the topic sentence and the supporting sentences, and return the paragraph to the writer.

Coherence

When you reassess, also check to ensure that your writing is **coherent.** A paragraph has coherence if all its sentences are arranged logically and connected so that the ideas flow smoothly. The two basic components of coherence are *transition* and *organization,* or order, of sentences.

Transitions   **Transitions** contribute to coherence because they show the connections, or relationships, among your ideas. To provide transitions for your readers, use these three techniques: (1) repeat key words and phrases; (2) use **synonyms**—words with a similar meaning; (3) use transitional words or expressions.

Repeating key words or replacing a key word with a synonym or pronoun helps to keep these ideas foremost in the reader's mind. These techniques, like transitional words and expressions, also tie ideas together.

The following common transitional expressions are grouped according to the kind of relationships between ideas they show.

Common Transitional Expressions to Illustrate or Show Cause and Effect

accordingly	consequently	indeed	particularly
after all	for example	in fact	specifically
as a result	for instance	of course	therefore
because	for one thing	overall	thus

EXAMPLE The special effects in that movie were outstanding. *Also,* the performances by the lead actors were excellent.

Common Transitional Expressions to Add, Restate, or Emphasize

again	finally	in conclusion	next
also	further	in other words	too
and	in addition	moreover	to sum up
besides			

EXAMPLE I enjoy spending time riding my bike, *and* I *also* enjoy hiking in the state forest.

Common Transitional Expressions to Show Time or Place

above	currently	now	to the right (left)
after	earlier	presently	under
as soon as	here	since	until
before	immediately	soon	when
below	lately	then	whenever
beyond	once	there	where

EXAMPLE The crowd waiting for the bus began to cheer as it drove up to the station. *As soon as* the door opened, people began pushing their way up the stairs and into the empty seats.

Common Transitional Expressions to Compare or Contrast

although	despite	likewise	though
and	even though	nevertheless	yet
as	however	on the other hand	
at the same time	in contrast	regardless	
but	in spite of	still	

EXAMPLE The shipment arrived late, *even though* Chris had paid extra for overnight delivery.

Take a look at the italicized and boldfaced words in the following paragraph:

My cousin Danny may be the most intense pro football fan I've ever met. *Once* football season arrives in the fall, Danny focuses on **his** favorite team, the New England Patriots. **His** fascination with **this team** affects his life in several ways. *For example,* **he** has season tickets on the 50-yard line. The stadium where the Patriots plays is new, so **his seat** costs as much as a two-week vacation at a beach resort. *Also,* Danny travels to at least one away game every year. Last year, *for instance,* **he** drove down to see the **Pats** play the Carolina Cougars. *Of course,* this **trip** required him to spend two nights in an overpriced hotel. *When* he can't travel to see the team play, Danny puts on his official Patriots jersey and hat, turns off the phone, and turns on the big-screen television **he** bought to watch **his favorite team.**

As you can see, in some sentences, the pronouns **he, his,** or **him** are used in place of *Danny.* In others, the synonyms **team** or **Pats** substitute for *New England Patriots,* and **seat** replaces *season tickets.* Also several transitional expressions, including *once, for example, also, for instance, of course,* and *when.* Together, these transitional devices help to hold the paragraph together and make the connections between ideas clear for the reader.

Exercise 4.3 **Defining Coherence and Transition**

1. When you reassess your writing for coherence, what are you checking for?

   When you reassess your writing for coherence, you check that your sentences and

   ideas are connected and arranged in logical order.

2. What are three techniques you can use to provide transition in your paragraph?

   1. Repeat key words and phrases; 2. use synonyms or pronouns; 3. use transitional

   words or expressions.

Exercise 4.4   Identifying Transition

Read the following paragraph:

Jeri's fear of insects and spiders has affected (her) life in many ways. For one thing, (she) always shakes (her) shoes before putting (them) on because somebody once told (her) that spiders hide (their) babies (there.) (She) is allergic to bee stings, so <u>whenever</u> Jeri goes on a picnic, (she) spends (her) time watching out for bees. <u>When</u> (she) is driving, Jeri worries about insects. Every morning, (she) checks (her) car for any (bugs) buzzing around or hiding under the seats. <u>Overall,</u> Jeri says a world without (bugs) would be wonderful.

Now, working with a classmate, underline the transitional expressions you find in each and circle any repeated words, synonyms, or pronouns in each paragraph. Use the paragraph on the pro football fanatic to guide you.

Exercise 4.5   Using Transition

1. On the following lines, write three related sentences about one of the following subjects: *cosmetic surgery* or *computer games.* In the brief passage you write, include at least two of the common transitional expressions listed on page 65:

   Answers will vary.

   _____

   _____

2. Exchange your brief passage with a classmate. In the sentences you receive, underline the transitional words. On the lines that follow, explain how this transition helps show the connection between the sentences.

   Answers will vary.

   _____

   _____

Challenge 4.2   Adding Transitions in Your Writing

1. Write a draft paragraph about your own or someone else's deep interest in some activity or hobby, using the paragraph on the pro football fanatic as a model.

2. Make a copy of your draft paragraph, and exchange it with a classmate. Assess the paragraph you receive in terms of transition. Underline any transitional expressions and circle any other uses of repeated words, synonyms, or pronouns and put a ✓ next to any spot that would be improved if transition were added. Return the paragraph to the writer.

Effective Organization   When you reassess your writing for coherence, you also check to be sure your ideas are organized so that readers can easily follow your point. You select the order for each piece of writing according to the subject. Three common methods of organization are *chronological order,* *spatial order,* and *emphatic order.*

Using Chronological Order   The word *chronological* refers to the order of time. When you arrange your writing in *chronological order,* you present events in sequence, or the order in which they occurred. With documents like instructions or recipes, which must be performed in a particular order, you use a variation of chronological order, called *linear order.* With both types of time order, you need to present the ideas so that a reader can easily follow and understand them.

Look at this paragraph about an encounter with the police:

> Yesterday I had one of those days that made me wish I'd stayed in bed. I left the house late, so I was driving over the speed limit to make up some lost time. Five minutes later, I looked in my rear-view mirror and saw flashing blue lights. The state trooper pulled me over and then asked for my license and registration. I handed her my registration, but when I reached in my pocket for my wallet, I realized that I had left it on the kitchen table. After she listened to my story, she smiled and handed me a ticket for $75 for speeding. Then she told me that I had an hour to produce my license at the state police barracks or she would double the fine.

As you can see, presenting the events in the order in which they occurred makes it easy to understand the entire experience. The writer was behind schedule and began driving over the speed limit. *A few minutes later,* a trooper pulled the writer over and *then* asked for license and registration. *When* the writer realizes that his license is at home, he explains what has happened. The trooper issued a ticket anyway and *then* warned the writer to produce the license or face an even higher fine.

Exercise 4.6   **Considering the Importance of Sentence Order**

1. Why is the organization of your sentences important?

The organization of your sentences is important because arrangement of information

helps the reader easily follow the point of the writing.

2. With what kind of writing task is linear order an appropriate way to arrange a piece of writing?

Linear order is an appropriate choice when you are dealing with some process that

must be performed in a particular step-by-step fashion to achieve the desired end.

Exercise 4.7   **Analyzing Organization**

1. Read the following paragraph. Then, on the lines that follow, summarize the sequence of events it describes.

The morning I went for my driver's license was a disaster. First, the instructor from the driving school arrived almost half an hour late. I therefore had no time for the lesson I was scheduled to have before the actual driving test. Then when we finally arrived at the Department of Motor Vehicles, the computer system was down, so the clerk couldn't process my application. As a result, I had to wait another 45 minutes in line, and I missed my scheduled test time. After all these delays, the inspector finally joined us in the car for the test. I turned the key, but the car wouldn't start. Fortunately, the driving school had a second car, so I was finally able to take my test and get my license. Once I made it home, I took a nap, hoping to forget all the headaches I endured just to get my license.

The driving school failed to pick up the writer at the appointed time, causing the can-

cellation of a scheduled lesson before the driving test. The processing of the writer's

paperwork was delayed because of a computer problem. The driving school car

wouldn't start, but the driver was able to use another car from the driving school to

take the test. The writer passed the test and headed home for a nap.

2. Working with a classmate, underline the transitional expressions, using the lists on page 65 to guide you. Then, on a separate sheet of paper, briefly explain how these expressions help the reader follow the order of the event.

Exercise 4.8   **Recognizing and Maintaining Chronological Order**

1. The following sentences are part of a paragraph on a holiday celebration. They are presented here out of chronological order. Working with a classmate, put the sentences in an order that makes sense, inserting numbers (1, 2, 3, etc.) in the spaces following the sentences.

Nobody takes the games seriously, so we spend most of the time yelling and laughing at our bad play.   _5_

We set up two gas grills and cook marinated steak, barbecued chicken and ribs, hot dogs, and the thickest, juiciest hamburgers around.   _2_

We have an afternoon of co-ed volleyball, croquet, and wiffle ball.   _4_

The mouth-watering aroma fills the whole neighborhood.   _3_

We all walk to Washington Park and join thousands of others who are waiting for the exciting fireworks display.   _6_

On the Fourth of July, my family hosts a big cook-out for about fifty people, including grandparents, aunts, uncles, cousins, and friends.   _1_

2. Now, working with a classmate, write out the paragraph on a separate sheet of paper, adding transitions to improve the flow. Use the list of transitional expressions on page 65 as a guide. (Answers will vary. Likely choices will include *Soon* at the beginning of sentence 3; *After that* at the beginning of sentence 4; and *Finally* at the beginning of sentence 6.)

Challenge 4.3   **Evaluating Your Use of Chronological Order**

1. Write a draft paragraph in which you tell the story of a particular holiday celebration you enjoyed yourself or witnessed. Use the paragraph on the Fourth of July party as a guide.

2. Make a copy of your draft paragraph and exchange it with a classmate. Assess the order of the paragraph you receive. Put a ✓ next to any point at which the time order isn't easy to follow and a transition would improve the flow. Return the paragraph to the writer.

Using Spatial Order   In writing, you will frequently find it necessary to explain the location of one object, person, or place in relation to another. The details must be presented in some logical, easy-to-follow method—bottom to top, front to back, left to right, and so on. Otherwise, the reader will be unable to visualize the scene.

Consider the use of spatial order in this paragraph about a campground:

> When I was five, my family stayed in a campground so beautiful that I can still remember it clearly today. At the entrance, there was a small shack where the owner sold food and camping supplies. Behind the shack was a playground area with a slide that seemed 50 feet high. To the left of the playground was a big grove of pine trees that gave the whole area its wonderful pine scent. Under the trees were picnic tables and stone fireplaces. To the right along a curving road were the campsites, each with water and electrical hookups in the front. At the end of that road was my favorite spot: the pond with the paddleboat that all the campers could use. For a child my age, no better place existed.

In this paragraph, spatial order makes it easy for the reader to visualize the entire campground. The store was *at the entrance*. The playground was *behind* the store, and a pine tree grove was to its *left*. Picnic tables and fireplaces were *under* these trees, and the campsites were on a curving road *to the right*. The pond was *at the end of that road*. Thanks to spatial order, the reader can take an imaginary stroll through the special place that the writer remembers so well.

Exercise 4.9   Defining Spatial Order

1. In your own words, explain spatial order.

   Spatial order is a method of arrangement through which you describe elements in
   terms of their location to each other.

2. With spatial order, in what ways can you present details so that they are logical and easy to follow?

   Answers will include bottom to top, left to right, and front to back.

Exercise 4.10   **Analyzing Spatial Order Transitions in a Paragraph**

1. Read the following paragraph. Then answer the questions about place that follow it.

> Vincent Van Gogh's *The Starry Night* is one of the most recognizable and most beautiful paintings in the world. Dominating (the left side) of the painting is a greenish gray form. The image resembles a bush, shattered tree trunk, or castle turret. The brush strokes make the form appear to be flowing (upward toward) the sky. (To the right) (below this shape,) a small village appears, set against a hillside. The violet and purple of the hillside seems to spill down onto the buildings, with small squares of yellow indicating the life within the little cottages. (Above the scene) is a sky of swirling blue, violet, yellow, and white brush strokes. Glowing yellow stars (surrounded by circles) of light hang in the sky. (In the upper right corner,) a yellow orange crescent moon casts its light on the world (below.) The scene is alive with color, so it's no wonder that the painting remains so popular.

a. Where is the crescent moon in relation to the village?

The crescent moon is to the right above the village.

_____

b. Where is the hillside in relation to the greenish gray shape?

The hillside is to the right of the greenish gray shape, rising up from the village.

_____

2. Working with a classmate, circle transitional words that help to maintain spatial order. Select one and then, on the lines below, briefly explain how this expression helps you visualize the painting.

Answers will vary, but students will generally note that the transitional expression

_____

specifies a particular area of the canvas.

_____

Exercise 4.11   **Using and Evaluating Spatial Order Cues**

1. Take a classmate on a brief tour of a room in your home by using spatial order to describe it. As you speak, have your partner make a diagram or sketch of the room on a separate sheet of paper. Then switch roles and repeat this activity.

2. Is the sketch or diagram that your classmate made accurate? On the lines that follow, explain.

Answers will vary.

3. What transitional expressions did your classmate use that helped you visualize the room? On the following lines, list them and then briefly explain how they help you get a sense of the layout.

Answers will vary.

Challenge 4.4   **Evaluating Spatial Order in Your Writing**

1. Write a draft paragraph in which you explain a particular location that you remember from your childhood. Use the paragraph from page 71 on the campground as a model.

COLLABORATION

2. Make a copy of your draft paragraph and exchange it with a classmate. Assess the order of the paragraph you receive. Put a ✓ next to any point at which the spatial order isn't easy to follow and a transition would help bring the scene into clearer focus. Return the paragraph to the writer.

Ordering for Emphasis   In some paragraphs, especially those in which the primary purpose is to persuade, you will want to present your supporting ideas in a way that provides the most impact. In other words, you will want to use *emphatic order*. With emphatic order, writers often begin with the least important details and end with the most significant information. This organization builds and holds the reader's interest in much the same way a play or story does—by building to a climax. Consider the order of the supporting ideas in this paragraph advocating the legalization of physician-assisted suicide:

Physician-assisted suicide for terminally ill patients should be legalized. First of all, these patients know they are dying, and they should be able to exercise some control over their situations. If they choose not to prolong their suffering when they have no hope for survival, that's their business. More important is the patients' concern for their family members. The around-the-clock care for people suffering from the advanced stages of cancer or degenerative muscular diseases is unbelievably expensive. The emotional toll from watching a loved one die by inches is even more costly. Most important of all is the patients' loss of dignity. The terminally ill face absolute dependence on others as well as tremendous pain, with no hope of recovery. Why should they be forced to linger in life when a humane alternative is available?

The supporting details and examples in this paragraph are arranged in emphatic order. A strong reason to legalize physician-assisted suicide is that it provides dying people some control over the lives they have left. A stronger reason is that it enables the afflicted individuals to protect their families from needless emotional pain and expense. But the strongest reason of all is it helps terminally ill people maintain their dignity in their final days. Arranged this way, these supporting details and examples draw and feed the reader's interest.

Exercise 4.12 — Defining Emphatic Order

1. On the following lines, briefly explain emphatic order.

   Emphatic order involves presenting supporting details and examples in a way that

   stresses their relative significance or importance.

2. Why is emphatic order a good choice with writings whose primary purpose is to persuade?

   Emphatic order is a good choice with persuasive writings because this arrangement

   draws and feeds the reader's interest.

Exercise 4.13 — Identifying Transitions That Emphasize Importance

1. Read the following paragraph that urges the banning of cigarette smoking in all restaurants.

   Cigarette smoking should be banned in all restaurants because of the problems smoking causes. First of all, even when restaurants have nonsmoking areas, the odor of smoking is often still present. The smell hangs in the air and gets on the clothes of both workers and patrons, making the whole experience much less pleasant for nonsmokers. Worse, smoking brings with it the risk of fire, and the crowded conditions in many restaurants would increase the risk of injury or death. Worst of all, however, smoking causes cancer and other health problems, such as emphysema. Smokers take the risk by choice, but other people in the restaurant don't. The people most affected by this problem are those waiting on tables and behind the bar who are exposed to second-hand smoke every time they go to work. (Therefore,) for the sake of everyone, including smokers themselves, smoking should be banned in all restaurants.

Do you agree with the order in which the supporting examples are given? On the lines below, briefly explain your reasoning.

Most students will agree that the order makes sense, since the first reaction is far

less serious than the other two and the third reason concerns actual health

problems that cigarette smoking in restaurants causes.

2. Circle the transitional expressions, using the lists on page 65 as a guide. Then, on the lines that follow, explain how these words help to maintain emphatic order.

Students will likely agree that the transitional expressions indicate an increasing level

of significance.

---

1. Write a draft paragraph in which you support or reject one of the following statements:

   a. High school and college students should have to perform public service work in order to graduate.

   b. Condoms should be distributed in middle and high schools without parental knowledge or permission.

   c. Marijuana should be decriminalized for medical use.

   Use the paragraph on physician-assisted suicide on pages 73–74 as a model.

COLLABORATION

2. Make a copy of your draft paragraph and exchange it with a classmate. Assess the order of the paragraph you receive. If you think the order should be adjusted to add particular emphasis to one of the supporting points, write a brief note explaining your reasoning. Also, put a + at any point where you think added transition will help the paragraph persuade, and then return the paragraph to the writer.

Effective Language

Your choice of words has a great impact on how well you communicate your ideas to your reader. When you reassess, you need to check your writing for **effective** use of **language.** Think of the words you choose as a window into your thoughts. A window that is all fogged up doesn't give anyone much of a view. Wipe that haze away, however, and the view is clear. To eliminate any fog in your writing, you need to use language that is specific and concise.

Making Your Writing Specific When you think of *dog*, what image comes into your mind? Chances are that when you close your eyes, you see a particular dog, perhaps one you've owned or one familiar to you. Regardless of what kind of dog you picture, it is unlikely that anybody else thinking of *dog* will have exactly the same picture in mind. That's because the word *dog* is a *general* word.

If you want your reader to visualize the same picture as you have in your mind, you need to replace general terms with *specific language.* To do this, you need to use words that are detailed and to the point. Instead of *dog*, write *the two-year-old, pure-bred, female cocker spaniel with the speckled eyes.* Then your reader will be able to share your specific image.

Which details in the following paragraph about a terrible work experience help you better understand what the writer went through?

> The dirtiest property I ever saw was a small cottage that I was hired to clean out last summer. The real estate agent who gave me the job had just purchased the one-acre plot on which the house was set. Her plan was to build another house on the property and convert the tiny 10-foot by 15-foot house into a garage. My job was to remove everything from the house and put it in a trash dumpster that was almost as big as the house. The doors and windows of the cottage had been locked up for ten years, so when I opened the door, dust began swirling around, filling the air. Two of the three tiny rooms contained broken-down furniture covered with a thick layer of dust. One room contained a love seat and recliner with torn and stained cushions. The other room contained a heavily scratched mahogany bed with matching bureau. The remaining room was filled with just odds and ends and junk. This collection included broken electrical appliances, empty paint cans, pieces of scrap wood and aluminum siding, and two truck tires. Bundles of old newspapers filled one wall from floor to ceiling. The whole job took me over ten hours and left me with aching muscles, grime-covered clothes, and dust-filled lungs.

Chances are that you identified a number of details. For instance, you probably noted the size of the house—10-foot by 15-foot—and the similarly sized dumpster. You also probably noted how long the house had been locked up—ten years—and the conditions that resulted from having the windows and door closed—dust-filled air. You also no doubt noted the stained, torn, scratched, and dust-covered furniture in two of the rooms and the listing of junk filling the third. Combined, these details make it easy to see what the writer faced on that long day of work.

Keeping Your Writing Concise   As you reassess your draft, you also need to ensure that your writing is *concise*—that is, brief but clear. To streamline what you have written, you need to eliminate any deadwood, vague or general words that add no real meaning to your writing. Words such as *definitely, quite, extremely, somewhat*, and *a lot* are examples of deadwood. General words such as *very* and *really* are also examples of deadwood, especially when they are coupled with weak or unclear terms such as *nice* or *good-looking*. Concentrate on selecting the best word or words for a particular situation, always avoid phrasing that is unnecessarily wordy. Here is a list of common wordy expressions, with alternatives that enable you to say the same thing more concisely:

Deadwood	Concise Version	Deadwood	Concise Version
due to the fact that	because	In order that	so
a large number	many	at the present time	now
in the near future	soon	take action	act
prior to	before	the month of October	October
completely eliminate	eliminate	give a summary of	summarize
come to the realization of	realize	mutual cooperation	cooperation
with the exception of	except for	make an assumption	assume

Now take a look at the following paragraph. What parts need to be made more concise?

The toughest part of being a teenager is always dealing with the constant peer pressure. As they are growing up, a large number of adolescents are unsure of themselves, and they really lack self-esteem. Some of these teenagers become sexually active or use drugs or alcohol due to the fact that they feel pressured to conform. They take chances to create an impression on others, but often end up feeling even less confident.

As you probably noted, several of the sentences are unnecessarily wordy. In the first sentence, for example, *always* is not needed because *constant* indicates the same thing. In the second sentence, *a large number* can be replaced with the more concise version *many*. Also, *unsure of themselves* can be replaced with *insecure*, and *really* doesn't add any meaning to the sentence and should be eliminated. Finally, in the third sentence, the wordy expression *due to the fact that* can be changed to *because*.

Make these changes, and you've got a more concise paragraph.

Exercise 4.14   **Defining Specific and Concise Language**

1. What can you do to make your writing more specific?

   Replace general words with words that are clear and precise and that offer enough

   detail.

2. What are two strategies you can use to make your writing more concise?

   Eliminate words or phrases that aren't necessary. I can avoid using two or more

   words when one word will do.

Exercise 4.15   **Identifying Overly General and Wordy Language**

COLLABORATION
Read the following paragraph. Then work with a partner or member of your writing group to complete the questions below.

> People with food allergies have to be careful when it comes to eating out. Due to the fact that it is prepared fresh each time, food at a restaurant doesn't come with a full list of ingredients. Restaurant patrons aren't always aware of what has been used to prepare the food. Many people are especially sensitive to certain things, but they don't come to the realization about what's in their food until they start to eat. In some cases, this situation can be bad. Last year, for example, a woman on vacation in Colorado died after eating at a small restaurant known for its award-winning chili. Her only food allergy was to peanut butter, so she made an assumption that the chili was OK. Unfortunately, one of the secret ingredients in the chili was peanut butter. She died before the ambulance arrived.

1. List the details you find specific enough as written.

   Woman in Colorado died after eating at a small restaurant known for its award-

   winning chili; only food allergy—peanut butter; a secret ingredient was peanut butter;

   she died before the ambulance arrived.

2. List those words or phrases that still need to be made more specific. Discuss with your classmate(s) how they might be improved.

   Many people are especially sensitive to *certain things*. This situation can be *bad*.

_____

_____

3. Refer to the list of wordy phrases and concise alternatives on page 77. List all deadwood that appears in this paragraph. Next to each phrase, list a suitable alternative.

due to the fact that—because
_____

come to the realization about—realize
_____

made an assumption—assumed
_____

_____

Exercise 4.16   **Writing Specific, Concise Language**

1. Revise these general words to make them concrete and specific.
Answers will vary. Representative answers are given.

a. a house

a five-story brick apartment building
_____

_____

b. a computer

a Macintosh iBook
_____

_____

2. Here is a paragraph explaining the effects that a fear of swimming can have. Working with a classmate, cross out any deadwood. Then, on a separate sheet of paper, write a more concise version. Rephrase portions if you agree that the paragraph will improve as a result.
Representative deletions and changes are shown.

Every time I would ~~go to~~ try swimming ~~in the water,~~ the same things would happen. My heart would begin to pound ~~really, really hard in my chest,~~ and I would start to ~~feel a choking in my throat.~~ choke. Then my fingers ~~on my hands~~ would become numb. I would start to ~~kind of~~ shake, and my feet would feel as if they were covered ~~over~~ with cement. Whenever I would walk toward the deeper water ~~where the water was over my head,~~ I would begin to feel as if I was going to pass out ~~or something.~~

Challenge 4.6 **Evaluating and Revising the Language in Your Writing**

1. Write a draft paragraph in which you discuss a difficult work experience. Use the paragraph from page 76 on cleaning out a filthy cottage as a model.

2. Make a copy of your draft paragraph and exchange it with a classmate. Assess the language of the paper you receive. Is it specific and concise? Circle any word or expression you think should be more specific or concise, and then return the paragraph to the writer.

Getting Feedback from an Objective Reader

In addition to reassessing your draft yourself, you should also ask another reader for a reaction. This kind of feedback can help you gauge how well your words communicate your ideas. Anyone you can count on to read your work with an unbiased eye and respond honestly—a classmate, friend, relative—can serve as your sounding board. Have your reader use the following Reader Assessment Checklist to make this task easier. The checklist focuses on concerns you have already considered. Therefore, answers from an objective reader to the same questions will help you establish how effectively you have made your point.

Reader Assessment Checklist

☐ Do you understand the point I am making?

☐ Do I stick to that point all the way through?

☐ Are all my ideas and examples clearly connected and easy to follow?

☐ Are the words I've used specific and concise?

☐ What changes do you think I should make?

Considering an Example: Peer Response

Consider again this first draft paragraph on life in the big city, featured at the end of the previous chapter:

Living in a big city can seem more like living in a small village. In my neighborhood, just about everything anybody could need is available within walking distance. There are several coffee shops, pizza places, bodegas, and small grocery stores. The area includes a small playground for children, its own branch library, and a small park with five benches and two picnic tables. The familiar faces on the streets, in the shops, and on the subway make the neighborhood seem like an extended family. The city recently increased the price of a weekly Public Transit Pass by 15 percent. Most residents live in really big apartment complexes. People get to know their neighbors and the shop owners and workers well. If you go into Izzy's, a small diner at the very center of the neighborhood, on a Friday or Saturday night, the tables and booths will be filled with people from the neighborhood. Many people spend a lot of time there. On most days, it all seems so comfortable that I forget that my neighborhood is just a small part of an enormous city.

Now consider this peer response to the draft:

> I like your paragraph—it gives me a good idea of what your neighborhood is like. I had never thought of a big city as a group of smaller places. Your topic sentence lets me know what you are focusing on, and your language is pretty much clear and easy to understand. I think you could make the paragraph even better if you make a few changes. For one thing, the sixth sentence, the one about the fee increase for the Public Transit Pass, is about a different subject, so you should probably get rid of it. Also, you don't explain much about what the people do in Izzy's, and it made me curious. I've put a ✓ where an additional transition would make your sentences flow better, too. I hope my comments help you.

As you can see, the insights of an objective reader can be very valuable. These kinds of comments help identify what is already effective in a piece of writing and what still needs work.

Exercise 4.17   **Understanding the Usefulness of Feedback**

1. Who is a suitable candidate to serve as your objective reader?

   Anyone who will read and react to your writing with an unbiased eye, including a

   classmate, friend, or family member, would make a good objective reader.

2. How can getting feedback from an objective reader improve your writing?

   The reaction of an objective reader gives you a sense of how clearly and effectively

   you have been in expressing your ideas, thus guiding you in improving your draft.

Exercise 4.18   **Analyzing Difficulties in Giving and Receiving Feedback**

1. Of the questions in the reader assessment checklist on page 80, which one do you think is the most difficult to answer? On the following lines, identify this category and explain your reasoning.

   Answers will vary. Many students will focus on the last question, noting that they

   don't always know exactly how to improve the writing.

2. Suppose your reader finds an area of your writing that still needs work. On the lines that follow, explain how getting this feedback about your work would make you feel?

   Answers will vary. Some students may feel unhappy or angry when faced with this

   feedback, while others will say that they look forward to a reaction that will help them

   improve their writing.

Challenge 4.7   **Providing and Receiving Objective Feedback**

1. In Challenge 3.6 on page 56 of Chapter 3, you completed a first draft paragraph. Now, make a copy of this draft or another draft paragraph you have created, and exchange it with a classmate.

COLLABORATION

2. Read through the draft you receive. Complete the following steps, using the Reader Assessment Checklist on page 80 as a guide.

   a. Put a **+** next to the topic sentence if it provides a clear direction. Put a **#** if this main idea still isn't clear.

   b. Underline any section or sentence that disrupts the unity because it is not relevant to the main idea of the paragraph.

   c. Put an ***** at any point where additional transition would make the writing more coherent. If sentences should be reordered, number them to show the change you would make.

   d. Circle all vague words and deadwood. Write any suggested substitutes above the words.

Return the copy to the writer.

Redrafting

Once you have reassessed your draft paragraph and had someone else assess it, and addressed its problems, you need to *redraft* it. In other words, you need to write a new version that addresses the problems you and your reader have noted.

Redrafting will be different for each paper you write. Sometimes, you'll have to make adjustments in only one category of the reader assessment list. Other times, you will need to make changes in several categories.

With some paragraphs, your task might be to *amplify*—to provide details and examples that more effectively answer the kinds of questions a reader might have. For instance, you might need to add details and examples to support your point. Or you might need to change the wording of a detail or example to enable your reader to visualize or understand it better. The extra work will be worth it because it will definitely improve your draft.

Here again is the first draft on life in the big city. This time, however, the sentences are numbered and annotations are included. These annotations indicate the problem spots that need to be addressed before the paper fulfills its promise:

Transition would help here.

Some transition would help here.

Some transition would help here.

Additional details would help here – Amplify.

This sentence isn't directly related to the topic – eliminate it.

This information is too vague and general – Amplify.

Some transition would help here.

This information is too vague and general – Amplify.

1. Living in a big city can seem more like living in a small village. 2. In my neighborhood, just about everything anybody could need is available within walking distance. 3. There are several coffee shops, pizza places, bodegas, and small grocery stores. 4. The area includes a small playground for children, its own branch library, and a small park with five benches and two picnic tables. 5. The familiar faces on the streets, in the shops, and on the subway make the neighborhood seem like an extended family. 6. The city recently increased the price of a weekly Public Transit Pass by 15 percent. 7. Most residents live in really big apartment complexes. 8. People get to know their neighbors and the shop owners and workers well. 9. If you go into Izzy's, a small diner at the very center of the neighborhood, on a Friday or Saturday night, the tables and booths will be filled with people from the neighborhood. 10. Many people spend a lot of time there. 11. On most days, it all seems so comfortable that I forget that my neighborhood is just a small part of an enormous city.

As these annotations, as well as the peer comments presented earlier, indicate, a number of changes need to be made. For one thing, the sixth sentence disrupts the unity of the paragraph because it isn't directly connected to the topic. Therefore, it should be eliminated. Amplifying in a few spots would also help the paragraph more effectively communicate its meaning. For instance, the following sentence improves the paragraph because it emphasizes how the people in the neighborhood help to make it special:

| **AMPLIFIED** | But it's the people who make my neighborhood special. |

In addition, sentence 7 isn't effective because the details it includes are too general and uninformative:

| **GENERAL AND UNINFORMATIVE** | Most residents live in really big apartment complexes. |

Improving this sentence is a matter of amplifying it so that it is more specific, as this version shows:

| **AMPLIFIED AND INFORMATIVE** | Most residents live in *apartment complexes that can house 50 or more families.* |

The same is true with sentence 10, which at this point is too general to provide a full sense of how patrons spend their time at the restaurant:

| **GENERAL AND UNINFORMATIVE** | Many people spend a lot of time there. |

The addition of some specific details makes it easy for the reader to see what goes on at this popular spot:

| **AMPLIFIED AND INFORMATIVE** | Many people spend *a couple of hours there, enjoying the great food, the small talk with Izzy and his wife, and the company of their neighbors.* |

Also, the coherence of the paragraph could be greatly improved by including additional transitions. In some cases, including a transitional expression is the answer, as this version of sentence 4 shows:

| **IMPROVED COHERENCE** | *In addition,* the area includes a small playground for children, its own branch library, and a small park with five benches and two picnic tables. |

In some cases, however, including more extensive transition is called for, as this version of sentence 3 shows:

| **IMPROVED COHERENCE** | *In an area that covers four blocks,* there are several coffee shops, pizza places, bodegas, and small grocery stores. |

Spending time redrafting is worth your time because the result will be an improved draft.

Exercise 4.19   Defining Redrafting

1. What do you do when you redraft a paragraph?

   When you redraft a paragraph, you write a clearer, stronger version of it, including

   the corrections and improvements gathered through reassessment.

2. Why is this step of revising important?

   It helps the writer turn something good into something better.

Exercise 4.20   Assessing and Redrafting a Paragraph

1. Read the following paragraph and act as an objective reader. Using the Reader Assessment Checklist on page 80 and the sample peer response on page 81 to guide you, suggest changes that could improve this paragraph. Write your suggestions on a separate piece of paper.

   > Insomnia is a very frustrating experience. I can't sleep. I worry about how I will feel the next day. I know I will feel terrible. The more I worry, the more I can't relax and go to sleep. Counting sheep or drinking warm milk doesn't help. The most frustrating thing about insomnia is that I can't do anything about it except listen to the clock tick and wait for the alarm to go off.

2. Exchange the list of suggestions you wrote for the insomnia paragraph with a classmate. Using your partner's suggestions, redraft the paragraph on a separate piece of paper.

Challenge 4.8   Redrafting Your Own Writing

1. For Challenge 4.7, a classmate reassessed a draft you have completed. Now review the comments and suggestions your classmate has provided.

2. Redraft your paragraph, addressing any weaknesses that you and your reader have identified. Use the redrafted examples from the paragraph on life in a big city as a guide.

Editing

Up to this point, your primary area of concentration has been the message of your paper: the content. Your goal has been to generate a main point—a topic sentence—and plenty of good supporting examples and details. In addition, you've focused on making sure that this material is unified, coherent, and effectively phrased.

But good content isn't enough to make a piece of writing effective. For a piece of writing to be wholly successful, it must be free from errors. In other words, the language you use must follow the rules of standard English.

This step in revising is especially important because errors in form can so negatively affect the response to your writing. Mistakes in form such as sentence errors or problems with agreement or spelling distract your reader. Instead of focusing on your good ideas, your reader is interrupted by the weaknesses in form. As a result, the quality of your content is overshadowed by the errors.

Using a Proofreading Checklist and Developing a Personal Proofreading System

It's simple: Good writing is the sum of solid content and correct form. Reassessing and redrafting ensure that your ideas are clear and complete. *Editing* enables you to express them correctly. Therefore, once you've identified and corrected problems with the content of your writing, you are ready to proofread for errors in grammar, usage, spelling, punctuation, and capitalization.

The secret to effective proofreading is timing. Fatigue and familiarity with your own material increase the chances that you will overlook errors. You will see what *you meant to write* rather than what you have *actually written*. That means you will see *quite* even though what's really there is *quiet*. In some cases, you may see a word that isn't even on the page. You *intended* to write the word, so when you read it over, you mentally insert it. It's important, then, to proofread when you are rested.

As you do more writing, you will discover which mistakes you are prone to make. For now, though, rely on the following Proofreading Checklist, which covers the most common mistakes writers make in form. Next to each listing is the abbreviation commonly used to identify the error when it appears in a paper.

Proofreading Checklist

☐ Have I eliminated all sentence fragments (*frag*)?

☐ Have I eliminated all comma splices (*cs*)?

☐ Have I eliminated all run-on sentences (*rs*)?

☐ Is the spelling (*sp*) correct throughout?

☐ Is the verb tense (*t*) correct throughout?

☐ Do all subjects agree with their verbs (*subj/verb agr*)?

☐ Do all pronouns agree with their antecedents (*pro/ant agr*)?

Although this list covers many common concerns, it doesn't cover all possible sources of errors. For instance, you may have trouble with double negatives or punctuation. Don't worry if you do not yet understand these problems or how to solve them. Parts 2 through 5 of this book provide practice in identifying and eliminating various errors in form. In addition, the Sentence Skill Locator on the inside back cover shows you where to look for help with particular problems.

As you gain experience in writing, you'll discover which of these categories you handle well and which ones still give you trouble. As you do, you can adapt the Proofreading Checklist so that it reflects your individual concerns. That way, you'll have a personal proofreading system you can use to check your final draft before you hand it in for evaluation.

Working with a Proofreading Partner

When it comes to checking your writing for errors, two sets of eyes are better than one. No matter how carefully you screen your own work, you sometimes overlook errors. A reader who hasn't invested the time and energy you have may be better able to find them. Although you might not notice that you wrote *beleive* when you meant to write *believe*, your proofreading partner probably will.

In short, working with a proofreading partner will benefit you in two ways. First, it will help make your paper error-free. And second, it will help you develop your own proofreading skills.

Using Computer Tools to Your Advantage

A computer can also help you find and correct errors, especially spelling mistakes. If you write on a computer or word processor, you probably have access to another proofreading tool: the *spell check* command. This function compares the words that you've used to the words in the computer's dictionary and lets you know when they don't match. If the computer detects an error but offers no alternative, you need to look the word up in a dictionary and then make the change.

In many cases, though, the function will offer a list of possible alternatives. Click on one, and the computer inserts that word in place of the misspelled one.

If this sounds too easy to be true, that's because it is. You need to consider the list of alternative words carefully. Remember—replacing a misspelled word with the wrong word is no improvement.

Computers don't reason the way that humans do—at least not yet. They don't know, for example, that you meant *calm* when you wrote, "The ocean had been especially *clam*, before the sudden storm struck." It also doesn't necessarily comprehend when one homophone is used in place of another, for example, "The woman running the courtesy booth went on her *brake* early, leaving the front of the story unattended." The correct word is *break*, but the computer can't catch the error.

The point of all this is simple. When it comes to proofreading, take advantage of all the tools available to you. Just make sure that you do one final proofreading, slowly and carefully, to catch any error the computer may have missed.

Exercise 4.21   **Defining Editing**

1. What effect do errors in form have on the overall effect of a piece of writing?

   Errors in form make a piece of writing less effective because it distracts the reader

   from the content.

2. How does editing differ from reassessing and redrafting?

   In reassessing and redrafting, you concentrate primarily on content. In editing, your

   focus is on matters of form.

Exercise 4.22   **Understanding Proofreading**

1. Why is it important to proofread when you are rested?

   You shouldn't proofread when you are tired because fatigue increases the chance

   that you will overlook some mistake in form.

2. How can you develop a personal proofreading system?

   To develop a personal proofreading system, you adapt the proofreading checklist by

   adding the particular problem spots that appear in your own writing.

3. How will working with a proofreading partner benefit you?

Working with a proofreading partner will benefit you in two ways. 1. A proofreading

partner will catch errors you miss. 2. You will become a better proofreader of your

own work as you practice on a partner's.

Considering Your Own Proofreading Strengths and Weaknesses

1. Which of the errors on the Proofreading Checklist on page 87 is a major problem spot in your writing? Why do you think you find this area difficult? Explain on the lines that follow.

Answers will vary.

2. Which of the problem spots on the Proofreading Checklist isn't a problem for you? Why do you think you find this aspect easy to deal with? Explain on the lines that follow.

Answers will vary.

Editing a Paragraph

1. Read the following paragraph. Put a ✓ or other marker above any errors.

Getting contact lenses has made a tremendous difference in my life. First of all, contacts are far more convenient than glasses. Now I don't have to contend with wet or fogged up glasses. I also don't have to keep pushing it up my nose when my face gets sweaty, in addition, contact lenses have improved my vision. For the first time that I can remember. I can now look out of the sides of my eyes and see something this feature have been particularly useful when I am involved in sports and other outdoor activities. Most of all, I love the change they have make in my appearance. I never liked the way I looked in glasses, so wearing contact lenses has also boosted my self-confidence.

2. Compare your findings with a classmate's. Then check your answers against the corrected version that appears on pages 94–95. Make a note of any errors you had originally missed.

Challenge 4.9 **Editing Your Paragraph**

1. For Challenge 4.8, you redrafted a paragraph. Make a copy of this paragraph and exchange it with a classmate. Then, using the Proofreading Checklist, proofread your own paragraph to identify any remaining errors.

2. Proofread your classmate's paper, using the Proofreading Checklist. Circle any errors and then return the paper to the writer.

3. Correct any errors that you and your proofreading partner have noted, and then submit the paper to your instructor. Did your partner find errors that you missed?

Considering a Final Draft

So what happens when you follow all these steps? Consider this final draft version of the paragraph on life in a big city:

Jamie McArdle
English 10.40 Basic College Writing
Dr. Kelly
January 25, 2004

The Little City within the Big City

Living in a big city can seem like living in a small village. In my neighborhood, for example, just about everything anybody could need is available within walking distance. In an area that covers four blocks, there are several coffee shops, pizza places, bodegas, and small grocery stores. In addition, the area includes a small playground for children, its own branch library, and a small park with five benches and two picnic tables. But it's the people of the neighborhood who make my neighborhood special. The familiar faces on the streets, in the shops, and on the subway make the neighborhood seem like an extended family. Most residents live in apartment complexes that can house 50 or more families. As a result, people get to know their neighbors and the shop owners and workers well. If you go into Izzy's, a small diner at the very center of the neighborhood, on a Friday or Saturday night, the tables and booths will be filled with people from the neighborhood. Many people spend a couple of hours there, enjoying the great food, the small talk with Izzy and his wife, and the company of their neighbors. On most days, it all seems so comfortable that I forget that my neighborhood is just a small part of an enormous city.

As you can see, the weaknesses identified during reassessing have been addressed during redrafting. The draft has also been carefully edited to eliminate any errors in form. Thanks to this hard work, the final draft version is clearly better than the first draft, as these instructor's comments indicate:

> Congratulations – this version shows much improvement, and your first draft was already good. The added examples bring those parts of your neighborhood into focus, particularly the material on the restaurant. Also additional transitions make the ideas flow so much more smoothly. I especially like the transitional phrases you added to the beginning of the third sentence. It helps the reader get a sense of the size of the area. Thanks for the insider's view of your neighborhood. It's an excellent first paper.

Incidentally, notice the **format,** the way the paragraph is arranged. Your instructor may prefer that you set up your paper in some other way. If your instructor has no preference, however, this arrangement is a good choice. As this example shows, list your name in the upper-left corner of the page, followed by the name of the course, your instructor's name, and the date you submit the paper. Leave at least a double space and then provide a title, centered from left to right. Indent at the beginning of the paragraph and then double space the paragraph.

Exploring Ideas through Journal Writing

As this chapter has shown, revising means carefully reconsidering a piece of writing with the goal of making it as good as it can be. Can you think of another situation in school, in your personal life, or at work when you reconsidered something and ended up with a better solution? Consider this subject and then spend 20 to 30 minutes exploring the subject in your journal.

SPOTLIGHT PIECE

Considering a Final Draft Writing

Here's a short essay by student Surrell Wells about how listening to a particular song affects her. The annotations to the left of Surrell's essay focus on the unity, coherence, and effective language featured in her writing. Read Surrell's essay and the annotations, and then answer the questions that follow the piece.

Blue in Green

Note her thesis, suggesting that Davis's music moves her to a different mental plane.

Music is a magical thing. Sometimes it's as if the musician stepped into your soul and wrote a song about your innermost thoughts and desires. At other times, music is a vehicle that can transport you to other worlds and other realities. That's what the piece "Blue in Green" by Miles Davis does for me. Whenever I pop in Miles's CD *Kinda Blue* and cue up song number three, I am transported to a special place.

Transition maintains coherence.

This paragraph maintains unity because it talks about how she moves to a different mental plane. Notice the effective specific language.

No matter the weather or the time of day, the music conjures up images of a mid-autumn day on the bay. It is a beautiful day. A strong noontime sun sits high in a blue sky as big white puffy clouds pass by. The sun's rays dance and sparkle on the blue-gray water and warm me from within. There is a mild, cool breeze moving my boat out to the middle of the bay. The weeping willows along the shore lazily sweep across the water as if dancing with the wind.

Transition maintains coherence.

Unity is maintained because this paragraph discusses a different mental plane.
Notice the effective specific language.

Notice the effective specific language.

Every time I push the play button, the calm, soothing notes of Miles Davis's trumpet wash over me like the waves lapping against the sides of the boat. My body, mind, and soul are floating on the rhythmic sounds of Coltrane's tenor sax, Bill Evans's piano, Paul Chamber's bass, and Jimmy Cobb's drum beat. Stress does not exist when I am in this place. Bills, school work, the stresses of trying to potty train my daughter, they belong to another world. I dreamily think about what the recording session for this album must have been like.

Transition maintains coherence.

Unity is maintained because this paragraph discusses a different mental plane.

Notice the effective specific language.

I can picture a cold March day in New York City in 1959. As it snows outside, the "cats" are warm in the studio, chatting, smoking cigarettes, and tuning up their instruments. It's time to record and everybody gets serious as Bill Evans begins to play the first notes of "Blue in Green."

Transition maintains coherence.
Unity is maintained because this paragraph discusses a different mental plane.

As I listen, I wonder what kind of person Miles Davis was. It's amazing how he could take an instrument with three simple keys and make it sound so complex. I don't know anything about music, but I know what I like, and I like him. I could stay in this state of euphoria all day, but inevitably, the CD stops and I drift back into reality.

Unity is maintained because these sentences reiterate the different mental plane that music takes her to.

Notice the effective specific language.

Whether I come back to my apartment and a pile of homework or back to a whining child, I am different. I am calm within. My soul is light and my mind is clear. I have been cleansed and I can face my responsibilities. I know that if the going gets tough, I can return to the world of "Blue in Green."

Exercise 4.25   **Exploring the Reading**

1. Surrell expresses her main idea for her essay in the last sentence of the introduction: **Whenever I pop in Miles's CD *Kinda Blue* and cue up song number three, I am transported to a special place.** On the lines that follow, briefly explain how the other paragraphs in the body of her essay support and explain her thesis.

   Answers will vary somewhat. Most students will note that the other paragraphs all

   discuss ways that the music takes her away from complications in her life.

2. Working with a classmate, identify three areas in Surrell's essay where you both feel that her use of transition is especially strong. Then, on the following lines, briefly explain your choices.

   Answers will vary. Likely choices will include the beginning of paragraph 3 (**Every**

   time I push the play button); the beginning of paragraph 5 (**As I listen**); and the be-

   ginning of the concluding paragraph (**Whether I come back to my apartment and a**

   pile of homework or back to a whining child). These transitional elements help tie

   the paragraphs together. Some students may focus on the transitions in the introduc-

   tion (**Sometimes, At other times,** and **Whenever**) because they improve its flow.

3. One of the strongest features in Surrell's essay is her effective use of language. In which paragraph do you think she best expressed her reactions to listening to "Blue in Green"? On the lines that follow, identify your choice and explain why you think this paragraph most effectively captures her meaning.

   Answers will vary, although many students will focus on paragraphs 2 or 3 because

   of the specific details she provides concerning how the music transports her.

Understanding the Subject through Writing

In her essay, Surrell spells out how she escapes from everyday pressures, difficulties, and annoyances by listening to the music of Miles Davis. On a separate sheet of paper, write a brief passage (50 to 100 words) in which you explain another strategy people can employ to deal with the stress they face every day.

Discovering Connections 4.1

Look at the photo below. What comes to mind? Does it make you think of someone you wish you had called—or someone you wish had called

you? Are you thinking about how annoying it can be to overhear cell phone conversations in public places? Perhaps you are thinking about communication in general and how hard it is to understand others and make others understand you. Have you had times when your "wires became crossed"—when someone completely misunderstood something you said?

For this assignment, focus on the photo and explore the ideas it suggests to you. After you prewrite and compose a draft, use the steps you practiced in this chapter to revise the paper.

Discovering Connections 4.2

For this assignment, consider the subject of letter writing. For instance, is there someone to whom you should have written a letter but because of anger, laziness, or embarrassment you haven't? Who is that person? Why have you hesitated, and what do you think would happen if you wrote now? Have you ever read a letter that wasn't intended for you and discovered something you shouldn't have? What did you discover? Do you feel guilty now? What's the best letter you ever received? What made it so good? If you were going to write yourself a letter offering advice, what would you say?

Explore some of the possibilities this topic suggests to you through prewriting. Once you discover a focus for writing, complete a draft. Then, using the steps in this chapter to guide you, revise your draft.

Corrected Version of Exercise 4.24

Getting contact lenses has made a tremendous difference in my

life. First of all, contacts are far more <u>convenient</u> ✓sp than glasses. Now I

don't have to contend with wet or fogged up glasses. I also don't have

to keep pushing <u>them up</u> ✓pro/ant agr my nose when my face gets sweaty. <u>In addi-</u> ✓cs

tion, contact lenses have improved my vision. <u>For the first time that</u> ✓frag <u>I</u>

<u>can remember,</u> I can now look out of the sides of my eyes and see

something. This feature <u>has</u> been particularly useful when I am involved in sports and other outdoor activities. Most of all, I love the change they <u>make</u> (or <u>have made</u>) in my appearance. I never liked the way I looked in glasses, so wearing contact lenses has also boosted my self confidence.

(margin annotations: ✓rs above "has"; ✓subj/verb agr above "has been"; ✓t above "make")

RECAP REVISING: REFINING YOUR DRAFT

New terms in this chapter	Definitions
● reassess	● to evaluate writing to see what works and what doesn't
● redraft	● to create a new version of a piece of writing by correcting problems and incorporating new material into the original draft
● amplify	● to add details or examples to make your meaning clearer
● edit	● to check language in a piece of writing to eliminate errors in grammar, usage, spelling, punctuation, and capitalization
● unified	● focused on one subject
● coherent	● clearly connected and effectively arranged or organized
● transitions	● words or expressions that connect ideas and show relationships between them
● synonyms	● words that are different from one another but have a similar meaning
● effective language	● language that is specific (detailed and to the point) and concise (brief but clear)
● format	● the way a document is arranged on a page

Steps to Revising Effectively

Reassess → unity + coherence + effective language

Redraft → additions + deletions + changes

Edit → personal proofreading system + proofreading partner

Chapter 5

Moving from Paragraph to Essay

Getting Started... **Q:** Up until now, I have had to focus on writing single paragraphs. Now I have to write an entire essay. I feel overwhelmed because writing an essay seems to be such an enormous job. What should I do to get over this feeling and start writing?

A: At this point, the thing you need to do is relax. When you write an essay, you follow the same process that you follow to write a paragraph. In other words, you prewrite, compose, and revise. The primary difference is in degree. A paragraph discusses a single facet of a subject in detail. An essay covers several facets of a subject, in much greater detail. This broader scope is a good thing, by the way, because it gives you the chance to explore a subject fully.

Overview: Understanding the Difference between a Paragraph and an Essay

Up to this point, the focus has been on writing paragraphs as a way to develop your skills. But as a college student and in your professional life, you will often be asked to prepare longer pieces of writing. Most college assignments call for multi-paragraph writings, called **essays,** that deal with a subject in greater detail than is possible in a single paragraph.

The most significant difference between a paragraph and an essay is *scope*. A paragraph can deal with a subject in a limited way. An essay can cover a subject more thoroughly, exploring its many facets and angles. You follow the same process in writing an essay, however, as you do in writing a paragraph. Therefore, what you have already learned about writing paragraphs will clearly help when it comes to writing essays.

In this chapter you will learn what you need to know about writing an essay, including

- the structure of an essay

- the stages of essay writing: prewriting, composing, and revising

- the importance of the thesis

- the importance of meeting your reader's needs

- the role of the introduction and conclusion

Understanding the Structure of an Essay

An essay consists of three parts: an *introduction*, a *body*, and a *conclusion*.

The Introduction

The **introduction** of an essay is usually a single paragraph that indicates the subject and direction of the paper. This paragraph sparks the interest of your readers and compels them to continue reading. The central part of the introduction is the **thesis,** the element that specifies the subject and focus of the entire essay. Just as a topic sentence serves as the main idea for a paragraph, the thesis serves as the main idea for an entire essay.

The Body

The **body** of an essay is the series of paragraphs that support and illustrate the thesis. How many paragraphs should be provided in the body of an essay depends on the specific focus and direction of the writing. The minimum number of paragraphs constituting the body of an essay is three, as with a type known as the **five-paragraph essay.** With such an essay, the introduction raises three specific points about a topic, and then each paragraph in the body discusses one of these three points in detail. This type of essay may prove to be especially useful with some timed writing assignments such as essay examinations or writing assessments. With other essays, the body may include ten paragraphs or more. The number of paragraphs depends on the focus and direction of the writing. Regardless of how many paragraphs are ultimately included, each must contain a clear topic sentence and supporting details, all relating to the thesis.

The Conclusion

The **conclusion** of an essay is a paragraph that strengthens the overall message expressed by the thesis and the supporting examples and details.

The conclusion brings the essay to a logical and appropriate end, summing up the *significance* of the essay. The following figure shows the structure of an essay:

The Structure of an Essay

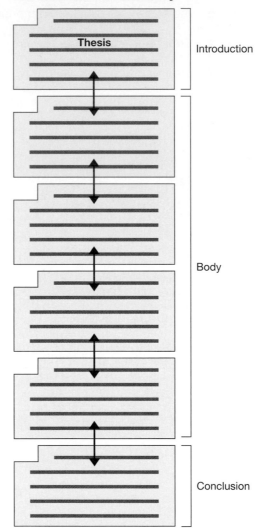

As you can see, the arrows between paragraphs point in both directions. The arrows signify that each paragraph relates to each other as well as to the main point expressed in the introduction and reemphasized in the conclusion.

Exercise 5.1 **Understanding Essay Structure**

1. Briefly explain the structure of the essay.

   An essay includes three sections: the introduction, which features the thesis; the

   body, which presents several paragraphs that support the thesis; and the conclusion,

   which restates the significance of the essay.

2. What role does the introduction play in an essay?

   The introduction presents the main idea and prepares the reader for the material to

   follow in the body.

3. What is the purpose of the conclusion?

   The conclusion serves to emphasize the significance of the points presented in the

   essay.

Challenge 5.1   Developing Essay Awareness

1. What do you think you will find the most difficult about writing an essay rather than a paragraph? Why? On the lines below, briefly explain your reasoning.

   Answers will vary. Most students, however, will admit to feeling intimidated about

   producing a paper that is considerably longer than the paragraphs they have

   developed so far.

2. Working with a classmate, choose a reading from Part Six, "Discovering Connections through Reading." After you both read the piece, write the title of the essay on a separate sheet of paper, and then below it, explain how the paragraphs in the body support the main idea expressed in the introduction.

Examining the Process of Writing an Essay

When you write an essay, you explore a subject far more than you do with a paragraph. To develop the essay, though, you still employ the same process: *prewriting, composing,* and *revising.* The process of writing an essay, like the process of writing a paragraph, often requires you to repeat some steps. In other words, the process is *recursive.*

Prewriting

The first stage of essay writing is prewriting, during which you generate the ideas you'll need to complete your essay. In Chapter 2, "Prewriting: Developing Ideas," you discovered which prewriting technique—or which combination of techniques—you prefer. When you write an essay, you also prewrite to develop a well-focused topic just as you do when you write a paragraph.

Composing

Once you have identified this well-focused topic, you move to the second stage of writing, *composing*. When you compose, you turn the ideas and examples you've generated during prewriting into sentences and arrange your sentences into paragraphs. You also focus on

- developing an effective thesis
- recognizing the needs of your reader
- creating an effective introduction and conclusion

Developing an Effective Thesis   During the composing stage, you also draft the **thesis.** Think of the thesis as a signpost in sentence form that lets the reader know what is to come in the rest of the paper. A topic sentence states the main idea of a paragraph, but a thesis states the main idea of the *entire* essay. An effective thesis, like a topic sentence, is also generally composed of two parts: a *subject* and the *writer's attitude or opinion about* or *reaction to* that subject.

Imagine that you had been asked to write about the most important characteristic a person can have. The subject appeals to you, because you have long believed that integrity—the quality of possessing honesty, fairness, and reliability—is the most important attribute a person can have. After prewriting, you identified the most promising ideas—that integrity plays an important role in friendships, in the workplace, and in the most intimate relationships. You therefore develop the following thesis:

EFFECTIVE THESIS

subject

Of all the qualities people need to succeed in life,

attitude or opinion

the most important one is integrity.

This thesis is effective because it features both a subject and an attitude or opinion about the subject.

One way to remember the characteristics of a good thesis is to remember what they *aren't*. An effective thesis is **not**

- an **announcement** of your intent, featuring words like *I plan, I intend,* or *This paper concerns:*

INEFFECTIVE THESIS

I want to talk about how important integrity is.

- a **statement of fact:**

INEFFECTIVE THESIS

Integrity is the quality of being honest, fair, and dependable.

- a **title:**

INEFFECTIVE THESIS

Integrity: The Quality That Sets a Person Off from the Rest

Recognizing Your Reader's Needs Creating an effective draft essay involves selecting the most promising prewriting ideas, grouping related points, and developing them fully. How you arrange the material is also important. Your goal is to present your ideas in the way that best expresses or supports the thesis.

The secret here is to keep your reader's needs in mind so that your writing will be *reader centered*. We discussed this idea in the context of sentences in Chapter 3 "Composing: Creating Topic Sentences and Supporting Sentences." As explained there, you often know a great deal about your subject, and it's easy to conclude that your reader has the same background and frame of reference as you. When you make this assumption, you fail to provide enough information, making your writing writer centered.

The secret to meeting the needs of your reader is to think of yourself *before* you learned what you know about the subject. For example, what specific examples and details did you need to understand how important integrity is in friendship or at work? How much information would you need to understand the vital role integrity plays in the relationship between spouses, partners, or girl- or boyfriends? Provide this kind of information, expressed in complete sentence form, and your writing will be reader centered.

Exercise 5.2   **Understanding the Thesis and the Needs of the Reader**

1. What are the two parts of the thesis?

   The two parts of the thesis are the subject and the writer's attitude or reaction to

   the subject.

2. Briefly explain the difference between reader-centered and writer-centered writing.

   Writer-centered writing makes sense to the writer only. It lacks the kinds of informa-

   tion that someone without the writer's background and experience needs to under-

   stand the point. Reader-centered writing contains sufficient information to allow

   someone without the writer's background to understand it.

Exercise 5.3 **Creating Effective Theses**

COLLABORATION

1. Working with a classmate or writing group, turn each of the following into an effective thesis: (Representative answers are shown.)

   a. The discharge of heated water from the Commonwealth Power Plant has been linked to a decline of two types of fish in the Taunton River.

   The owners of the Commonwealth Power Plant should be forced to pay a fine

   and restore the stocks of two types of fish that discharge waters have reduced.

   _____

   b. I plan to show that reading to toddlers will help them develop a love of books.

   Reading to toddlers can go a long way in helping them develop into lifetime

   readers.

   _____

   c. Many newspapers are now publishing a complete electronic version of their paper, available before the paper copy.

   The move by a number of major U.S. newspapers to publish a complete elec-

   tronic version may mean the beginning of the end for traditional paper news-

   papers.

   d. Cooperative Education: Gaining Academic Credit and Valuable Work Experience

   Cooperative education courses represent a great way to learn and to develop

   job skills.

   _____

   e. I want to show that directors of youth leagues should enact strict rules regarding the behavior of parents at games.

   Directors of youth sports leagues should establish strict codes of behavior for all

   spectators, including misguided parents.

   _____

2. Choose one of the theses, and, on a separate sheet of paper, prewrite to develop at least three supporting ideas.

Challenge 5.2   **Developing Support for a Thesis**

1. Consider the following thesis:

   The Internet is the most important technical innovation of the last 50 years.

   Working with a classmate or writing group, make a list on a separate sheet of paper of several details and examples that could be used to support this thesis.

2. What do you think the most important personal quality is? Do some prewriting, and then, on a separate sheet of paper, isolate the most promising ideas, and develop a thesis that addresses this issue. Use the sample thesis on integrity as a guide.

Creating an Effective Introduction and Conclusion   As noted, an essay contains two paragraphs that perform specialized functions: the **introduction** and the **conclusion.** The introduction contains the thesis, engages the reader, and previews the structure of the essay. Often the best way to develop a solid introduction is to make the thesis the first or second sentence of the introduction. This way, your reader knows the point of the essay right from the start, as with this introduction for the essay about integrity:

> Of all the qualities people need to succeed in life, the most important one is integrity. When people have this kind of honesty and dependability, all aspects of their lives fall into place. But without integrity, they have little chance of enjoying success with friendships, on the job, or in personal relationships.

You have some other techniques available to help you develop an effective introduction. For example, along with the thesis, you can include

- an **anecdote**—a brief, entertaining story that emphasizes the thesis
- pertinent facts or statistics
- a relevant saying or quotation
- a **rhetorical question**—a type of question designed not to be answered, but to provoke thought or discussion

The conclusion summarizes the point of the essay and brings it to a logical and appropriate end. It is the writer's last word on the subject, a final thought or a question for the reader to consider. In general, conclusions don't present new information in detail. The place to develop new thoughts and ideas fully is the body, not the conclusion.

As with an introduction, sometimes an anecdote that embodies the point of the paper can conclude an essay. Other times a relevant question or quotation will be the best alternative. The technique you ultimately choose should depend on the particular situation. Here, for instance, is the conclusion for the essay on integrity:

> Of all the qualities that a person needs to succeed in life, none is more vital than integrity. When you have integrity, the people you interact with every day know they are dealing with someone who is dependable and honorable. When you lack integrity, people don't expect much from you. They are used to being disappointed.

With conclusions, whatever technique helps you bring an essay to an effective close is the correct choice for that essay.

Exercise 5.4   **Understanding Introductions and Conclusions**

1. How can you ensure that your reader knows the point of your essay right from the start?

   You can ensure that your reader knows right from the start what an essay is about

   by making the thesis the first or second sentence in the introduction.

2. What techniques do writers often use in combination with a thesis to create an effective introduction?

   Writers often use one or more of the following techniques: an anecdote, pertinent

   facts or statistics, a relevant saying or quotation, or a rhetorical question.

3. Why should you generally not include new information in the conclusion of an essay?

   You generally don't include new ideas in the conclusion because they can't be

   developed fully. The place for such development is in the body.

Challenge 5.3   **Examining Introductions and Conclusions**

COLLABORATION

1. For Challenge 5.1 (page 99), you and a classmate were asked to read one of the essays from Part Six, "Discovering Connections through Reading." If you completed that activity, now answer the following questions on a separate sheet of paper:

   a. What is the thesis of this essay? Write it down.

b. Does the writer use any special techniques to introduce or conclude the essay? Explain.

2. Working with a classmate, choose one of the techniques for developing an introduction. Then, on a separate sheet of paper, compose an alternative introduction featuring this technique for the essay on integrity.

Revising

Once you have completed a draft of your essay, take a break of a day or so. This way you will bring a rested and refreshed eye to the final stage of the writing process: **revising.** When you revise, you refine and polish your draft. You follow the same steps to revise an essay that you follow to revise a paragraph. First, you reassess, then you redraft, and finally you edit.

Reassessing   As with a paragraph, when you reassess an essay, you make sure it is

- *unified*—all examples and details must be directly connected
- *coherent*—all the material must have clear transitions and be expressed in standard English and arranged in a logical order
- *effectively worded*—all ideas must be specific and concise

Asking an objective reader for a reaction to your paper is also a great idea. Unlike you, this person is not involved in writing the paper and so can offer a fresh view. Choose someone who will respond honestly and intelligently to your work and then suggest that your reader use the following Essay Assessment Checklist to evaluate your draft.

Essay Assessment Checklist

☐ Do you understand the point I am making? Does my thesis clearly state the subject along with my opinion or attitude about it?

☐ Do I stick to that point all the way through?

☐ Are all my ideas and examples clearly connected and easy to follow?

☐ Are the words I've used specific and concise?

☐ What changes do you think I should make?

Here, for instance is one paragraph from the first-draft version of the essay on integrity:

Integrity is vital in the workplace. Whether the setting is a retail business, a restaurant, or a telecommunications giant, customers and clients expect fairness and honesty. So many people have cell phones today that pay phones are almost not necessary anymore. When the people who these customers and clients deal with don't have integrity,

the consequences can be severe.

Generally, the paragraph is related to the thesis about integrity, so it doesn't disrupt the unity of the essay. Still, some changes could be made that would greatly improve it.

For one thing, because this paragraph follows another, the overall flow of the essay would be improved by adding some transition to the topic sentence. In addition, the third sentence shifts away from the main topic, so it disrupts the unity of the paragraph. Once this sentence is eliminated, the paragraph will be unified. Finally, the fourth sentence suggests that those who run business enterprises face consequences when they act without integrity but never specifies them. Adding details—**amplifying**—will address this problem.

Comments from an objective reader address some of these same points:

> I definitely agree with you about integrity - that's one thing I look for in the people I come in contact with. I think your main point is clear, and your whole introduction is good. So is your conclusion. I found a couple of spots that you might want to go back over. In the third paragraph, I don't think the sentence about the cell phones fits. Also, what happens to guys who run businesses and who cheat? You hint that something bad happens, but you never say exactly. I think the paragraph would be better with this information. That's about it from me.

Redrafting   With the weaknesses in your essay identified, you can begin *redrafting.* When you redraft, you address any problems that you or your objective reader identified in terms of unity, coherence, logical order, and specific language. In many cases, you also *amplify,* providing additional examples and details to bring a scene or situation into better focus for your reader.

Consider this redrafted version of the first draft paragraph on the importance of integrity in the workplace:

> Integrity is *also* vital in the workplace. Whether the setting is a retail business, a restaurant, or a telecommunications giant, customers and clients expect fairness and honesty. When the people who these customers and clients deal with don't have integrity, the consequences can be severe. In most cases, customers will simply go elsewhere. Eventually, corporations that manufacture shoddy products or cheat their customers and stockholders can expect to go out of business. The executives and managers involved and the employees often face public scorn, thousands of dollars in fines, and many years in prison.

A number of changes that improve the paragraph have been made, as the highlighted sections show. The transitional word *also* has been added to the first sentence to serve as a bridge from the previous paragraph. In addition, the sentence about cell phones has been eliminated, which helps to maintain unity in the paragraph. But the most significant change is the addition of the final three sentences. This amplified material outlines consequences that officials may face, thus helping to meet the needs of the reader.

Editing   The final step in revising an essay, as in writing a paragraph, is *editing*. The purpose of this part of the revising process is to eliminate any remaining grammatical errors. The Proofreading Checklist that appears in Chapter 4, "Revising: Refining Your Draft" (page 87) lists several of the most common writing problems. Use that list to identify specific weaknesses in your essay.

You may find that you've mastered certain items on the checklist. At the same time, your paper may contain errors not covered on the list. Therefore, the best thing to do is adapt the list so that it covers your own particular problem spots. Then use this *personal proofreading list* every time you write, whether it's an essay, a term paper, or a letter.

Working with a proofreading partner (someone who can look for errors with a fresh perspective) is also a great idea. If you are using a computer, take full advantage of any spell checking or style checking features. As noted in Chapter 4, always proofread your paper one more time after using these functions, however, to make sure that all errors have been corrected.

Exercise 5.5   **Understanding Editing**

1. Why should you give yourself a break between the composing and revising stages of writing?

    You should take some time between composing and revising in order to bring a

    rested eye to the process.

2. What does it mean to *amplify?*

    To amplify means adding or specifying details and examples.

3. How can having an objective reader help you improve your draft?

    An objective reader has not been involved in writing the essay and so can offer a

    fresh perspective.

4. Briefly explain the purpose of editing.

The purpose of editing is to eliminate any remaining errors in form.

Examining the Process of Writing an Essay: A Sample Essay

The following figure summarizes the process you follow when you write an essay:

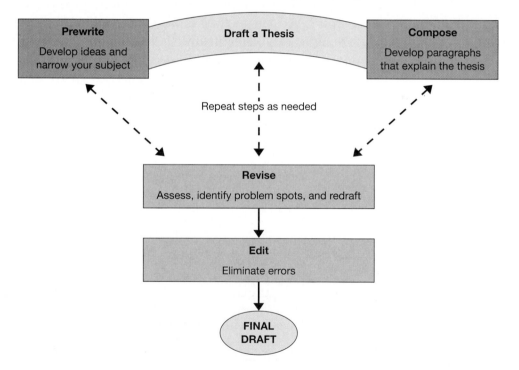

The Process of Writing an Essay

The arrows in the figure indicate the recursive nature of the process. In other words, as you discover a gap or weakness during reassessing, you return to prewriting to generate material to address this problem. Then you move again to composing to turn these ideas into complete sentences.

Here is an example of the product that results from this process: the final draft essay about the most important personal quality. Note the annotations, which emphasize the key points in the essay.

Integrity: Don't Leave Home without It

Thesis

Note how this introduction prepares the reader for the paragraphs to follow.

Of all the qualities people need to succeed in life, the most important one is integrity. When people have this kind of honesty and dependability, all aspects of their lives fall into place. But without integrity, they have little chance of enjoying success with friendships, on the job, or in personal relationships.   *Note the key ideas to be developed.*

Note how this first paragraph of the body discusses the first key idea: integrity as a vital component in friendship.

When it comes to having a solid friendship, integrity is an essential characteristic. For a friendship to thrive, the people involved have to know for sure that they can depend on each other. For example, friends with integrity keep secrets and personal matters confidential. They also follow through on their promises. If they agree to lend a garment, repay money, or provide a ride, they always do it. Their word is their guarantee.

Note how this second paragraph in the body discusses the second key point: the importance of integrity in the workplace.

Integrity is also vital in the workplace. Whether the setting is a retail business, a restaurant, or a telecommunications giant, customers and clients expect fairness and honesty. When the people who these customers and clients deal with don't have integrity, the consequences can be severe. In most cases customers will simply go elsewhere. Eventually, corporations that manufacture shoddy products or cheat their customers and stockholders can expect to go out of business. The executives and managers involved and the employees often face public scorn, thousands of dollars in fines, and many years in prison.

Note how this third paragraph in the body covers the third key point: the role integrity plays in the most personal relationships.

But nowhere is integrity more important than in the personal relationships people have with girl- or boyfriends, partners, or spouses. The foundation of all relationships is trust. No personal relationship can survive without it. Rearing children, handling finances, or owning or caring for property are all profoundly affected by the trust and integrity of the people involved. When either party finds that the other can't be depended on to act responsibly or honestly, the relationship begins to die.

When either person fails to honor these basic obligations, the fundamental lack of integrity destroys the relationship.

This conclusion restates the significance of the role integrity plays in people's lives.

Of all the qualities a person needs to succeed in life, none is more vital than integrity. When you have integrity, the people you interact with every day know they are dealing with someone who is dependable and honorable. When you lack integrity, people don't expect much from you. They are used to being disappointed.

Clearly, this essay is a successful piece of writing, as these instructor's comments indicate:

Congratulations—you have done a fine job revising your paper. Since I saw the first draft a week ago in conference, you made a number of great changes, especially the new examples. The new details concerning personal relationships are especially good. This paragraph is now your strongest. If you want to develop the paper further, you might consider adding another category or two in which integrity plays an important role, for example, in politics or law enforcement. Remember—an essay doesn't have to be only five paragraphs long. In any case, what you have here is already good—you should consider submitting it for our class anthology.

Exercise 5.6   **Considering the Essay-Writing Process**

1. On the lines below, briefly explain the recursive nature of essay-writing.

   The recursive nature of writing means that writers generally need to return to earlier

   stages in the writing process to eliminate weaknesses identified during reassessing.

2. Working with a classmate, review the essay on integrity. Assume that it has been written by someone else in class. On a separate sheet of paper, briefly give your reaction to the essay and list any suggestions for change.

Challenge 5.4   **Writing a Complete Essay**

1. Now it's your turn. For Challenge 5.2, you did some prewriting on what you considered the most important personal quality, isolated the key

ideas, and developed a thesis. Now, with this material as your foundation, create an essay of at least five paragraphs. Use the essay on integrity as a model.

2. Exchange draft essays with a classmate. Evaluate the draft you receive, using the Essay Assessment List on page 105 and return the draft to the writer.

3. Redraft your essay, considering the assessment your objective reader has supplied.

4. Exchange your redrafted essay with a classmate who has not previously seen it. Check the essay you receive for any remaining errors in form, using the Proofreading Checklist on page 87 in Chapter 4. Return the draft with your comments to the writer.

5. Correct any errors in form identified by your reader and hand the paper in for grading.

Exploring Ideas through Journal Writing

The move from paragraph writing to essay writing involves covering a subject far more thoroughly. Consider some other situation that involves a movement from something limited to something more extensive. For example, was there a time when you moved from working part time to full time? Or did you go from playing a sport or music as a hobby and then become part of an organized team, league, band, or organization? Maybe it was a personal relationship that went from being casual to serious and exclusive. What did the change from one stage to the other feel like? Consider this subject and then spend 20 to 30 minutes exploring it in your journal.

SPOTLIGHT PIECE:

Considering a Final Draft Writing

Here's a short essay by student José Gouveia about the tragic death of his younger brother. The annotations to the left of José's writing focus on the elements that make up an essay. Read José's essay and the annotations, and then answer the questions that follow the writing.

Hero

José's introduction prepares the reader for the story he will tell.

Thesis

My brother Eddy was killed on October 30, 1999, at the age of 18. A man named Carlos shot him in the head with a handgun. What happened to Eddy that night changed everything for my whole family, and I'm still trying to adjust to the changes today.

Continued

The paragraphs in the body present the series of events making up José's traumatic experience.

Witnesses say Eddy arrived at the house at 164 Blackstone Street at approximately 3:00 A.M. to pick up his friend who was drunk. Eddy asked Carlos for a drink, but Carlos refused.

Carlos approached Eddy about ten minutes later and offered him a drink. Eddy refused it because he had seen Carlos put white powder in the drink. Carlos and his brother took offense, and there was a fight. Eddy defended himself, but it was two against one. Eddy was pushed to a bedroom where he tripped over the carpet and fell.

When he got up, Carlos had a gun pointed at his head about eight to twelve inches away. Eddy asked Carlos to put the gun away. Carlos just pulled the trigger and shot him in the head.

At 3:15 A.M., we received a call from Saint Anne's Hospital. Some lady claimed to be a nurse from the hospital. She wanted to speak with my mother. I told her that my mother did not speak any English. She told me to wake my mother up and bring her to the hospital A.S.A.P. She refused to explain. She said, "I'm not supposed to say anything. Just wake up your mom and come to the hospital." I didn't believe her, so I told my mother that someone was playing a joke on us and to go back to bed.

At about 4:30 A.M. the phone rang again, and it was the same lady. I was already upset because this lady had ruined my sleep a second time, so I started to curse at her. She said, "I'm sorry but your brother has been shot and your family should come here immediately." I asked her if he was OK, but she refused to answer. She told me she couldn't say anything over the phone. She told me to take the family to the hospital.

When we arrived at the hospital, the doctor said, "I tried everything. I'm very sorry. I couldn't do anything for him. He was already dead when the EMTs tried to revive him. They were hoping for some kind of miracle, but the bullet had damaged his brain."

Then he asked me to go and identify the body. When I saw him, my heart began beating like I had never felt before. He looked like he was sleeping, but when I tried to wake him, he didn't move. When I lifted the bandage, his face was swollen, and just a little above his right eye, I saw the bullet hole. My heart dropped, and I could not stop crying. I wanted him back.

After Eddy's death, I became a different person. I didn't care about anybody. I said to myself on many occasions, "I left Mozambique for this?" I did not know how to live my life without him. Eddy was very important to me. We used to do many things together, especially play soccer. He was my younger brother, and he had been a role model for many of his friends, and especially for our younger brother Agostinho.

Even today, I don't believe he's gone. I'm just learning to live my life without him. I take it one step at a time and pray to God to protect his soul. He was one of my heroes.

Exploring the Reading

1. On the lines that follow, briefly explain how José's introduction prepares his reader for the story he is about to tell.

   José's introduction tells his reader that his brother was murdered and that this tragic

   event had terrible effects on him that continue even today.

2. In your view, which paragraph in the body of José's essay contains the most compelling details and examples? On the following lines, explain your choice.

   Answers will vary, although many students will focus on paragraph 8, in which José

   tells what it was like to have to identify his brother's body.

3. The role of the conclusion is to bring an essay to a logical and appropriate end. Sometimes it summarizes the point of the essay, offering the writer's final thought on the issue. Working with a classmate, examine José's conclusion, and then on the lines that follow, explain how José's conclusion brings his essay to an effective close.

   Answers will vary somewhat, but most students will note that the conclusion reminds

   the reader of the extent of the trauma he has faced and of the way he felt about his

   brother.

Understanding the Subject through Writing

In his essay, José tells of an event so terrible that it has shattered his family. The story is powerful because José provides powerful, specific details. On a separate sheet of paper, write a brief passage (50 to 100 words) in which you discuss a traumatic event that you have witnessed or experienced.

Discovering Connections 5.1

Take a look at this photo. What ideas does this image represent to you? Do you have a problem that needs unraveling? Do you feel trapped by obligations and responsibilities, or do you enjoy the ties that bind you to others? Perhaps this image suggests other kinds of tie-ups, whether traffic jams or complications in school or at work.

Use the image to help you explore this topic. Once you have completed your prewriting, refer to the material in this chapter, especially the sample essay on integrity, to guide you as you turn these ideas into a 400-to-500-word essay.

Discovering Connections 5.2

The word *stereotype* comes from printing and originally referred to a plate from which numerous identical copies could be made. In more general usage, *stereotype* refers to common conceptions people hold about groups of other people. Why do you think some people judge entire groups on the basis of a stereotype? Think of a group you are in. In what ways do you differ from others in that group? In your view, what is the best way to make people see others as individuals, not just as stereotypes?

Prewrite on one of these aspects of stereotypes. Then use the material as the basis for a 400-to-500-word essay. Use the material in this chapter, especially the sample essay on integrity, as a guide as you work through the stages of the essay-writing process.

RECAP   MOVING FROM PARAGRAPH TO ESSAY

New terms in this chapter	Definitions
● essay	● a multi-paragraph writing that deals more extensively with a subject than a paragraph does
● five-paragraph essay	● an essay that introduces three points in the opening paragraph that are discussed one at a time in the body with the conclusion reiterating them
● introduction	● a paragraph that opens an essay, providing a clear thesis and engaging the reader

New terms in this chapter	Definitions
● **thesis**	● the sentence in the introduction that specifies the main subject of the essay and the writer's attitude or position on it
● **body**	● the series of paragraphs that provide support and illustration for a thesis
● **conclusion**	● a paragraph that closes the essay, summarizing the essay's point and bringing it to a logical and appropriate end
● **anecdote**	● a brief, entertaining story, often used to make a point An anecdote may be used effectively in an introduction or a conclusion.
● **rhetorical question**	● a question designed not to be answered, but to provoke thought or discussion A rhetorical question may be used effectively in an introduction to engage readers.
● **amplifying**	● the process of providing additional, specific details and examples

The Process of Writing an Essay

Prewrite on a **topic.**
Identify a **focus.**
Develop a **thesis.**

Arrange the most promising prewriting ideas in a logical order and turn them into **supporting sentences.**
Develop the supporting sentences into **paragraphs.**
Write paragraphs for an **introduction** and **conclusion.**

Reassess your draft for **unity, coherence** (transitions and organization), and **effective language.**
Redraft to eliminate any weaknesses identified in reassessing.
Edit to eliminate any **grammatical** or **spelling errors.**

Writers' Café

Is it worth the hard work necessary to become a better writer?

Absolutely. Write well in school and on the job and you will . . .

- earn better grades
- earn the respect of coworkers, clients, customers, and supervisors

It's that simple.

Will developing writing skills also enhance critical thinking skills?

Definitely. Writing well requires that you thoroughly understand what you have experienced, witnessed, or read about. Writing effectively means . . .

- considering the people, events, situations, or conditions themselves
- recognizing how they relate to each other

Therefore, each time you write, you develop critical thinking skills.

Does talking about writing with other writers help people become better writers?

Without a doubt. When it comes to writing, experience can be one of the best teachers, and other writers have faced the same experiences with writing that you have. Other writers can . . .

- serve as a great audience for your own writing, offering an immediate assessment of your success with a draft
- identify problem spots and provide different strategies and techniques for dealing with problems

When writers talk writing with other writers, everyone benefits.

Is there anything I can do to deal with writer's block?

Yes. Writer's block—the feeling that you have nothing to say about a subject, no ideas to develop, and no ways to explore them—is no joke. To combat writer's block, remember that with writing . . .

- it is normal to feel overwhelmed sometimes
- it is a messy process, involving starts, stops, and stumbling before you complete an effective draft
- you can't revise something that doesn't exist, so force yourself to write—even if you are initially disappointed with the results

Half the solution to writer's block is to recognize the complexity of the writing process. The other half is to, as the popular Nike slogan states, *just do it* and worry about quality later.

Effective Sentences: Constructing Meaning

Chapter 6

Subjects and Verbs

Getting Started... **Q:** I've done my prewriting and identified my main point and supporting ideas. I know how important it is for me to present my good ideas correctly. What do I do now to make sure that I express them all in complete sentence form?

A: You've already done the hard work—generating ideas, identifying a focus, and selecting and shaping the strongest supporting points. Now, to ensure that the sentences you write are correct, you need to turn your attention to the basics: verbs and subjects. Each unit you write must contain a verb and a subject so that each expresses a complete thought.

Overview: Understanding Elements of a Complete Sentence

"Always write in complete sentences."

You have probably heard this directive many times, but you may have found it hard to follow.

To follow this instruction, you need to understand what makes a sentence complete. By definition, a **sentence** is a series of words that expresses a complete thought through a subject and a verb. The **subject** is the doer of the action or the focus of the verb. The **verb** shows action or otherwise completes the statement. To express your ideas so that your reader understands them, you must understand the role of these two parts of a sentence.

> *This chapter helps you learn the proper use of subjects and verbs. To help you express your thoughts in complete sentences, you will learn to identify and use*
>
> - action verbs, linking verbs, verb phrases, and compound verbs
>
> - simple subjects, complete subjects, and compound subjects

Consider the following quotation:

Imagination is more important than knowledge.

—*Albert Einstein*

Or consider this photo.

Now, using the prewriting technique you prefer, do some prewriting about your reaction to the quotation or photo. Save your work.

Identifying Action Verbs

In most sentences, subjects come before verbs. However, it's more helpful to go to the heart of the sentence and consider verbs first. Most verbs indicate some action on the part of the subject. They are called **action verbs.** To identify the action verb in a sentence, ask yourself *what word shows action?*

Look at these sentences:

EXAMPLE   My friend works at the Women's Center.

EXAMPLE   Suddenly, the dishes crashed to the floor.

In the first sentence, the verb is *works,* and in the second, it is *crashed.* These words show action in the sentences.

Verbs can show different kinds of action. Some verbs, such as *works* and *crashed,* show action that can be witnessed. Other verbs, such as *think, judge, desire,* or *wonder,* show thought or implied action.

Exercise 6.1   **Practice Identifying Action Verbs**

Underline all the action verbs in the paragraph below. Use the example as a guide.

EXAMPLE   Maria's fingers <u>tapped</u> the keyboard quickly during the word processing exam.

(1) In his spare time, my Uncle Joe <u>tends</u> the community vegetable garden. (2) Early in the morning, he <u>pulls</u> the weeds between the rows of vegetables. (3) Often this task <u>takes</u> him a half an hour or more.

(4) He also <u>monitors</u> the irrigation system every day. (5) Uncle Joe <u>knows</u> from experience the dangers of overwatering. (6) One year, one whole section of the garden <u>died</u> from excess water. (7) On his day off during the week, Joe also <u>loosens</u> the dirt from around the plants. (8) Year after year, Uncle Joe's efforts <u>pay</u> off in the form of an abundance of produce.

Exercise 6.2 **Working with Action Verbs**

Choose ten action verbs from the following list. On a separate sheet of paper, write ten sentences using these verbs. Use the example to guide you.

EXAMPLE That electrician <u>installs</u> alarm systems in buildings.

talk	run	think	write	drive
wonder	laugh	imagine	paint	read
ask	consider	call	visit	cook

Challenge 6.1 **Recognizing the Role of Action Verbs**

Here is a short poem by Langston Hughes, written in 1951. Read it, and then answer the questions that follow.

Harlem

What happens to a dream deferred?

Does it dry up
like a raisin in the sun?
Or fester like a sore—
And then run?
Does it stink like rotten meat?
Or crust and sugar over—
like a syrupy sweet?

Maybe it just sags
like a heavy load.

Or does it explode?

1. Find the action verbs in the poem. On a separate sheet of paper, list each verb and write what you believe it means as Hughes has used the word. Use the following example as a guide.

action verb	meaning

EXAMPLE   happens   comes to be; occurs by chance

2. Discuss with your classmates what you think the "dream deferred" may be. Do you think Hughes chose effective verbs to express his idea? Why?

Identifying Linking Verbs

A second type of verb does not show action. Most **linking verbs** are forms of the verb *to be* (*is, are, were, will be, might have been*, and so on). They link or connect the subject to some other word that restates or describes the subject. Look at these sentences. Which words provide the links?

EXAMPLE   My opponent for the match was my old friend.

EXAMPLE   Alice Walker's novel *The Color Purple* is truly powerful.

In the first sentence, the linking verb *was* connects the subject *My opponent for the match* with the words that rename it: *my old friend*. In the second sentence, the linking verb *is* connects the subject, *Alice Walker's novel The Color Purple* with the words that describe it: *truly powerful*.

The following verbs usually serve as action verbs, but they can also be used as linking verbs:

appear	feel	look	sound
become	grow	seem	taste

Look at these sentences:

action verb

EXAMPLE   Robins *appear* again in spring.

linking verb

EXAMPLE   The lines *appear* crooked from this angle.

In the first sentence, the action verb *appear* tells what the robins do. In the second, however, the word *appear* acts much like the verb *are*. It is a linking verb used to connect the subject *lines* with the describing word *crooked*.

Exercise 6.3   **Identifying Linking Verbs**

Underline the linking verbs in the paragraph on the following page. Remember—linking verbs connect the subject with a word that restates or describes it. Use the example to guide you.

EXAMPLE   The effects of positive reinforcement <u>are</u> immediately noticeable.

(1) Fetal alcohol syndrome <u>is</u> a serious problem for some children. (2) This preventable syndrome <u>is</u> a result of a mother's alcohol intake during pregnancy. (3) The effects of the syndrome <u>are</u> devastating. (4) From the moment of their birth, babies with fetal alcohol syndrome <u>are</u> behind their peers in every mark of development. (5) For example, children with fetal alcohol syndrome <u>are</u> smaller and thinner than most kids their age. (6) As a result of physical weaknesses, they <u>are</u> frequent victims of viruses and other communicable diseases. (7) In school, children with fetal alcohol syndrome <u>are</u> almost always far behind their peers. (8) Learning, especially with higher level skills like reading and mathematical computation, <u>is</u> extremely difficult for them.

Exercise 6.4   **Working with Linking Verbs**

Complete the paragraph below. Fill in the blanks with appropriate linking verbs taken from the following list. In some cases, more than one verb will fit the sentence. You may use each verb more than once. Use the example as a guide. (Answers may vary slightly in some cases.)

was	were
will be	have been
seemed	appeared
be	became
are	grew
has been	

EXAMPLE   Scorpions ____*are*____ relatives of spiders.

(1) Professional sports leagues for women ____are____ a new phenomenon in North America. (2) Women's sports leagues ____have been____ successful in other parts of the world. (3) However, the idea ____has been____ less popular in North America. (4) Still, many women in North America ____are____ upset that they did not have the opportunity to compete on a professional level in the sports of their choice. (5) They ____were____ weary of watching their male counterparts receive all of the glory.

Exercise 6.5   **Choosing Appropriate Action and Linking Verbs**

Fill in the blanks in the following paragraph with appropriate action or linking verbs. Label action verbs with an *A* and linking verbs with an *L*. Then exchange and discuss your work with a classmate. As you compare your responses, consider these questions: Did you use similar action verbs? What made you choose those action verbs? Which ones seem most effective? Why? Did you choose the same linking verbs? What are the differences between your choices? (Answers may vary in some cases. Representative answers are given.)

EXAMPLE   Wolves _____*travel*_____ in packs.

(1) Gabriel García Márquez _____is_____ a popular writer of contemporary fiction. (2) He _____began_____ his writing career as a journalist in his hometown of Aracataca, Columbia. (3) As a young man, García Márquez _____attended_____ the University of Bogotá, where he studied journalism. (4) After he graduated from college, he _____took_____ a job as a reporter for a Columbian newspaper. (5) Later in his life, García Márquez _____moved_____ to Mexico City, where he began to write literature. (6) *One Hundred Years of Solitude, Love in the Time of Cholera,* and *Of Love and Other Demons* _____are_____ some of his most famous works of fiction. (7) Readers of his work _____admire_____ him for the way he weaves realism and fantasy in his stories and novels. (8) In 1982, he _____won_____ the Nobel Prize for literature.

Challenge 6.2   **Considering Your Own Verb Use**

1. Choose a draft of a writing you created for an earlier assignment. If you prefer, draft a new writing to support the following topic sentence:

   Reality television shows reflect changing attitudes among viewers.

2. Make a copy of your writing and exchange it with a classmate. On the copy you receive, underline the linking verbs and circle the action verbs.

Identifying Subjects

The subject, you remember, is the doer of the action or the focus of the verb. Often the subject is a **noun,** a word that names a person, place, or thing. But it may be a **pronoun,** a word that substitutes for a noun, such as *he, she,* or *it.* Ask yourself *who or what is doing the action or being discussed?* The answer to this question is the subject. Look at these sentences:

EXAMPLE   The running back spiked the football in the end zone.

EXAMPLE   Friday nights are always the busiest times at the store.

To discover the subject in these sentences, follow these simple steps.

1. Identify the verb.
2. Ask *who or what did this?* or *who or what is being described?*

In the first sentence, the verb is *spiked.* Who or what spiked the football? The answer to the question, and therefore the subject of the sentence, is *The running back.*

In the second sentence, the verb is *are.* Who or what are always the busiest times at the store? The answer, and therefore the subject of the sentence, is *Friday nights.*

Exercise 6.6   **Identifying Subjects**

Underline the verbs in the following sentences. Then find the subjects by asking who or what is doing the action or being described. Circle each subject. (It may be more than one word.) Use the example as a guide.

EXAMPLE   My (Uncle Milt) tripped over the cat in front of the couch.

(1) In the last few years, (meditation) has become increasingly popular in the United States. (2) People from many walks of life now (meditate) on a daily basis. (3) Regular (meditation) offers a number of benefits. (4) This ancient (practice) improves overall health, including circulation and respiration. (5) As a result, (meditators) enjoy a higher overall level of energy. (6) Also (meditation) is a safe stress reliever. (7) According to some research findings, (blood pressure) goes down after only fifteen minutes of meditation a day.

Exercise 6.7   **Providing Appropriate Subjects**

The subjects are missing from the sentences in the following paragraph. Fill in the blanks in each sentence with appropriate nouns or pronouns. Use the example to guide you.

EXAMPLE   On weekdays, __the bakery__ closes at 8 P.M.

(Answers may vary. Representative answers are given.)

(1) Last Sunday, __everyone__ came out to the park to enjoy the beautiful fall day. (2) __The parking lot__ was filled with cars. (3) __The lawn__ was covered with blankets, radios, and coolers. (4) __Teenagers__ threw frisbees and footballs along the lakefront. (5) __Children__ played on the swings and seesaw in the playground. (6) Meanwhile, __families__ ate at the picnic tables nearby. (7) In a small grove of pine trees, __my parents__ sat and quietly talked. (8) A __little girl__ flew a kite in the little league field.

Challenge 6.3   **Focusing on Subjects**

1. Choose a draft of a writing you created for an earlier assignment. If you prefer, draft a new writing to support the following topic sentence:

   To make sure that the right person is convicted, police investigators need to pay more attention to DNA evidence.

   Make a copy of your writing and exchange it with a classmate. On the copy you receive, underline the subjects. Put an X in front of any sentence in which you think a subject is missing.

2. Check any sentences your reader has identified as missing a subject and make necessary adjustments.

Finding the Simple Subject within the Complete Subject

Every sentence has a **simple subject.** It is the one noun or pronoun that answers the who or what question. The **complete subject** includes the simple subject plus any words or phrases that describe or modify it.

In the following example sentences, the verbs and complete subjects are identified:

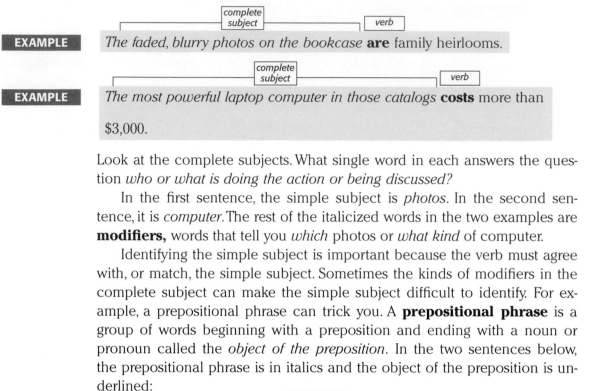

EXAMPLE

The faded, blurry photos on the bookcase **are** family heirlooms.

EXAMPLE

The most powerful laptop computer in those catalogs **costs** more than $3,000.

Look at the complete subjects. What single word in each answers the question *who or what is doing the action or being discussed?*

In the first sentence, the simple subject is *photos.* In the second sentence, it is *computer.* The rest of the italicized words in the two examples are **modifiers,** words that tell you *which* photos or *what kind* of computer.

Identifying the simple subject is important because the verb must agree with, or match, the simple subject. Sometimes the kinds of modifiers in the complete subject can make the simple subject difficult to identify. For example, a prepositional phrase can trick you. A **prepositional phrase** is a group of words beginning with a preposition and ending with a noun or pronoun called the *object of the preposition.* In the two sentences below, the prepositional phrase is in italics and the object of the preposition is underlined:

EXAMPLE

The faded, blurry photos *on the <u>bookcase</u>* are family heirlooms.

EXAMPLE

The most powerful laptop computer *in those <u>catalogs</u>* costs over $3,000.

When the object of the preposition comes right before the verb, as it does in these examples, it's easy to mistake it for the subject. You can avoid this mistake if you remember a simple rule: the noun or pronoun following a preposition *cannot* be the subject of a verb. Learning to recognize these common prepositions will give you an advantage:

about	behind	during	on	to
above	below	except	onto	toward
across	beneath	for	out	under
after	beside	from	outside	underneath
against	besides	in	over	unlike
along	between	inside	past	until
among	beyond	into	since	up
around	but (except)	like	than	upon
as	by	near	through	with
at	despite	of	throughout	within
before	down	off	till	without

Once you can recognize prepositional phrases, you can cross them out and find the subject more easily.

Exercise 6.8   Focusing on the Simple Subject

Underline the complete subject in each sentence below. Then find and circle the simple subject. Remember—the complete subject includes the simple subject plus any words that describe it. Use the example as a guide.

EXAMPLE   In the store, the video (monitor) behind the counter shows any movement in the aisles.

(1) A violent (storm) on a summer night can really get your attention. (2) Two weeks ago, a fierce (thunderstorm) with accompanying hail hit my town, shaking everyone up. (3) (People) in my area suffered property losses during the storm. (4) For example, the picnic (table) next to my neighbor's driveway flipped and broke into pieces. (5) The shattered (pieces) of the table flew over the fence and into our yard. (6) A (branch) of a maple tree above my neighbor's car crashed through the windshield. (7) The (damage) to the glass led to water damage inside the car. (8) In addition, a huge (section) of shingles on the building across the street blew off the roof.

Exercise 6.9   Identifying the Simple Subject

Circle the complete subject in each sentence in the following paragraph. Then underline all prepositional phrases in each complete subject. Last, cross out all other modifiers. Refer to the list of prepositions to help you identify prepositional phrases. Use the example to guide you.

EXAMPLE   (The large package in the hallway) was filled with discarded toys.

(1) (The small bookstore in the Student Union) is always crowded. (2) (The overworked staff of the bookstore) tries to keep the lines of people moving. (3) Unfortunately, (the one narrow doorway from the Student Union) slows the flow of traffic. (4) Yesterday, (several students with big armloads of books) were blocking the entrance. (5) (The huge piles of new books next to the registers) also get in everyone's way.

1. On a separate sheet of paper, write five sentences with subjects with no modifiers except for the *articles* (*a, an,* or *the*).

2. Exchange your sentences with a classmate. Underline the subjects in the sentences you receive. Then, above the subjects you have identified, add suitable modifiers—words or phrases or both.

3. Rewrite your sentences, including the modifiers your classmate has suggested or modifiers of your own choice.

Recognizing Verb Phrases and Compound Verbs

Not all verbs are one word. Many sentences contain verb phrases or compound verbs. A **verb phrase** is a *main* verb plus one or more *helping verbs.* Various forms of *be, have,* and *do* serve as helping verbs. Can you find the verb phrases in the following sentences?

EXAMPLE   We are discussing the Vietnam War in my American History class.

EXAMPLE   Michelle can study for six hours on Mondays.

In the first sentence, *discussing* is the main verb. Note that *discussing* cannot fully communicate the action by itself. It needs the helping verb *are* to do that. Therefore, the verb phrase is *are discussing.*

The situation is similar in the second sentence. The main verb *study* needs the helping verb *can* to communicate the full meaning of the action. The two words together, *can study,* constitute the verb phrase.

Here is a list of common helping verbs:

am	can	had	might	were
are	could	has	must	will
be	did	have	shall	would
being	do	is	should	
been	does	may	was	

Some sentences express more than one action or state of being. These sentences have **compound verbs,** two or more action verbs connected by the conjunctions *and* or *or.* (For more on conjunctions, see Chapter 8, "Subordination," and Chapter 9, "Coordination.") Can you identify the compound verbs in the following sentences?

EXAMPLE   Tyrone draws, paints, and plays the piano.

EXAMPLE   All participants register the week before the tournament or pay a late fee.

In the first sentence, three verbs connected by *and* (*draws, paints,* and *plays*) make up the compound verb. In the second sentence, the verbs *register* and *pay* are connected by the conjunction *or*. The compound verb is *register* or *pay*.

Exercise 6.10   **Recognizing Verb Phrases and Compound Verbs**

Find and underline the verb phrases and compound verbs in the following passage. With the compound verbs you identify, circle the conjunctions *and* and *or*. Use the example as a guide.

EXAMPLE   The instructor <u>guided</u> the young student through the first steps of the dance (and) then <u>sat</u> down to watch.

(1) I <u>have been coaching</u> a softball team of 9 to 12 year old girls for the past two years. (2) This season, the kids <u>played</u> hard (and) <u>won</u> all but two regular season games. (3) Katrina, the youngest girl on the team, <u>pitched</u> (and) <u>hit</u> better than anybody else. (4) She also <u>showed</u> great leadership (and) <u>demonstrated</u> good sportsmanship throughout the season. (5) She always <u>cheered</u> (or) <u>encouraged</u> her teammates, even following occasional bad plays. (6) During the playoffs, Katrina and the other girls <u>concentrated</u> (and) <u>played</u> even better. (7) For the championship game, they <u>were determined</u> to play at the same level. (8) By the end of the second inning in this game, they <u>had</u> already <u>scored</u> seven runs, ultimately celebrating a 7 to 0 championship victory.

Exercise 6.11   **Identifying Verb Phrases and Compound Verbs**

COLLABORATION

Work with a classmate to complete the sentences below. Write a verb phrase or a compound verb in each blank. Refer to the list of common helping verbs on page 130. Use the example to guide you.

EXAMPLE   Without considering what the people around us would think, Greg _yelled at me and stomped angrily away_ .

(Answers may vary. Representative answers are shown.)

(1) Extremely bad economic conditions in my community _have hurt_ (verb phrase) my family directly. (2) Because the employees at my brother's plant didn't get a raise this year, they _protested and struck_ (compound verb). (3) The manager _has filled_ (verb phrase) their positions with workers who will work for lower wages. (4) Because of declining sales, one of the small independent grocery stores in my neighborhood _lost money and closed_ (compound verb). (5) My mother _can shop_ (verb phrase) at another store, but it is not convenient. (6) Many other companies _have moved_ (verb phrase) to other parts of the state where business is better. (7) In these conditions, how will my father, who is unemployed, _find and keep work_ (compound verb)? (8) My family _has felt_ (verb phrase) the effects of tough times in other ways, too.

Exercise 6.12   **Writing Sentences with Verb Phrases and Compound Verbs**

COLLABORATION

1. Below is a list of verb phrases and a list of compound verbs. Working with a classmate, select five verb phrases and five compound verbs from the lists. Then on a separate sheet of paper, write ten sentences, each with one of your chosen word groups.

Verb Phrases	*Compound Verbs*
have thought	smile or laugh
can speak	washed, dried, and ironed
am trying	memorize and study
must return	screamed and jumped
can understand	call or write
might arrive	push, pull, or lift
is crying	sat and rested

2. Choose one of the sentences, and on a separate sheet of paper write at least three sentences related to the same idea. Underline all the verbs and circle their subjects.

Challenge 6.5   **Working with Verb Phrases and Compound Verbs**

1. Choose a selection from Part Six, "Discovering Connections through Reading." After reading the essay, select a four-paragraph passage, and on a separate sheet of paper, list all verbs, verb phrases, and compound verbs.

2. Working with a classmate, choose five verbs from each of your lists and on a separate sheet of paper use these verbs to write sentences.

Recognizing Compound Subjects

You've already seen that complete subjects can contain many words. The simple subject within that complete subject may be a single noun or pronoun or it may be several. A **compound subject** is two or more nouns or pronouns connected by *and* or *or*. Identify the compound subjects in these sentences:

EXAMPLE   Donald, Paul, or Lew borrowed that book.

EXAMPLE   The flowers and hedges in the cemetery were trimmed neatly.

In the first sentence, the verb is *borrowed*. The answer to the question *who or what borrowed?* is the compound subject, *Donald, Paul, or Lew*. In the second sentence, the verb is *were trimmed*, and the answer to the question *who or what were trimmed?* is the compound subject, *flowers and hedges*.

Exercise 6.13   **Identifying Compound Subjects**

Underline the compound subjects in the following paragraph. Use the example as a guide.

EXAMPLE   In many cases, fruit juice or water is more refreshing than carbonated

drinks.

(1) Shelley and Shannon are identical twins with totally different personalities. (2) At first glance, their eyes, the shape of their faces, and

their lips look almost identical. (3) In addition, their speaking voices and their laughs seem exactly the same. (4) But their smiles and some facial expressions are quite different. (5) Also, their interests and attitudes are completely different. (6) Sports, dancing, and music fascinate Shelley. (7) She and her friends regularly go out to sporting events and dance clubs, especially on karaoke nights. (8) For Shannon, however, books, movies, and politics are her main interests.

Exercise 6.14 **Focusing on Compound Subjects**

Some of the sentences below have compound subjects and some do not. Before you begin, review the differences between simple and complete subjects. Then underline each compound subject and circle each simple subject, using the examples below to guide you.

EXAMPLE   Most action movies have little character development.

EXAMPLE   Pollen, mold, and dust can cause breathing difficulties for people with allergies.

(1) Golf and fishing are comparatively boring to watch on TV for several reasons. (2) For one thing, the announcers on these programs speak in a quiet monotone. (3) Even the reaction of the crowd at the location is subdued. (4) Spectators usually have to avoid breaking the participants' concentration. (5) The fans, cheerleaders, and bands are part of the fun of watching other sports, such as football and basketball. (6) In contrast, fishing tournaments and golf matches take a long time to complete. (7) Also, the action and pace of these sports are slow.

Exercise 6.15 **Using Compound Subjects**

Below is a list of compound subjects. Choose ten of these subjects, and on a separate sheet of paper, write a sentence using each.

basketball and football	computers and CD-ROMs
apartments and condominiums	ice and snow
bottles or cans	cars, buses, or trains
books and magazines	tables, chairs, and desks
fruit and vegetables	glasses or contact lenses
beards and mustaches	family and friends

Challenge 6.6   **Working with Compound Subjects**

1. On a separate sheet of paper, write four sentences with simple subjects, one subject a person, one a place, one a thing, and one an idea or concept.

2. Exchange your sentences with a classmate. On a separate sheet of paper, rewrite the sentences, turning each of the simple subjects into appropriate compound subjects.

Subjects and Verbs Checklist

☐ Have you made sure that every group of words you intend as a sentence contains either an action or linking verb?

☐ Have you asked "Who or what is doing this or who or what is being described" to make sure that each verb has a subject?

☐ Have you used an appropriate helping verb to form any verb phrases?

☐ Have you connected compound verbs by using an appropriate conjunction such as *and* or *or*?

☐ Have you connected compound subjects by using an appropriate conjunction like *and* or *or*?

Discovering Connections 6.2

1. For Discovering Connections 6.1 on page 121, you began prewriting in response to a quotation by Albert Einstein or a photo. Now, continue your prewriting on one of these options:
   a. Do you agree with Einstein about imagination versus knowledge? Why or why not? Explain.
   b. How would you define imagination? In what ways does imagination play a role in day-to-day existence for most people?
2. Evaluate your prewriting material, identify a focus, and create a draft of about 100 words.

3. Exchange your draft with a writing partner. Using the material in this chapter as a guide, evaluate the draft you receive, and note any problems with subjects and verbs as well as any other weaknesses. Return the draft to the writer.
4. Revise your draft, eliminating any errors that your reader identified.

Exploring Ideas through Journal Writing

As this chapter shows, the way to communicate your ideas effectively is to express them in complete sentences. Can you think of something you have witnessed or thought about that doesn't make sense unless you have the full picture? What is or was the missing element? Why was there such a difference without it? For example, the extreme was a friend reacted to a phone call in a way that didn't match her normal behavior. Then you discovered the significance of the message she received over the phone. Consider this topic and then spend 20 to 30 minutes exploring it in your journal.

Chapter Quick Check:
Subjects and Verbs

Find all the subjects and verbs in the following essay. Circle each simple subject, and underline each verb, including the conjunctions for compound verbs and the helping verbs in verb phrases.

(1) Thanks to the unusual efforts of some horse lovers, a (lookalike) for an extinct breed of horse has been created. (2) The (horse) is the Tarpan, a short, stocky breed with a rounded belly and a distinctive, stand-up mane. (3) Many prehistoric (artifacts) and (cave paintings) contained images of the Tarpan's earliest ancestors, with the same rounded bellies and distinctive mane. (4) These (horses) lived and thrived throughout the Middle East and Europe following the last Ice Age. (5) According to the Wisconsin-based American Tarpon Studbook Association, the (number) of wild Tarpans dwindled over many centuries and then died out in the 1890s. (6) Within a couple of decades, a few (breeders) and horse (lovers) began attempts to develop a horse closely resembling the extinct Tarpan. (7) (They) eventually accomplished their aim and produced a Tarpan by mating horses sharing Tarpan-like physical characteristics. (8) Other modern-day (breeders) have taken a more controversial road to create a Tarpan by focusing attention on herds of wild mustangs in the U.S. West. (9) According to these breeders, the (ancestry) of these mustangs extends to horses with Tarpan genes belonging to Spanish explorers. (10) By breeding mustangs with strong Tarpan features, these horse (lovers) have created a horse closely resembling the Tarpan, including the distinctive stand-up mane.

Summary Exercise: Subjects and Verbs

Find all the subjects and verbs in the following essay. Circle each simple subject, and underline each verb, including the conjunctions for compound verbs and the helping verbs in verb phrases.

(1) My next-door (neighbor) is running for the city council. (2) Over the past two years, (Madeleine) has been involved in several political campaigns. (3) After working for other people, (she) has become a candidate herself. (4) (She) truly believes in the power of the vote to create change.

(5) (Bumper stickers and signs) for Madeleine are posted all over the city. (6) Every day, (she) visits another neighborhood and introduces herself to the people. (7) Fortunately, (she) isn't shy. (8) Instead, (she) looks right at the people, smiles, and explains her positions on various issues. (9) For the most part, (people) have been friendly to her.

(10) Of course, a serious political (campaign) costs money. (11) As a result, (Madeleine) has held several fund-raisers. (12) Neighborhood (breakfasts or block parties) draw the biggest crowds. (13) For these fund-raisers, campaign (volunteers) make and sell a variety of food. (14) (Madeleine) goes from table to table and introduces herself to the voters. (15) So far (she) has held five of these events. (16) (They) have raised money for her campaign signs and several newspaper advertisements.

(17) The (election) is a month away. (18) Madeleine has knocked on doors in every part of the city. (19) (She) has worked hard. (20) The (rest) is up to the voters.

RECAP   SUBJECTS AND VERBS

New terms in this chapter	Definitions
● **sentence**	● series of words containing a subject and verb and expressing a complete thought
● **subject**	● doer of the action or focus of the verb
	Continued

New terms in this chapter	Definitions
	● answer to the question *who or what is doing the action or being discussed?* *Example* Petra asked a question.
● **verb**	● word that shows action or completes a statement
● **action verb**	● word expressing action *Example* Mike accidentally *broke* the window.
● **linking verb**	● word connecting the subject with other words that restate or describe it *Example* Sally *is* a volunteer in the tutoring center.
● **noun**	● a word that names a person, place, or thing *Example* The *mountain* was covered with heather.
● **pronoun**	● a word that substitutes for a noun *Example* *She* was concerned about the cast on Lauren's arm.
● **simple subject**	● main word or group of words that answers the question *who or what is doing the action or being discussed?*
● **complete subject**	● simple subject plus any words or phrases that describe or modify it *Example* The <u>streets</u> around the campus are crowded.
● **modifier**	● a word or group of words that tells you which or what kind when used with a noun or pronoun *Example* The *rusty* nail lay on the ground.
● **prepositional phrase**	● a group of words beginning with a preposition and ending with a noun or pronoun called the object of the preposition ● Prepositional phrases often come between the simple subject and verb. *Example* The pancake mix *in the cupboard* is two months old.
● **verb phrase**	● a main verb plus a helping verb *Example* Teresa *is learning* her Spanish vocabulary.
● **compound verb**	● two or more verbs connected by a conjunction *Example* Steve *slipped <u>and</u> fell* on the ice.

New terms in this chapter	Definitions
● **compound subject**	● a subject consisting of two or more nouns or pronouns connected by a conjunction
	Example <u>Dogs and cats</u> remain America's favorite pets.

The Structure of a Sentence

Subject   +   verb   →   expression of a complete thought

Chapter 7

Sentence Fragments

Getting Started... **Q:** I understand what a sentence is supposed to be. I'm just not always confident that I know how to write them. How can I make sure that I don't end up with fragments instead of complete sentences?

A: The way to make sure that you write sentences, not sentence fragments, is to focus on each unit that you have set off as a sentence. Check the unit—if it contains a subject and verb and expresses a complete thought, then you have a sentence.

Overview: Recognizing and Writing Complete Sentences

A *fragment* is a piece of something. It's not complete or whole. A **sentence fragment** is an incomplete piece of a sentence. It doesn't express a complete idea and cannot stand alone. As a writer, you must transform sentence fragments into complete thoughts, or sentences, that communicate your ideas fully and clearly to readers.

Several types of sentence fragments appear in writing. Writers may accidentally omit a subject or verb, or they might mistake a phrase or a subordinate clause for a complete sentence. The subordinate clause is discussed in detail in Chapter 8, "Subordination." However the error arises, it results in a failure to communicate the meaning the writer intended.

> *This chapter helps you to discover ways to recognize and correct sentence fragments. You will learn that sentences must include*
>
> ● an action verb or a linking verb that communicates a complete action or meaning
>
> ● a subject that answers the question *who or what is doing the action or being discussed?*
>
> ● a complete thought that can stand on its own

Discovering Connections 7.1

Consider the following quotation:

A child's life is like a piece of paper on which every passerby leaves a mark.

—*Chinese proverb*

Or consider this photo.

Now, using the prewriting technique you prefer, do some prewriting about your reaction to the quotation or photo. Save your work.

Recognizing and Correcting Fragments with Missing Verbs

As you saw in Chapter 6, "Subjects and Verbs," a group of words must contain a verb and subject in order for it to be a sentence. When one of these elements is missing, the group of words won't express your thoughts fully. You must therefore check the sentences you write to make sure that each contains a verb and a subject.

First, identify the verb. As you have seen, it can be either an action verb or a linking verb. Without a verb, the group of words is a fragment, not a sentence.

Look at the two groups of words below:

FRAGMENT   Those expensive disposable contact lenses.

FRAGMENT   The runaway car with ten other cars on the highway.

Both groups of words lack verbs. You correct each sentence fragment by adding a verb and completing the thought, in this way:

SENTENCE   Those expensive disposable contact lenses *are* not good for the environment.

SENTENCE   The runaway car *collided* with ten other cars on the highway.

Sometimes a group of words contains a verb form that doesn't communicate a complete action or meaning. For example, some verb forms are not complete unless they have helping verbs. (See Chapter 6, page 130 for a discussion about helping verbs.)

Read the following examples:

FRAGMENT   The professor always *trying* to make us comfortable.

FRAGMENT   On the day of the concert, the afternoon *grown* especially warm.

Trying and *grown* do not communicate the action fully, so these word groups are sentence fragments. To correct the fragments, add a helping verb to create a verb phrase, or use the present form of the verb.

SENTENCE   The professor *is* always *trying* to make us comfortable.

or

The professor always *tries* to make us comfortable.

SENTENCE   On the day of the concert, the afternoon *had grown* especially warm.

or

On the day of the concert, the afternoon *grew* especially warm.

Turn to Part Three, "Verbs: Conveying Action and Time," for more practice in using verbs correctly.

Sometimes words that normally act as verbs take another role in a sentence. **Verbals** are words formed from verbs, but they function as nouns, adjectives, or adverbs. Look at these examples:

EXAMPLE   *To err* is human; *to forgive* is divine.

EXAMPLE   We could hear the wind *howling*.

In the first sentence, the verbals *to err* and *to forgive* are used as nouns. (They are subjects.) In the second, the verbal *howling* is used as an adjective describing the wind.

These forms may cause confusion because you may at first glance think that a fragment contains a verb, when in fact it contains a verbal.

FRAGMENT   My best friend *to meet* David Letterman someday.

The thought is incomplete, because *to meet* does not function as a verb here, but as a noun. Add a verb, and consider the words again.

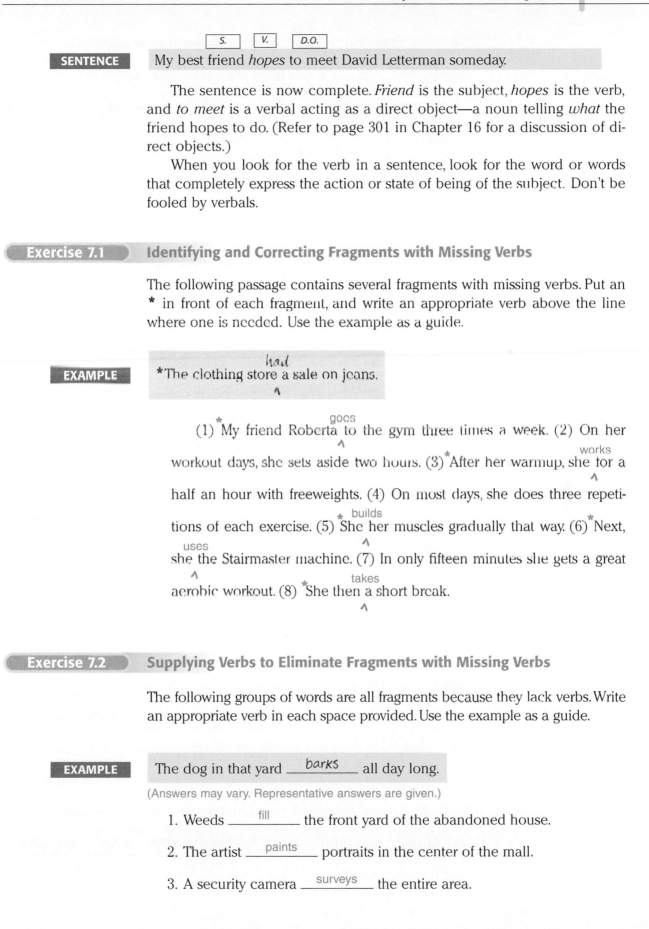

SENTENCE

$\boxed{S.}$ $\boxed{V.}$ $\boxed{D.O.}$

My best friend *hopes* to meet David Letterman someday.

The sentence is now complete. *Friend* is the subject, *hopes* is the verb, and *to meet* is a verbal acting as a direct object—a noun telling *what* the friend hopes to do. (Refer to page 301 in Chapter 16 for a discussion of direct objects.)

When you look for the verb in a sentence, look for the word or words that completely express the action or state of being of the subject. Don't be fooled by verbals.

Exercise 7.1   **Identifying and Correcting Fragments with Missing Verbs**

The following passage contains several fragments with missing verbs. Put an * in front of each fragment, and write an appropriate verb above the line where one is needed. Use the example as a guide.

EXAMPLE

*The clothing store had a sale on jeans.

(1) *My friend Roberta goes to the gym three times a week. (2) On her workout days, she sets aside two hours. (3) *After her warmup, she works for a half an hour with freeweights. (4) On most days, she does three repetitions of each exercise. (5) *She builds her muscles gradually that way. (6) *Next, she uses the Stairmaster machine. (7) In only fifteen minutes she gets a great aerobic workout. (8) *She then takes a short break.

Exercise 7.2   **Supplying Verbs to Eliminate Fragments with Missing Verbs**

The following groups of words are all fragments because they lack verbs. Write an appropriate verb in each space provided. Use the example as a guide.

EXAMPLE

The dog in that yard *barks* all day long.

(Answers may vary. Representative answers are given.)

1. Weeds fill the front yard of the abandoned house.

2. The artist paints portraits in the center of the mall.

3. A security camera surveys the entire area.

4. Every afternoon, the cat ___takes___ a nap on the windowsill.

5. Lenny ___plays___ tennis three afternoons a week.

6. My new backpack ___has___ a special compartment for pens and pencils.

7. Her leg ___is___ in a cast.

8. The new convenience store ___opens___ next week.

Exercise 7.3   **Finding and Eliminating Fragments with Missing Verbs**

Some groups of words in the passage below are fragments because they lack an appropriate verb. Identify each of these fragments by underlining them. Then, on a separate sheet of paper, turn each fragment into a sentence by supplying a verb. Use the example to guide you. Some fragments may be corrected in several ways.

EXAMPLE   Meals from fast food restaurants still often containing high degrees of fat.

Meals from fast food restaurants still often contain high degrees of fat.

(1) Every year, some areas of the United States ^(can expect) to face serious water problems as a result of drought. (2) In fact, in many recent years, more than half the nation has experienced moderate to severe drought conditions. (3) Ruined crops and forest fires ~~being~~ (are) just a couple of the more serious effects of prolonged drought. (4) In terms of severity, experts point to the summer of 1934 as the worst in modern times. (5) In that summer, 80 percent of the United States ^(suffered) from moderate to severe drought. (6) But a close examination of some historical data ~~pointing~~ (points) to even worse drought conditions than in the summer of 1934. (7) For example, natural signs, such as rings in the trunks of trees, indicate several periods of sustained severe drought in the 1700s. (8) At one point during the 1800s, drought ~~afflicting~~ (afflicted) the country for seven years straight.

Challenge 7.1)   **Avoiding Fragments with Missing Verbs in Your Writing**

COLLABORATION

Working with a writing partner, choose one of the topic sentences below, and draft a paragraph that supports it. As you write, be sure to include a verb in each sentence. Save your work for Challenge 7.2.

1. Knowing how to use a computer is essential for anyone looking for a good job.

2. Responsible pet owners must provide daily care to have a healthy animal.

Recognizing and Correcting
Fragments with Missing Subjects

Once you have determined that a group of words has a verb, your next step is to check whether it has a subject. As you learned in Chapter 6, you can find the subject by asking *who or what is doing the action or being discussed?* The word or group of words that answers that question is the subject.

Look at the two groups of words below:

FRAGMENT   Mailed the package yesterday.

FRAGMENT   In the middle of the mall, sat on a bench alone.

Neither group of words is a sentence. The first group has a verb—*mailed.* However, it has no word that answers the question *who or what mailed the package yesterday?* The second group also has a verb—*sat*—but there is no word that answers *who or what sat alone on a bench in the middle of the mall?* Neither group of words has a subject, so both are fragments.

You can correct both fragments the same way, by adding subjects, as these versions show:

SENTENCE   *Consuela* mailed the package yesterday.

SENTENCE   In the middle of the mall, *a frail old man* sat on a bench alone.

Exercise 7.4)   **Identifying and Correcting Fragments with Missing Subjects**

The following passage contains several fragments that lack subjects. Put an ***** in front of each fragment. Where a subject is called for, write an appropriate subject above the fragment. Make changes in capitalization as needed. Use the example as a guide.

EXAMPLE

> * *The used car salesperson lied*
> ~~Lied~~ about the number of miles the car had been driven.
> ^

(Answers may vary somewhat.)

(1) My favorite class in middle school was art. (2) *This class made* ~~Made~~ me look forward to school. (3) My teacher, Mrs. Joseph, loved her job. (4) *She inspired* ~~Inspired~~ us
all to learn. (5) My favorite class project was a family collage. (6) We had
to collect pictures and other family keepsakes. (7) Then *we* cut and glued
the material to big sheets of white cardboard. (8) *I still have* ~~Have~~ it in a closet
somewhere. (9) Mrs. Joseph taught her classes more than just art, however. (10) *We learned* ~~Learned~~ to take our work and ourselves seriously.

Exercise 7.5   **Correcting Fragments by Supplying Subjects**

The following groups of words are all fragments because they all lack subjects. Write an appropriate noun or pronoun in each space provided. Use
the example as a guide. (Answers may vary.)

EXAMPLE

_____*The minister*_____ conducted the special memorial service.

1. Every summer _____workers_____ clean(s) the streets throughout the city.

2. _____The Gap_____ is having a big sale.

3. _____Television_____ is a very popular form of entertainment.

4. _____Babies_____ demand a lot of attention.

5. _____My best friends_____ have now become vegetarians.

6. _____A Polartec jacket_____ costs $100 less than the competing brand.

7. _____Everyone_____ should have access to quality health care.

8. _____A window_____ was broken during the demonstration at City Hall.

Exercise 7.6 **Identifying Fragments with Missing Subjects**

Check for fragments in the paragraph below. Find these sentence fragments and underline them. Then write their numbers on a separate piece of paper. Beside their numbers, rewrite these fragments by adding a subject. Use the example first to guide you.

EXAMPLE

After her workout at the gym, rewarded herself with a sundae.

After her workout at the gym, Marlene rewarded herself with a sundae.

(Answers may vary.)

(1) Disc jockey Alan Freed is an important figure in the history of American popular music. (2) In the early 1950s, Freed began to play what people then called "Negro music" on his program at station WJW in Cleveland. (3) Meanwhile, at other stations, disc jockeys would not play rhythm and blues music by black musicians on their radio shows. (4) Freed found his audience of white teenagers wanted to hear this music. (5) These kids appreciated Appreciated the beat, strong singers, and emotion of the music Freed played. (6) In a few years, Freed moved to New York City. (7) His show was ~~Was~~ syndicated around the country. (8) Other DJs then began to play the music of Chuck Berry, Little Richard, Bo Diddley, and other performers on their radio shows. (9) Freed named the new music "rock 'n' roll." (10) Freed encouraged and influenced future generations.

Challenge 7.2 **Identifying Fragments with Missing Verbs or Subjects**

COLLABORATION

1. Exchange the paragraph that you and your partner completed in Challenge 7.1 for a paragraph written by another pair of writers. On the paragraph you receive, underline the verb and subject in each of their sentences. Return the paragraph.

2. Correct any of your sentences that do not have a subject or verb.

Recognizing and Correcting Phrase Fragments

Another kind of fragment involves phrases mistakenly used as sentences. By definition, a **phrase** is two or more words acting as a single unit but lacking a subject–verb combination. The phrase *under the maple tree,* for example, consists of a preposition plus its object and modifiers. It contains no subject or verb. (See page 128 in Chapter 6 for a discussion of prepositional phrases and a list of common prepositions.) The phrase *talking loudly,* has a verb, and an adverb that describes the verb, but it lacks a subject. (See page 130 in Chapter 6 for more on verb phrases.)

Look at the following examples:

FRAGMENT At the finish line.

FRAGMENT Has agreed.

The first example is a prepositional phrase, which lacks both a subject and a verb. The second example is a verb phrase, which lacks a subject. To create sentences from these fragments, you need to supply the missing elements.

|subject| |verb| |prepositional phrase|

SENTENCE The *Nigerian sprinter passed* the U.S. runner *at the finish line*.

|subject| |verb phrase|

SENTENCE *Jackie has agreed* to serve as club president.

Exercise 7.7 **Correcting Phrases Incorrectly Used as Sentences**

The following passage contains several phrase fragments. Put an * in front of each fragment. Then, on a separate sheet of paper, add the missing sentence elements, turning the fragments into sentences. Make changes in capitalization as needed. Use the example to guide you.

EXAMPLE The nurse was   the doctor's instructions to the patient.
              *Was repeating,
(Answers may vary.)

(1) Being a professional athlete is more complex than is commonly
                              These stars will
thought. (2) *Will earn millions. (3) Many of these athletes make addi-
                                              *and
tional money from endorsements, (4) For personal appearances at sports
                                                    They keep themselves in
memorabilia shows. (5) Of course, these stars work hard. (6) *In superb

shape. (7) Sometimes they have no guarantee of being on the team for
Even a star could
the next season. (8) *Could be traded.
∧

Using Phrases Correctly within Sentences

The following groups of words are all fragments because they are phrases.
On a separate sheet of paper, turn these phrases into sentences. Some need
only a subject and some need both a subject and a verb. Use the example
as a guide.

EXAMPLE   was watching

My grandmother was watching a game show.

(Answers will vary.)

1. behind the building

2. should be studying

3. through the entire store

4. between two huge trees

5. are cleaning

6. will be speaking

7. over the bridge

8. have bought

Challenge 7.3   **Correcting Phrase Fragments in Your Writing**

COLLABORATION

1. Make a copy of a writing you are working on and exchange it with a
classmate. On the paper you receive, identify and underline any prepositional phrases and verb phrases. Then make sure each sentence that includes a prepositional phrase also includes a subject and a verb. Also
check to be sure each sentence with a verb phrase contains a subject.
Return the writing to your classmate.

2. Correct any fragments your classmate has identified.

Recognizing and Correcting Appositive Phrase Fragments

Another group of words that is sometimes used incorrectly as a sentence is
an **appositive phrase.** An appositive phrase is a group of words placed
next to a noun or pronoun in order to identify or explain it.

EXAMPLE

appositive phrase

Clarice was glad to see Shari, *her best friend from the old neighborhood.*

Some appositive phrases are long. Without thinking, some writers set them off as sentences. However, these phrases cannot stand alone and should never be separated from the word that they identify. They are a part of the sentence in which that word appears.

SENTENCE AND FRAGMENT

appositive fragment

The local hangout was Mugsy's. *A neighborhood greasy spoon with a juke box and great fries.*

The appositive phrase *a neighborhood greasy spoon with a jukebox and great fries* identifies the noun *Mugsy's.* It should be placed next to this noun, set off by a comma.

CORRECTED SENTENCE

The local hangout was Mugsy's, a neighborhood greasy spoon with a juke box and great fries.

Exercise 7.9 **Dealing with Appositive Fragments**

The following passage contains several fragments resulting from appositive phrases incorrectly used as sentences. Put an ***** in front of each fragment. Then correct the errors by joining the fragments to the sentences of which they are a part. Remember to use capitals and punctuation correctly. Use the example as a guide.

EXAMPLE

, the
I never go to school in the summer, ~~The~~ prime time for earning tuition

money.

(1) Two years ago, I worked as a driver's assistant for Express Wishes, *, a*

(2) ~~A~~ ***** delivery service specializing in overnight delivery. (3) My main task
, a*
was to bring the packages to the door. ~~(4) A~~ pretty simple job. (5) I would
,the*
ring the doorbell and have the customer sign for the package. ~~(6) The~~

most important part of the transaction. (7) Heavy packages were a prob-

lem in multi-level office buildings and warehouses. (8) Of course these

places receive the most deliveries. (9) After four hours, the driver and I
, a*
would take a break at Dot's. ~~(10) A~~ small coffee shop on the route.

Exercise 7.10   **Writing Sentences with Appositive Phrases**

The following groups of words are all appositive phrases. On a separate sheet of paper, write a sentence in which you include each appositive. Check each sentence to be sure it expresses a complete thought and sets off the appositive phrase with a comma. Use a pair of commas if you put the phrase in the middle of your sentence. Use the example as a guide.

EXAMPLE

my counselor and mentor

On my first day back on campus, I met with Jenny, my counselor and mentor, to get advice and support.
(Answers will vary.)

1. the most civilized form of transportation

2. the best spot in the stadium

3. a big hit with the crowd

4. the smallest child in the school

5. a secluded spot in the city

6. the most popular sports figure of the past decade

7. a rusty, broken-down bus

8. a priceless piece of art

Challenge 7.4   **Identifying and Evaluating Appositive Phrases**

COLLABORATION

Working with a partner, read one or more of the selections in Part Six, "Discovering Connections through Reading." Find at least three sentences that use appositive phrases. Write the sentences that contain these elements on a separate sheet of paper. Underline the appositives. Be ready to explain how they contribute to the ideas in the sentences that contain them.

Recognizing and Correcting Subordinate Clause Fragments

Having a subject and verb is not enough to make a group of words a sentence. A sentence must also express a complete thought. Check the following example for a subject and verb:

FRAGMENT

Because the lighting was poor.

As you can see, this example has a verb (*was*) and a subject (*lighting*).

However, it isn't a sentence because it doesn't express a complete thought. Instead, it is a subordinate clause. A **subordinate clause** is a group of words that contains a subject and verb but doesn't make sense on its own. It is called *subordinate* because it is written to explain or describe a main clause. Alone, a subordinate clause fails to communicate the whole idea. It leaves the reader waiting for more information. *What happened* because the lighting was poor?

Subordinate clauses are introduced by subordinating conjunctions, words that provide connections or links between parts of a sentence, and show how those parts are related. For more information about subordinate clauses, turn to Chapter 8, especially the list of some common subordinating conjunctions.

There are various methods of correcting subordinate clause fragments. One possibility is to restate the clause or to add or delete words. For example, to turn the example above into a sentence, you could drop the subordinating conjunction *because*.

SENTENCE   The lighting was poor.

Dropping the subordinating conjunction has made the statement complete on its own. Notice that you no longer expect additional information when you finish the sentence.

Another option is to join the subordinate clause to a main clause. A main clause is a group of words that can stand alone, but it is joined to a subordinate clause to finish a thought. This kind of correction introduces more complex thinking into your writing, since it shows relationship. Study the following two possible corrections:

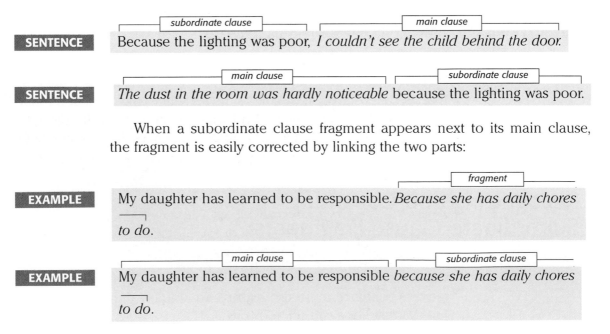

SENTENCE   Because the lighting was poor, *I couldn't see the child behind the door.*

SENTENCE   *The dust in the room was hardly noticeable* because the lighting was poor.

When a subordinate clause fragment appears next to its main clause, the fragment is easily corrected by linking the two parts:

EXAMPLE   My daughter has learned to be responsible. *Because she has daily chores to do.*

EXAMPLE   My daughter has learned to be responsible *because she has daily chores to do.*

|—————————————— fragment ——————————————|

EXAMPLE

After I pay the rent, buy food, and pay the minimum on my charge card. The

cash I have left is very limited.

|—————————————— subordinate clause ——————————————|

EXAMPLE

After I pay the rent, buy food, and pay the minimum on my charge card, the

|—— main clause ——|

cash I have left is very limited.

When you join a subordinate clause fragment to a main clause, be sure to make any necessary changes in punctuation and capitalization. When the subordinate clause comes before the main clause, you need a comma to separate them. When the subordinate clause follows the main clause, no comma is needed.

Exercise 7.11   Correcting Subordinate Clause Fragments

The following passage contains several subordinate clauses incorrectly used as sentences. Put an * in front of each of these fragments. Then change each fragment into a sentence. If two numbered word groups should be joined, join them. Check to be sure you use punctuation and capitals correctly. Use the example as a guide.

EXAMPLE

, nobody

*Although most people enjoy going to the movies, ~~Nobody~~ wants to pay a
                                                            ^

huge amount of money for a ticket.

(1) Even sun-worshippers can learn to protect themselves against skin cancer. (2) You should be smart about when you sunbathe. (3) It is best to avoid the sun if possible between the hours of 10 A.M. and 3 P.M.

, because

~~(4) Because~~ that is when ultraviolet rays from the sun are strongest. (5)

, you

Whenever you go out into the sun for a prolonged period, (6) ~~You~~ should apply a good sunscreen to exposed skin. (7) If your skin is fair, you need sunscreen with an SPF, or sun protection factor, of 15 or higher. (8) Finally, you should watch for changes in moles. (9) *Whenever a mole

it

or skin spot begins to darken, itch, or change in appearance, (10) ~~It~~ is time to see a doctor right away to have it checked.

Exercise 7.12   **Turning Subordinate Clause Fragments into Sentences**

The following groups of words are all fragments because they are subordinate clauses. On a separate sheet of paper, turn these subordinate clauses into sentences. Remember—you may restate the clause, add or subtract words, or join it to a main clause. Use the example to guide you.

EXAMPLE

whenever Karen feels a tightness in her chest

Whenever Karen feels a tightness in her chest, she uses her asthma inhaler.

(Answers will vary.)

1. after the class was over

2. that has scratched several children in the neighborhood

3. whenever the alarm goes off

4. if the hurricane causes severe high tides

5. who wants to major in early childhood education

6. that decorate the health office

7. until the semester ends

8. which indicate permission to park in a restricted area

Challenge 7.5   **Correcting Subordinate Clause Fragments in Your Writing**

COLLABORATION

1. Take a paragraph you have recently drafted, and exchange it with a classmate. On the paper you receive, make note of any groups of words that do not express a complete thought. Pay particular attention to any subordinate clauses.

2. Return the paper to the writer, and make whatever changes are necessary on your own paper.

Sentence Fragments Checklist

Have you made sure

- ☐ that each unit you have set off as a sentence contains a verb?
- ☐ none of the words you have chosen as verbs are actually verbals?
- ☐ you have supplied a subject for each verb?
- ☐ you haven't incorrectly set off a phrase as a sentence?
- ☐ you haven't incorrectly set off an appositive as a sentence?
- ☐ you haven't incorrectly set off a subordinate clause as a sentence?

Exploring Ideas
through Journal Writing

A sentence fragment is a piece of a sentence. It doesn't tell the entire story. You need to add something to it—or add it to something—before it will do that. Think of a small part of something else, for instance, an item of clothing, a ticket stub, or a cash register receipt—something that represents a fragment of a story. Consider this subject, and then spend 20 to 30 minutes with your journal, exploring the role this fragment of a story played in the entire incident.

Chapter Quick Check:
Sentence Fragments

The following passage contains several fragments. Put an * in front of any fragment. Then, in the space above each fragment, add corrections, using the various techniques discussed in the chapter. Remember—fragments can be corrected in more than one way. (Representative answers are shown.)

(1) New Zealanders with a taste for adventure can get their fix in a unique, fun way: Zorbing. (2) To take part in Zorbing, a person climbs into a tiny enclosure within a Zorb. **, an** * (3) An enormous 12 foot tall clear plastic sphere. (4)* Once the Zorbing assistants close the sphere with a huge rubber plug, **, they** (5) They push the giant globe over the edge of a hill. (6) Inside the Zorb, the rider tumbles around, **, like** (7)* Like clothes in a dryer. (8) The flat area at the bottom of the slope hundreds of feet away slows the Zorb to a gradual stop. (9)* Since its invention in 1995, **Zorbing** has grown in popularity, attracting thousands of riders each year. (10) With no Zorbing center in the United States, curious Americans will have to travel to the other side of the world to enjoy a roll in a Zorb.

Discovering Connections 7.2

1. For Discovering Connections 7.1 on page 141, you began prewriting in response to a Chinese proverb or photo. Now, continue your prewriting on one of these options:
   a. Aside from parents, who has the greatest opportunity—or the greatest responsibility—to influence a child's life?
   b. What is the best lesson adults can mark on the paper of a child's life?
2. Evaluate your prewriting material, identify a focus, and create a draft of about 100 words.
3. Exchange your draft with a writing partner. Using the material in this chapter as a guide, evaluate the draft you receive, and note any problems with sentence fragments as well as any other weaknesses. Return the draft to the writer.
4. Revise your draft, eliminating any errors that your reader identified.

Summary Exercise: Sentence Fragments

The following passage contains a number of fragments. Put an * in front of any fragment. Then, in the space above each fragment, add corrections. Use the techniques discussed in the chapter. Remember—fragments can be corrected in more than one way. (Answers may vary.)

(1) I still remember the most exciting day in my fifth grade class. (2) A bookcase fell on my friend Laura's foot and broke her toe. (3) *The whole school was in an uproar.

(4) *The accident happened at lunchtime, (5) When when our teacher was out of the classroom. (6) At the back of the room, one of the boys pinched Laura. (7) She bumped into the big bookcase full of textbook, (8) *The , the big heavy ones for geography and reading. (9) It started to fall on Laura, (10) Who *, who was trying to get away.

(11) The bookcase crashed down on her foot. (12) A couple of the boys lifted it, so Laura could free her foot. (13) Blood was already soaking her sock, (14) *From from her crushed toe.

(15) At that point, the true craziness began. (16) Laura started to

scream/ (17) ~~Because~~ she was in so much pain. (18) Then Mrs. Leio
                because

came back into the room/ (19) ~~From~~ the teachers' room down the hall.
                              from

(20) Mrs. Leio immediately sent for the nurse and called Laura's father. (21)
              sent

~~Came~~ to take her to the hospital. (22) Meanwhile, the rest of us cleaned
He came

up the room.

(23) At the hospital, she was treated for a deep cut and a broken big

toe. (24) The next day we were relieved to see her in school. (25) Her experi-
                    were

ence was the subject of discussion for the rest of the year.

RECAP SENTENCE FRAGMENTS

New terms in this chapter	Definitions
● **sentence fragment**	● a group of words that is incomplete as a sentence because it does not express a complete thought and cannot stand alone *Example* *After the class was over.*

● **verbal**	● a verb form that functions as a noun, adjective, or adverb in a sentence
	
	Verbals *cannot* act as verbs in sentences.
	
	                   adverb
	Examples The driver stopped *to ask* directions.
	           adjective
	            A *worried* face is not a happy face.

● **phrase**	● two or more words acting as a single unit but lacking a subject–verb combination Correct by adding the missing subject or verb, or inserting of the phrase in a sentence. v. phrase prep. phrase *Example* The children *were looking* *for the crayons.*
● **appositive phrase**	● a group of words identifying or explaining a noun or pronoun next to it Correct an appositive fragment by including it in the sentence with the noun or pronoun it identifies. Set the appositive phrase off with commas. *Continued*

New terms in this chapter	Definitions
	Example The crossing guard, *a retired police officer*, escorted the children across the street.
● **subordinate clause**	● a group of words containing a subject, verb, and subordinating conjunction, but not expressing a complete thought Correct a subordinate clause fragment by (a) joining it to a main clause to complete its thought, or (b) adding or subtracting words to make a complete thought in itself. *Example* The child who had screamed suddenly laughed.

To Identify a Fragment

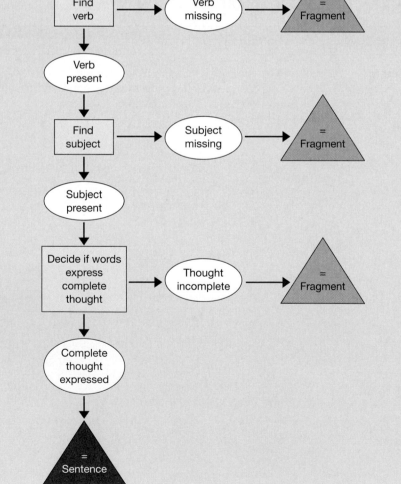

Chapter 8

Subordination

Getting Started... **Q:** I'd like to make my sentences more interesting by extending the ideas in them. How can I do this but not lose the focus of the main idea?

A: The answer you may be looking for is subordination. With subordination, you use a subordinating conjunction or relative pronoun to combine subject–verb units. These words make one of the ideas dependent and thus focus greater attention on the other unit.

Overview: Creating Complex Sentences with Supporting Clauses

In Chapter 6, "Subjects and Verbs," and Chapter 7, "Sentence Fragments," you've seen the importance of expressing your ideas in complete sentences. There are many ways to compose sentences so that your ideas will stand out and be clearly understood.

One way to connect ideas and show their relationship is to use **subordination.** This technique involves combining an idea in a main clause with an idea in a subordinate, or supporting, clause. The main clause conveys a complete idea. The subordinate clause supports the main clause and depends upon the main clause for its full meaning. Exploring subordination can help you express your good ideas more clearly.

> ***This chapter gives you the opportunity to discover more about subordination. You will learn***
>
> ● to distinguish between simple and complex sentences
>
> ● to identify, use, and correctly punctuate complex sentences
>
> ● to use subordinating conjunctions that connect and show relationships
>
> ● to identify relative pronouns used to introduce subordinate clauses that describe or specify a noun or pronoun

Consider the following quotation:

Hold fast to dreams, for if dreams die, life is a broken-winged bird that cannot fly.

—*Langston Hughes*

Or consider this photo.

Now, using the prewriting technique you prefer, do some prewriting about your reaction to the quotation or photo. Save your work.

Distinguishing between Simple and Complex Sentences

As you've learned in the previous chapters, a sentence is a group of words containing a subject and verb and expressing a complete thought. A **simple sentence** consists of only *one* subject–verb unit (even though its subject or verb may be compound). Here are some examples of simple sentences:

SIMPLE
| subject | verb |

Tia often *visits* the art museum.

SIMPLE
| subject | verb | | verb |

The *landlord changed* the lock on my apartment and *installed* dead-bolt locks. *[The verb is compound but there is still only one subject–verb unit.]*

A simple sentence conveys a main idea. When it is combined with a **subordinate clause,** which contains supporting information, then the simple sentence becomes the **main clause** of the new sentence. (Subordinate clauses are introduced in Chapter 7, "Sentence Fragments.") A subordinate clause combined with a main clause is called a **complex sentence.** Here are examples of two complex sentences:

COMPLEX
| main clause | | subordinate clause |

Tia often visits the art museum *because she wants to learn more about modern art*.

COMPLEX
| subordinate clause | | main clause |

After the building was burglarized, the landlord changed the lock on my apartment and installed deadbolt locks.

Without the main clauses, the subordinate clauses would be fragments. But when they are added to main clauses, the subordinate clauses become part of a larger, complete sentence.

In the preceding example, notice that the subordinate clause appears before the main clause. It is equally correct for the subordinate clause to follow the main clause:

|main clause| |subordinate clause|

EXAMPLE The landlord changed the lock on my apartment *after the building was burglarized*.

No matter which clause comes first, the ideas in each are related or linked by the subordinating conjunction. When the subordinate clause comes before the main clause, you need a comma to separate them. When the main clause comes first, as in this last version, no comma is needed.

Exercise 8.1   **Identifying Subordinate Clauses**

The following sentences are complex—meaning that they contain both a main clause and a subordinate clause. Underline the subordinate clause in each complex sentence, using the example as a guide

EXAMPLE <u>Even though we were prepared</u>, the hurricane did extensive damage to our home.

(1) Gambling in one form or another is a pastime <u>that has existed since civilization itself began</u>. (2) <u>As widespread exposure to gambling advertising increases</u>, more people than ever are gambling as a recreational pastime. (3) Most people <u>who buy lottery tickets or visit a casino</u> are able to gamble for fun. (4) <u>Before some people know it</u>, however, they are suddenly facing addiction. (5) Unfortunately for them, scientists have found this kind of addiction difficult to overcome <u>unless the victims are highly motivated</u>.

Exercise 8.2   **Identifying Simple and Complex Sentences**

The following exercise contains both simple and complex sentences. Identify each sentence. Put an *S* on the line in front of each simple sentence and a *CX* in front of each complex sentence.

EXAMPLE __*CX*__ That building is being restored because it was designed by a famous architect.

S   1. My diet isn't very nutritious.

CX   2. For one thing, I don't eat any vegetables because I hate the taste.

S   3. I'm also not too fond of milk and other dairy products.

CX   4. I will even avoid ice cream unless I am especially hungry.

S   5. In addition, I eat a lot of red meat and fried foods.

S   6. Sweet foods appeal to me as well.

CX   7. Whenever I have the chance, I have doughnuts or other pastries for lunch.

CX   8. Even though this kind of food is high in fat and calories, I'm not overweight.

Challenge 8.1   **Evaluating the Use of Simple and Complex Sentences**

1. The passage in Exercise 8.2 discusses dietary habits. What is your own diet like? Consider this subject and then write a passage of about ten sentences.

COLLABORATION

2. Make a copy of your draft and exchange the copy with a classmate. On the paper you receive, circle any simple sentences and underline any complex sentences. Remember—a complex sentence contains a main clause and a subordinate clause.

Understanding and Using Subordinating Conjunctions

Subordinate clauses are introduced by **subordinating conjunctions.** *Conjunctions* are words that provide connections or links. A subordinate clause is linked to a main clause by the subordinating conjunction. Here is a list of subordinating conjunctions:

Common Subordinating Conjunctions

after	before	since	whenever
although	even though	so that	where
as	if	though	wherever
as if	in order that	unless	whether
as soon as	once	until	while
because	rather than	when	

In addition to connecting clauses, subordinating conjunctions indicate a relationship between the main clause and the subordinate clause. Look at the following sentences, with the subordinating conjunctions underlined. What relationship does the subordinating conjunction suggest in each?

EXAMPLE

We will have to cancel the party <u>unless</u> we can raise some money.

EXAMPLE

<u>Although</u> the temperature had grown cold, the children remained in the pool.

In the first sentence, *unless* indicates a contingency relationship. The party won't occur *without* additional funds. In the second, *although* suggests a contrasting or contradictory relationship. The children's swimming continued *despite* the cold.

In a complex sentence construction, the main clause has the most emphasis. Notice how the emphasis changes depending on the placement of the subordinate clause:

EXAMPLE

Omar bought his plane ticket before the prices increased.

EXAMPLE

After Omar bought his plane ticket, the prices increased.

The first sentence emphasizes buying the ticket. The second emphasizes the increase in prices. When you write a complex sentence, be sure the idea you want to emphasize is in the main clause.

Exercise 8.3 **Using Subordinating Conjunctions**

Each complex sentence in the paragraph below needs a subordinating conjunction. Choose the subordinating conjunction from the list on page 162 that you think best connects the clauses and shows their relationship. Write it on the line provided. Use the example to guide you.

EXAMPLE

Rachael works overtime _____*whenever*_____ her boss at the restaurant asks her to.

(1) _____Before_____ the Nineteenth Amendment was passed on August 26, 1920, American women did not have the right to vote. (2) We should not take that right for granted _____because_____ many women

struggled for over seventy years to obtain it. (3) The movement began before the Civil War, and it ended _____ as _____ World War I was being fought. (4) _____ When _____ women mark a ballot, they should remember the efforts of Elizabeth Cady Stanton, Susan B. Anthony, Lucretia Mott, Carrie Chapman Catt, and Alice Paul. (5) These and other suffragettes wrote, marched, endured ridicule, and spent time in prison _____ so that _____ women could participate in the democracy.

<u>**Exercise 8.4**</u>   **Developing Sentences Using Subordinating Conjunctions**

Below is a list of subordinate clauses. On a separate sheet of paper, write each clause. Then add a main clause to make each a complex sentence. Use appropriate capitalization and punctuation. Use the example as a guide.

EXAMPLE

because the other restaurants had closed

We finally settled on a small diner because the other restaurants had closed.

1. whenever I have the chance

2. after gold was discovered in California

3. because Nick was late

4. if the building is condemned

5. unless the city enforces the ban on outside water use

6. before I go to bed

7. although the movie had some funny parts

8. since Jacqueline started playing the piano

<u>**Exercise 8.5**</u>   **Creating a Different Meaning by Using Subordinating Conjunctions**

Following are three simple sentences, each followed by two subordinating conjunctions. On a separate sheet of paper, write two versions of each sentence, adding a dependent clause beginning with the conjunction supplied. Use the example as a guide.

EXAMPLE

One of my coworkers won't be in for a week **because**

after

One of my coworkers won't be in for a week because she has jury duty.

(Answers will vary.)

1. The worst thing about moving to a new apartment is packing **unless**

if

2. Computer literacy is important **before**

whenever

3. The federal government should offer new businesses tax breaks **until**

so that

Challenge 8.2   **Writing and Evaluating Complex Sentences Featuring Subordinating Conjunctions**

1. Choose five of the following ten subordinating conjunctions and use each to write a complex sentence:

because	whenever	unless	if	before
as	until	although	where	after

2. Exchange these sentences with a classmate. On a separate sheet of paper, copy three of the sentences you receive, reversing the order of the clauses. Below the sentences, indicate which order—the original one or the new one you have created—is better in your view and why.

Understanding and Using Relative Pronouns

Not all subordinate clauses are introduced by subordinating conjunctions. Some are introduced by *relative pronouns*, like those listed below:

Relative Pronouns

that	who
what	whom
which	whose

A subordinate clause that begins with a relative pronoun describes or specifies a noun or pronoun in the main clause.

Look at the following examples:

subordinate clause

EXAMPLE

Any high school or college athletic coach *who hits one of his or her players* should be fired immediately.

subordinate clause

EXAMPLE

Merchandise *that is marked with a red tag* is half price.

In the first sentence, the relative pronoun *who* introduces the subordinate clause. This clause specifies which athletic coaches should be fired. In the second sentence, the relative pronoun *that* introduces the subordinate clause. This clause describes which items are half price.

Exercise 8.6 **Identifying Relative Pronouns in Subordinate Clauses**

Each sentence in the following paragraph contains a subordinate clause introduced by a relative pronoun. Underline each subordinate clause and circle the relative pronoun. Use the example to guide you.

EXAMPLE

Professor Malone, (who) is my adviser, will be retiring at the end of the semester.

(1) My sister Dawn, (who) is in her ninth month of pregnancy, is preparing for her baby's arrival. (2) She has furnished a nursery with a rocking chair, a dresser, and a crib (that) she bought at a flea market and repaired. (3) The crib, (which) she washed and painted, now looks almost new. (4) Dawn also made curtains (that) will keep the bright morning sun out of the nursery. (5) Any baby (whose) mother prepares for her with so much love will be a lucky child.

Exercise 8.7 **Using Relative Pronouns in Subordinate Clauses**

Below is a list of subordinate clauses that begin with relative pronouns. On a separate piece of paper, add a main clause to each subordinate clause to create a complex sentence. Use the example as a guide.

EXAMPLE

that is in front of the building

The burned-out car that is in front of the building belongs to my uncle.

1. that the trooper pulled over for speeding

2. which has been abandoned for ten years

3. who will take phone calls and handle complaints

4. whose job has been cut

5. that can cause damage

6. which had been bright blue

7. who received the letter

8. which was found in the dumpster behind the restaurant

Exercise 8.8   **Understanding and Using Subordinate Conjunctions and Relative Pronouns**

Most paragraphs contain a variety of simple and complex sentences. The following paragraph, however, is composed of only simple sentences. On a separate piece of paper, revise it, joining ideas to create complex sentences. Use subordinating conjunctions and relative pronouns to introduce subordinate clauses. Be sure that the ideas you want to emphasize are in the main clauses of your new sentences. You may decide to leave some simple sentences just as they are. (Answers will vary.)

(1) Larry Bird is considered by many to be one of professional basketball's greatest all-around players. (2) He was born in French Lick, Indiana. (3) Bird played as a forward for Indiana State University. (4) In 1979, he was chosen as College Player of the Year. (5) That same year, he joined the Boston Celtics of the National Basketball Association. (6) In 1980, he was named the NBA's Rookie of the Year. (7) Bird led the Celtics to NBA championships in 1981, 1984, and 1986. (8) He was named the league's most valuable player in 1984, 1985, and 1986. (9) Bird and his rival Magic Johnson helped to revive the game's popularity in the 1980s. (10) Bird and Johnson brought excitement to professional basketball.

Challenge 8.3   **Using Subordinate Conjunctions and Relative Pronouns in Your Writing**

1. Make a copy of the paragraph that you revised in Exercise 8.8, and exchange the copy with a classmate. Compare your classmate's revision with your own. Put a + in front of sentences that you have both combined in the same way.

2. Put an ***** in front of any remaining sentences on your classmate's paper that would be more effective if they were combined through subordination. Underneath the essay or on the back of the paper, briefly explain why you feel subordination would help. Then return the paper to your classmate.

3. Consider what your classmate has suggested. If you agree, make the changes in your own paper.

Punctuating Subordinate Clauses Introduced by Relative Pronouns

As you may have noticed, some subordinate clauses beginning with a relative pronoun are set off by commas. Others are not. How can you decide when commas are needed? As a general rule, if the clause is used to describe or add extra information about a noun or pronoun, it is set off by commas. Sometimes these clauses are called nonrestrictive because they don't restrict or change the essential, or basic, meaning of the sentence.

EXAMPLE

subordinate clause

Vincent van Gogh, *whose paintings now sell for millions of dollars,* was

penniless during his lifetime.

Ask yourself *would the sentence have the same general meaning if the subordinate clause were left out? Would it make sense?* The example would read *Vincent van Gogh was penniless during his lifetime.* The meaning remains the same. The clause should be set off by commas.

However, if the clause is essential to the meaning of the sentence, then it specifies or restricts the noun or pronoun. In this case, *do not* use commas.

Recall these sentences about the athletic coach and the red tag sale:

EXAMPLE

subordinate clause

Any high school or college athletic coach *who hits one of his or her*

players should be fired immediately.

EXAMPLE

subordinate clause

Merchandise *that is marked with a red tag* is half price.

What happens if you leave out the subordinate clauses in these sentences?

EXAMPLE

Any high school or college athletic coach should be fired immediately.

EXAMPLE   Merchandise is half price.

Without the subordinate clauses, these sentences have very different meanings. The first sentence now suggests that all coaches should be fired. The second now implies that everything in the store has been discounted. Clearly, these versions don't reflect the writer's meaning. The subordinate clauses are essential to meaning and should not be set off with commas.

Exercise 8.9   **Punctuating Subordinate Clauses Introduced by Relative Pronouns**

As you read the following paragraph, consider the underlined clauses. Add commas before and after the underlined clauses that need them. Remember—set off a clause if it describes a noun but does not change the meaning of the sentence. Use the examples to guide you.

EXAMPLE   The mall's senior discount day, which falls on the first Tuesday of every month, has boosted sales dramatically. *[Subordinate clause gives extra, describing information; add commas.]*

EXAMPLE   A frog that is poisonous makes a dangerous pet. *[Subordinate clause gives essential meaning to sentence; no commas needed.]*

(1) According to my high school business teacher, all students who study regularly will succeed. (2) Study skills that are practiced often are the only ones to become life-long habits, she stressed. (3) This teacher, whose advice I ignored, was right. (4) I learned by experience, which can be the hardest teacher, to review each day's lessons every night. (5) Students learn what is important by practice.

Exercise 8.10   **Using and Punctuating Subordinate Clauses Introduced by Relative Pronouns**

In the space provided, add a subordinate clause beginning with a relative pronoun to each of the following sentences. If the clauses you supply are nonrestrictive, add commas.

EXAMPLE   The part of the movie _that scared me most_ was the closing scene.

[*Subordinate clause gives essential meaning to sentence; no commas are needed.*]

(Answers will vary. Representative answers are shown.)

1. My friend Barry _____, who never seemed to care about his weight,_____ has lost over 60 pounds in the last year.

2. The emergency room _____, which didn't exist two years ago,_____ recently received a citation for high quality service.

3. The movie _____ that I thought was very funny _____ received bad reviews.

4. Two cars _____ that had skidded on the ice _____ were blocking the exit.

5. The newest museum exhibit is an ancient mummy _____ _____ that was discovered last year _____.

6. Their last concert _____, which drew a huge audience,_____ was over a year ago.

7. The books _____ that did not sell well _____ are on sale.

8. Last year's drought _____, which was completely unexpected,_____ has affected the price of fresh fruit and vegetables.

Challenge 8.4   **Punctuating Subordinate Clauses in Your Writing**

1. Working with a classmate, choose one of the sentences from Exercise 8.9 and, on a separate sheet of paper, turn it into a paragraph by adding five to seven related sentences.

2. Exchange your paragraph with a paragraph prepared by another pair of classmates. Check the paragraph you and your partner receive to make sure it has commas around relative clauses that are not required. Use the discussion on pages 168–169 about comma use with restrictive and non-restrictive clauses to guide you. Circle any commas that you and your

partner feel are unnecessary, and then return the paragraph to the class-mates who created it.

Subordination Checklist

☐ Are you clear on the differences between a simple and a complex sentence?

☐ With any subordinating conjunctions you have used, have you carefully considered the relationship they suggest between the main clause and the subordinate clause?

☐ Have you carefully considered the order of clauses in complex sentences featuring subordinating conjunctions so that you provide the emphasis you want?

☐ Are you clear on the differences between a restrictive and a nonrestrictive clause in complex sentences featuring relative pronouns?

☐ Have you distinguished between restrictive and nonrestrictive clauses and used commas to enclose only the nonrestrictive ones?

Exploring Ideas through Journal Writing

As this chapter illustrates, subordination involves combining ideas to make one part dependent to some degree on the other. Now consider other relationships in life that involve dependence, for example, a parent and child, a new employee and an experienced worker, an owner and a pet, or a teacher and kindergarten students. Focus on one of these subjects and then spend 20 to 30 minutes in your journal exploring what can be good about such a subordinate relationship and what can be troubling or problematic.

Chapter Quick Check: Subordination

The following passage contains both simple sentences and complex sentences. Put an * in front of each simple sentence and circle each complex sentence, underlining the subordinate clauses.

(1) Archeologists are now one step closer to finding the answer to a mystery about Egypt's Great Pyramid that has long been a puzzle. (2)

*This pyramid was built some 4,500 years ago by the Pharaoh Khufu.

(3) While nineteenth-century explorers were examining the inner chambers of the Great Pyramid, they discovered four, eight-inch square shafts rising at angles from the chamber area within the pyramid. (4) The purpose of these shafts has mystified Egyptologists for many years since they don't appear in other Egyptian pyramids. (5) Researchers pursued the mystery because they were particularly interested in what was behind a small limestone door with brass handles at the top of one of the shafts. (6) *The door is at the end of the shaft about 200 feet above the floor of an inner chamber. (7) Engineers designed a tiny robot with special treads that enabled the robot to grip the walls of the shaft in order to reach the door. (8) *The research team then used the robot to drill a hole in the door and insert a tiny light and camera. (9) When they got their first glance inside, they found a space leading to another door instead of a chamber or artifacts of some kind. (10) Although the mystery remains, researchers hope to continue the exploration of this unique feature of the Great Pyramid.

Discovering Connections 8.2

COLLABORATION

1. For Discovering Connections 8.1 on page 160, you began prewriting in response to a quotation by Langston Hughes or a photo. Now continue your prewriting on one of these options:
   a. Why are dreams so important in our lives?
   b. What can people do to ensure that their dreams don't die?
2. Evaluate your prewriting material, identify a focus, and create a draft of about 100 words.
3. Exchange your draft with a writing partner. Using the material in this chapter as a guide, evaluate the draft you receive, and note any problems with subordination as well as any other weaknesses. Return the draft to the writer.
4. Revise your draft, eliminating any errors that your reader identified.

Summary Exercise: Subordination

The following passage contains both simple sentences and complex sentences. Put an * in front of each simple sentence and circle each complex sentence, underlining the subordinate clauses.

(1) *Spanish painter, sculptor, and graphic artist, Pablo Picasso, was one of the most famous artists in the history of painting. (2) *He was a central figure in the artistic movement known as Cubism. (3) *Picasso was born on October 25, 1881, in Malaga, Spain. (4) *At age 15 he attended the School of Fine Arts in Barcelona. (5) Because he was impatient and did not enjoy this formal training, the young Picasso went to Paris in 1900. (6) After Picasso had lived in Paris for a few months, he became interested in the city's street life. (7) *Between 1900 and 1906, Picasso tried out many styles of contemporary painting. (8) When he discovered the work of the Spanish painter El Greco, twenty-year-old Picasso began to sink into a depression. (9) *His work at the time reflected his feelings of misery and despair. (10) This was known as Picasso's Blue Period, since most of these paintings were dominated by various shades of blue and gray. (11) *Picasso's Blue Period of deep depression began to change to a mild sadness in 1904. (12) The colors that he chose for this group of paintings were more natural, with many red and pink tones. (13) *This period is called Picasso's Pink Period. (14) After 1906, Picasso began to paint in a style that deviated from his earlier styles. (15) *The faces of the people in some of these paintings can be seen from the front and side at the same time.

(16) *Picasso's most celebrated painting is called *Guernica*. (17) Guernica is a Spanish city that was destroyed by bombs in the Spanish Civil War. (18) Picasso used only black, white, and gray paints to show the pain and anger that he felt about the bombing of Guernica. (19) *After

World War II, Picasso moved to the south of France. (20) Today he is universally recognized as an artistic genius <u>who dominated his field.</u>

RECAP SUBORDINATION

New terms in this chapter	Definitions
● **subordination**	● a way to combine ideas, show their relationship, and add emphasis in a sentence
● **simple sentence**	● one complete thought containing one subject–verb unit, set apart by a beginning capital letter and an ending punctuation mark *Example* The skunk wandered across the busy highway.
● **subordinate clause**	● a subject–verb unit that doesn't express a complete thought by itself Subordinate clauses are often introduced by *subordinating conjunctions.* *Example* *Before that volcano erupted last week,* it had been dormant for 50 years. Subordinate clauses may also be introduced by *relative pronouns: that, who, what, which, whom, whose* *Example* The chili *that caused her allergic reaction* has peanut butter in it.
● **main clause**	● a subject–verb unit that expresses a complete idea and that has been combined with a subordinate clause
● **complex sentence**	● a unit consisting of a main clause and one or more subordinate clauses main clause *Example* The protesters plan to remain outside city hall *until* subordinate clause *the mayor agrees to meet with them.*
● **subordinating conjunction**	● a word that connects and shows a relationship between clauses: *after, although, as, as if, because, before, even though, if, in order that, rather than, since, so that, than, though, unless, until, when, whenever, wherever, whether, while*

Structure of Two Sentences with Subordinate Clauses				
1.	main clause	+ subordinating conjunction	+	subordinate clause
2.	main clause	+ relative pronoun	+	subordinate clause

Chapter 9

Coordination

Getting Started... **Q:** When I write, it doesn't always sound smooth. I know it's because many of my sentences are short, but I'm not sure how to eliminate the problem. How can I make my sentences flow?

A: One way to increase the smoothness in your writing is to use coordination. With this technique, you use a coordinating conjunction or a semicolon to join subject–verb units. When you connect ideas this way, both units share equal importance and focus, and you eliminate choppiness.

Overview: Creating Compound Sentences by Joining Ideas

The use of many choppy, short sentences in writing inhibits the smooth flow of ideas. One way to give your writing this smoothness is coordination. **Coordination** involves the joining of simple sentences that express equally important, related ideas. They are joined either by a conjunction, which shows their relationship, or by a semicolon. Coordination can help you better communicate your ideas to your reader.

> *This chapter helps you see how coordination can make your writing more effective. You will learn to join two simple sentences and create one compound sentence by using*
>
> - a coordinating conjunction and a comma
>
> - a semicolon
>
> - a semicolon and a conjunctive adverb

Discovering Connections 9.1

Consider the following quotation:

Education is what remains when we have forgotten all that we have been taught.

—*Lord Halifax*

Or focus on this photo.

Now, using the prewriting technique you prefer, write about your reaction to the quotation or photo. Save your work.

Using Coordinating Conjunctions

As you learned in Chapter 8, "Subordination," a simple sentence consists of one subject–verb unit that stands on its own. Sometimes, two or more simple sentences are connected by a **coordinating conjunction,** a word that is used to link words, phrases, or sentences of equal importance. This combination of equal ideas or sentences is called a **compound sentence.** Here are the coordinating conjunctions:

Coordinating Conjunctions

and	nor	so
but	or	yet
for		

The statements on either side of a coordinating conjunction are equally important, or balanced. Writers show the relationship between these equally important ideas by choosing an appropriate coordinating conjunction:

- *And* suggests that one idea is added to another.
- *But* and *yet* suggest a difference between the two ideas.
- *So* suggests that one idea happens as a result of another.
- *For* suggests that one idea is a reason for the other happening.
- *Or* and *nor* suggest that the two ideas offer a choice.

Identify the two complete thoughts in each of the following compound sentences, and identify the coordinating conjunction that connects them:

EXAMPLE   Jason had to find a way to get help, or he would be stranded on the darkened highway.

EXAMPLE   No one answered the knock at the door, so the delivery person left.

In the first example, the coordinating conjunction is *or*, and in the second, the coordinating conjunction is *so*. As these examples show, a comma is always placed before the coordinating conjunction.

What is the advantage of using coordination? Consider the following sets of simple sentences:

SIMPLE   The breeze at the beach was chilly. The water was warm.

SIMPLE   Carlos runs three miles each morning. He runs another three miles each evening.

Notice how choppy these sets seem.

Now read the compound sentences below, which combine each set of sentences:

COMPOUND   The breeze at the beach was chilly, *but* the water was warm.

COMPOUND   Carlos runs three miles each morning, *and* he runs another three miles each evening.

The compound sentences flow much better than the simple sentences alone. They are also easier to understand. When using a compound sentence, a writer balances two equally important ideas and shows how they are related.

Exercise 9.1   **Creating Compound Sentences with Coordinating Conjunctions**

Combine each pair of simple sentences in the paragraph below using coordination. Change the period between them to a comma, and add a coordinating conjunction *and, nor, so, but, or, yet,* or *for.* Use the conjunction that will best show the relationship between the two ideas. Change capitalization as needed. Use the example as a guide.

EXAMPLE   Matthew wants to play the guitar in an R&B band, ~~He~~ , so he practices for an hour every day.

(1) Sal loves to cook Italian food, ~~He~~ , and he likes to serve it to his friends.

(2) He says this hobby helps him relax, ~~He~~ , for he can concentrate on a new

recipe instead of on his problems. (3) He usually begins a meal with an

antipasto of roasted vegetables, ~~Sometimes~~ he starts with a pasta course.

, but sometimes
∧

(4) Sal always includes a meatless dish, ~~His~~ vegetarian friends enjoy the

, so his
∧

food, too. (5) I don't like to miss one of Sal's dinners, I even cancel other

, and
∧

plans to join him for supper.

Using Coordinating Conjunctions to Create Compound Sentences

On the lines provided, complete each of the following sentences. Add another clause to the clause and coordinating conjunction that are given to create a compound sentence. Remember that the material you add must be able to stand as a sentence by itself. Use the example to guide you.

(Answers will vary. Representative answers are shown.)

EXAMPLE   The man's shoes were wet, *and*   _his pants were muddy_   .

1. The movie was good, *but* _my friend Ellie talked through the whole thing_

    _____ .

2. _We were too tired to hike anymore_ , *so* we walked back to the car.

3. The small dog must have run away from its owner, *or* _____it_____

    must have become lost somehow .

4. _Nobody had taken in the mail_ , *nor* had anyone picked up the
   trash outside the house for weeks.

5. An accident had blocked the main street, *so* _____traffic was_____
    at a standstill .

6. My cousin Terry is a nurse, *and* _her children want to work in the_
    medical field, too .

7. _Everybody else in my family is a hockey fan_ , *but* I am more interested
   in soccer.

8. _____ The city better fix these potholes soon _____, *or* they will have to repave the entire street.

Exercise 9.3   **Revising a Paragraph for Appropriate Coordination**

1. The following paragraph suffers from too much coordination. Some ideas that have been joined would communicate better standing alone. Decide which ideas you want to separate.

2. Rewrite the paragraph on a separate piece of paper so that the writer's ideas are expressed through a variety of compound and simple sentences.
   (Answers will vary.)

(1) Obtaining health insurance can be difficult for many reasons, and many people have to take their chances without it. (2) Some insurance plans are very expensive, but these policies may be the only options available for people without employee health benefits, so they have to pay high premiums. (3) People with certain health problems, such as high blood pressure, can't even find insurance, or the price is too expensive, so they couldn't buy it anyway. (4) A deductible is the amount of a bill an insured person will pay, and the higher the deductible is, the lower the cost of a policy, so many people will promise to pay a high deductible, yet they can't afford to pay that either. (5) Some insurance policies limit the amount of coverage for some illnesses, and that hurts people with chronic illnesses, or they won't pay for certain procedures.

COLLABORATION

3. Share your revised paragraph with a classmate. Explain the changes you made.

Challenge 9.1   **Identifying and Evaluating the Use of Coordination in a Piece of Writing**

COLLABORATION

Make two copies a four-paragraph passage from one of the readings in Part Six, "Discovering Connections through Writing." Exchange a copy with a classmate, and then circle any compound sentences in the passage you selected and the one you received from a classmate.

Using Semicolons

Another way to create a compound sentence is to use a *semicolon* (;) as a connector. A semicolon has the same power to connect as a coordinating conjunction, but the semicolon calls attention to the connection in a different way.

Look at the two versions of the same sentence below:

EXAMPLE   The food at Billy J's Sports Bar is bad, *but* the service is even worse.

EXAMPLE   The food at Billy J's Sports Bar is bad; the service is even worse.

In the first version, the coordinating conjunction *but* points out the contrast between the linked thoughts: The service is worse than the food. In the second example, the use of the semicolon makes the connection between the simple sentences more dramatic. It emphasizes the writer's annoyance.

It's important to remember that both of the examples above are correct. They represent differences in *style*. You can experiment with both coordinating conjunctions and semicolons to add variety to your writing.

Exercise 9.4   **Creating Compound Sentences with Semicolons**

The following compound sentences are composed of independent clauses connected by coordinating conjunctions. On a separate sheet of paper, rewrite each sentence, crossing out the coordinating conjunction and substituting a semicolon. Beneath each of these new sentences, explain which version—the original with the coordinating conjunction or the new version with the semicolon—you believe is better and why. Use the example as a guide.

EXAMPLE   The caffeine in coffee keeps me awake; I don't drink it after five o'clock.

1. Exercise at any age improves health. It is especially good for people over
   the age of fifty-five.
   , but it

2. According to current research, exercise slows down aging. ~~People~~ live
   longer and feel better because of exercise.
   , and people

3. In addition, physically fit elderly people recover from illness quickly. ~~They~~
   go to hospitals less often and for shorter times.
   , and so they

4. Older people don't have to be sedentary. ~~They~~ can train for and enjoy
   most sports.
   , and they

, and competing

5. Exercise can keep our muscles working well, ~~Competing~~ in sports can
   ∧

change our attitude about getting old.

Exercise 9.5 **Using Semicolons to Create Compound Sentences**

On each line of this exercise, add a clause to complete the compound sentence. The semicolons have already been provided. Remember that the idea you add must be able to stand as a sentence by itself and should have a strong connection to the clause already present. Use the example to guide you.

(Answers will vary. Representative answers are shown.)

EXAMPLE The day had been long and hot; *all I wanted to do was go for a swim* .

1. The broken hydrant gushed water ; before long,

the street was flooded.

2. After two weeks, the truth about the murder was discovered;

the story was hard to believe .

3. Resistance would have meant death ; the clerk had no

choice but to turn over the money to the woman with the gun.

4. The canned goods drive was a great success for the club; _____

the food will be donated to a homeless shelter .

5. We filled the empty gas tank ; the car still wouldn't start.

6. The luggage on the baggage carousel had broken open; _____

someone's clothes were spilling out .

7. Luis loves sports ; his brother loves

theater and movies.

8. The employment counselor's office is always crowded; _____

company after company is downsizing .

Challenge 9.2 **Comparing Different Methods of Coordination**

1. For Exercise 9.4, you used semicolons to combine pairs of sentences in a passage. Evaluate the combined units, and choose the two or three that you decided would be as or more effective if they were connected with

a coordinating conjunction. Then copy the passage on a separate sheet of paper, making these changes.

2. Compare your version with your classmate's. Below your own passage, explain which version you think is better and why.

Using Conjunctive Adverbs

Another way to combine ideas of equal importance is by using a **conjunctive adverb** and semicolon. These are the conjunctive adverbs:

Common Conjunctive Adverbs

also	however	similarly
besides	instead	still
consequently	meanwhile	then
finally	moreover	therefore
furthermore	nevertheless	thus

Conjunctive adverbs point out the relationship between two simple sentences. Notice, however, that they are not called *conjunctions*. Because conjunctive adverbs do not function as joining words, they require a semicolon to make the connection. Place a semicolon before the conjunctive adverb and a comma after it.

Look at these two examples:

EXAMPLE   *The Fat-Free Cookbook* is expensive; *however,* it contains hundreds of great recipes for people concerned about their health.

EXAMPLE   On vacation, we didn't visit the White House; *instead,* we spent the time visiting various museums and monuments.

In each case, the semicolon establishes the connection between the two ideas. The conjunctive adverb, however, emphasizes the difference between them.

Exercise 9.6   **Using Conjunctive Adverbs in Compound Sentences**

For each compound sentence below, add the conjunctive adverb that best suggests a relationship between the ideas. (See the list of conjunctive adverbs above.) Remember to add a comma after the conjunctive adverb. Use the example to guide you.

EXAMPLE   My math assignment was very confusing; *nevertheless,* I struggled to finish it.
                                                            ^

however,
1. A movie makes money when people buy a ticket to see it; that is not the
   ^
   only way movies make money.

2. People rent or buy DVDs or videocassettes even after the movie leaves
   therefore,
   the theaters; producers keep earning money.
   ^

   consequently,
3. Premium cable TV stations pay producers to air the movies; this is an-
   ^
   other way movies make money.

   moreover,
4. Advertisers also pay to have their products appear in movies; some com-
   ^
   panies buy the right to produce products based on movie characters.

5. For example, toy companies don't have to think of new ideas for best-
   instead,
   selling toys and games; they just pay producers for the rights to make
   ^
   and sell action figures and other merchandise.

Exercise 9.7 **Creating Compound Sentences with Semicolons and Conjunctive Adverbs**

On the lines provided, complete each of the following sentences. Choose one of the conjunctive adverbs in parentheses, and add a related thought. (The semicolon is already provided.) Add a comma after the conjunctive adverb. Remember—the clause you add must be capable of standing alone. It must also carry through the relationship suggested by the conjunctive adverb you choose. Use the example as a guide. (Note: Either conjunctive adverb is a possible choice, depending upon the relationship of your two thoughts.)

(Answers will vary. Representative answers are shown.)

EXAMPLE

Fall is probably the best season of the year; _____*however,*_____

_____*I still prefer summer*_____ . (moreover, however)

1. Working in a restaurant is hard work; _____nevertheless, I enjoy it_____

_____ . (still, nevertheless)

2. Over a hundred gallons of gasoline spilled into the stream; __consequently, all the fish died__ . (consequently, however)

3. College classes should always be interesting; __furthermore, they should make you think__ . (furthermore, instead)

4. The explosion destroyed the front of the building; __nevertheless, the company remained open for business__ . (moreover, nevertheless)

5. The press secretary spoke to the room full of reporters; __meanwhile, the president walked into the room__ . (meanwhile, then)

6. Serving on a jury is demanding; __besides, it can be time consuming__ . (besides, nevertheless)

7. I waited two hours to be seen at the emergency room; __moreover, I had to stand in a crowded waiting room for an hour__ . (finally, moreover)

8. Several stray cats live in my neighborhood; __however, no one seems to mind__ . (furthermore, however)

Using Coordination to Improve a Paragraph

The paragraph below is composed of simple sentences. Decide where it would be improved through coordination. Use a coordinating conjunction with a comma, or a semicolon with a conjunctive adverb and a comma, to create compound sentences. Rewrite the revised version of the paragraph on a separate piece of paper. You may decide not to change some sentences. (Answers will vary.)

(1) Rude behavior is becoming more and more common. (2) I can't stand this trend. (3) I saw a woman combing her hair at a restaurant table. (4) She didn't seem to mind all the people staring at her. (5) Another very rude person works at my bank. (6) This man, a teller, snaps his chewing gum loudly. (7) His customers can't hear what he has to say. (8) Maybe our schools should teach manners. (9) Training

should begin early. (10) Businesses could offer refresher courses. (11) Ongoing education might cut down on rude behavior.

Challenge 9.3   **Evaluating Your Use of Coordination**

COLLABORATION

1. Using coordination to join simple sentences presents writers with several style options. Share the paragraph you revised in Exercise 9.8 above with a partner. Compare the choices you each made.

2. Answer these questions as you talk about the paragraphs:

   ● Where are your choices similar?
   ● Where are they different?
   ● What ideas did you leave as simple sentences?
   ● Why did you join the ideas you joined?
   ● Did you use commas and semicolons correctly?

Coordination Checklist

☐ Are you clear on how coordinating conjunctions allow you to indicate relationships between subject and verb units while also keeping them equal in importance?

☐ Do you understand how semicolons function?

☐ Can you see how the connection a semicolon provides differs from the connection a coordinating conjunction provides?

☐ Are you clear on the different roles played by coordinating conjunctions and conjunctive adverbs?

☐ Do you understand the additional link you can suggest between subject–verb units by using a semicolon to connect them and adding a conjunctive adverb?

Exploring Ideas through Journal Writing

Coordination is a kind of balancing act, one that involves combining subject–verb units so that each unit has the same general level of importance. What else in your life depends on maintaining balance? a personal relationship? School, work—or both? What about your own physical health or well-being? Focus on some aspect of balance and then spend 20 to 30 minutes in your journal exploring its importance or effects.

Chapter Quick Check:
Coordination

The following passage contains a series of simple sentences presented in sets of two within brackets. Turn each pair of simple sentences into a compound sentence, using one of the techniques illustrated in this chapter. Write the revised sentences on a separate sheet of paper.

(Representative answers are shown.)

(1) [Thomas Edison probably never envisioned it. ~~The~~ *, but the* sheer amount of electric light in our modern world can be a real problem.] (2) [In big cities, the problem is particularly bad. ~~Except~~ *, except* during a power blackout, residents never experience a natural level of evening darkness.] (3) [The sun goes down. ~~Lights~~ *, and lights* all over these cities go on.] (4) [Portions of large office buildings remain lit long after closing. ~~Many~~ *, and many* also have extensive exterior lighting.] (5) [Few stores and fast food restaurants ever shut off their lights. ~~They~~ *, or they* keep them on until 1 or 2 A.M. even during the week.] (6) [On the clearest nights, the excess light makes it nearly impossible to see most stars. ~~Any~~ *, and any* clouds completely obscure the sky.] (7) [The amount of illumination in the sky has also increased in other areas. ~~Even~~ *, even* tiny cities and towns have far more external lighting than in any time in the past.] (8) [Amateur astronomers find the excess light a genuine problem. ~~They~~ *, so they* have to travel far from home to view stars and planets through their telescopes.] (9) [Bright lights illuminating some Florida beachfront hotels have also created problems. ~~This~~ *, and this* situation underscores the seriousness of light pollution. (10) [Turtle hatchlings instinctively follow the light of the full moon to the safety of the water. ~~Unfortunately~~ *, but unfortunately* some have been known to head toward the bright lights of the hotels to their deaths.]

Discovering Connections 9.2

COLLABORATION

1. For Discovering Connections 9.1 on page 177, you began prewriting in response to a quotation by Lord Halifax or a photo. Now continue your prewriting on one of these options:
   a. Is an education only what you remember from school? Or is it much more? Explain.
   b. What lesson from your education has most impressed you thus far?
2. Evaluate your prewriting material, identify a focus, and create a draft of about 100 words.
3. Exchange your draft with a partner. Using the material in this chapter, evaluate the draft you receive, and note any problems with coordination as well as any other weaknesses. Return the draft to the writer.
4. Revise your draft, eliminating any errors that your reader identified.

Summary Exercise: Coordination

The following passage contains a series of simple sentences presented in sets of two within brackets. Turn each pair of simple sentences into a compound sentence, using one of the techniques illustrated in this chapter. Write the revised sentences on a separate sheet of paper.

(1) [Almost everything about Sacajawea, the Shoshoni woman, is a
     , but she
mystery. ~~She~~ remains a compelling figure.] (2) [Sacajawea's experiences
                                                 , so she
raised the Native American woman to a new level of admiration. ~~She~~ is
often credited with shattering long-held stereotypes.]

(3) [The Shoshoni (also spelled *Shoshone*) lived in Idaho, parts of
                                    , and it
Utah, and parts of Northern Nevada. ~~It~~ is believed that Sacajawea was
born in what is now Salmon, Idaho.] (4) [When she was ten years old,
                                          ; they
Sacajawea was captured by a rival tribe. ~~They~~ carried her to their
camp near the border of North Dakota.] (5) [The tribe sold Sacajawea
                                          , and he
to a French-Canadian fur trader named Charbonneau. ~~He~~ took her as
his wife.]

(6) [Lewis and Clark, the famous explorers of the American Pacific
                                    ; he
Northwest, hired Charbonneau as a guide. ~~He~~ was very knowledgeable

about the region they wanted to explore.] (7) [Lewis and Clark told
Charbonneau to bring Sacajawea and her baby boy, John Baptiste, ~~They~~
, for they
knew that Sacajawea had useful knowledge of the languages, customs,
and tribes of the country.]

(8) [Sacajawea's knowledge of the land and mountain passes saved
weeks of travel time, ~~Her~~ , and her ability to speak and trade with native tribes allowed the expedition to get fresh horses and food all along the way.] (9)
[The expedition ended successfully, ~~Lewis~~ , and Lewis and Clark named a river
Sacajawea in her honor.] (10) [According to some historians, Sacajawea
took her son to live with Clark in St. Louis, ~~Clark~~ , and Clark raised the boy as his
own.] (11) [One account says that Sacajawea died of a putrid fever at
age 25, ~~Clark's~~ ; however, Clark's own account of the members of his expedition marks her
as dead.] (12) [Native accounts and Shoshoni oral history tell a different
story, ~~One~~ , and one such account tells of Sacajawea marrying several more times.]
(13) [In these stories, she had a number of children, ~~She~~ ; furthermore, she met up with her
son Jean Baptiste in Wind River, Wyoming.] (14) [This account suggests
that Sacajawea died at age 96, ~~It~~ , and it describes how she was buried in the
white cemetery at Fort Washakie.] (15) [Her final resting place represents a final show of respect for her assistance to Lewis and Clark and to
the Shoshoni tribe, ~~It~~ , so it is a significant part of the story.]

RECAP COORDINATION

New terms in this chapter	Definitions
● coordination	● the combining of simple sentences into compound sentences to eliminate choppiness and repetition
● coordinating conjunction	● one of a set of words used to join other words or groups of words: *and, but, for, nor, or, so, yet* *Continued*

New terms in this chapter	Definitions
	A coordinating conjunction can be used to join simple sentences to make a compound sentence.
	Place a comma before the coordinating conjunction in a compound sentence.
	Example Joe always eats hot dogs, *but* Mary prefers Polish sausage.
● **compound sentence**	● a sentence created by joining simple sentences with a connector: a coordinating conjunction and comma a semicolon a semicolon, conjunctive adverb, and comma
● **conjunctive adverb**	● one of a set of words used with a semicolon to join simple sentences: *also, besides, consequently, finally, furthermore, however, meanwhile, instead, moreover, nevertheless, similarly, still, then, therefore, thus*
	A conjunctive adverb cannot connect simple sentences by itself, but it does emphasize the connection provided by a semicolon.
	Place a comma after the conjunctive adverb used with a semicolon to join simple sentences.
	Example Cheetahs are an endangered species; *however*, many cheetahs were born at zoos last year.

Three Ways to Make a Compound Sentence

1. simple sentence + comma and coordinating conjunction + simple sentence

2. simple sentence + semicolon + simple sentence

3. simple sentence + semicolon with conjunctive adverb and comma + simple sentence

Chapter 10

Comma Splices and Run-On Sentences

Getting Started... **Q:** I know how important it is to express my ideas in correct sentence form. The problem is that I'm not always sure how. Sometimes I'm not sure my sentences end when they should, and other times I think I let one run into the next. How can I make sure I set off each of my sentences in the correct way?

A: Once you have come up with good ideas, you've done most of the hard work. The errors you are worried about are called comma splices and run-on sentences, and they occur when you incorrectly link sentences. To avoid these errors, you need to examine each subject–verb unit and ask yourself if you want to separate it from the next one or connect it. If you want to separate sentences, then use a period, question mark, or exclamation point. If you want to connect sentences, use a conjunction with a comma or a semicolon. It's as simple as that.

Overview: Avoiding Sentence-Combining Errors

As Chapters 8 and 9 have shown, *subordination* and *coordination* are important techniques in writing. Connecting ideas clarifies meaning and eliminates choppiness.

Sometimes these techniques can be tricky. Even very experienced writers may make errors when they combine sentences. Two of the most common sentence-combining errors are the comma splice and the run-on sentence. A **comma splice** occurs when two sentences are joined by only a comma. A **run-on sentence** occurs when two sentences are run together with no punctuation or conjunction. Discovering how to recognize and eliminate these problems is crucial if you want to make your ideas clear to your reader.

This chapter provides the opportunity to explore ways to avoid both comma splices and run-on sentences. You will learn options to correct these sentence errors by using

●   a coordinating conjunction and a comma

●   a semicolon

●   a period

●   a subordinating conjunction

Discovering Connections 10.1

Consider the following quotation:

The purpose of life is to believe, to hope, and to strive.

—Indira Gandhi

Or focus on this drawing.

    Now, using the prewriting technique you prefer, do some prewriting about your reaction to the quotation or to the illustration. Save your work.

Recognizing Comma Splices and Run-On Sentences

Eliminating comma splices and run-on sentences begins with a quick check. If you have written what you think is a compound sentence, first see whether you have combined two simple sentences. Remember—every simple sentence has its own subject and verb.

    Look at the example below:

subject	verb	subject	verb

EXAMPLE   My New Year's *party was* a flop, *I could*n't *wait* for my friends to leave.

    As you can see, the sentence contains two separate sets of subjects and verbs. Next, check to see whether each part of the sentence can stand alone. Put a slash (/) between the two subject–verb units, as shown below.

EXAMPLE   My New Year's party was a flop, / I couldn't wait for my friends to leave.

    Both parts can stand on their own, so each is a simple sentence. Here, the writer used a comma to connect them. As Chapter 9, "Coordination," explained, a coordinating conjunction in addition to a comma is required to connect two simple sentences. **Commas alone cannot serve as connectors.** This first sentence is a *comma splice*.

The example below shows a similar kind of problem. A / has been placed between the two main parts of the sentence.

EXAMPLE

subject	verb		subject	verb

Her *clothes were* torn and dirty / *she was* obviously disoriented.

As you can see, the sentence also consists of two simple sentences. Here, the writer did not use anything, not even a faulty comma, to connect them. The two simple sentences just run right into one another. That is why this kind of error is called a *run-on sentence*. In the rest of this chapter, four options to correct both comma splices and run-ons are discussed.

Exercise 10.1 **Recognizing Comma Splices and Run-Ons**

Find the comma splices and run-ons in the paragraph that follows. First, underline and label the subject and verb in each clause. Then put a / between clauses that make sense on their own. Use the example to guide you.

EXAMPLE

S V

The equipment in the schoolyard needs replacing,/for example, the

S V

swing's plastic seat is cracked.

(1) The first atomic bomb was dropped more than 50 years ago /people still argue about that decision. (2) In World War II, atomic bombs killed more than 250,000 people/thousands died as a result of radiation poisoning. (3) According to some people, the attack on Hiroshima and Nagasaki ended the war,/many more people on both sides would have died in an invasion of Japan. (4) Historians will study the impact of the bomb in the future,/we should remember its lessons forever. (5) Humans have a terrifying capacity for destruction,/we need to keep talking.

Exercise 10.2 **Identifying Comma Splices and Run-Ons**

The following paragraph contains several run-on sentences. Put an * in front of each run-on. Then put a / where one sentence should end and the next should begin. Use the example as a guide.

EXAMPLE *My first babysitting job was terrible/six-year-old Michelle cried for her mother all night.

(1) Being a lifeguard isn't easy or glamorous. (2)*First of all, the heat gets to be unbearable/you can't jump in the water to cool down while on duty. (3) Instead, you spend the day sweating and roasting. (4) You have to be on duty on cold days, too. (5)*On these cold days, you have to stand there freezing in your bathing suit/you still have to be ready for any emergency. (6)*Sometimes the job can also be boring/only a few people are in your assigned area on weekdays, for example. (7) On weekends the job is almost too much to handle. (8)*On sunny days, people start arriving early in the morning/they keep pouring in until noon.

Challenge 10.1 **Checking Your Writing for Comma Splices and Run-Ons**

1. Select one of the journal entries you have completed and make a copy of it.

2. Exchange the copy of your entry with a classmate. Identify the subjects and verbs in each sentence of the entry you receive. Check for any subject–verb units that are incorrectly connected or run together. Put an ***** in front of any sentence that you suspect is incorrect, and then return the entry to the writer.

3. Check the sentences your classmate has identified. Make necessary corrections.

Using Coordinating Conjunctions to Correct Comma Splices and Run-Ons

One way to correct a comma splice or run-on is to use a coordinating conjunction, such as *and, but,* or *or,* to connect the two simple sentences. (See page 177 in Chapter 9 for a list of coordinating conjunctions.) As Chapter 9 explained, a coordinating conjunction links independent thoughts to eliminate choppiness.

Look at these examples, which have a / between the clauses:

RUN-ON

Lines for the concert tickets ran all around the block / some people had even set up tents.

COMMA SPLICE

Walter usually plays practical jokes on others, / he was the victim this time.

In the first example, the first simple sentence ends with *block*, and the second begins with *some*. Because nothing connects or separates them, it is a run-on. The second sentence contains two independent clauses separated by a comma. **Commas cannot connect,** however, so this example is a comma splice.

Now consider the versions below, with coordinating conjunctions linking the clauses:

COMPOUND SENTENCE

Lines for the concert tickets ran all around the block, *and* some people had even set up tents.

COMPOUND SENTENCE

Walter usually plays practical jokes on others, *but* he was the victim this time.

The clauses are now joined by coordinating conjunctions: *and* and *but*. The sentences flow better, and they are correct. Remember—when you use a coordinating conjunction to link simple sentences, place a comma before the conjunction.

Exercise 10.3   **Using a Coordinating Conjunction to Connect Clauses**

The paragraph below contains some run-ons and comma splices. Find these errors, and put a / between clauses that are not correctly connected. Then, between these clauses, add the coordinating conjunction (*and, or, but, for, nor, so,* or *yet*) that best connects the thoughts. Check each sentence to be sure commas are used correctly. Use the example as a guide.

EXAMPLE

My computer is now out-dated/most new software will not run on it.
 (,so above the /)

(1) Kitty Genovese was murdered outside her apartment in Queens, New York, in 1964. (2) Thirty-eight people watched from their windows/no
(but above the /)

one called the police or tried to help her. (3) The assailant followed Miss

, and

Genovese from her car/he stabbed her. (4) He went away he/came back to

, but he

yet

find her, stabbing her two more times. (5) She cried for help,/her neighbors

didn't respond.

Exercise 10.4   **Connecting Clauses Using a Coordinating Conjunction**

The following paragraph contains several comma splices and run-ons. Put an * in front of each comma splice or run-on. Then choose an appropriate coordinating conjunction (*and, but, for, or, nor, so,* or *yet*), and write it above the place where the correction is needed. Use the example to guide you.

EXAMPLE   *, but*
*Rose wanted to start school with me she had to find a full-time job.

(1) Just about every region of the United States was affected by last year's severe drought. (2) *In the Midwest, farmers had trouble irrigating

and

their fields, they also had to plow some crops under. (3) In the Far West, ranchers had to deal with wildfires. (4) *In some cases, firefighters from

, but

neighboring states were called in to help fight the fires/they couldn't do much to stop them. (5) All along the East Coast, cities imposed strict water bans. (6) *In some places, residents had to cut back outdoor water

or

use/they would face stiff fines and possible termination of water service.

but

(7) *People were allowed to water their vegetable gardens/they could do so only three times a week for a half hour at a time. (8) For some reason, the South wasn't affected by the drought this time.

Challenge 10.2   **Evaluating the Use of Coordinating Conjunctions in a Piece of Writing**

1. Underline each independent clause in the following passage.

The lake was the heart of the resort. Rustic old cottages nestled in the trees along its shore, and hills rose in tiers around it. Generous porches with big picture windows behind them had been placed on the water side, for everyone wanted to make the most of the view. The

<u>big lodge sat on a hill rather than on the water's edge,</u> but <u>it, too, gazed out on the shining water.</u> From first light to starlight, <u>the sight of water offered repose,</u> and <u>the sound offered comfort.</u>

2. Working with a classmate, evaluate each compound sentence, discussing which would be better: leaving the sentence as it is or turning it into two simple sentences. Then, on a separate sheet of paper, write your version of the paragraph as well as a brief explanation of your decisions.

Using Semicolons to Correct Comma Splices and Run-Ons

A second way to eliminate a comma splice or run-on is to use a semicolon (;) to connect the two simple sentences. As Chapter 9 discussed, a semicolon has the same power to connect as a conjunction plus a comma. Using a semicolon emphasizes the connection between the simple sentences.

Look at these examples, which have a / between the simple sentences:

COMMA SPLICE   The old woman in the wheelchair was sleeping, / her husband stood sadly at her side.

RUN-ON   I just wanted a fast cup of coffee / things didn't work out that way, though.

Correcting these errors is a simple matter of inserting semicolons between the simple sentences, as these versions show:

COMPOUND SENTENCE   The old woman in the wheelchair was sleeping**;** her husband stood sadly at her side.

COMPOUND SENTENCE   I just wanted a fast cup of coffee**;** things didn't work out that way, though.

As Chapter 9 also showed, semicolons can be used with conjunctive adverbs like *also, however,* and *therefore* to suggest a relationship between the simple sentences. (See page 183 in Chapter 9 for a list of conjunctive adverbs.)

Look at these examples:

EXAMPLE   The movie was entertaining; *however,* it was very violent.

> **EXAMPLE**   Shirley went inside to look for a wrench; *meanwhile*, Chuck crawled under the car.

In both, the semicolon provides the connection, and the conjunctive adverbs provide an additional dimension to the connection. Notice that a comma follows the conjunctive adverb.

Exercise 10.5   **Using a Semicolon to Connect Clauses**

Identify the independent clauses in the paragraph below, and put a / between them. If commas are used incorrectly, cross them out. Then insert a semicolon alone or with a conjunctive adverb and comma to connect the clauses and show their relationship. Use the example as a guide.

> **EXAMPLE**   For more than thirty years, the popular magazine *Reader's Digest* did not
> [;] or [; instead,]
> carry advertising/subscriptions paid for the publication.

(1) Many animal lovers criticize the use of animals for medical re-
[;] or [; however,]
search/there is another side to the controversy. (2) Some research is nec-

essary. (3) Research may help find a cure to a serious illness such as
[;] or [; on the other hand,]
AIDS/other studies investigate genetic problems. (4) Laboratories are not
[;] or [; in fact,]
necessarily miserable places to be/they are clean and comfortable. (5)
[;] or [; in addition,]
Moreover, not all experiments are cruel/painkillers and medical care are

given when needed.

Exercise 10.6   **Connecting Clauses Using a Semicolon**

The following paragraph contains several comma splices and run-on sentences. Put an * in front of each comma splice or run-on. Correct each error by inserting a semicolon, or a semicolon and a conjunctive adverb, above the place where correction is needed. Use the example to guide you.

> **EXAMPLE**   *
> [;] or [; however,]
> Management presented their last, best offer or the workers rejected it and
> ^
>
> returned to the picket line.

[;]

(1) *A lot of people lump insects and spiders together as "bugs" actually, they are quite different. (2) *Insects typically have one or two pairs of
[;] or [; however,]
wings/spiders have none at all. (3) Look closely at the bodies of insects
and spiders. (4) *You will see that insects always have three distinct body
[;]
segments, or divisions/in contrast, spiders have only two. (5) *Every insect
[;]
has three pairs of legs these grow from its second body segment. (6) *A
[;] or [; moreover,]
spider's legs grow from its first body segment/it always has four pairs of
legs. (7) You might need a magnifying glass to see the final difference.
[;] or [;however,]
(8) *Insects have antennae, or "feelers," on their first body segment spiders
lack these delicate sensory organs.

Exercise 10.7   **Connecting Sentences with Coordinating Conjunctions and Semicolons**

Put an * in front of each comma splice or run-on that you identify in the paragraph below. Decide how you want to correct these errors. On a separate piece of paper, rewrite the paragraph by inserting a coordinating conjunction, a semicolon, or a semicolon and conjunctive adverb where you decide is best. Be sure you use commas where they are needed.

(1) One of this century's greatest musicians and composers was
Edward Kennedy "Duke" Ellington. (2) *When he died in 1974, he left an
, and
amazing legacy of achievements musicians today continue to learn from
his innovative style. (3) Fans can still hear Ellington's creative genius in
recordings such as "Take the A Train" and "Mood Indigo." (4) *Recordings
;
were not the only way Ellington expressed himself he also composed
music for movies, such as *Anatomy of a Murder*. (5) In addition, he wrote
an autobiography, *Music Is My Mistress* (6) *Ellington led many accom-
; in addition,
plished musicians in his bands/ he wrote most of the music his band
played. (7) *Ellington's music was heard in Harlem's Cotton Club and

and

Carnegie Hall, Ellington was at home in both places. (8) *His music

∧

brought together jazz, blues, ballads, ragtime, and other types of music ;

American music is richer as a result.

Challenge 10.3   **Using Coordinating Conjunctions and Semicolons**

COLLABORATION

Share the paragraph you revised in Exercise 10.7 with a classmate, and discuss the changes that each of you made. Together, revise the paragraph another time. Use the sentences that you both agree are most effective.

Using Periods to Correct
Comma Splices and Run-Ons

Another sure way to eliminate comma splices and run-ons is to add a period and create two separate sentences. If the simple sentences are short, using a period to separate them may make your writing sound choppy. When the sentences are long, however, splitting them up may be a good option.

Look at these examples, which have a / between the simple sentences:

COMMASPLICE

The flight to Miami was the longest part of my vacation journey last year, / the connecting flight to Aruba was an hour and a half shorter.

RUN-ON

Ali's new job is much easier than her old job at the self-service gas station / now she works in the florist department at a supermarket.

In each example, two independent thoughts have been joined incorrectly. These errors could be eliminated by using a conjunction and a comma or a semicolon. However, both examples are fairly long, and long sentences can be difficult to follow. Therefore, using a period to separate the simple sentences in them is a better option, as these versions show:

REVISED

The flight to Miami was the longest part of my vacation journey last year. The connecting flight to Aruba was an hour and a half shorter.

REVISED

Ali's new job is much easier than her old job at the self-service gas station. Now she works in the florist department at a supermarket.

Exercise 10.8 **Using a Period to Separate Independent Thoughts**

The paragraph below contains run-ons and comma splices. Put a / between the incorrectly joined clauses. Then insert a period and a capital letter where each is needed. Use the example to guide you.

EXAMPLE

A planet is a large, fairly cool body traveling in a path around a star,/often

smaller bodies called satellites or moons orbit planets.

(1) Pelé, whose real name is Edson Arantes Do Nascimento, is often

called the greatest soccer player of his time,/he was largely responsible

for popularizing soccer in the United States. (2) Pelé was famed for his

powerful kicking,/he was also known for his brilliant field strategy. (3) He

was born in Três Corações, Brazil. (4) He began playing as an inside left

forward for the Santos Football Club in 1956,/in 1962 the team won its

first world club championship. (5) Pelé retired in 1974,/he had scored

1200 goals in 1253 games.

Exercise 10.9 **Separating Independent Thoughts with a Period**

The following paragraph contains several comma splices and run-on sentences. Put an * in front of each comma splice or run-on. Insert a period where the first sentence should end. Then capitalize the first letter of the word that begins the second sentence. Cross out any incorrect commas. Use the example as a guide.

EXAMPLE

*People with a mental disorder may lead uncertain, disrupted lives,/the

most ordinary events may be an ordeal.

(1) Panic attacks are unbelievably frightening. (2) For no apparent

reason, you begin to feel an overwhelming sense of fear. (3) *Then your

heart begins to pound,/it feels like a heart attack. (4) *At this point, you become even more scared,/ y̶o̶u̶ [. You] feel completely out of control. (5) Sometimes, you even end up in an emergency room. (6)[*]Doctors often prescribe medications to control panic attacks c̶o̶u̶n̶s̶e̶l̶i̶n̶g̶ [. Counseling] and relaxation techniques have better results. (7) With this kind of treatment, most people can return to their regular lifestyle. (8) They don't have to live in fear any more.

Challenge 10.4   **Evaluating Different Ways of Correcting Comma Splices and Run-Ons**

1. For Exercise 10.2 on page 193–194, you identified several comma splices or run-on sentences. Working with a classmate, evaluate this paragraph. Then decide what would be the best way to correct the errors: connecting them with a coordinating conjunction or semicolon (with or without a conjunctive adverb) or separating them with a period.

2. On a separate sheet of paper, prepare a corrected version of the paragraph.

Using Subordinating Conjunctions to Correct Comma Splices and Run-Ons

A final way to correct a comma splice or run-on is to use a *subordinating conjunction* like *after, because, if,* and *unless* to connect the two subject–verb units. (See page 162 for a list of subordinating conjunctions.) As Chapter 8, "Subordination," showed, the resulting sentence is called a *complex sentence*.

As Chapter 8 also explained, a subordinating conjunction indicates a relationship between the ideas it connects. The simple sentence introduced by the conjunction becomes the *subordinate clause,* and the other sentence becomes the *main clause*.

Look at these examples, which include a / between the two subject–verb units.

COMMA SPLICE   Darrell volunteered to coach the church youth soccer team, / no one else wanted to do it.

| RUN-ON | Two parents of youth soccer players had a fight during a game, / league officials banned all spectators. |

These sets of simple sentences have been joined but not properly *connected*. **Remember—a comma cannot connect.** These sentences require connectors that show their relationship if they are to be left together. Now look at these versions, with subordinating conjunctions added:

| COMPLEX SENTENCE | Darrell volunteered to coach the church youth soccer team *because* no one else wanted to do it. |

| COMPLEX SENTENCE | *After* two parents of youth soccer players had a fight during a game, league officials banned all spectators. |

In each case, the subordinating conjunction links the simple sentences and also indicates the relationship between them. Darrell will coach *because* no other parent volunteered. Parents fought; officials banned spectators from the sidelines after. Notice where punctuation is needed. When the subordinate clause comes first, set it off with a comma.

Exercise 10.10   **Using a Subordinating Conjunction to Connect Clauses**

Correct the comma splices and run-ons in the following paragraph. First, identify the incorrectly joined clauses and put a / between them. Then add a subordinating conjunction that shows the relationship between the clauses and corrects the error. Remember—you can place a subordinating conjunction *before* the first clause or *between* the clauses. See page 162 in Chapter 8 for a list of subordinating conjunctions. Add a comma wherever one is needed, and cross out any unneeded commas. Use the example as a guide.

| EXAMPLE | Televisions were once a symbol of luxury, but now almost every American household has at least one television. |

Although he
(1) He was born Cassius Clay, / we know the world's most famous boxer as Muhammad Ali. (2) Ali changed his name, after he became a member of the group known as the Black Muslims. (3) Ali is known as "The

because
Greatest," he was the first boxer in history to win the heavyweight cham-

When
pionship three times. (4) Ali retired from boxing in 1979 he had only lost

Even though he
three bouts in his career. (5) He retired in 1979, he returned in 1980 to

challenge and lose to heavyweight champion Larry Holmes.

Exercise 10.11   Connecting Clauses using a Subordinating Conjunction

The following paragraph contains several comma splices and run-ons. Put
an * in front of each comma splice and run-on. Then choose an appropriate subordinating conjunction from the list on page 162, and write it above
where one sentence should end and the next should begin. Change punctuation as necessary. Use the example to guide you.

EXAMPLE

because
* Our world unwittingly sets up many obstacles for people with disabilities,

it is built for the convenience of able people.

because
(1) * My friend Donnie has trouble getting around school she is in a

wheelchair (2) * Many of the doorways inside the buildings are very nar-
even though
row federal regulations call for wide doors and corridors. (3) She faces

other obstacles on campus. (4) For example, the crushed stone walkways
when
cause her difficulty. (5) * She sometimes becomes stuck the wheels of her

chair sink in the loose stone. (6) Also, in some of the buildings, the desks
until
are bolted to the floor. (7) * She can't enter or leave these rooms, all the

other students leave. (8) Most of the desks on campus are the wrong

height for her to use. (9) * She has to use a big textbook on her lap as a
unless
desktop, the instructor requests a special desk for her. (10) Without her

determination, she would have dropped out long ago.

Exercise 10.12   **Using a Period or Subordinating Conjunction to Correct Comma Splices and Run-Ons**

Identify the comma splices and run-ons in the paragraph below. Mark each with an *****. On a separate sheet of paper, rewrite the paragraph, revising the incorrectly connected sentences by inserting a period or a subordinating conjunction where you think is best. Check your work for correct use of punctuation and capitals.

(1) With an optimistic outlook, a person will live a much happier life. (2) *Some people see a partially filled glass and call it half empty, the people I admire see it half full. (3) *Pessimistic people never seem satisfied they often have all they need and more. (4) One woman with whom I work is always complaining. (5) *On Monday she is tired after the weekend, and she dreads the start of a new work week, she should be grateful she has her job and good health to enjoy the weekend. (6) By Wednesday, she begins to whine about the work piled on her desk. (7) *A new project comes her way, she moans about being overworked. (8) *An optimist would see the added responsibility as a sign of the boss's confidence this type of upbeat attitude will make a person happier in the long run. (9) Most of the things the pessimist complains about cannot be changed. (10) *They should be more like optimists, they should look for opportunities in what comes their way.

Challenge 10.5   **Using Periods and Subordinating Conjunctions**

Share the paragraph you revised in Exercise 10.12 with a classmate, and discuss the changes that each of you made. Together, revise the paragraph another time. Use the sentences that you both agree are most effective.

Comma Splices and Run-On Sentences Checklist

☐ Have you remembered that commas cannot serve as connectors?

☐ Have you checked all subject–verb units to determine which ones can stand as simple sentences?

☐ Are you clear on how the connection supplied by a semicolon differs from the connection supplied by a coordinating conjunction?

☐ Have you considered situations for which using a period to separate sentences would be a better choice than connecting them?

☐ Have you considered the dependent relationship created when you use a subordinating conjunction to connect subject–verb units?

Exploring Ideas through Journal Writing

As this chapter shows, comma splices and run-on sentences occur when sentences are incorrectly joined. Eliminating these errors involves correctly linking subject–verb units or correctly separating them. In other words, it's a matter of connection or separation. Now consider connection and separation as they exist in the world. What is the most difficult part of either of these experiences? Think of an incident you've seen or experienced in which connection or separation played an important role. In what ways can either have a positive effect on a person's life—or a negative one? Select some aspect of separation or connection and explore it for 20 to 30 minutes in your journal.

Chapter Quick Check: Comma Splices and Run-On Sentences

The following passage contains a number of commas splices and run-ons. First identify any errors by putting an * in front of each faulty sentence. Then, using the techniques discussed in this chapter, correct the comma splices and run-ons. Check your work to be sure you have used punctuation and capitals correctly.

(Answers may vary. Representative answers are shown.)

(1)*For the past several years, astronomers and scientists have turned their attention far away from Earth ; they have largely ignored regions ∧ closer to home. (2) Meanwhile, our own solar system is still ripe for study and exploration. (3)*For example, a few years ago, some astronomers ar-

. Their

gued for removing Pluto from the list of planets ∧ their reasoning was

based on several criteria common to planets, including Pluto's size. (4)

Now astronomers from the California Institute of Technology have dis-

covered an object some 1 billion miles beyond Pluto. (5)* Experts don't

because

feel the object is a planet ∧ it appears to be only about half the size of

Pluto. (6) It was discovered in an area called the Kuiper Belt. (7)*This

which

area is a cold, dark region, it̶ ∧ extends from Neptune to the edges of the

solar system. (8)* The object ranks as the largest body found in the solar

. Astronomers

system in over 70 years a̶s̶t̶r̶o̶n̶o̶m̶e̶r̶s̶ ∧ have named it Quaoar (pro-

nounced KWA-wahr). (9) This name is drawn from the mythology of na-

tive Americans who originally inhabited the Los Angeles areas. (10)

∧Astronomers are enthusiastic about the possibility of additional discover-

. In

ies in Quaoar's distant neighborhood, i̶n̶ ∧ fact, some scientists look for-

ward to the eventual discovery of objects as large as the Earth in the

Kuiper Belt.

Discovering Connections 10.2

1. For Discovering Connections 10.1 on page 192, you began prewriting
   in response to a quotation by Indira Gandhi or a drawing. Now continue your prewriting on one of these options:
   a. Indira Gandhi offers one view of the purpose of life. Do you agree
      with her, or do you prefer another definition? Explain your own
      view.
   b. In your view, what connections exist between believing, hoping,
      and striving? How can they together affect what one achieves in
      life?
2. Evaluate your prewriting material, identify a focus, and create a draft
   of about 100 words.
3. Exchange your draft with a writing partner. Using the material in this
   chapter as a guide, evaluate the draft you receive, and note any
   comma splices or run-on sentences as well as any other weaknesses.
   Return the draft to the writer.
4. Revise your draft, eliminating any errors that your reader identified.

COLLABORATION

Summary Exercise: Comma Splices and Run-On Sentences

The following passage contains a number of comma splices and run-ons. First, identify any errors by putting an * in front of each faulty sentence. Then, using the techniques discussed in this chapter, correct the comma splices and run-ons. Check your work to be sure you have used punctuation and capitals correctly. (Answers may vary. Representative answers are shown.)

(1) Last year, I went snow skiing for the first time. (2) *Skiing sounded easy enough to me‸before long, I discovered the truth.
                  ; however,

(3) My friend Pat and I left early in the morning and drove up to the mountains. (4) *He already knew how to ski,‸he kept telling me to stop worrying. (5) *He even talked me out of taking a professional lesson‸he promised to teach me himself.
  so   ;

(6) *At the resort, I rented my equipment‸and I also bought a lift pass.
              , and

(7) Pat took me to the beginner's slope first. (8) This area had an old-fashioned rope tow. (9) *He didn't warn me about letting the rope slide through my hands,‸I ended up flat on my face.
  so

(10) Meanwhile, Pat waited for me at the top of the beginner's slope. (11) He demonstrated "snowplowing," a technique for slowing by turning the ski tips inward. (12) *I tried to follow his instructions‸I just went faster.
              , but

(13) Finally, I fell down on purpose to stop myself. (14) *One of my skis fell off and went down the slope by itself‸I had to take off the other ski and walk the rest of the way to the bottom.
              .

(15) I spent the remainder of the morning mastering the beginner's slope. (16) *I finally made a few runs down the hill without falling, I still didn't know how to stop very well. (17) At least I felt a little more confident.
  Although

(18) Then Pat talked me into going on the intermediate slope. (19) *I rode the chair lift to the top of the slope and looked down‸the slope
              ;

seemed more like a cliff than a hill. (20) *Pat told me to ski from side to
side down the mountain, ; he then left me there. (21) I started slowly and
∧
purposely fell to stop myself when necessary. (22) *At the end of my trip
and
down the mountain, I was wet and sore, I just wanted to go home.
∧   , and
(23) *I've been skiing several times since that first trip I'm getting to
∧
be a much better skier. (24) I regularly use the intermediate slope now.
;
(25) *Still, I'll never forget my first time skiing, I couldn't sit down for three
∧
days afterwards.

COMMA SPLICES AND RUN-ON SENTENCES

New Terms in this Chapter	Definitions
● comma splice	● a sentence-combining error in which two simple sentences are joined by only a comma
	Example The wall was covered with graffiti, the ground was covered with litter.
● run-on sentence	● a sentence-combining error in which two simple sentences run together without any punctuation to separate or conjunction to connect them
	Example The nurse took the patient's blood pressure the doctor stitched the wound.

To Identify Comma Splices and Run-On Sentences
1. Identify all subject–verb units.
2. Establish that these units can stand alone.

Four Ways to Correct Comma Splices and Run-On Sentences
1. simple sentence + comma and coordinating conjunction + simple sentence
2. simple sentence + semicolon (+ conjunctive adverb and comma) + simple sentence
3. simple sentence + period + simple sentence
4. simple sentence + subordinating conjunction + simple sentence

Writers' Café

Is there a way that I can feel as comfortable with writing as I do with talking?

Probably not, for a couple of reasons:

- You have been speaking much longer and have done it far more often than you have been writing.
- Writing involves far more rules and conventions—things like punctuation and spelling—than talking does.

But you can certainly become more comfortable with writing, and the answer is ridiculously simple:

- Write more. The more you write, the more ordinary it will seem.

The way I talk doesn't always sound like published writing. Is it all right for me to write the way I talk?

Actually, it depends on how much *slang*—words and expressions used in a different way than most people use them—is involved. Too much slang is a problem because . . .

- slang is understood by some groups but not by others
- slang often violates the conventional rules of grammar and usage

An occasional slang word or expression isn't usually a problem, but more than that can keep your writing from clearly communicating your ideas.

Is there a difference between creative writing and college writing?

Yes, although the labels don't really explain the differences. Both types involve creativity, and both can be part of the writing people do in college. Creative writing aspires to be considered art as well as to express ideas. It appears in forms such as . . .

- short stories
- plays
- novels
- poems
- memoirs

College writing generally focuses on the significance of the information it presents, including

- paragraphs
- essays
- summaries
- research projects
- answers to essay questions

How can I make sure my writing sounds authentic and genuine, not stuffy or overly formal?

Make it sound like *you*, but not as you would talk to your closest family and friends. Instead, think of someone who is one level less familiar than these people, for instance . . .

- your boss
- a new classmate
- a stranger asking you for directions

Then present your ideas in a way that is normal for you, including . . .

- the kind and level of vocabulary you customarily use
- a sentence length that approximates the way you explain things when you speak

You should find the writing that results to be more relaxed and natural-sounding.

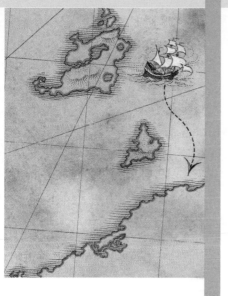

Verbs: Conveying Action and Time

Chapter 11

Maintaining Subject–Verb Agreement

Getting Started... **Q:** Sometimes after I write a sentence and read it back, I notice something doesn't sound right. When I check, I find that the subject and verb don't match up. What can I do to make sure that the subjects and verbs I write are always in agreement?

A: That you are noticing problems in your subject–verb agreement means you are already doing something vital to success as a writer: effective proofreading. But to catch the error before you make it, focus on the verb and the subject in each sentence. If it's a present tense verb, make sure it matches the subject in number. Do that with every sentence you write and you'll be all set.

Overview: Making Sure Subjects and Verbs Agree in Number

For your sentences to be clear and understandable, you must make each subject agree with each verb in terms of number. In other words, singular subjects call for a singular form of a verb, and plural subjects call for a plural form of a verb. This is called **subject–verb agreement.** Although this sounds simple, writers tend to have difficulty with subject–verb agreement in certain kinds of sentence constructions. They may become confused when the verb precedes the subject or when several words come between the subject and the verb. Certain indefinite pronouns, collective nouns, and singular words that appear to be plural can also confuse writers. Subject–verb agreement errors are serious problems for writers because they distract readers from interpreting the meaning of the writing.

In this chapter, you will discover how to avoid agreement problems with

- subjects following verbs

- sentences beginning with *There* or *Here*

- subjects and verbs separated by other words

- compound subjects

- indefinite pronouns, collective nouns, and singular nouns ending in *-s* used as subjects

Discovering Connections 11.1

Consider the following quotation:

Advice is what we ask for when we already know the answer but wish we didn't.

—*Erica Jong*

Or look at this photo.

Now, using the prewriting technique you prefer, do some prewriting about your reaction to the quotation or photo. Save your work.

Maintaining Agreement When the Subject Follows the Verb

In the majority of the sentences you write, the subject comes before the verb. But in many direct questions, part of the verb comes before the subject:

|verb|subject|verb|

EXAMPLE   What *did Ted say?*

|verb|subject| |verb|

EXAMPLE   *Did Joanie* really *turn* him down?

Although maintaining subject–verb agreement with questions is generally not too difficult, the contraction *don't* can sometimes trip you up. For example, look at the use of *don't* in the following questions:

FAULTY   *Don't* Ted *know* how to deal with such a delicate matter?

FAULTY   *Don't* she *understand* how to turn a person down?

Both sentences are incorrect because *don't* is a shortened form of two words: *do not.* But *do* is the verb that agrees with plural subjects, not singular subjects like *Ted* and *she.*

CORRECTED *Doesn't Ted know how to deal with such a delicate matter?*

CORRECTED *Doesn't she understand how to turn a person down?*

Exercise 11.1 **Choosing the Correct Verb When the Subject Follows the Verb**

Fill in the blanks in the questions below with the correct verb taken from the following list, and underline the subject of that verb.

Hasn't *or* Haven't   Does *or* Do   Has *or* Have
Was *or* Were   Doesn't *or* Don't

EXAMPLE ___*Were*___ many good <u>seats</u> still available for the concert on Sunday?

1. ___Have or Haven't___ you enjoyed yourself tonight?

2. ___Does or Doesn't___ that old refrigerator need to be replaced?

3. ___Has or Hasn't___ the leader of our study group called you yet?

4. ___Was___ Karrie the winner of the scholarship?

5. ___Do or Don't___ those in-line skates cost $200?

Exercise 11.2 **Identifying Subjects and Verbs When Subjects Follow Verbs**

All the sentences in the following passage are questions. First circle the proper verb for each sentence from the pair in parentheses, and then underline the subject of that verb.

EXAMPLE (Doesn't, (Don't)) <u>Terry and Lucy</u> want to go with us tonight to see if we can find the comet?

(1) (Doesn't, Don't) people know how easy it is to shop online? (2) (Is, Are) they aware that this kind of shopping is among the fastest-growing areas of the U.S. economy? (3) (Hasn't, Haven't) they received a gift purchased through the Internet or heard of someone who has? (4) (Isn't, Aren't) the many stories of satisfied customers enough to make them at least curious about the type of e-commerce? (5) (Is, Are) concerns about releasing a credit card number stopping them from investigating some of the fine companies doing business over the Internet? (6) Or (has, have) they had a negative experience in the past with some mail-order business? (7) (Isn't, Aren't) they aware that major companies are working hard to make online shopping simple, easy, and fun? (8) (Is, Are) they interested in using their computers for more than just word processing?

Exercise 11.3   **Making Subjects and Verbs Agree When Writing Questions**

Write ten questions on a separate sheet of paper, including five questions that contain the contraction *don't* or *doesn't*. Make sure that you maintain agreement between the subject and verb in each question. (Answers will vary.)

Challenge 11.1   **Checking for Errors with Subjects That Follow Verbs**

Exchange the questions you wrote in Exercise 11.3 with a classmate. Rewrite each question as a statement to verify that the subjects agree with the verbs in each sentence. Suggest any revisions that are necessary to maintain agreement, and return the paper to the writer. (Answers will vary.)

Correcting Errors in Sentences Beginning with *There* and *Here*

Sentences beginning with *there* or *here* occasionally present problems for writers. Only a noun or pronoun can be the subject of a sentence. *There* and *here* are both adverbs, so they can't be subjects. In sentences beginning with either of these words, the subject always comes *after* the verb. A common error is to use the singular form of the verb with a plural subject, as these examples show:

FAULTY   There is several reasons for her success.

FAULTY   Here comes my brothers.

In the first sentence, *is* is a singular verb. *There* can't act as the subject, so you must look for a noun or pronoun that answers the question *there is who or what?* In this case, the answer is *reasons,* which is plural. In the second sentence, the verb is also singular: *comes. Here* can't act as a subject, so the subject follows the verb. Ask *here comes who or what?* and you'll find that the subject is *brothers,* which is plural.

Once you find an error in subject–verb agreement, you'll find it easy to correct. Simply make the two parts agree by changing one of them:

CORRECTED   There *are* several *reasons* for her success.

   or

CORRECTED   There *is* one main *reason* for her success.

CORRECTED   Here *come* my *brothers.*

   or

CORRECTED   Here *comes* my *brother.*

You might also restate the sentence and eliminate *there* or *here* completely:

CORRECTED   Several *reasons* have led to her success.

CORRECTED   My *brothers* are coming.

Exercise 11.4   **Working with Sentences Beginning with *There* or *Here***

Each of the following sentences calls for either *is* or *are.* Underline the subject, and then write the appropriate verb in the space provided.

EXAMPLE   There _____*are*_____ elaborate <u>costumes</u> to make for Lawanda's

performance next week.

(1) There _____are_____ many <u>ways</u> a person can improve study skills. (2) Here _____is_____ <u>one</u> of the best methods to increase reading comprehension: preparing a brief summary of a passage. (3) There _____is_____ <u>something</u> to be gained through restating the ideas of an author in your own words. (4) For one thing, there _____is_____ the <u>value</u> of the work involved in reducing the original passage, which forces you to identify the most important material. (5) Also, there _____is_____ the additional <u>advantage</u> in terms of extra writing practice.

Identifying Subjects and Verbs in Sentences Beginning with *There* or *Here*

In each of the sentences in the following passage, underline the subject and circle the correct verb.

EXAMPLE   There (is,(are)) several <u>reasons</u> why a person might drop out of school.

(1) For anyone seeking a vacation that combines sun and fun, there ((is,) are) no <u>shortage</u> of possible destinations. (2) First, there ((is,) are) <u>Disney World</u>. (3) ((Is,)(Are)) there <u>people</u> in this world who wouldn't want to spend time in the Magic Kingdom and Epcot, with all the wonderful rides and exhibits? (4) Then there (is,(are)) the <u>islands</u> in the Caribbean. (5) Whether it's Aruba or the Virgin Islands, there (is,(are)) many <u>things</u> for tourists to do. (6) There (is,(are)) <u>swimming, snorkeling, deep sea fishing, and sailing,</u> to name only a few. (7) However, there ((is,) are) a <u>vacation</u> destination that ranks at the top of the list for millions each year: Hawaii. (8) There ((is,) are) <u>everything</u> a tourist could ever want to do on this island paradise.

Challenge 11.2 **Eliminating *There* or *Here* Sentence Openings**

Restating a sentence eliminating *there* or *here* can help you maintain agreement. Eliminating these words also can help you write more concise and direct sentences. Working with a classmate, revise five of the sentences in Exercise 11.5, eliminating *there* or *here*. Then, on a separate sheet of paper, explain which version of each sentence is more effective and why.

Maintaining Agreement When Subjects and Verbs Are Separated by Other Words

Often problems with subject–verb agreement occur because words appear between the subject and the verb. In the sentence below, which of the two verbs is correct?

EXAMPLE

> The old scrapbook in the closet under the storage boxes (belongs, belong) to my grandmother.

What is confusing about sentences like this one is that a plural word, *boxes*, comes right before the verb. So you might incorrectly select *belong* because it agrees with *boxes*. But the focus of the sentence is the *scrapbook*, not *boxes*. Therefore, the proper verb choice is *belongs*.

In this sentence, the words that come between the subject and verb are **prepositional phrases:** *in the closet* and *under the storage boxes*. As Chapter 6, "Subjects and Verbs" (page 128), explains, a prepositional phrase consists of a preposition and some noun or pronoun following it that serves as the *object of the preposition*. The *object* of a preposition cannot be the *subject* of a verb. The word *boxes* is the object of the preposition *under*, another reason it cannot be the subject in this sentence.

Here again is the list of *common prepositions,* as well as a list of *common compound prepositions:*

Prepositions

about	before	by	into	over	under
above	behind	despite	like	past	underneath
across	below	down	near	since	unlike
after	beneath	during	of	than	until
against	beside	except	off	through	up
along	besides	for	on	throughout	upon
among	between	from	onto	till	with
around	beyond	in	out	to	within
as	but (except)	inside	outside	toward	without
at					

Compound Prepositions

according to	because of	instead of
along with	in addition to	in the place of
aside from	in front of	next to
as to	in spite of	out of

To ensure that you don't mistake the object of a preposition for the subject of a sentence, always identify any preposition you've used. Once you find a preposition, look for the noun or pronoun following it, and you'll have the complete prepositional phrase. Then put some imaginary parentheses around the phrases, and you may find it easier to identify the real subject, as this version of the sentence shows:

EXAMPLE

The old *scrapbook* [subject] (in the closet) (under the storage boxes) [prepositional phrases]
belongs [verb] to my grandmother.

Another construction that might confuse you is when compound prepositions such as *along with* and *in addition to* introduce prepositional phrases that come between the subject and verb. In the following sentence, which is the correct verb?

EXAMPLE

Dr. Fiscus, along with Dr. Howard and Dr. Fine, (has, have) an office in this building.

If you look at the sentence quickly, you might conclude that because three doctors are mentioned, the verb should be *have*. But the compound preposition *along with* introduces a prepositional phrase. *Dr. Howard* and *Dr. Fine* are the objects of that preposition, so these doctors can't also be part of the subject. Put imaginary parentheses around the prepositional phrase, and ask the question *who or what has/have an office in this building?* The answer is *Dr. Fiscus,* so the correct verb in the sentence above is *has*.

Sometimes, subordinate clauses may come between subjects and verbs, too. A subordinate clause is a group of words that contains a subject and verb but cannot stand on its own. (For more on subordinate clauses, see Chapter 7, page 152.) Which of the verbs in parentheses is the proper choice?

EXAMPLE

The security guards who had been hired at the beginning of the week (was, were) asleep in the back room of the unfinished building.

To check subject–verb agreement in sentences like this, follow the same basic routine: Find the verb in the main clause, put imaginary parentheses around the subordinate clauses, and then ask the question *who or what?* Look at this version of the sentence in the previous example, with the subordinate clause in parentheses:

EXAMPLE

> The *security guards (who had been hired at the beginning of the week)* *were* asleep in the back room of the unfinished building.

(*subject* is labeled above *security guards*)

As you can see, once the subordinate clause is isolated, you can more easily see the essence of the sentence. Now ask the question *who or what was/were asleep?* The answer is *security guards*, which is plural. Therefore, the proper verb choice is *were*.

Exercise 11.6   **Choosing the Correct Verb When Subjects and Verbs Are Separated by Other Words**

In each sentence in the following passage, underline the subject and circle the correct verb.

EXAMPLE

> My <u>relatives</u> from Virginia, who haven't seen my parents in years, (is, (are))
>
> planning to visit us this year.

(1) Electronic <u>books</u>, which a few years ago were just part of science fiction, (is, (are)) now widely available. (2) <u>Technology</u> in development for many years ((has), have) now made it possible for a consumer to use one device to read thousands of paperless books. (3) Some <u>e-books</u>, which are roughly the same size and weight as a hardcover book, (holds, (hold)) as many as 100 books in their memory. (4) <u>Many</u> of these devices (allows, (allow)) a user to download other texts and to add other documents to the text. (5) Right now, the <u>cost</u> for these devices ((runs), run) to $200 or more, but prices are dropping as the technology improves.

Exercise 11.7   **Working with Subjects and Verbs Separated by Other Words**

On a separate sheet of paper, write ten sentences using the prepositional phrases or subordinate clauses listed below to separate the subject and verb. Be sure that your subjects and verbs agree, as the example shows. (Answers will vary.)

EXAMPLE

next to me on the bus

The boy next to me on the bus was asleep.

1. according to educators
2. who worked overtime every day
3. in spite of the discounted price
4. aside from the small fines
5. at the end of each month
6. except for his overdue library books
7. after ten great years
8. next to the chairs in the back of the room

Challenge 11.3   **Evaluating Sentences with Subjects and Verbs Separated by Other Words**

Exchange the sentences you worked on in Exercise 11.7 with a classmate. Underline the subjects, and circle the verbs in the sentences. Suggest any revisions that are necessary to maintain agreement, and return the paper to the writer. (Answers will vary.)

Avoiding Problems with Compound Subjects

Not all the subjects you'll use are individual words. As Chapter 6 shows (page 133), many sentences have *compound subjects*, more than one noun or pronoun connected by a coordinating conjunction. Like subjects that are individual words, some compound subjects are singular and some are plural. The difference depends on what conjunction connects them.

Look at these examples:

EXAMPLE

A small sign and a campaign button (is, are) the only indication of the candidate's presence.

EXAMPLE

Marc or Shelly (know, knows) the address.

For the first sentence, ask the question *who or what was/were the only indication of the candidate's presence?* You'll find that the subject is *A small sign and a campaign button.* These two parts of the subject, *sign* and *button*, are connected by *and,* the conjunction that indicates more than one. Compound subjects connected by *and* are almost always plural. (The exceptions are subjects that are commonly thought of as one, such as pork and beans, peanut butter and jelly, peace and quiet, ham and eggs, and rock and roll.) Therefore, the proper verb choice for this sentence is *are.*

In the second sentence, the situation is different. By connecting the subjects with *or,* you are indicating that only one of them knows the address. Both parts of the compound subject are singular, so for this sentence, the proper verb choice is *knows.* But if the two alternatives were plural, then the proper verb choice would be plural:

EXAMPLE   *Books or magazines make* time spent in a doctor's office easier to bear.

Both parts of the subject are plural, so *make* is the correct verb.

When the compound subject consists of one singular word and one plural word connected by *or,* the verb agrees with the alternative closest to it. What's the correct verb in the following example?

EXAMPLE   The captain or the firefighters (is, are) meeting with the television crew.

Because *firefighters* is closer to the verb, the correct choice is the form that agrees with *firefighters: are.* But if the parts of the subject were reversed, then the proper choice would be *is:*

EXAMPLE   The firefighters or the captain *is* meeting with the television crew.

Exercise 11.8   **Choosing the Proper Verbs for Compound Subjects**

In each sentence in the following passage, underline the subject and circle the correct verb.

EXAMPLE   Either the college president or the union chief (is, are) to blame for the current impasse in contract negotiations.

(1) Neither my brother nor my sister (cares, care) about keeping the house or their own clothes clean. (2) The shirts and pants they wear (is, are) always wrinkled unless someone else irons for them. (3) In addition, Sammy's school-work or books (is, are) always in a disorganized pile in his room. (4) Carla's brushes and makeup (is, are) always spread out

across her bureau. (5) Neither Sammy nor Carla (seems, seem) to be bothered by the messes that result.

Exercise 11.9   **Writing Sentences with Compound Subjects**

On a separate piece of paper, write a sentence for each of the compound subjects below. Make sure you maintain agreement between the subject and verb in each sentence.   (Answers will vary.)

1. Love and marriage
2. The Super Bowl and the World Series
3. Watching television or reading romance novels
4. Math, science, and foreign language
5. The negatives and finished prints
6. Neither the law nor their consciences
7. Red meat, whole eggs, cheese, and nuts
8. Either my parents or my brother

Challenge 11.4   **Evaluating Subject–Verb Agreement with Compound Subjects**

Exchange the sentences you have written for Exercise 11.9 with a classmate. Underline the subjects and verbs in the sentences you receive to check for any errors in subject–verb agreement, and then return the sentences to the writer. (Answers will vary.)

Maintaining Agreement with Indefinite Pronouns

Another potential problem spot with subject–verb agreement concerns the use of **indefinite pronouns.** Writers use indefinite pronouns to refer to general rather than specific persons and things.

The following indefinite pronouns are always singular:

Singular Indefinite Pronouns

another	each	everything	no one	somebody
anybody	either	neither	nothing	someone
anyone	everybody	nobody	one	something
anything	everyone			

Whenever you use one of these singular indefinite pronouns, use a singular verb. Words such as *each, everybody,* and *everyone* may confuse you because they seem to be plural. But they are singular, so they require singular verbs:

EXAMPLE *Everyone* around the accident scene *was* silent.

EXAMPLE *Each is* tricky, but the tenth hole is probably the worst.

Other indefinite pronouns are always plural:

Plural Indefinite Pronouns

both   many
few   several

Whenever you use one of these plural indefinite pronouns, use a plural verb:

EXAMPLE Of the musicians who start groups, *few* ever really *make* any money.

EXAMPLE *Several* of the smaller cars *have received* good ratings from safety agencies.

Still other indefinite pronouns are either singular or plural, depending on the word they refer to in the sentence:

Indefinite Pronouns Affected by the Words That Follow Them

all   more   none
any   most   some

The words on the list above can be either singular or plural depending on what they refer to.
Consider these examples:

SINGULAR *All* of his strength *was* gone.

PLURAL *All* of their jewels *were* missing.

SINGULAR *Some* of her anger *is* justified.

PLURAL *Some* of these regulations *are* ridiculous.

In the first example, *All* refers to *strength,* a singular word, so the proper verb choice is *was*. In the second, though, *All* refers to *jewels,* a plural word, so the proper verb choice is *were*. In the third sentence, *Some* refers to *anger,* a singular word, so the proper verb choice is *is*. But in the final sentence, *Some* refers to *regulations,* a plural word. So *are* is the proper verb choice.

Copyright ©2004 by Pearson Education, Inc.

Exercise 11.10   **Choosing the Correct Verbs for Indefinite Pronoun Subjects**

In each of the sentences in the following passage, underline the subject and circle the correct verb.

> **EXAMPLE**   Nobody at the station (seems, seem) concerned that the train hasn't arrived on time.

(1) Maintaining the proper weight is a lifelong struggle for millions of Americans, and many of the problems these people encounter in life (is, are) related to their weight. (2) For many of these people, it seems as if nobody else (understands, understand) what it is like to be overweight. (3) They often begin to question whether everybody (prejudges, pre-judge) them as lazy or gluttonous just because of their weight. (4) For many overweight people, neither of these adjectives (is, are) accurate. (5) Even though these individuals exercise regularly, nothing (seems, seem) to help them lose weight.

Exercise 11.11   **Working with Indefinite Pronouns as Subjects**

In each of the sentences in the following passage, underline the subject and circle the correct verb.

> **EXAMPLE**   When each of the customers (is, are) more considerate, there won't be so much trash on the floor of the movie theater.

(1) Each mission into space (provides, provide) NASA scientists with more information about the universe. (2) Everyone (has, have) to agree

that initiatives like the Hubble Space Telescope have given us views of the universe that would otherwise not be possible. (3) Right now, however, nobody (seem, *seems*) to be concerned about the threat of budget cuts in this area. (4) Many members of the Congressional Budget Committee (is, *are*) openly critical of NASA. (5) In addition, several members of the committee (argues, *argue*) that the many millions of dollars spent on a single initiative could help to solve real problems here on earth. (6) Yet, as politicians debate the issue, no one (*appears*, appear) to recognize the way that space exploration has changed our world. (7) Many of the advances in the field of communication (is, *are*) the direct result of NASA's work. (8) For example, anyone who watches television broadcast from distant nations (*is*, are) enjoying one small benefit of space exploration.

Challenge 11.5   **Working with Indefinite Pronouns**

"Anything is possible." Have you heard this saying before? Notice that the subject of the sentence, *anything*, is a singular indefinite pronoun and the verb *is* is also singular. Remembering this expression can help you remember that *anything* is singular. Working with a classmate, make a list on a separate sheet of paper of three other familiar sayings or expressions that include indefinite pronouns. Underline the subjects and verbs for each saying you record. (Answers will vary.)

Maintaining Agreement with Collective Nouns, Singular Nouns Ending in -*s*, and Words Indicating Amounts

If a word refers to a group of items or individuals, you might naturally assume that the word would require a plural verb. But for a group of words called *collective nouns,* this is not the case. Collective nouns like *audience, class, committee, faculty, flock, herd, jury, swarm,* and *team* take singular verbs:

EXAMPLE   This season's basketball *team has* already won more games than last year's team.

EXAMPLE   The entire *flock was sitting* on the power line.

Certain animal names can also be confusing because the name for a single animal is the same as the name for a group of animals. For example, *antelope, deer, fish, sheep,* and *trout* might all refer to either one animal or a group of animals. Whether you use a singular or plural form of the verb depends on whether you mean one or more than one, as these examples show:

EXAMPLE   That *moose has broken* out of its holding area.

EXAMPLE   Those *moose look* so peaceful as they stand together near the water tank.

The first sentence deals with *one* moose, so the proper verb choice is a singular verb form, *has broken.* The second sentence deals with many moose, so the proper verb choice in the first clause is the plural verb *look.*

Another confusing group of words are those that look plural but are actually singular. You make most nouns plural by adding *-s.* For this reason, it is easy to make a mistake with nouns that end in *-s* but are nevertheless singular. These words include nouns like *economics, ethics, mumps, measles, mathematics, news, physics,* and *politics.* All of these words are singular and require a singular verb:

EXAMPLE   *Economics is* a difficult subject for the beginner.

EXAMPLE   Because of vaccines perfected over the past 30 years, *measles is* no longer a serious threat to children.

Nouns that writers use to refer to *measurements, money, time,* and *weight* are also singular and call for singular verbs:

EXAMPLE   *Fifty dollars is* much more than any ticket is worth.

EXAMPLE   *Ten minutes was* as long as I could stand the complete quiet.

EXAMPLE   *Forty points was* too big a lead to overcome.

In each of the examples, the subject refers to a unit, so the verb is singular.

Exercise 11.12   **Working with Collective Nouns, Singular Nouns Ending in -s, and Words Indicating Amounts as Subjects**

In each sentence in the following passage, underline the subject and circle the correct verb.

EXAMPLE

I don't understand what all the fuss is about, because I think physics (is, are) the easiest course around.

(1) Last year, Nehi Regional High School was shut down for two weeks; measles (was, were) the reason. (2) When the epidemic first started, the school committee (was, were) unsure what to do. (3) When the committee held an open meeting, the audience (was, were) ready to fight to close the school for two weeks. (4) The committee (was, were) very quiet during the presentations. (5) "Ten days (is, are) a long time, but I guess we don't have a choice," said the committee head after the two-hour meeting.

Exercise 11.13   **Choosing the Correct Verb for Collective Nouns, Singular Nouns Ending in -s Used as Subjects, and Words Indicating Amounts**

In each sentence in the following passage, underline the subject and circle the correct verb.

EXAMPLE

After seeing the marks on the mid-term, the class (was, were) convinced that the instructor was grading unfairly.

(1) Athletics (plays, play) a big part in the life of many Americans, even after their high school and college years. (2) According to several national surveys, forty-five minutes of some kind of athletic activity three times a week (is, are) the amount of time reported by a large percentage of adults. (3) On every night of the week in cities across the United

States, teams of grown men and women (suits, suit) up in organized basketball, hockey, softball, or volleyball leagues. (4) In a recent national news story focusing on a co-ed volleyball league in a mid-sized city, the scheduling committee (acknowledges, acknowledge) the difficulty of keeping up with the number of adults wanting to play. (5) The news story also highlighted how politics (is, are) involved in team selection, with some adults trying to arrange the schedule to make it easier for them to win a championship. (6) Apparently, an audience (motivates, motivate) many of the middle-aged athletes in this league, so they make the league a family affair. (7) League officials noted that fifty fans (is, are) the average crowd. (8) After a big game, the winning team (heads, head) to Phil's, a little diner not far from the health club where the games are played.

Challenge 11.6   **Using Collective Nouns, Singular Nouns Ending in -s, and Words Indicating Amounts as Subjects**

COLLABORATION

Working with a classmate, write sentences on a separate sheet of paper in which you use the following words as subjects:

fifty dollars	news
audience	committee
mathematics	ethics
jury	audience
flock	politics

Maintaining Subject–Verb Agreement Checklist

☐ Have you double checked any questions, especially those beginning with *Don't*, to ensure that subjects and verbs agree?

☐ Have you checked after the verb for any sentences beginning with *there* or *here* to make sure you have identified the actual subject?

☐ Have you made sure you have selected the actual subject of a verb and not a word from a phrase or clause coming between subject and verb?

Continued

■ Have you checked to ensure that you have chosen the correct verb for any compound subjects?

■ Have you used an appropriate verb with any indefinite pronoun used as a subject?

■ Have you double checked your choice of verb with any collective noun, singular noun ending in -s, or noun indicating amount used as a subject to make sure that the subject and verb agree?

Exploring Ideas through Journal Writing

As this chapter shows, written communication fails when subjects and verbs don't match up. It's clear, then, that subject–verb agreement is vital if you want to achieve your goal in writing. How about in life in general? Is it necessary for people on a team, at work, in a relationship, or in a family to agree all the time in order for the individuals to succeed? Is it possible to achieve your goal by holding to your position even if others involved don't agree with you? Explore some aspect of this subject for 20 to 30 minutes in your journal.

Chapter Quick Check: Maintaining Subject–Verb Agreement

The following passage contains various errors in subject–verb agreement. Using the examples throughout the chapter to guide you, identify any errors in agreement. Then correct the errors by writing the correct form over the incorrect one. Some sentences are correct as they are.

(1) The field of biomimicry, one of the most fascinating areas of science to emerge in the past few years, ~~involve~~ *involves* examining some natural process or structure in order to imitate it. (2) Although the name may be new, there ~~are~~ *is* a long history of humans' developing products or procedures based on nature. (3) For example, Velcro, among today's most popular fasteners, ~~owe~~ *owes* its existence to the common cocklebur. *OK* (4) In the 1940s, a Swiss engineer noticed how cockleburs stick to clothing and

hair, studied the process, and developed a system that mimics it. (5) In

other cases, the behaviors or abilities of a particular creature ~~serves~~ as
(serve)

the source for inspiration. (6) For instance, anybody who has observed

the behavior of reptiles ~~know~~ that geckos can cling effortlessly to a vari-
(knows)

ety of surfaces. (7) Now researchers studying this natural phenomenon

~~hopes~~ to imitate the process in order to manufacture reusable adhesive
(hope)

tape. (8) Spider silk, the threads used to create webs that are both elabo-

rate and durable, ~~rank~~ among the strongest and most flexible substances
(ranks)

in all of nature. (9) A Canadian company has recently taken biomimicry
_(OK)_

to a new level by taking the web genes from spiders and inserting them

in the fertilized eggs of goats. (10) The theory behind these efforts ~~hold~~
(holds)

that the milk produced by these goats will contain the makings of spider

silk, to be extracted and used to make lightweight but incredibly strong

fabrics.

Discovering Connections 11.2

COLLABORATION

1. For Discovering Connections 11.1 on page 215 you began prewriting in response to a quotation by Erica Jong or a photo. Now, continue your prewriting on one of these options.
   a. Jong suggests that when people say they want advice, they are really just hoping that what they know is true isn't. Do you agree with Jong's assessment? Why or why not?
   b. Why are some people often unwilling to accept advice that might help them?
2. Evaluate your prewriting material, identify a focus, and create a draft of about 100 words.
3. Exchange your draft with a writing partner. Using the material in this chapter as a guide, evaluate the draft you receive, and note any problems with subject–verb agreement as well as any other weaknesses. Return the draft to the writer.
4. Revise your draft, eliminating any errors that your reader identified.

Summary Exercise: Maintaining Subject–Verb Agreement

The following passage contains various kinds of errors in subject–verb agreement. Using the examples throughout the chapter to guide you, identify any errors in agreement. Then correct the errors by writing the correct form over the incorrect one. Some sentences are correct as they are.

(1) Of all the cars I have owned, my first car, the one in which I had
plenty of good times, ~~were~~ [was] the best. [OK] (2) I owned it for only a year, but

during that year I had plenty of fun with it.
[OK]
(3) When you have a nice car, you worry about it all the time. (4) For

example, if you take it to the mall, you park it carefully so that nobody
else ~~dent~~ [dents] the doors. (5) If it gets dirty, there ~~are~~ [is] a compulsion to clean it

right away. (6) Accidents or a breakdown ~~make~~ [makes] you feel as if a good

friend has been hurt.

(7) A car that has already suffered a few mishaps ~~are~~ [is] a different

thing, as I discovered with my first car. (8) All the people in my neighborhood ~~was~~ [were] a little embarrassed to see it parked in front of my house. (9)
The engine and the transmission ~~was~~ [were] pretty good, but the body was quite

rusty. (10) The interior was pretty worn, too; the stuffing in all the seats
~~were~~ [was] coming out. [OK] (11) In addition, the front seat wouldn't lock in place,

so the passenger in the front moved back and forth whenever the car

stopped and started.

(12) The car, which already had dents in all the doors, ~~were~~ [was] further

damaged a month after I bought it when another car went through a

stop sign and hit the passenger's door broadside. (13) I needed the

money I got from the insurance company for bills, so the door along
with the rest of the damage ~~were~~ [was] never fixed. (14) That left me with only

Does

one door that worked in the front. (15) ~~Do~~ that sound like a luxury limo

to you?

OK

(16) I finally had to get rid of the car after a year when it wouldn't

was

pass inspection. (17) I felt as if a jury ~~were~~ condemning that car to

death. (18) A junkyard in town that specialized in shredding old cars

was

~~were~~ its last destination; my girlfriend and I drove it to its graveyard. (19)

wasn't

Twenty-five dollars ~~weren't~~ much money for a vehicle that had given me

OK

so much fun. (20) My friends told me I was lucky I didn't have to pay the

junkyard to take such an ugly car.

RECAP ## MAINTAINING SUBJECT–VERB AGREEMENT

New terms in this chapter	Definitions
● **subject–verb agreement**	● a state in which the subject and verb agree in number Use the singular form of a verb with a singular subject. Use the plural form of a verb with a plural subject.
● **prepositional phrase**	● a unit consisting of a preposition and a noun or pronoun following it, serving as the object of the preposition
● **indefinite pronoun**	● a pronoun that refers to general rather than specific people and things

Ways to Maintain Agreement

1. When the subject follows the verb:

   in a question ⟶ *Does* Roy *know* the words to that song?

   in a sentence beginning with *There* or *Here* ⟶ There *are* four days left until vacation.

   Identify the verb and ask *who or what?* to find the subject.

2. When the subject and verb are separated by other words:

   prepositional phrases ⟶ The *kitten* (across the hall) *cries* all night.

   subordinate clauses ⟶ The *director* (who treats a cast well) *earns* respect.

   Identify the verb and ask *who or what?* to find the subject.

Continued

Ways to Maintain Agreement

3. When the subject is compound:

with *and* the subject is usually plural ⟶ *Morris and Shirley are* friends.

unless the compound is considered one ⟶ *Bacon and eggs is* his favorite meal.

with *or* the subject can be singular ⟶ *Running or swimming is* my usual daily activity.

with *or* the subject can be plural ⟶ *Muffins or bagels are* good for breakfast.

Find the conjunction and determine what is being connected.

4. When the subject is an indefinite pronoun:

singular ⟶ *Everybody is* well-rested now.

plural ⟶ *Both* of my cousins *are* quite tall.

Use singular verbs with singular pronouns and plural verbs with plural pronouns.

5. When the subject is a collective noun or singular noun ending in -*s*:

collective noun ⟶ The *audience chooses* the contestants.

singular noun ending in -*s* ⟶ *Economics is* known as the dismal science.

If the subject is a unit, use a singular verb.

Singular Indefinite Pronouns

another	each	everything	no one	somebody
anybody	either	neither	nothing	someone
anyone	everybody	nobody	one	something
anything	everyone			

Plural Indefinite Pronouns

both	many
few	several

Indefinite Pronouns Affected by the Words That Follow Them

all	more	none
any	most	some

Chapter 12

Forming Basic Tenses for Regular Verbs

Getting Started... **Q:** I sometimes find it frustrating to figure out the right endings for verbs. In some cases, I add a *-d* or an *-ed* where one isn't needed, and other times I don't add an ending where one is needed. And I'm not always sure when I should put *will* in front of a verb form. Why are there so many forms anyway? More important, how can I keep them straight?

A: The confusion you are facing stems from the fact that verbs have the power to signify different times. This ability enables you to explain what has already happened, what is happening at this moment or on a regular basis, and what will happen. This aspect of verbs, then, works to your advantage as a writer. The secret to avoiding confusion is to identify what general period of time—past, present, or future—you are discussing and check back as you write to make sure that you consistently use the verb ending that signifies that time.

Overview: Understanding the Basic Tenses

As Chapter 6, "Subjects and Verbs," explained, verbs are words that either convey action or indicate a relationship between the subject and other words in a sentence. When you think about it, no words are more important to you as a writer. Without verbs, you would be unable to communicate about events that actually happen or about ideas or possibilities.

Verbs also express time. In other words, they show when an action or situation occurs: in the present, future, or past. The time expressed by a verb is called the **verb tense.** As verbs change their time, or tense, they also change their form. Most verbs are regular, meaning that their tenses change in consistent ways. Using verb tenses correctly is one way to ensure that your writing will convey your ideas clearly.

In this chapter, you'll discover the correct ways to form six basic tenses for regular verbs. You will learn how to use

● present tense to describe an action or situation that is happening now

● future tense to describe an action or situation that has not occurred yet

● past tense to describe an action or situation that has already occurred

● past perfect, present perfect, and future perfect tenses

Discovering Connections 12.1

Consider the following quotation:

There are two ways of meeting difficulties: you alter the difficulties, or you alter yourself to meet them.
—*Phyllis Bottome*

Or look at this photo.
Now, using the prewriting technique you prefer, do some prewriting about your reaction to the quotation or the photo. Save your work.

Using the Present Tense

Writers use the **present tense** to describe a fact, an action that is happening at the moment, or a situation that happens habitually. For regular verbs, the present tense is the same as the basic form, or the word you would use to complete the simplest sentence beginning with *I: I laugh. I climb. I talk.* Look at the following sentences shown in the present tense:

> **EXAMPLE**   My friend *laughs* at all the instructor's bad jokes.

> **EXAMPLE**   Most children *watch* too much television.

For regular verbs, the form of the present tense varies according to the subject. If the subject is singular, it refers to one person or thing. For present tense singular, you add *-s* (or *-es* if the verb ends in *-sh, -ch,* or *-x*) to the end of the basic verb. In the first example, the singular subject *friend* requires a verb ending in *-s: laughs.* (Pronoun subjects follow different guidelines, which are discussed next.)

When the subject is plural, it refers to more than one person or thing. For present tense plural, add nothing to the verb. In the second example, the plural subject *children* means that the basic verb form doesn't change: *watch.*

If these subjects were to change, so would the verbs:

EXAMPLE   My friends *laugh* at all the instructor's bad jokes.

EXAMPLE   The average child *watches* too much television.

In the first example, the plural subject *friends* calls for the basic form *laugh*. In the second, the singular subject *child* now needs a verb with the *-es* ending: *watches*.

Sometimes the subject of a sentence is a *pronoun,* a word that replaces a noun that has been used earlier. In that case, the form of the present tense will vary depending upon which pronoun is used. Look at the table below.

Present Tense Verbs with Pronoun Subjects		
	Singular	**Plural**
First person	I climb.	We climb.
Second person	You climb.	You climb.
Third person	He, She, It climbs.	They climb.

As you can see, you need to add an *-s* or *-es* to the end of the basic verb only when you use the third person singular pronouns *he, she,* or *it.* Even though *I,* the first person pronoun, and *you,* the second person pronoun, are singular, do not add an *-s* to the basic verb form. See Chapter 11, "Maintaining Subject–Verb Agreement," for more information about matching subjects and verbs.

Exercise 12.1   **Working with Subjects and Present Tense Verbs**

Circle the subject, and then underline the correct form of the verb of the two in parentheses in the sentences below. Remember—most singular subjects take a verb ending in *-s* or *-es.* Use the example as a guide.

EXAMPLE   The (birds) (eat, eats) at my backyard feeder every morning.

(1) My (father) (record, records) everything possible using his new video camera. (2) (He) (love, loves) to get our embarrassing moments on tape. (3) Our resident (humorist) (catch, catches) our pants splitting and our bikes falling. (4) (Guests) always (hide, hides) at birthday parties because (they) (know, knows) that Dad is ready and waiting with his

camera. (5) Even though the joke is usually on us, (we) (smile, smiles) at the scenes when we see them.

Exercise 12.2 **Matching Subjects and Present Tense Verbs**

In the following paragraph, choose the verb form that matches the subject. If the subject is singular, circle the singular form of the verb. If it is plural, circle the plural form. Use the example as a guide.

EXAMPLE There is little doubt that Americans (love, loves) going to the movies.

(1) Fast-food chains (need, needs) to find ways to cut their operating costs. (2) One way they (save, saves) money is by opening a restaurant inside another company's store. (3) For example, Starbucks Coffee Company (set, sets) up coffee bars in Barnes & Noble bookstores. (4) Customers in many Wal-Mart stores (take, takes) a break and (enjoy, enjoys) a McDonald's hamburger. (5) This strategy (work, works) well for the fast-food chains. (6) They (lower, lowers) their cost of doing business because they split operating expenses with the other company. (7) In other words, the fast-food restaurant (pay, pays) only part of such expenses as equipment, taxes, and security protection. (8) In exchange, the host company (get, gets) the financial contribution of the fast-food restaurant.

Exercise 12.3 **Working with Subjects and Present Tense Verbs**

In the following paragraph, subjects and verbs are italicized. Rewrite the paragraph on a separate piece of paper. Change the singular subject in each sentence to a plural subject. Then make any change needed to make the verb agree with the subject. Change other words as necessary to make the sentences sensible. Use the example to guide you.

EXAMPLE My *roommate shares* household and grocery expenses with me.

My roommates share household and grocery expenses with me.

(1) A single *mother faces* many challenges caring for her children. (2) This *responsibility requires* energy and dedication. (3) For example, *she plays* the role of both mother and father. (4) This means that on a typical day *she nurtures, disciplines, educates,* and *entertains.* (5) Her *job* never *stops,* either. (6) A *baby demands* around-the-clock care, and a single *mother learns* to live without much sleep. (7) Even a school-aged *child needs* a lot of love and attention. (8) A limited *income increases* a single mother's daily challenges, also. (9) Nevertheless, a single *mother finds* ways to make ends meet. (10) *She sacrifices* and *puts* her own needs last.

Challenge 12.1   Analyzing Present Tense Verbs in Directions

Sometimes present tense verbs are used in directions or process explanations. Read the following paragraph about precautions when you jump-start your car. Then follow the instructions below the paragraph.

Your vehicle's *battery* discharges if *you* leave the lights or any electrical equipment on after *you* turn the engine off. If *this* happens, *you* jump-start your vehicle from a booster battery. WARNING: *Batteries* contain sulfuric acid, which burns skin, eyes, and clothing. If battery *acid* touches someone's skin, eyes, or clothing, *you* immediately flush the area with water for at least fifteen minutes.

1. Working with a classmate, identify the present tense verbs that match the *italicized* subjects in this paragraph. List each of these subjects and verbs on a separate piece of paper.

2. Circle the verbs that end in *-s* or *-es.* Why do they have these endings?

3. Do you think the present tense is the best one to use when giving directions? Explain your answers on the same sheet of paper.

Using the Future Tense

Writers use **future tense** to describe an action that has not occurred yet or a relationship that is to come. You can change regular verbs to future tense by adding *will* to the basic verb.

Note the present tense verb in the following sentence:

PRESENT The hamsters *enjoy* their new, spacious cage.

Now here is the same sentence, with the verb in the future tense.

FUTURE The hamsters *will enjoy* their new, spacious cage.

The sentence now conveys a new meaning. The hamsters do not have a new home yet, but when they get one, they will like it.

In the future tense, the verb endings *-s* and *-es* are not needed. Singular and plural forms are the same. For example, if we give the sentence above a singular subject, the verb ending will stay the same.

FUTURE The hamster *will enjoy* its new, spacious cage.

This means that if you change a sentence written in the present tense with a singular subject to future tense, you need to drop the *-s* or *-es* ending from the verb.

PRESENT Ben *commutes* to work.

FUTURE Ben *will commute* to work.

Exercise 12.4 **Working with Future Tense Verbs**

Change the underlined present tense verbs in the paragraph below to future tense. When you make the change, remember to drop any *-s* or *-es* endings. Write your answers above the underlined verbs. Study the example first.

EXAMPLE
    will buy
Rosemary <u>buys</u> groceries for her elderly neighbors.

  (1) Because of new developments in technology, mass media
will improve   *will transmit*
<u>improve</u>. (2) High definition television <u>transmits</u> clear, sharp video im-
         will hear
ages. (3) Radio listeners <u>hear</u> sounds as sharp as the music on their CDs
       will read
at home. (4) A subscriber <u>reads</u> newspapers delivered to a computer, not
     will buy
a newsstand. (5) We <u>buy</u> books in new digital formats, too.

Exercise 12.5   **Using Future Tense Verbs Effectively**

What do you think will happen in the future? Complete each of the following sentences by adding a future tense verb and a completing thought on the lines provided. Use the example as a guide. (Answers will vary.)

EXAMPLE   The population of cities in Asia and Africa ___*will grow quickly in the*___ *next century* .

1. Even though rap music is controversial, it _____ .

2. Housing prices in cities with a lot of high-tech industry _____ _____ .

3. Even though it's a rugged, risky sport, rock-climbing _____ _____ .

4. Rather than spending eight hours a day, five days a week in the office, more and more workers _____ _____ .

5. College tuition _____ _____ .

6. When they need to search for employment, job hunters _____ _____ .

7. By the year 2020, the U.S. population _____ _____ .

8. Diseases such as cancer and heart disease _____ _____ .

Challenge 12.2 **Analyzing the Use of Future Tense**

Have you used the future tense in your own writing? Bring a paragraph you have written to class. Underline the topic sentence of the paragraph, and list the future tense verbs you used. If you have not used this tense, select a paragraph from one of the reading selections in Part Six, "Discovering Connections through Reading," and use it to complete this challenge. Write its topic sentence, and list its future tense verbs on a separate piece of paper.

Using the Past Tense

Writers use the **past tense** to describe an action or situation that has already occurred. For regular verbs, you can form the past tense by adding *-ed* to the basic verb form. If the basic form ends in *-e,* add *-d.* The endings for singular and plural forms are the same. How would you change the following present tense verbs to the past tense?

EXAMPLE   After midnight, the waitress *cleans* all the sticky tables.

EXAMPLE   The mayoral candidates *promise* to end all corruption at city hall.

In the first sentence, the basic form of the verb is *clean.* Dropping the *-s* and adding *-ed* will change the verb to the past tense: *cleaned.* In the second sentence, the verb *promise* already ends in *-e.* Simply add a *-d* to change it to past tense: *promised.*

The present, future, and past tenses discussed above are called *simple tenses.* Use the following table to review ways to form them.

How to Form Simple Tenses for Regular Verbs (Example verb—walk)

Tenses	Basic or "I" Form	Form for Plural Subjects	Form for Singular Subjects
For the **simple present tense,** use the basic verb form. Add *-s* or *-es* for singular subjects.	I *walk* a mile every day.	Harvey and Sheila *walk* a mile every day.	Norton *walks* a mile every day.
For the **simple future tense,** use the basic verb form plus *will.* Use the same verb form for both singular and plural subjects.	I *will walk* a mile every day.	Harvey and Sheila *will walk* a mile every day.	Norton *will walk* a mile every day.
For the **simple past tense,** use the basic verb form plus *-d* or *-ed.* Use the same verb form for both singular and plural subjects.	I *walked* a mile every day.	Harvey and Sheila *walked* a mile every day.	Norton *walked* a mile every day.

Exercise 12.6   **Working with Past Tense Verbs**

The underlined verbs in the sentences below are in the present tense. Change them to the past tense by adding -d or -ed. You may first have to drop the -s or -es ending if the verb is singular. Write the past tense verbs in the space above each present tense verb. Use the example as a guide.

EXAMPLE

hesitated
I hesitate too long at that busy intersection, and the light changes.
changed

created   baked
1. Gwenetta creates a masterpiece when she bakes a cake.
included
2. The cake includes both vanilla and chocolate layers.
frosted
3. She frosts each layer with a rich chocolate cream.
decorated
4. Fresh raspberries decorate the top.
looked   tasted
5. The final result looks delicious and tastes even better.

Exercise 12.7   **Using Past Tense Effectively**

Use the following list of verbs to complete the paragraph below. Put all verbs into the past tense by adding -d or -ed. Write the past tense verb in the appropriate blank.

arrive	disagree	happen	post	repair
ask	fill	install	print	

(1) Recently the highway department ___repaired___ a very dangerous road. (2) Road crews ___filled___ the potholes. (3) They also ___installed___ guardrails along the sides of the road. (4) All of this mending ___happened___ only after thirty-four people had been killed or injured over a period of seventeen years. (5) The situation continued so long because state officials and county officials ___disagreed___ about who was responsible for maintaining the road. (6) Local citizens finally ___asked___ the federal government to get involved. (7) They formed a committee that ___printed___ flyers and ___posted___ them on bulletin boards all over the county. (8) Their

efforts paid off when the highway department crew _____arrived_____ to

make Route 6 safe for motorists.

Challenge 12.3   **Analyzing the Use of Past Tense**

Do you use the past tense in your writing? Bring a paragraph you have written to class. Underline the topic sentence, and list the past tense verbs. If you have not used any, find examples of past tense verbs in a paragraph from one of your textbooks or a magazine article to complete this challenge. Write out the topic sentence and list the past tense verbs on a separate piece of paper.

Using the Perfect Tenses

Writers use another verb form called the **past participle** to form additional tenses: past perfect, present perfect, and future perfect. All of the perfect tenses are formed by adding one of the helping verbs shown below to the past participle of a verb. For regular verbs, the past participle is the same as the simple past tense: the basic verb form plus -d or -ed.

This chapter discusses, perfect tense verbs that use *has, have,* or *had* as helping verbs. Chapter 15, "Additional Elements of Verb Use," will discuss progressive tense verbs that use *am, is, was,* and *were* as helping verbs.

To form the perfect tense of a regular verb, add a helping verb to the past participle (the *-ed* form) as shown below.

Helping Verbs That Form Perfect Tenses

Helping Verb	+	Past Participle	→	Perfect Tense
had		walked		had walked
has		walked		has walked
have		walked		have walked

Past Perfect Tense

As the time line below shows, the **past perfect tense** indicates actions or situations that happened a little further back in time than actions in the simple past tense. For regular verbs, form the past perfect tense by adding *had* to the past participle.

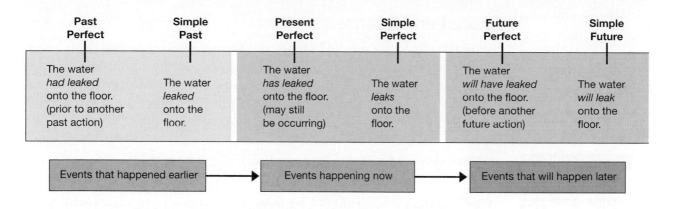

Look at the following pairs of sentences:

SIMPLE PAST   We *planned* the surprise party.

PAST PERFECT   We *had planned* the surprise party before Jack said he didn't want one.

SIMPLE PAST   We *sent* out invitations.

PAST PERFECT   We *had sent* out invitations, too.

As you can see, the simple past and the past perfect forms of these verbs express slightly different meanings. In each instance, the past perfect tense expresses an action that was completed in the past, *before* some other past action. Jack said he wanted no party. Before that, the party planners had already planned the party and sent out invitations.

Present Perfect Tense

When you add *has* or *have* to a past participle, the resulting verb expresses an action that occurred at some indefinite time in the past, or that occurred in the past and is still going on. These verbs are in the **present perfect tense.** Look at these sentences:

PRESENT PERFECT   The park workers *have cleaned* up the playground.

PRESENT PERFECT   My friend Maya *has studied* dance for ten years.

The present perfect verb in the first sentence shows that the workers have completed their task, although the time of completion is indefinite. In the second sentence, the present perfect verb states that Maya's dance lessons began in the past and still continue.

Future Perfect Tense

As the time line on page 247 shows, the **future perfect tense** refers to actions or events that you expect to be completed in the future before some other future event or action. For regular verbs, this tense is easy to form. Just add the word *will* to the *have* form of the present perfect tense. Look at the example below:

PRESENT PERFECT   A lot of eerie events *have happened* on Halloween night.

FUTURE PERFECT   A lot of eerie events *will have happened* by the end of Halloween night.

In the first sentence, *have happened* is a verb in the present perfect tense. It describes events that were completed in the past at unspecified times. In the second sentence, the future perfect tense verb *will have happened* describes events that will occur in the future. However, they will occur before the end of Halloween night, which is even further in the future.

Exercise 12.8   **Using Perfect Tenses**

Change the present tense verb in parentheses in each sentence below to a perfect tense verb. Add a helping verb (*has, had,* or *have,* plus *will* for future perfect tense) to the past participle of the verb. Use the examples as a guide.

EXAMPLES   Tre (works) ___has worked___ in his journal every week for the past year.

Jeannetta (fills) ___will have filled___ two journals by the end of the year.

(1) Very severe headaches (plague) ___have plagued___ my life for the past year. (2) Even though the doctor (administers) ___has administered___ several tests, including a CAT scan, she cannot diagnose the source of my pain. (3) Since last Thursday, I (suffer) ___have suffered___ from a headache. (4) Thank goodness I (call) ___had called___ the doctor to ask for a new prescription just before this headache began. (5) If the medication doesn't block the pain, I (stay) ___will have stayed___ home from work a total of six days by next Monday.

Exercise 12.9   **More Practice Using the Perfect Tense**

The following paragraph contains some errors in verb tense. In some cases, the participle form of the verb is incorrect. In other cases, the participle form is correct, but the helping verb (*have, has,* or *had*) is either incorrect or missing. Put a line through any incorrect verb form, and write the correct form above it.

EXAMPLE

> Throughout history, the president of the United States ~~have~~ *has* always been a man.

(1) Gun control legislation ~~have~~ *has* become a highly controversial topic. (2) Many people ~~has~~ *have* suggested laws that would require guns to be registered or laws that would restrict the number of guns one person can purchase. (3) Other people said that guns should be banned altogether. (4) Congress ~~have~~ *has* ᐱ proposed a number of gun control measures, but not one of the measures has been approved yet. (5) Despite the heated debate, studies ~~has~~ *have* shown that both gun owners and non gun owners in the United States favor gun control measures.

Exercise 12.10   **Using the Basic Tenses in Your Writing**

COLLABORATION

Working with a writing partner, select *two* of the following topic sentences. Draft a paragraph of at least five sentences for *each* topic. As you write, be sure you use verbs in the appropriate tense to signify when the action or situation occurs.

1. The content of television shows will change for the better in the future.

2. I manage my time away from my classes very well.

3. When I was a child, I loved to celebrate Halloween.

4. Rude people in public places like restaurants have annoyed me for years.

Challenge 12.4 **Analyzing Verb Tense Use in Others' Writing**

Exchange one of the paragraphs you completed in Exercise 12.10 with another pair of writing partners. Underline each verb, and identify its tense. Return the paragraph, and suggest any changes needed in verb tense or subject–verb agreement.

Forming Basic Tenses for Regular Verbs Checklist

☐ Have you used an appropriate present tense verb when discussing a situation or relationship that is happening now or that happens regularly?

☐ Have you chosen the appropriate ending—an -s for singular subjects—for all present tense verbs?

☐ Have you used an appropriate future tense verb, including *will*, when discussing a situation or relationship that has yet occurred?

☐ Have you used an appropriate past tense verb—with the correct -d or -ed ending—when discussing a situation or relationship that has already occurred?

☐ Have you used an appropriate perfect tense—with the correct form of *to have* and the past participle or -ed form of the verb—when discussing a situation or relationship that (1) has happened and may still be happening or (2) will happen before some other situations or relationships in the future?

Exploring Ideas through Journal Writing

When it comes to writing, *tense* refers to *time*. By shifting tense, writers can take control of time. In life in general, it's not so easy. Time is a commanding force, one that no one can challenge or control. Clocks tick, and time passes. There is no stopping it, and there is no getting it back. In what aspect of your life does time play the greatest role? What do you do to help manage time? Does time pass more quickly for a child? For someone who is elderly? For someone like yourself? Consider one of these questions or some other aspect of time, and then explore it in your journal for 20 to 30 minutes.

Chapter Quick Check: Forming Basic Tenses for Regular Verbs

Underline the verbs in the following sentences. Then write the name of the verb tense above the verb.

present
(1) Of all the senses, smell possesses the greatest power to recreate

present perfect
sensations. (2) Until recently, business and industry have failed to take

advantage of these characteristics. (3) Today, however, a number of com-

present perfect
panies have begun to experiment with odor in their day-to-day opera-

present
tions. (4) For example, one international airline pumps the aroma of cut

present
grass into their lounges. (5) This pleasant fragrance gives passengers

waiting for a flight the sensation of a world far beyond the concrete and

past
asphalt runways. (6) Drivers often used to talk about new car odor as

one of the highlights of the process of buying a car. (7) Soon, in addi-

future
tion to new car smell, some cars will have aroma systems to calm the

driver in the face of traffic jams or other irritating situations. (8) The

present
technology to deliver a variety of aromas on demand already exists. (9)

present
The scenting device, with more than 100 odors available, links up to a

present
computer. (10) At the push of a button, the aroma system enhances the

user's work environment.

Discovering Connections 12.2

1. For Discovering Connections 12.1 on page 238, you began prewriting in response to a quotation by Phyllis Bottome or a photo. Now, continue your prewriting on one of these options:
   a. Phyllis Bottome offers two options for dealing with difficulties. Which of the two options is more difficult to achieve? Why?
   b. When you face a difficult situation, what solution do you routinely pursue? Explain.
2. Evaluate your prewriting material, identify a focus, and create a draft of about 100 words.
3. Exchange your draft with a writing partner. Using the material in this chapter as a guide, evaluate the draft you receive, and note any problems with the simple tenses of regular verbs as well as any other weaknesses. Return the draft to the writer.
4. Revise your draft, eliminating any errors that your reader identified.

COLLABORATION

Summary Exercise: Forming Basic Tenses for Regular Verbs

Underline the verbs in the following sentences. Then write the name of the verb tense above the verb.

(1) Undisturbed, most teenagers will sleep [*future*] late in the morning. (2) They also like [*present*] nightlife. (3) Parents hope [*present*] for an early teen bedtime, usually with no success. (4) Scientists have discovered [*present perfect*], though, that teens' biological clocks contribute [*present*] to this pattern. (5) This new theory joins [*present*] the information that scientists have accumulated [*present perfect*] about sleep.

(6) We know [*present*] a lot about sleep now. (7) For example, without sleep we cannot think [*present*] clearly. (8) Sleep requirements depend [*present*] on age, however. (9) Babies sleep [*present*] the most, and adults will need [*future*] less as they age. (10) No one stays [*present*] still when he or she sleeps [*present*]. (11) The movement helps [*present*] our circulation. (12) If a muscle cramps [*present*], we usually wake up [*present*].

(13) Scientists have studied [*present perfect*] dreams, too. (14) We all dream [*present*] every night. (15) Researchers have watched [*present perfect*] rapid eye movements beneath a sleeper's eyelids. (16) These movements occur [*present*] only during dreams. (17) Scientists have determined [*present perfect*] that women and children dream [*present*] more than men, and dreams get [*present*] longer as the night goes [*present*] on. (18) People will yawn [*future*] and feel [*future*] wider awake. (19) A yawn increases [*present*] oxygen supply. (20) No one knows [*present*] why the yawn is [*present*] contagious.

RECAP   **FORMING BASIC TENSES FOR REGULAR VERBS**

New terms in this chapter	Definitions
● **verb tense**	● the form of a verb that indicates when the action or situation occurs: in the past, present, or future

New terms in this chapter	Definitions
● **present tense**	● the basic form of the verb plus *-s* or *-es* if the subject is singular ● used to show a fact, an action, or a situation now going on or occurring habitually Change the form of the verb to match the subject. *Example* The cat *cries* all night outside my window. The cats *cry* all night outside my window.
● **future tense**	● the basic form of a verb plus *will* ● used to show action or state of being that will occur later *Example* The cat *will* stay inside tonight.
● **past tense**	● the basic form of a verb plus *-ed* or *-d* ● used to show action or state of being that has already occurred *Example* The cat *stayed* outside and *cried*.
● **past participle**	● for regular verbs, a form created by adding *-d* or *-ed* to the basic form ● used with a helping verb to form the perfect tenses *Example* Martha had *ended* the relationship months ago.
● **past perfect tense**	● the past participle plus the helping verb *had* ● used to express action completed in the past, before some other past action *Example* The cat *had eaten* all its food and cried for more.
● **present perfect tense**	● the past participle plus the helping verb *has* or *have* ● used to express action completed at some indefinite time in the past or occurring in the past and still continuing *Example* The cat *has eaten* all its food. *Continued*

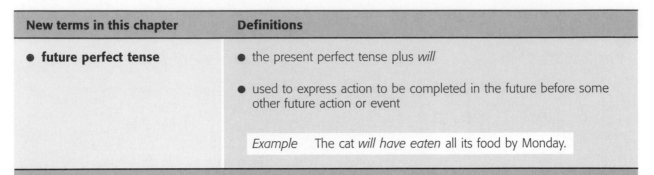

New terms in this chapter	Definitions
● **future perfect tense**	● the present perfect tense plus *will* ● used to express action to be completed in the future before some other future action or event *Example* The cat *will have eaten* all its food by Monday.

Forming the Simple and Perfect Tenses

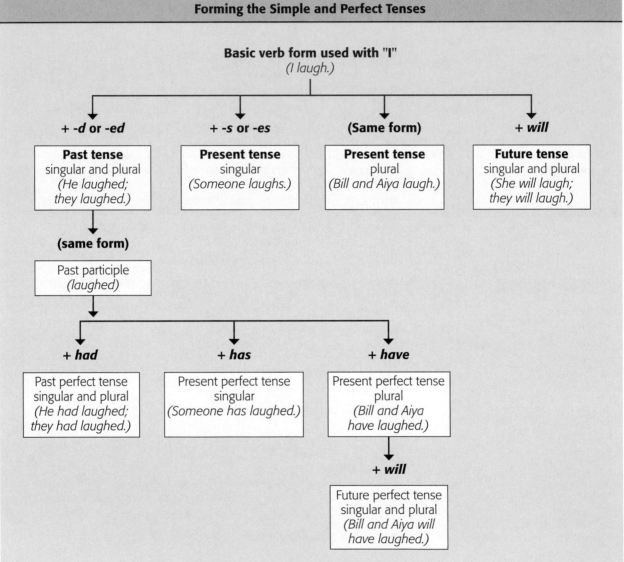

Basic verb form used with "I"
(I laugh.)

+ -d or -ed

Past tense
singular and plural
*(He laughed;
they laughed.)*

+ -s or -es

Present tense
singular
(Someone laughs.)

(Same form)

Present tense
plural
(Bill and Aiya laugh.)

+ will

Future tense
singular and plural
*(She will laugh;
they will laugh.)*

(same form)

Past participle
(laughed)

+ had

Past perfect tense
singular and plural
*(He had laughed;
they had laughed.)*

+ has

Present perfect tense
singular
(Someone has laughed.)

+ have

Present perfect tense
plural
*(Bill and Aiya
have laughed.)*

+ will

Future perfect tense
singular and plural
*(Bill and Aiya will
have laughed.)*

Chapter 13

Using Irregular Verbs Correctly

Getting Started... **Q:** Of the verbs I use, I have the most trouble with the irregular ones. The regular verbs, the ones that end in *-d* or *-ed*, I can handle just fine. But the verbs that don't follow the rules are really confusing. Without consistent rules to guide me, how can I keep the forms for irregular verbs straight?

A: You are correct—keeping the forms of irregular verbs straight is a big challenge for writers. And, true, there is no rule to guide you in using them, as there is for regular verbs. The only good news is that you probably don't have difficulty with all irregulars. To master the verbs you do have difficulty with, go through the list of common irregulars in this chapter. Highlight the ones you have trouble with, and then memorize them. This strategy isn't foolproof, but it will go a long way in helping you master this difficult aspect of writing.

Overview: Learning to Use Verbs That Do Not Follow the Rules

In Chapter 12, "Forming Basic Tenses for Regular Verbs," you learned how to form verbs in the six basic tenses. The rules explained there work for regular verbs, but English is a complicated language. A number of the verbs you will use in your writing are irregular. **Irregular verbs** do not follow these rules. Fortunately, you do not have to memorize all the irregular verb tenses in order to use them effectively in your writing. In fact, you already know the basic tenses of many irregular verbs that you use often. As you learn more about these verbs, you'll discover new ways to form sentences that describe past, present, and future actions.

> ***To help with your writing, this chapter provides a list you can use to look up unfamiliar irregular verbs. You will learn***
>
> ● the present, past, and past participle forms of irregular verbs
>
> ● some helpful strategies for grouping and remembering irregular verbs

Copyright ©2004 by Pearson Education, Inc.

Consider the following quotation:

Nothing in life is to be feared. It is only to be understood.

—*Marie Curie*

Or look at this photo.

Now, using the prewriting technique you prefer, do some prewriting about your reaction to the quotation or photo. Save your work.

A List of Irregular Verbs

You should keep the following list handy whenever you write. Refer to it to check how to form the past tense or past participle form of a verb. If the verb you are searching for is not on the list, it is probably regular. In that case, you can use the rules you learned in Chapter 12. If you are still unsure about whether your verb is regular or irregular, however, you can look it up in the dictionary. The past tense will appear in brackets right after the listing for the word.

As you read through the list below, remember that all irregular verbs use a helping verb with the past participle to form the perfect tense.

Irregular Verb Forms

Present Tense	Past Tense	Past Participle (+ *had, has, have*)
am/is/are	was, were	been
arise	arose	arisen
awaken	awoke, awaked	awoke, awaked
become	became	become
begin	began	begun
bend	bent	bent
bind	bound	bound
bite	bit	bitten, bit
bleed	bled	bled
blow	blew	blown
break	broke	broken
bring	brought	brought
build	built	built
burn	burned, burnt	burned, burnt
burst	burst	burst
buy	bought	bought
catch	caught	caught

Irregular Verb Forms (continued)

Present Tense	Past Tense	Past Participle (+ *had, has, have*)
choose	chose	chosen
cling	clung	clung
come	came	come
cost	cost	cost
creep	crept	crept
cut	cut	cut
deal	dealt	dealt
dig	dug	dug
dive	dived, dove	dived
do/does	did	done
draw	drew	drawn
dream	dreamed, dreamt	dreamed, dreamt
drink	drank	drunk
drive	drove	driven
eat	ate	eaten
fall	fell	fallen
feed	fed	fed
feel	felt	felt
fight	fought	fought
find	found	found
flee	fled	fled
fling	flung	flung
fly	flew	flown
forbid	forbade, forbad	forbidden
forget	forgot	forgotten, forgot
freeze	froze	frozen
get	got	got, gotten
give	gave	given
go/goes	went	gone
grind	ground	ground
hang	hung	hung
hang (execute)	hanged	hanged
have/has	had	had
hear	heard	heard
hide	hid	hidden, hid
hold	held	held
hurt	hurt	hurt
keep	kept	kept
kneel	knelt, kneeled	knelt, kneeled
knit	knit, knitted	knit, knitted
know	knew	known
lay	laid	laid
lead	led	led
leap	leaped, leapt	leaped, leapt
leave	left	left
let	let	let
lie	lay	lain
light	lighted, lit	lighted, lit

Continued

Irregular Verb Forms (continued)

Present Tense	Past Tense	Past Participle (+ *had, has, have*)
lose	lost	lost
make	made	made
mean	meant	meant
meet	met	met
mistake	mistook	mistaken
pay	paid	paid
plead	pleaded, pled	pleaded, pled
prove	proved	proved, proven
put	put	put
quit	quit	quit
raise	raised	raised
read	read	read
ride	rode	ridden
ring	rang	rung
rise	rose	risen
run	ran	run
say	said	said
see	saw	seen
seek	sought	sought
sell	sold	sold
send	sent	sent
set	set	set
sew	sewed	sewn, sewed
shake	shook	shaken
shine	shone, shined	shone, shined
shine (polish)	shined	shined
shoot	shot	shot
show	showed	shown, showed
shrink	shrank, shrunk	shrunk, shrunken
shut	shut	shut
sing	sang, sung	sung
sit	sat	sat
sleep	slept	slept
slide	slid	slid
sling	slung	slung
slink	slunk, slinked	slunk, slinked
sow	sowed	sown, sowed
speak	spoke	spoken
speed	sped, speeded	sped, speeded
spell	spelled	spelled
spend	spent	spent
spit	spit, spat	spit, spat
spring	sprang, sprung	sprung
stand	stood	stood
steal	stole	stolen
stick	stuck	stuck
sting	stung	stung
stink	stank, stunk	stunk
stride	strode	stridden

Irregular Verb Forms (concluded)

Present Tense	Past Tense	Past Participle (+ *had, has, have*)
strike	struck	struck, stricken
string	strung	strung
strive	strived, strove	striven, strived
swear	swore	sworn
sweat	sweat, sweated	sweat, sweated
swell	swelled	swelled, swollen
swim	swam	swum
swing	swung	swung
take	took	taken
teach	taught	taught
tear	tore	torn
tell	told	told
throw	threw	thrown
understand	understood	understood
wake	woke, waked	woken, waked, woke
wear	wore	worn
weave (make cloth)	wove, weaved	woven, weaved
weave (sway)	weaved	weaved
weep	wept	wept
win	won	won
wind	wound	wound
wring	wrung	wrung
write	wrote	written

Strategies for Mastering Irregular Verbs

As you can see, it would be hard to memorize all the irregular verb forms. You may want to use a few strategies to help you remember certain words, however. One strategy is to identify and group irregular verbs that follow the same pattern. Some keep the same form for present tense, past tense, and past participle:

Present	*Past*	*Past Participle*
burst	burst	burst
cut	cut	cut
let	let	let
read	read	read

A number of other irregular verbs have the same form for both past tense and past participle:

Present	Past	Past Participle
bring	brought	brought
feel	felt	felt
mean	meant	meant
teach	taught	taught

Other irregular verbs change the same way as they move from present to past tense. In the list below, note that all the present tense forms have an *i*, all the past tense forms have an *a*, and all the past participles have a *u*:

Present	Past	Past Participle
begin	began	begun
drink	drank	drunk
ring	rang	rung
sing	sang	sung

Still other irregular verbs have past participles that are formed by adding an *-n* at the end of the present tense:

Present	Past	Past Participle
blow	blew	blown
grow	grew	grown
know	knew	known
throw	threw	thrown

Going through the entire list of irregular verbs and completing these groupings may help you remember them better.

If these lists seem confusing, keep in mind that you probably use most of the irregular verbs properly when you speak. Therefore, another technique is to identify and highlight those verbs that do give you trouble. Then, rather than wasting time on words you already know, you can focus on your smaller list of troublesome verbs.

An effective way to learn irregular verbs is to write a series of related practice sentences using the three forms of the verb. For the verbs *feel* and *sell,* for instance, you could write sentences like these:

EXAMPLE   I *feel* happy today. Yesterday, I *felt* sad. On many occasions, I *have felt* even sadder.

EXAMPLE   My aunt *sells* cars. Yesterday, she *sold* a Jeep. On many occasions, she *has sold* luxury cars.

Exercise 13.1   **Working with the Tenses of Irregular Verbs**

Complete the following paragraph by writing an appropriate verb in each blank. Change each irregular present tense verb in parentheses to the past participle form, and add a helping verb (*has, had,* or *have*) to create a perfect tense verb. Refer to the list on pages 256–259 if you need help. Use the example as a guide.

EXAMPLE

When you have learned to manage time, you (lay) _____ *have laid* _____

the foundations for success.

(1) Now that I (take) _____ have taken _____ a study skills course, I am no longer scared by the thought of a history test. (2) Before, even though I knew I (read) _____ had read _____ the chapter in the textbook, I did not feel prepared. (3) I (spend) _____ had spent _____ time studying, but I had studied the wrong way (4) I learned in study skills how to connect information in the new chapter with material I (understand) _____ had understood _____ in the previous chapter. (5) This course (teach) _____ has taught _____ me how to analyze ideas.

Exercise 13.2   **Using the Tenses of Irregular Verbs Effectively**

Practice using the forms of the irregular verbs listed below. On a separate sheet of paper, write three related sentences using the present tense, past tense, and the past participle with *have, has,* or *had* to create a perfect tense verb. Use the example to guide you. (Sentences will vary.)

EXAMPLE

write

I write letters to my girlfriend in the Navy every day.

I wrote letters to my girlfriend in the Navy when she was overseas.

I had written letters to my girlfriend in the Navy before we broke up.

1. grow	3. keep	5. shut	7. dream	9. rise
2. go	4. stand	6. begin	8. win	10. leave

Exercise 13.3   **Mastering the Tenses of Irregular Verbs**

Help yourself learn the forms of irregular verbs by grouping them into "families" that follow the same pattern. Find and write verbs from the list on pages 256–259 that fit under each of the following headings:

1. Verbs with the Same Form for Present Tense, Past Tense, and Past Participle

2. Verbs with the Same Form for Past Tense and Past Participle

3. Verbs with an *i* in the Present Tense, an *a* in the Past Tense, and a *u* in the Past Participle Form

Now, study these lists and decide which irregular verbs cause you the most trouble. Compile your own list of "problem verbs," and keep it within easy reach for reference.

Challenge 13.1   **Sorting Irregular Verbs by Pattern**

1. Write a paragraph that uses at least five of the following verbs in the present tense form:

to do	to feel	to wash
to have	to need	to see

2. Exchange your paragraph with a partner. Rewrite your partner's paragraph, substituting a past participle form and helping verb for each present tense verb. For help with the irregular verbs, consult the list on pages 256–259.

Forming Basic Tenses for Irregular Verbs Checklist

- ☐ Have you checked any irregular verb to make sure you have used the correct form?

- ☐ Have you included the correct form of *to have* (*has, have,* or *had*) with any irregular past participles you have used as verbs?

- ☐ Have you made yourself familiar with the irregular verbs that keep the same form for present, past, and past participle and used them properly?

- ☐ Have you made a note of the irregular verbs that have the same past and past participle form and used them correctly?

- ☐ Have you considered the irregular verbs that follow the same pattern for present, past, and past participle and used them properly?

- ☐ Have you memorized the irregular verbs that have past participle ending in *-n* and used them correctly?

Exploring Ideas through Journal Writing

With verbs, irregular means that these words don't follow predictable patterns as they change form. But in life in general, irregular has many other meanings. For instance, garments that are marked *irregular* have some defect or blemish. If it is a small problem, irregular can mean a big bargain. If a financial report is irregular, however, it means big trouble for someone. When it comes to the way we behave, irregular means unusual or other than ordinary. Consider these and other meanings of *irregular* and then write in your journal for 20 to 30 minutes on the consequences when some aspect of life doesn't conform to the typical pattern.

Chapter Quick Check: Using Irregular Verbs Correctly

Complete each sentence in the following passage with the correct verb form. Fill in the blank with the past or perfect form (past participle plus *have, has,* or *had*) of the verb in parentheses. Refer to the list of irregular verbs in this chapter for help.

(Answers may vary somewhat between past and perfect forms.)

(1) No doubt bullying or other cruel behavior always (take) _____ has taken _____ place among middle and high school age students. (2) In recent years, though, some experts (write) _____ have written _____ about this conduct among pre-teen and teenage girls in particular. (3) The stories in these books and reports (make) _____ made, have made _____ the public aware of a world of fierce competition, great cruelty, and intense insecurity. (4) The girls at the top of the pecking order (take) _____ have taken, took _____ advantage of their popularity to control the behavior and loyalty of others. (5) From their position in this hierarchy, the most popular girls (recognize) _____ recognized, have recognized _____ the girls with the greatest desire for popularity. (6) Within a brief period of time, this second group of girls, desperate to be accepted, (become) _____ has become, became _____ the agents of the girls at the top. (7) Soon, the two

groups of girls (begin) __have begun, began__ campaigns of negative behavior, including spreading rumors, name-calling, and shunning, against other girls in the school. (8) None of the victims (do) __did, had done__ anything to earn this abuse. (9) Rather, the other two groups (choose) __had chosen, chose__ to victimize this third group to maintain their own positions in this strange hierarchy. (10) Their experiences (show) __showed, had shown__ them the consequences awaiting those at the bottom of the heap.

Discovering Connections 13.2

COLLABORATION

1. For Discovering Connections 13.1 on page 256, you began prewriting in response to a quotation by Marie Curie or a photo. Now, continue your prewriting on one of these options:
   a. What point is Marie Curie making about the relationship between knowledge and fear?
   b. What kinds of things would people no longer fear if they understood them better?
2. Evaluate your prewriting material, identify a focus, and create a draft of about 100 words.
3. Exchange your draft with a writing partner. Using the material in this chapter as a guide, evaluate the draft you receive, and note any problems with irregular verbs as well as any other weaknesses. Return the draft to the writer.
4. Revise your draft, eliminating any errors that your reader identified.

Summary Exercise: Using Irregular Verbs Correctly

Each sentence in the following passage should be completed with the correct verb form. Fill in each blank with the past tense of the verb in parentheses. Most of the verbs are irregular; refer to the list of irregular verbs in this chapter for help.

(1) In Greece, drama (begin) __began__ as early as the sixth century B.C. (2) The original form it (take) __took__ is not

known for certain. (3) Probably a chorus danced, (tell) _____told_____

stories, or (give) _____gave_____ speeches as part of ceremonies

honoring the god Dionysus. (4) Eventually, the playwrights (add)

_____added_____ one, two, and then three actors who (talk)

_____talked_____ to this chorus. (5) Citizens (come) _____came_____ to

watch plays during a religious festival in the spring. (6) The festival,

called the Dionysia, (last) _____lasted_____ four days.

(7) The audience (sit) _____sat_____ very far away from the ac-

tors. (8) The theaters (are) _____were_____ huge. (9) Because the

Greeks (build) _____built_____ them on the side of a hill, spectators

sat in tiers, looking down. (10) One theater in the city of Epidaurus

(hold) _____held_____15,000 people. (11) The audience (look)

_____looked_____ down on actors and the chorus, who (stand)

_____stood_____ in a flat, circular area called the *orchestra*. (12) The

only set (is) _____was_____ a building known as the *skene*. (13) The ac-

tors (wear) _____wore_____ masks that made their voices louder when

they (speak) _____spoke_____ their lines. (14) The audience (read)

_____read_____ the actors' emotions by the expression on the masks.

(15) Masks also (hide) _____hid_____ the fact that the actors (is)

_____were_____ all men. (16) The audience (hear) _____heard_____

and (understand) _____understood_____ the plays very well.

(17) Unfortunately, the world (lose) _____lost_____ most of these

plays long before scholars had the chance to study them. (18) However,

the plays that survived (become) _____became_____ some of the most

beloved of all time. (19) We still enjoy the plays of Aeschylus, Sophocles,

and Euripides thousands of years after these great playwrights (write)

_____wrote_____them. (20) They (bring) _____brought_____ the legend

of their culture alive.

RECAP

USING IRREGULAR VERBS CORRECTLY

New term in this chapter	Definition
● irregular verbs	● verbs that do not form their tenses in regular, or typical, ways The past participle is used with a helping verb to form the perfect tenses.

Categories of Irregular Verbs			
	Present	**Past**	**Past Participle**
All tenses use the	cut	cut	cut
same form	read	read	read
Past tense and past participle	bring	brought	brought
use the same form	teach	taught	taught
In each tense, one letter changes	begin	began	begun
	sing	sang	sung
In past tense, one letter changes; in past participle, one letter is added	grow	grew	grown
	know	knew	known

Using Passive Voice and Progressive Tenses, and Maintaining Consistency in Tense

Getting Started... **Q:** I never realized how much was involved in verb use. I understand what *voice* means when I speak, and I also understand that when some people discuss writing and writers, they talk about *voice* as the tone and language used. But what does *voice* mean when it comes to verbs? And what is the progressive tense? Overall, how can I do a better job of being consistent in verb use?

A: You are correct—there is plenty involved in using verbs, and the voice of a verb is one of them. When the subject is doing the action, the verb is in the *active* voice. But when the subject is acted on, the verb is in the *passive* voice. Having these two voices gives you the chance to record a condition, situation, or individual in more exact terms. Having the progressive tense, which enables you to show actions that are, were, or will be ongoing, allows further precision. And regardless of the tense involved, the best way to maintain consistency is to focus on the time period you are discussing—past, present, or future—and then check the verbs to ensure that they all express that period of time.

Overview: Understanding Passive Voice and Progressive Tense

Chapter 12, "Forming Basic Tenses for Regular Verbs," and Chapter 13, "Using Irregular Verbs Correctly," discussed verb tenses that use some form of the irregular verb *to have* as a helping verb. This chapter will discuss tenses that use some form of the irregular verb *to be* as a helping verb.

For example, a form of *to be* combined with the past participle of another verb creates a verb in the *passive voice*. The subject of a sentence using passive voice is acted upon rather than acting. In many cases, the active voice, in which the subject is the doer of the action, is the correct choice. The passive voice is useful, however, when you need to focus on the receiver of action.

The *progressive tense* combines a form of the helping verb *to be* with the *present participle* form of another verb. This tense is useful to describe actions that are ongoing.

> **In this chapter, you will explore these verb uses and discover ways to use all tenses consistently when you write. You will learn**
>
> ● how to form and when to use passive voice verbs
>
> ● how to form and use the progressive tenses for ongoing actions
>
> ● how to make the tense of verbs consistent throughout a paragraph

Discovering Connections 14.1

Consider the following quotation:

It's easy to have principles when you're rich. The important thing is to have principles when you're poor.

—*Ray Kroc*

Or look at this photo.

Now, using the prewriting technique you prefer, do some prewriting about your reaction to the quotation or the photo. Save your work.

Using the Passive Voice

Verbs may be in the active voice or the passive voice. If the subject of a sentence performs the action, the verb is in the **active voice.** If the subject of the sentence receives the action, the verb is in the **passive voice.** To create a verb in the passive voice, add a form of *to be* to the past participle of another verb, as this chart shows:

To Form the Passive Voice				
Present Tense	**or**	**Past Tense**	**+ Past Participle of Another Verb**	**Examples**
am is		was	eaten, checked, taken	Every morsel of cake *was eaten* by the time I arrived.
are		were		"Sorry, those seats *are taken*," said the usher.
				All of the rings and valves *were checked* by an ace mechanic.

Most of the examples in Chapters 12 and 13 illustrate active voice. To understand an important difference between active and passive voices, consider the following examples:

ACTIVE VOICE   Unfortunately, Barbara had closed the corner deli for the weekend.

PASSIVE VOICE   Unfortunately, the corner deli was closed for the weekend.

In the first sentence, the verb is in the active voice because the subject (*Barbara*) has performed the action (closing the deli). In the second sentence, the verb is in the passive voice. The subject (*deli*) has been acted upon. After all, a deli cannot close itself.

Here is another pair of examples:

ACTIVE VOICE   The reporter spelled several words incorrectly in the article.

PASSIVE VOICE   Several words were spelled incorrectly in the article.

In the first sentence, the subject (*reporter*) does something (misspells words). We know who spelled the words incorrectly. Notice how the focus of the sentence shifts away from the doer in the passive voice example. When the subject *words* is acted upon, or receives the action, we no longer know who made the mistake. Writers usually choose the active voice because it describes things more clearly and directly and makes the communication more energetic.

There will be times, however, when you do want to focus on the receiver of the action. Look at the pairs of sentences below. Which version of each sentence is more effective?

PASSIVE VOICE   Last night, the windshield on my new car was smashed.

ACTIVE VOICE   Last night, someone smashed the windshield on my new car.

PASSIVE VOICE   After the heavy snowfall, school was canceled.

ACTIVE VOICE   After the heavy snowfall, the principal canceled school.

In these sentences, the passive voice is more effective. In the first pair, it emphasizes the subject *windshield*, rather than the unknown person who damaged it. The same is true for the second pair of sentences. It is more important to know that school is canceled than to know who canceled it.

Be careful with your use of the passive voice. It can easily emphasize the wrong noun or pronoun. Consider the following sentences:

PASSIVE VOICE   The referee was approached by the furious player.

ACTIVE VOICE   The furious player approached the referee.

Here, the sentence loses effectiveness in the passive voice. The emphasis should be on the angry player who is carrying out the action.

Exercise 14.1   **Identifying Passive and Active Voice**

Find all uses of the passive voice in the following paragraph. First, underline the subject and verb in each clause. Check to see if the subject receives the action. If it does, the verb is in the passive voice. Write a *P* above verbs in the passive voice. Use the example as a guide.

EXAMPLE
P

The shelves in the gift shop <u>were dusted</u> carefully every week.

(1) The chemistry <u>experiment</u> <u>was completed</u> [P] by most of the students before the end of the class. (2) The <u>results</u> <u>were calculated</u> [P], and then the <u>data</u> <u>were submitted</u> [P] to the lab instructor. (3) After <u>she</u> <u>reviewed</u> the procedures the next day, the lab <u>instructor</u> <u>assigned</u> a written lab report. (4) A <u>groan</u> <u>was heard</u> [P] from the students when <u>they</u> <u>got</u> the assignment. (5) <u>They</u> <u>must complete</u> the report over the spring vacation.

Exercise 14.2   **Working with Passive Voice**

In the paragraph below, fill in each blank with a passive form of the verb given in parentheses. Use the example to guide you.

EXAMPLE   When she arrived at the old homestead site, she (tell) __was told__ that it had been torn down.

(1) When other major American cities (compare) __are compared__ with Boston, Boston seems to deserve its nickname, "Tiny Town." (2) Often we (lead) __are led__ to believe that bigger is better, but Boston's small size is one reason that the city is such a major tourist attraction. (3) The earliest Boston buildings (plan) __were planned__ on a small scale. (4) One reason that Boston buildings stayed small for so long is that the

building of skyscrapers (discourage) __was discouraged__ by area architects and urban planners. (5) We (remind) __are reminded__ of the importance of colonial Boston when we see its old neighborhoods. (6) The houses (build) __were built__ close together and with careful attention to detail. (7) The smaller scale of their city (like) __is liked__ by most Bostonians. (8) With numerous new skyscrapers on the scene, however, some claim that the small-scale charm of Boston (lose) __is lost__ .

Challenge 14.1   **Evaluating the Effectiveness of Passive versus Active Voice**

Working with a classmate, revise the paragraph in Exercise 14.1 so that every sentence uses a verb in the active voice. Then answer the following questions about both versions of the paragraph. Discuss your answers with the class.

1. Who or what is the subject in each sentence?

2. Who or what should be emphasized in each sentence?

3. Which version of each sentence do you think is more effective? Why?

Using Progressive Tenses

The **progressive tenses** are formed by adding some form of the verb *to be* to the **present participle** of another verb. For both regular and irregular verbs, you form the present participle by adding *-ing* to the basic verb form—for example, *watching, eating, driving,* as this chart shows:

To Form the Progressive Voice				
Present Tense	**or** **Past Tense**	**+**	**Past Participle of Another Verb**	**Examples**
am ⟍ is ⟋	was		eating, checking, taking	I *am eating* less meat these days. He *was checking* the roof for leaks when it began to rain.
are	were			My cousins *were taking* swimming lessons while their pool was being built.

The progressive forms show continuing actions or situations that are or were ongoing.

Verbs in the *past progressive tense* (*was* or *were* + the present participle) show action that was ongoing at some time in the past:

> **EXAMPLE** The traffic light *was changing* from yellow to red when I hit the brake.

> **EXAMPLE** Icicles *were forming* on the side of the cliff as we climbed.

In the first sentence, the verb *was changing* indicates that the signal was in the process of changing (not changed) when the driver applied the brake. In the second, the verb *were forming* indicates that ice development was in progress (not complete) and continuing during the climb. All these actions occurred in the past.

When you combine the helping verbs *am, is,* or *are* with a present participle, you create a *present progressive tense.* The helping verbs are in the present tense, so the progressive verb form indicates something that is currently ongoing, or in progress.

Note the present progressive verbs in the following sentences:

> **EXAMPLE** I *am studying* algebra and geometry for the first time.

> **EXAMPLE** In many cities, gangs *are driving* customers away from downtown stores.

In the first sentence, the verb is *am studying.* It indicates that the mathematical study is happening now. In the second sentence, the verb is *are driving,* and it indicates that the disruption in the downtown area is occurring now and continues.

When you combine the helping verbs *will be* with a present participle, you create a *future progressive tense.* The helping verbs are in the future tense, so the progressive verb indicates something that will be ongoing in the future. Find the future progressive verbs in the following sentences:

> **EXAMPLE** Forecasters predict the snow *will be falling* all through the night.

> **EXAMPLE** Before you know it, your daughter *will be asking* to borrow your favorite clothes.

In both sentences, the verbs indicate that the action will happen continuously in the future.

Exercise 14.3   Using the Progressive Tenses

Change the present tense verbs in the following sentences to progressive tense verbs. Change the verb in parentheses to the present participle form, and add a *to be* form as a helping verb. Use the example to guide you.

EXAMPLE   The folk choir (sing) ____*is singing*____ at the Sunday morning service.

(1) Many parents believe that teens who spend hours at a mall (form) ____are forming____ bad habits. (2) They think that teens (waste) ____are wasting____ time that would be better spent studying or working, and that they (lose) ____are losing____ ambition. (3) In addition, mall merchants (complain) ____are complaining____ about teens who (intimidate) ____are intimidating____ customers. (4) Last month, mall security officers removed several groups who (congregate) ____were congregating____ near the mall entrances. (5) Teens, however, (try) ____are trying____ to convince their parents that the mall is a good place to socialize.

Exercise 14.4   Working with the Progressive Tenses

Add a form of the helping verb *to be* to each blank in the sentences below to complete the progressive tense verbs. Consider whether the action is on-going in the past, present, or future to help you choose the correct helping verb. Use the example as a guide.

EXAMPLE   Until the wedding, I ____*will be*____ counting my calories.

1. Suzanne and Mark ____are____ going to the student theater production together.

2. The last time I checked, the volunteer sign-up sheets ____were____ filling up fast.

3. The class ____was____ taking the exam when the fire alarm sounded.

4. I _____was_____ crossing the intersection against the light when the accident happened.

5. She _____is_____ practicing her flute every day to prepare for the recital.

6. My daughter's award for academic achievement _____is_____ hanging in a place of honor in our living room.

7. If my financial aid package is sufficient, I _____will be_____ attending the university this fall.

8. Mayor Connors _____was_____ announcing his candidacy for governor when the sound system failed.

Exercise 14.5   **Mastering the Progressive Tense**

From the following list of ten verbs, choose five or six. On another sheet of paper, write a paragraph that uses each of the verbs in a progressive tense form. Remember—these tenses call for the present participle plus a form of the helping verb *to be*. Use the example as a guide.

| to measure | to alter | to cut | to mend | to stitch |
| to hem | to sew | to shorten | to tailor | to pin |

EXAMPLE   to measure

The seamstress is measuring the customer's shoulders right now.

Challenge 14.2   **Using Several Tenses in Your Writing**

Choose two verbs from the list of irregular verbs in Chapter 13 and two regular verbs. Write a sentence using each verb in the present tense, the past tense, and a progressive tense. Exchange your writing with a partner. Underline the verbs in your partner's paper, and identify the tense used in each sentence.

Maintaining Consistency in Tense

When you write, it is important to maintain **consistency** in your verb tenses. If you're writing about something that happened in the past, use past tense verbs throughout. If it is happening now, use present tense verbs. If it will happen in the future, then future tense verbs are appropriate. Sudden switches in tense can cloud the meaning of your ideas and confuse your reader. Consider the tense of the verbs in the following two sentences:

EXAMPLE   The bouncer at the door of the club *checks* licenses or other IDs. A cop *stood* behind him in case of any trouble.

Do these sentences make you feel confused about time? In the first sentence, the verb *checks* is present tense. In the second, the verb *stood* is past tense.

To correct this error, make both verbs the same tense:

PRESENT   The bouncer at the door of the club *checks* licenses or other IDs. A cop *stands* behind him in case of any trouble.

or

PAST   The bouncer at the door of the club *checked* licenses or other IDs. A cop *stood* behind him in case of any trouble.

Both versions are correct. Which tense should be used? That will depend on what you are trying to describe. Are you telling what happened in the past or describing what goes on today? Always have a clear sense of the time line for the events you are describing before you begin to write.

Exercise 14.6   **Maintaining Consistency in Tense**

Verb tense has been used inconsistently in the following paragraph. Read it, and decide which tense works best. Then underline the verbs in the sentences. Cross out and change any verb whose tense is not consistent with the tense you have chosen. Study the example first.

EXAMPLE   Soon more people <u>will communicate</u> using e-mail.
                                            will talk
Some people think we <u>~~talked~~</u> to each other less.

(Present tense answers are shown.)

                                                                        love
(1) My dog <u>gives</u> me a lot of trouble, but I still <u>~~loved~~</u> him. (2) Paco
                                            digs
runs after my neighbor's cat and <u>~~will dig~~</u> up her flower garden. (3) When
                                                                brings
it <u>rains</u>, Paco <u>rolls</u> in the mud and <u>~~has brought~~</u> dirt into the house. (4) He
                                    take
<u>drags</u> on his leash when I <u>~~took~~</u> him for a walk. (5) However, nothing <u>~~will~~</u>

beats

~~beat~~ the good feeling I get when Paco ~~welcomed~~ me home at the end of

the day.

Exercise 14.7 Employing the Proper Verb Tense

The following paragraph should use three tenses. Decide which tenses are correct. Then change the verbs in parentheses to match those tenses. In the space above each verb, identify its tense. Study the example first.

EXAMPLE

present
When most people (remembered) _____remember_____ the 1960s, they

past
think first of the Beatles. They (is) _____were_____ the most popular

musical group of their day.

---

present
(1) Sometimes when I (daydreaming) _____daydream_____ , I (seeing)

present
_____see_____ the house where I grew up. (2) It (is)

past
_____was_____ on a new suburban street surrounded by prairies

past
where pheasants (hunt) _____hunted_____ for food in the grasses. (3)

past
When my family first (moving) _____moved_____ in, the cottonwood tree

past
in our backyard (is) _____was_____ just a sapling. (4) The maples in

past
front (are) _____were_____ thin and frail. (5) By the time I (growing)

past perfect
_____had grown_____ big enough to climb, the cottonwood (offers)

past
_____offered_____ the perfect place. (6) Its thick trunk (splits)

past perfect
_____had split_____ a short leg's length from the ground, so even my worry-

past
wart of a mother never (worries) _____worried_____ when I (scrambling)

past   *present*
_____scrambled_____ up. (7) I (picture) _____picture_____ the inside of my

house, too, especially my room. (8) The wallpaper with pink roses and

present
the speckled white floor (lingers) _____linger_____ in my memory.

Exercise 14.8 Ensuring Consistency in Tense and Effective Voice

Edit this article from a college newspaper to make verb tenses consistent with the time frame of the particular sentence. Cross out any verbs that are incorrect, and write the correct verb forms above them. Also, revise any sentences in the passive voice that you think would be more effective in the active voice.

(1) Yesterday, a new cafeteria manager ~~begins~~ [began] his work at Western Community College, Margaret O'Neill, dean of administration, announced. (2) This appointment ~~will conclude~~ [concluded] a long search process. (3) "I will cut prices and ~~increases~~ [increase] hours of operation," the new manager, Victor Rodriguez, vowed. (4) ~~Complaints about the prices and hours~~ [For two semesters students had] complained to the administration about the prices and early closing hours at the ~~at the cafeteria were made to the administration for two semesters by~~ cafeteria. ~~students~~.

(5) Before the management ~~change~~ [changed], most students boycotted the cafeteria and ~~are refusing~~ [refused] to buy any food or beverages there. (6) As a result of that protest, student leaders ~~have~~ won the right to interview candidates for the new manager position.

(7) The administration also ~~agrees~~ [agreed] to meet with a student review board once a semester. (8) From now on, the board will bring student concerns to the administration for action.

Challenge 14.3   **Achieving a Consistent Tense in Your Writing**

Select a paragraph of your own writing, and make sure the verb tense is consistent. First, decide if your paragraph talks about what happened in the past, what is happening today, or what will happen in the future. Next, underline the verbs in your paragraph, and write them on a separate piece of paper. Is the tense consistent? If not, change the verbs, revising the sentences if you need to. Refer to Chapter 6, "Subjects and Verbs," to Chapter 12, "Forming Basic Tenses for Regular Verbs," and to the list of irregular verbs in Chapter 13, "Using Irregular Verbs Correctly," to help you review different types of verbs and their tenses.

Voice, Progressive Tenses, and Consistency in Tense Checklist

- ☐ Have you used active voice for those sentences in which you want your reader to know immediately who is, was, or will be doing some action?

- ☐ Have you preferred the passive voice for any sentence in which the focus should be on the receiver of the action rather than on the subject?

- ☐ Have you rechecked any sentences featuring passive voice to ensure that the active voice wouldn't be a better choice?

- ☐ Have you used the progressive tense, including the correct form of *to be* (*am, is, are, was, were*), to signify actions or events that are ongoing in some period of time?

- ☐ Have you identified the general time period—past, present, or future—you are writing about and then checked all verbs to make sure that their tenses match that time?

Exploring Ideas through Journal Writing

When it comes to verbs, as this chapter indicates, *active* indicates the subject is doing the action. *Passive* indicates the subject is being acted on, while *progressive* means the action is ongoing. But in other contexts—in other situations—these words have other meanings. For instance, consider your own day-to-day activities. What time of the day are you most or least active? Why? Have you been in a situation where you were passive when you should have been more active? Why did you choose passivity? Do you wish you had acted differently now? How about your plans for the future—are they progressing as you wish they were? Are they progressing better now than they had been progressing earlier? How will they be progressing five years from now? Consider one of these questions and explore it in your journal for 20 to 30 minutes.

Chapter Quick Check: Using Passive Voice and Progressive Tenses, and Maintaining Consistency in Tense

Each of the following sentences contains a blank line preceded by a verb in parentheses. Fill in each blank with either a progressive or passive form of the verb in parentheses. Some of the verbs are irregular, so refer to pages 256–259 of Chapter 13 if you are unsure about the correct forms of these words.

(1) In 2001, the world of personal transportation experienced a dramatic change when the Segway Human Transporter (introduce) _____was introduced_____ . (2) Soon, if the inventors are correct, thousands of

people (cruise) _____will be cruising_____ through cities and towns on these futuristic devices. (3) As demonstrations of the Segway across the nation have shown, people climb aboard a machine that resembles an old-fashioned two-wheeled lawn mower, and in a matter of seconds they (ride) _____are riding_____ along. (4) A platform or shelf above the Segway's wheels (provide) _____is provided_____ on which the rider stands. (5) The Segway (control) _____is controlled_____ by the motions of the rider's body, so as soon as the driver leans forward, the Segway takes off. (6) While the Segway (move) _____is moving_____, a series of internal gyroscopes keeps it from tipping over. (7) At the Segway's top speed, the rider (propel) _____is propelled_____ at 12.5 miles per hour. (8) Slowing down or stopping (achieve) _____is achieved_____ when the driver leans back. (9) More than 30 states already permit Segway use on sidewalks, and the developers (hope) _____are hoping_____ that the other states will eventually legalize it. (10) The developers (plan) _____are planning_____ to adapt the technology of the Segway for other personal vehicles, including wheelchairs.

Discovering Connections 14.2

1. For Discovering Connections 14.1 on page 268, you began prewriting in response to a quotation by Ray Kroc or a photo. Now continue your prewriting on one of these options:
   a. When it comes to principles, what difference does the absence of money create?
   b. In your view, what principle is most important to have, regardless of your financial status?
2. Evaluate your prewriting material, identify a focus, and create a draft of about 100 words.
3. Exchange your draft with a writing partner. Using the material in this chapter as a guide, evaluate the draft you receive, and note any problems with passive voice, progressive tenses, or consistency in verb tense. Return the draft to the writer.
4. Revise your draft, eliminating any errors that your reader identified.

COLLABORATION

Summary Exercise: Using Passive Voice and Progressive Tenses, and Maintaining Consistency in Tense

Each of the following sentences contains a blank line preceded by a verb in parentheses. Fill in each blank with either a progressive or passive form of the verb in parentheses. Some of the verbs are irregular, so refer to pages 256–259 of Chapter 13 if you are unsure about the correct forms of these words.

(1) Right now, I (learn) ___am learning___ about herbs. (2) I (study) ___am studying___ the ways they are used as medicine, for teas, and in food. (3) Today's consumers (discover) ___are discovering___ what earlier generations knew about these interesting and beautiful plants.

(4) Herbal remedies for ailments (grow)___are growing___ in popularity with many people. (5) Ointments (make) ___are made___ from thyme and summer savory to soothe insect bites. (6) Parsley juice (apply) ___is applied___ to bites to stop itching, too. (7) An infusion of chamomile flowers, fennel, or sage leaves (believe) ___is believed___ to help people with colds. (8) Black eyes (relieve) ___are relieved___ by a compress of hyssop leaves and stems.

(9) Herbal teas (become) ___are becoming___ popular, too. (10) Stores (sell) ___are selling___ herb teas with fancy packaging and names that promise to soothe, relax, or invigorate people. (11) Some teas (make) ___are made___ simply and inexpensively at home. (12) Dried or fresh herbs (place) ___are placed___ in a cup, and boiling water is then poured over them. (13) The tea (strain) ___is strained___ after steeping for five minutes. (14) It (serve) ___is served___ hot or chilled.

(15) Cooks also (experiment) ___are experimenting___ with herbs to add flavor and nutrition to foods they prepare. (16) They (find) ___are finding___ that herbs can reduce or even replace sugar and salt in some recipes and can aid digestion. (17) Culinary herbs (dry) ___are dried___ carefully

to retain their essential oils and salts. (18) They (find) _____are found_____ in markets everywhere.

(19) I (encourage) _____was encouraged_____ to begin studying herbs by my grandmother. (20) I now (plan) _____am planning_____ to grow my own herbs. (21) I also (look) _____am looking_____ forward to teaching my children what I know.

 RECAP

USING PASSIVE VOICE AND PROGRESSIVE TENSES, AND MAINTAINING CONSISTENCY IN TENSE

New terms in this chapter	Definitions
● **active voice**	● a term used to describe a verb whose action is *performed* by the subject *Example* A robber broke into my apartment.
● **passive voice**	● a term used to describe a verb whose action is *received* by the subject *Example* My apartment was robbed.
● **present participle**	● a verb form created by adding *-ing* to the basic form of regular and irregular verbs *Example* The snow was *falling* steadily by rush hour.
● **progressive tenses**	● tenses formed by adding some form of *to be* to the present participle of another verb They convey actions or situations that are, were, or will be ongoing. *Example* I *am learning* to control my temper. *Example* Rita *was singing* at the top of her lungs. *Example* Janet *will be using* her own bat in the softball game.

Continued

New terms in this chapter	Definitions
● **consistency**	● a condition of agreement among parts Verb tense is consistent when it agrees throughout a piece of writing. *Inconsistent* I caught the ball that was thrown. *Consistent* I catch the ball that was thrown.

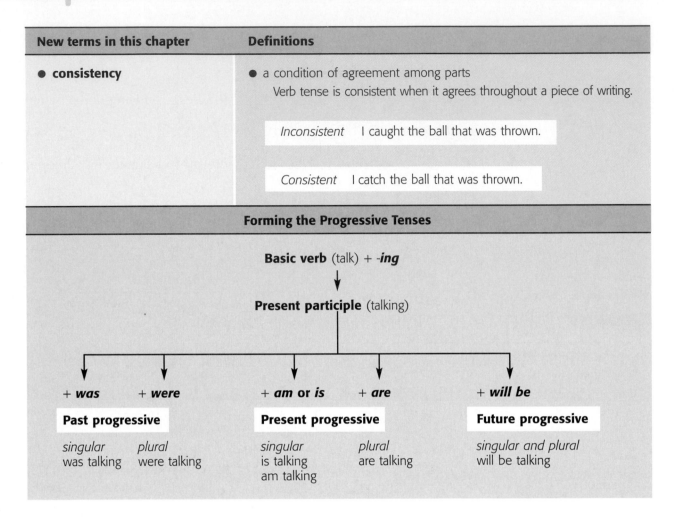

Forming the Progressive Tenses

Basic verb (talk) + *-ing*

Present participle (talking)

+ *was*   + *were*   + *am* or *is*   + *are*   + *will be*

Past progressive   **Present progressive**   **Future progressive**

singular   *plural*   *singular*   *plural*   *singular and plural*
was talking   were talking   is talking   are talking   will be talking
                          am talking

Chapter 15

Dealing with Additional Elements of Verb Use

Getting Started... **Q:** Some irregular verbs give me more trouble than others. I'm not always sure when I should use *can* and when I should use *could*. The same thing is true about *will* or *would*. It's even worse with the different forms of *to be*. What's the best way to make sure I always choose the correct forms of these irregular verbs?

A: It's no surprise that these verbs give you trouble. A number of factors, including the time period and the circumstances involved, determine whether *can* or *could* or *will* or *would* is correct. Therefore, you need to take a few moments and memorize the guidelines concerning their use. And *to be* is especially challenging to use because it has more forms than any other verb. The key to selecting the correct form of any of these verbs is to identify the time and condition you're discussing. Once you've determined these factors, choosing the correct form of these verbs will be far easier.

Overview: Avoiding Special Problems with Verbs

There's no doubt about it: understanding verb use is crucial to good writing. As the preceding chapters have shown, writers need to include a verb in every sentence, choose the proper tense, and be consistent about the tense.

When you write, you also need to steer clear of errors in verb use that can distort the meaning of what you write. Several common types of verb errors make it difficult for readers to understand what you intend to say.

> ***In this chapter, you will discover ways***
>
> - to choose correctly between pairs of confusing words such as *can/could* and *will/would*
>
> - to use correctly the most irregular of irregular verbs: *to be*

Discovering Connections 15.1

Consider the following quotation:

The significance of man is not what he attains, but rather in what he longs to attain.

—*Kahlil Gibran*

Or look at this photo.

Now, using the prewriting technique you prefer, do some prewriting about your reaction to the quotation or photo. Save your work.

Choosing between *Can* and *Could*

Writers have trouble choosing correctly between *can* and *could* as helping verbs. These two verbs both mean *to be able to*. *Can* is used to indicate present tense, and *could* is used to indicate past tense. Look at these two versions of the same sentence:

EXAMPLE   At this point, Sascha *can* run five miles in thirty minutes.

EXAMPLE   Last summer, Sascha *could* run five miles in thirty minutes.

In the first sentence, the verb indicates that Sascha is *now* able to run at that pace. In the second sentence, the verb indicates that Sascha *used to be* able to run at that pace. As you can see, correctly choosing between *can* and *could* is important because the meaning of the sentence changes, depending on the verb.

Sometimes, writers also use *could* to indicate a possibility or hope of being able to do something, as this sentence shows:

EXAMPLE   Sascha wishes she *could* run five miles in thirty minutes.

Sascha isn't able to run five miles, but she'd like to be able to do so.

Exercise 15.1   **Using *Can* and *Could* Correctly**

Circle the verb that is correct in each of the following sentences. Use the example to guide you.

EXAMPLE   Shaunna (can, could) pass the exam to become a firefighter.

(1) Timothy (can, could) entertain everyone with his piano playing.

(2) When I listen to him, I find myself wishing I (can, could) play as well.

(3) I (can, could) tell that he blocks out the world around him as he

plays. (4) At his last performance, the audience (can, could) see his

body sway with the beat of the music, and they knew that was all he

heard. (5) Only after years of practice (can, could) someone master an

instrument as Timothy has mastered the piano.

Exercise 15.2   **Working with *Can* and *Could***

Correct the errors in the use of *can* and *could* in the following paragraph.
Cross out the incorrect word, and write the correct one above it. If a sentence is correct as written, mark it *OK*. Use the example as a guide.

EXAMPLE   If I bought a zip drive, ~~can~~ *could* I throw away my floppy disks?

(1) Contact lenses ~~could~~ *can* be worn by most people. (2) These lenses
~~could~~ *can* correct the most common vision problems. (3) They can be tinted *OK*
in a variety of colors. (4) For example, if you have brown eyes, you ~~can~~ *could*
change your eye color to blue. *OK* (5) If you want to sleep with your lenses
in, you can buy extended-wear lenses. (6) If you don't want to fuss with
cleaning, you ~~could~~ *can* choose hard lenses. (7) They are also the best *OK*
choice if you can't spend a lot of money. (8) Replacing a lost contact
lens ~~could~~ *can* be cheaper and easier than replacing a pair of glasses.

Exercise 15.3   **Using *Can* and *Could* in Your Writing**
(Answers will vary.)

1. What can you do? Think about your skills or areas of expertise. On a separate sheet of paper, write three sentences that begin this way: I can
_____.

2. What would you like to be able to do? What skills or expertise would you like to develop? Write three more sentences that begin this way: I wish I could _____ .

Challenge 15.1   **Analyzing the Use of *Can* and *Could***

Read the following passage from "Two Kinds," a chapter in Amy Tan's novel, *The Joy Luck Club,* and discuss the questions that follow with your classmates.

> My mother believed you could be anything you wanted to be in America. You could open a restaurant. You could work for the government and get good retirement. You could buy a house with almost no money down. You could become rich. You could become instantly famous.
>
> "Of course, you can be prodigy, too," my mother told me when I was nine. "You can be best anything."

1. Why did Tan use *could* in the first paragraph instead of *can?* Why did she use *can* in the next paragraph?

2. Do you agree with the mother's beliefs? Use some examples to support your opinion.

Choosing between *Will* and *Would*

Deciding between the helping verbs *will* and *would* is another choice that baffles many writers. Both verbs are used to indicate the future. However, each links the future with a different period of time.

Look at the sentences below with the verbs italicized:

PRESENT TENSE   Maria *thinks* that she *will major* in accounting.

PAST TENSE   Maria *thought* that she *would major* in accounting.

As the first sentence shows, *will* points to the future from the *present. Right now,* Maria intends to focus on accounting at some future time. As the second sentence shows, *would* points to the future from the *past. At an earlier time,* Maria intended to study accounting in the future.

In some instances, *would* is also used to indicate a hope or possibility rather than a certainty, as this sentence shows:

EXAMPLE   Many people *would* feel better if they changed their diets.

It is possible that people's health would improve, but this depends on a change in eating habits.

Understanding the distinction between *will* and *would* is important. Each verb refers to a different time. Making the right choice will ensure that your readers understand your meaning clearly.

Exercise 15.4   **Using *Will* and *Would* Correctly**

Circle the verb that is correct in each of the following sentences. Use the example to guide you.

EXAMPLE   My brother Luis hopes he ((will) would) graduate in the top 10 percent of his class.

(1) The weather forecasts predict it ((will) would) rain this evening. (2) If this were to happen, it (will, (would)) be good news for farmers. (3) Many crops (will, (would)) be saved. (4) In June, the agriculture experts predicted that farmers (will, (would)) produce bumper crops this year. (5) It is likely that they ((will) would) revise those predictions soon.

Exercise 15.5   **Working with *Will* and *Would***

Correct the errors in the use of *will* and *would* in the following paragraph. Cross out the incorrect word, and write the correct choice above it. If a sentence is correct as written, mark it *OK*. Use the sample as a guide.

EXAMPLE   I can see why many people ~~will~~ *would* be reluctant to try using a computer.

OK
(1) Many people would like to learn to use a computer. (2) However, they are afraid that it ~~would~~ *will* break if they make a mistake. (3) Actually, you ~~will~~ *would* almost have to throw the machine against a wall to break it.
OK   OK
(4) Computers will take a lot of abuse. (5) The fearful would be better off if they could overcome their fears and learn the fun of computing. (6) For example, ~~will~~ *would* you like to design and print your own greeting

OK or would
cards? (7) With your own computer and basic software, the job ~~will~~ be

would
easy and fun. (8) I ~~will~~ like to make a prediction. (9) If you get a com-

will
puter, you ~~would~~ find it hard to resist. (10) In fact, you may begin to love

will
using it so much that you ~~would~~ spend too much time on it.

Working with Forms of *to Be*

The most irregular of the irregular verbs is the verb *to be*. Writers often have difficulty using this verb properly. Here is a table that shows the most common forms of *to be:*

Common Forms of the Verb *to Be*

When the subject is . . .	the present tense is . . .	the past tense is . . .	the future tense is . . .	the present participle is . . .	the past participle is . . .
I	am	was	will be	being	been
he, she, or it	is	was	will be	being	been
we, you, or they	are	were	will be	being	been

Working with the forms of *to be* is easier than you might think at first glance. As the right side of this chart shows, not *all* the forms are irregular. *Will be*, *being*, and *been* are used with all subjects (although the helping verbs do change for the participles). To help yourself master the use of the verb *to be*, focus on just those forms that *do* change. Use this abbreviated table to help yourself learn them:

When the subject is . . .	the present tense is . . .	the past tense is . . .
I	am	was
he or she	is	was
we, you, or they	are	were

Keep these forms straight, and you'll find that you experience far fewer problems with this verb.

Refer to the following example sentences to see how all the forms in the complete table above are used.

PRESENT   I *am* late.

Alonso *is* tired.

You *are* confused about the new rules. We *are* confused about them, too. They *are* also confused.

PAST   Sheila *was* tired. I *was* tired, too.

The people around the pool *were* relaxed. We *were* relaxed, and you *were*, too.

FUTURE   You *will be* glad that you are taking that self-defense class. Your family *will be* pleased, and I *will be*, too.

PRESENT PARTICIPLE   We were *being* entertained. The crowd was *being* silly. Even now, the girl in the front row is *being* silly.

PRESENT PARTICIPLE   The youth center has *been* planning a talent night. The performers have *been* rehearsing for a month. At first, I had *been* reluctant to try out.

One common error in the use of *to be* is to use *been* without one of the helping verbs *has, have,* or *had:*

FAULTY   For the past two weeks, we *been* especially busy at work.

FAULTY   The arson suspect *been* accused of the same crime a year earlier.

You do hear this usage in casual conversation and street talk, but it is not acceptable in college or professional writing. Both of these units are *fragments* because they lack a complete verb. (For more on fragments and complete verbs see Chapter 7, "Sentence Fragments," page 141). In each sentence, *have* or *had* must be added to *been* to create a complete verb:

REVISED   For the past two weeks, we *have been* especially busy at work.

REVISED   The arson suspect *had been* accused of the same crime a year earlier.

Using *be* by itself as the verb in a sentence is another common error in writing, as these examples show:

FAULTY	We *be* upset with the mess that the plumbers left in the kitchen.

FAULTY	He *be* the reason for this party.

This use also occasionally occurs in informal speech, but it is not acceptable in writing for college or work. To correct this error, change *be* to another form of *to be*, as these versions show:

REVISED	We *are* upset with the mess that the plumbers left in the kitchen.

REVISED	He *is* the reason for this party.

Exercise 15.6   Working with Forms of *to Be*

Supply the correct form of the verb *to be* in each sentence of the paragraph below. Refer to the table on page 288 for help in choosing the correct form. Study the example first.

EXAMPLE	The fishing boat *is* late returning to the harbor.

(1) The Internet ___is___ a worldwide connection of computer networks. (2) Using the Internet, we ___are___ able to write and send a letter instantly to someone thousands of miles away. (3) If a person joins a newsgroup or forum on the Internet, he or she ___is___ put in touch with people who share similar interests. (4) I ___am___ connected to the Internet through my subscription to America Online. (5) It ___is___ one of several online services that connect users to the Internet for a fee.

Exercise 15.7   Using the Correct Forms of *to Be*

Some sentences in the following paragraph use *been* or *be* without a helping verb. Correct these errors by adding the appropriate helping verbs or by substituting another form of the verb *to be*. Cross out the incorrect form first, if necessary. Then write your revision in the space above the line. Use the example as a guide.

EXAMPLE   *has been*
The cost of living ~~been~~ increasing each year.

has been
(1) Recently, the term *cloning* ~~been~~ in the news a great deal. (2)
is
Cloning ~~be~~ a technique that makes exact copies of living cells. (3) In the
have been
past few years, scientists called genetic engineers ~~been~~ able to take a
gene and make several exact copies of that gene. (4) These scientists
have been
~~been~~ using this cloning technique to discover how to grow new organs
have
and limbs for patients who need transplants. (5) Scientists ᴧ not yet been
successful in this goal of growing new "spare parts," however. (6) Cloning
has been   *have been*
~~been~~ successful in other ways, though. (7) Some genetic engineers ~~been~~
are
working on copying single genes and cells. (8) Others ~~be~~ working on
copying whole sets of genes. (9) After several experiments on copying
were
whole sets of genes ~~been~~ successful, the scientists decided to try cloning
a whole animal. (10) Finally, after years of hard work, genetic engineers
were
in Scotland ~~be~~ able to successfully clone a sheep, which they named
Dolly, who was finally euthanized in 2003.

Challenge 15.2   **Analyzing the Use of *to Be***

Choose a paragraph of an assignment you are currently writing, and exchange it with a writing partner. Underline forms of the verb *to be* in your
partner's paragraph. Put an *X* in the margin next to each verb that is used
incorrectly. Return the paragraph, and revise any errors on your own paper.

As an alternate challenge, choose a reading from the selections in Part
Six, "Discovering Connections through Reading." Read it, and find at least
five places where the verb *to be* is used. List these verbs, and exchange lists
with a writing partner. Write the name of the form of the verb next to each
verb on the list. Then return the paper to its owner. You may find the table
on page 288 helpful for your labeling.

Additional Elements of Verb Use Checklist

☐ Have you selected *can* as a helping verb to indicate actions or situations in the present?

☐ Have you used *could* as a helping verb to show actions or situations in the past or to indicate a hope or possibility of achieving some action or situation?

☐ Have you selected *will* as a helping verb to signify actions or situations that *right now* are expected to occur in the *future*?

☐ Have you used *would* as a helping verb to discuss actions or situations that *in the past* were expected to occur in the *future* or something that might happen under particular circumstances?

☐ Have you made sure you have included *have, has,* or *had* each time you have used *be* or *been* as the verb in a sentence?

Exploring Ideas through Journal Writing

As this chapter shows, one verb can indicate different conditions depending on the situation. In some cases, *could* means at one time being able to accomplish something. In other cases, *could* means a hope or possibility that something could be accomplished. Sometimes *would* indicates a plan for the future made in the past. Other times, *would* suggests something that might occur if something else did. Now consider circumstances in life for which you might use these verbs to describe or explain. For example, is there something that you could do once that you wish you could still do? What happened? Is it possible for you to regain this skill or ability? Or, if you could, what one event in your life would you change? Why? What difference do you think this change would make? Consider one of these questions, and explore it in your journal for 20 to 30 minutes.

Chapter Quick Check: Dealing with Additional Elements of Verb Use

The following passage contains errors in the use of *can* and *could, will* and *would*, and forms of the verb *to be*. Read the passage, and correct these errors. Cross out the incorrect word or words, and write your revision in the space above the line. Above any sentence that is correct as written, write *OK*.

(1) History has shown that the names companies choose for prod-

ucts ~~could~~ can make a huge difference in the ultimate success of the prod-

uct. (2) When it comes to developing a brand name for a product, one primary goal ~~be~~ [is] instant identification. (3) Usually, firms choose names for their products that hold positive connotations. (4) That's the technique that been followed [has] by the company that produces Beneful dog food. (5) The marketing department of this corporation actually created a word that suggests *benefit* so that people ~~will~~ [would] view this product in a positive light. (6) The makers of the pain reliever Celebrex had the same thing in mind and named their product with the hopes that consumers ~~will~~ [would] associate their product with a celebration. (7) Sometimes a company ~~would~~ [will] even take the unusual step of changing a brand name in order to alter the public's perception. (8) So that it ~~can~~ [could] broaden its appeal nationally, the cable company The Nashville Network decided a few years ago to change its name. (9) The cable network kept its familiar initials—TNN—so that it ~~can~~ [could] capitalize on existing name recognition, but it is now known as The National Network. (10) This brand name game will continue as long as there ~~be~~ [are] new products to bring to the marketplace.

Discovering Connections 15.2

COLLABORATION

1. For Discovering Connections 15.1 on page 284, you began prewriting in response to a quotation by Kahlil Gibran or a photo. Now, continue your prewriting on one of these options:
   a. Why do you think Gibran argues that what people desire to do is more important than what they actually accomplish?
   b. What led you to establish your own goals? How do your aspirations affect the way you live?
2. Evaluate your prewriting material, identify a focus, and create a draft of about 100 words.
3. Exchange your draft with a writing partner. Using the material in this chapter as a guide, evaluate the draft you receive, and note any mistakes with *can* or *could, will* or *would,* or forms of *to be,* as well as any other weaknesses. Return the draft to the writer.
4. Revise your draft, eliminating any errors that your reader identified.

Summary Exercise: Dealing with Additional Elements of Verb Use

The following sentences contain errors in the use of *can* and *could, will* and *would*, and forms of the verb *to be*. Read the passage, and correct these errors. Cross out the incorrect word or words, and write your revision in the space above the line. Above any sentence that is correct as written, write *OK*.

(1) *Plagiarism* is using someone else's words, opinions, or ideas in your [OK]

own writing without giving the original author credit. (2) Plagiarism ~~could~~ [can]

be avoided. (3) There ~~was~~ [is] no excuse for stealing other writers' words.

(4) Learning about a school's regulations concerning plagiarism ~~was~~ [is]

a good idea. (5) If they checked, they ~~will~~ [would] find that colleges and universi-

ties condemn plagiarism. (6) Many instructors ~~would~~ [will] take time in class

to discuss this important ethical issue. (7) In my science class, we ~~been~~ [have been]

studying methods scientists use to report their own research. (8) They ~~is~~ [are]

careful about crediting the work of other scientists.

(9) Next semester, I ~~would~~ [will] have to write a research paper in history.

(10) I will be learning how to show which ideas ~~is~~ [are] someone else's and

which ones belong only to me.

(11) Professional writers, such as reporters, ~~be~~ [are] concerned with pla-

giarism, too, for many reasons. (12) Many reporters would be suspended [OK]

or fired if they borrowed material from another source without giving

credit. (13) Reporters ~~will~~ [would] not be trusted if they could not be believed.

(14) Readers ~~be~~ [are] suspicious of stories that don't name sources.

(15) Plagiarism always ~~been~~ [has been] an important ethical issue for fiction

writers, too. (16) They avoid using story ideas that could be considered [OK]

another author's property. (17) Some ~~will~~ [would] argue that stealing an idea is

far more serious than stealing another person's watch or car.

RECAP — DEALING WITH ADDITIONAL ELEMENTS OF VERB USE

Verb pairs often confused

- *can/could*
  - helping verbs that mean *to be able to*

    Use *can* to show present tense.

Example	Jose *can* win the contest.

    Use *could* to show past tense, or the possibility or hope of being able to do something.

Example	If I *could* sing, then I *could* join the chorus.

- *will/would*
  - helping verbs that indicate the future

    Use *will* to point to the future from the present.

Example	Howard promises he *will* return before midnight.

    Use *would* to point to the future from the past.

Example	Howard promised he *would* return before midnight.

The irregular verb *to be*

- using *to be* correctly
  - Always use *has, have,* or *had* with *been.*

  - Never use *be* alone as a verb.

  - Follow the chart below for forms of *to be.*

Common Forms of the Verb *to Be*

When the subject is . . .	the present tense is . . .	the past tense is . . .	the future tense is . . .	the present participle is . . .	the past participle is . . .
I	am	was	will be	being	been
he, she, or it	is	was	will be	being	been
we, you, or they	are	were	will be	being	been

Writers' Café

Can working on a computer really help me as a writer?

Without a doubt. A computer isn't magic. It can't develop ideas for you. But using a computer word-processing program can . . .

- make it easier for you to record your good ideas during prewriting
- manipulate the order of your sentences and paragraphs as you develop and revise a draft
- check your writing for errors through spelling and grammar checking features

If the computer is linked to the Internet, you gain additional advantages, including the ability to . . .

- send and receive documents, making it easier to seek or provide reaction to a draft
- research any topic you could imagine

In addition, if you e-mail, including any instant message programs— and you pay attention to grammar and usage as well as the ideas you are communicating— you gain extra practice with writing while doing something that you enjoy.

Are there steps I can take to improve my word power?

Yes, there are several. Some are pretty standard, including . . .

- studying lists of vocabulary words
- consulting a *thesaurus*—a book containing lists of synonyms for words—regularly and learning alternate words for the words you customarily use

But a step you might not be thinking of to strengthen your vocabulary is simple. No matter what you are reading,

- write down or highlight any word whose meaning you don't already know
- look it up
- write a brief sentence in which you use the word in context

Once you have actually used the word yourself, you will be on your way to a full understanding of it

When it comes to longer pieces of writing, is there an easy way to know when to start a new paragraph?

There is no foolproof method, but you might try this. First, consider all the things you are trying to tell your reader. While the entire piece of writing should deal with one main subject, different parts of your discussion deal with different aspects. Ask yourself . . .

- what parts of my discussion belong in the same "box"?
- what transitional words indicate that I've moved on to another idea?

Does it make a difference when I choose to do my writing?

It may, but the actual time really depends on you. What time of the day or night are you most alert? That's the time to do an activity calling for great concentration and energy. To increase your efficiency during your peak period, identify other factors that make you most comfortable, including . . .

- the most appropriate location
- level of noise preferred
- other factors—food, beverages, music, etc.—that help to complete your ideal writing environment

Sentence Elements: Striving for Precision

Chapter 16

Working with Nouns

Getting Started... **Q:** Of all the words I use when I write, the ones that name people, places, things, and ideas dominate. How can I make sure that I always use these words properly?

A: Words that name—nouns—do appear often in writing, so concentrating on using them effectively and correctly makes sense. For the most part, doing so is easier than you might think. The biggest problem is determining the number of the word, that is, identifying if the word is singular or plural. Focus on recognizing cue words that signal number and on providing the correct plural form and you'll be all set.

Overview: Understanding Words That Name

To keep the world straight, we name everything around us, and the names we assign are **nouns.** Nouns are classified into two groups. **Common nouns** name nonspecific people or things—an executive, a state, a novel. **Proper nouns** name particular people or things—Jeremy Wright, Wisconsin, *Of Mice and Men*—and these are always introduced by a capital letter. Nouns also have two forms, *singular* for those nouns referring to individual persons or things and *plural* for those referring to several. As a writer, you must understand nouns because you will use them in every sentence you compose.

> **In this chapter, you will learn how to**
>
> ● turn a singular noun into a plural one
>
> ● recognize singular nouns that end in *–s*
>
> ● work with collective nouns
>
> ● use cue words to identify the number of a noun

Discovering Connections 16.1

Consider the following quotation:

Forget the past. No one becomes successful in the past.

—Anonymous

Or consider this photo.

Now, using the technique you prefer, do some prewriting about your reaction to the quotation or the photo. Save your work.

Reviewing the Function and Form of Nouns

Of the parts of speech in English, nouns are the most versatile. Even though you probably won't think of this while you are writing, nouns perform six distinct functions in a sentence. Nouns can serve as

- a **subject:**

`subject`

EXAMPLE   *History* remains a popular choice of study for many college students.

- a **predicate nominative,** the word that answers **Who or What?** after a linking verb:

`predicate nominative`

EXAMPLE   My best friend is an outstanding *guitarist.*

- a **direct object,** the word that answers **Whom or What?** *after* an action verb:

`direct object`

EXAMPLE   Caitlyn opened the *package* left on the counter.

- an **indirect object,** the word that answers **To Whom or For Whom, To What or For What?** *after* an action verb:

`indirect object`

EXAMPLE   The sales representative gave the *woman* a brochure explaining the DVD player's warranty.

- an **object of a preposition,** the word that follows a preposition and completes a **prepositional phrase:**

`object of a preposition`

EXAMPLE   The photograph on the *desk* is almost 100 years old.

- an **appositive,** a word that helps to explain or illustrate another noun:

appositive

EXAMPLE   The speaker held onto his good-luck charm, a small *keychain*.

Regardless of a noun's function, you must always select the proper form—singular or plural—for each situation. The good news, however, is that changing nouns from singular to plural is generally easy. To make most nouns plural, simply add *-s* to the singular form:

Singular	Plural
basketball	basketball**s**
chair	chair**s**
plan	plan**s**

Not all nouns form their plurals the same way, though. For example, to make most words that end in *-ch, -sh, -x,* or *-s* plural, you must add *-es:*

Singular	Plural
box	box**es**
bush	bush**es**
church	church**es**
glass	glass**es**

To make words that end in a consonant and *-y* plural, you must change the *-y* to *-i* and add *-es:*

Singular	Plural
baby	bab**ies**
butterfly	butterfl**ies**

To make many words that end in *-f* or *-fe* plural, you must change the ending to *-ves:*

Singular	Plural
half	hal**ves**
knife	kni**ves**

To make combined or hyphenated words plural, you must add *-s* to the main word:

Singular	Plural
maid of honor	maid**s** of honor
passerby	passer**s**by
sister-in-law	sister**s**-in-law

To make some common words plural, you must *change letters within the word:*

Singular	*Plural*
foot	f**ee**t
mouse	m**ice**
tooth	t**ee**th
woman	wom**en**

Some words have the same singular and plural forms:

Singular	*Plural*
antelope	**antelope**
deer	**deer**
fish	**fish**
sheep	**sheep**

Still other variations exist. For example, some words that end in *-o,* such as *piano* and *radio,* form their plural by adding *s.* Other words that end in *-o,* such as *tomato* and *hero,* form their plural by adding *-es.* Some words from foreign languages, like *analysis* and *crisis,* form their plurals in keeping with their original language: *analyses* and *crises.*

When you are in doubt about the plural form for a noun, turn to the dictionary. It gives the plural ending in boldface for nouns that do not form a plural simply by adding -s.

Exercise 16.1 **Identifying the Function of Nouns**

In each of the following sentences, two nouns are underlined. Using the discussion of the function of nouns to guide you, write the function of each underlined noun above it, as the example shows:

EXAMPLE

subject   predicate nominative
The <u>owner</u> of that truck is the former <u>mayor</u> of the city.

subject
(1) A major <u>figure</u> in the world of contemporary literature is Sandra

Cisneros, perhaps best known for *The House on Mango Street,* her first
appositive   object of the preposition
<u>novel</u>. (2) More than 2 million copies of this <u>work</u> are in print, and the
subject
<u>book</u> is required reading in many high school and college classrooms.
object of the preposition   direct object
(3) In the <u>novel</u>, which was first published in 1983, she discusses <u>life</u> in
predicate nominative
the Hispanic area of Chicago. (4) Cisneros is also the <u>author</u> of several

volumes of poetry, a bilingual children's book, and two other works of fiction, including *Caramelo,* her most recent <u>work</u>, published in 2002. (5)

In this book, Cisneros tells her <u>readers</u> the <u>story</u> of three generations of

the Reyes family through the words of granddaughter Celaya.

appositive (above "work")

indirect object (above "readers")   *direct object* (above "story")

Exercise 16.2   **Making Nouns Plural**

Change the underlined singular nouns in the paragraph below to their plural forms. Cross out each singular noun and write the plural noun above it. Review the various rules for forming plural nouns. Use the example as a guide.

EXAMPLE   We saw many *kinds* <u>kind</u> of *butterflies* <u>butterfly</u> during our walk at the arboretum.

(1) The ~~holiday~~ [holidays] are especially hectic for those who both work and care for ~~home~~ [homes] and ~~family~~ [families]. (2) ~~Employee~~ [Employees] at many service ~~job~~ [jobs] get busier as demand increases. (3) More folks head to the ~~mall~~ [malls] to shop and to their favorite ~~restaurant~~ [restaurants] for holiday ~~party~~ [parties]. (4) Even after a busy day at work, people can't relax but instead turn to their holiday ~~task~~ [tasks]. (5) They wrap gift ~~box~~ [boxes], mail ~~package~~ [packages], and decorate their ~~house~~ [houses] or ~~apartment~~ [apartments]. (6) Also, ~~child~~ [children] are excited about the ~~celebration~~ [celebrations] ahead, and the ~~treat~~ [treats] and ~~present~~ [presents] they will soon receive. (7) It's no wonder that by the end of a typical day in December, many ~~man~~ [men] and ~~woman~~ [women] have aching ~~foot~~ [feet] and pounding ~~head~~ [heads].

Exercise 16.3   **Using Plural Nouns**

On a separate sheet of paper, write the plural form of seven of the following nouns. Then write at least five sentences using these plural forms correctly. Use the example sentence provided as a guide.

maid of honor	glass
wife	woman
knife	box
cake	solo
pew	family

EXAMPLE   At the wedding I attended yesterday, the maids of honor were dressed in blue.

Challenge 16.1   **Working with Singular and Plural Forms**

1. Select a piece of your own writing, and identify ten singular nouns. List them on a separate piece of paper, and write the plural form next to each noun on the list. Check in a dictionary if a word doesn't fit the guidelines presented in this chapter.

2. Exchange your list with a classmate, and use a dictionary to check the list you receive. Correct any errors you find.

Working with Singular Nouns Ending in -s and Collective Nouns

It's true that you add -s to make many nouns plural, but it's also true that *not* all nouns that end in -s are plural. This group of nouns includes the following:

economics	mathematics	mumps	physics	statistics
ethics	measles	news	politics	

Because these words end in -s, you may incorrectly select a plural verb form. As this example shows, however, these words are singular and thus take a singular verb form:

EXAMPLE   In terms of academic majors, *mathematics provides* students with a background to move into several areas, including engineering, chemistry, and medicine.

Collective nouns, words that stand for groups of items or people, can also be confusing in terms of number. Here is a list of common collective nouns:

Common Collective Nouns

audience	department	government	office
class	faculty	group	school
committee	family	herd	team
congregation	flock	jury	troop

Collective nouns generally call for a singular form of a verb, as these examples show:

EXAMPLE   Barbara's *family provides* emotional support whenever she is stressed out about her classes.

EXAMPLE   Our *team has* already won more games this season than we won for the whole season last year.

In the first sentence, the correct verb for the collective noun *family* is the singular form, *provides*. In the second sentence, the correct verb for the collective noun *team* is the singular form of the helping verb, *has*.

Recognizing Cue Words That Identify Number

Some of the words you include in your sentences can help you decide whether a noun is singular or plural. When these **Cue words** refer to nouns used as subjects, recognizing them can help you determine whether to use a singular or plural verb.

The following words can signal that a singular noun follows:

Common Singular Cue Words

a, an	every
another	neither
each	one
either	

EXAMPLE   *Each* deer in the photograph *looks* startled.

EXAMPLE   *One* luxury car in the showroom *costs* more than $55,000.

In the first sentence the cue word *each* signals a singular subject. The singular subject *deer* requires a singular verb, *looks*. In the second sentence, the cue word *one* signals a singular subject. The singular subject *car* requires a singular verb, *costs*.

The following cue words usually signify that a plural subject follows:

Common Plural Cue Words

all	many
both	several
few	some

EXAMPLE   *Several* deer *are* feeding in my backyard every evening.

EXAMPLE   *Both* children in the news *come* from my neighborhood.

In the first sentence, the cue word *several* signifies a plural subject. The plural subject *deer* requires a plural verb, *are.* In the second sentence, the cue word *both* indicates a plural subject, *children,* which requires a plural verb, *come.*

The singular and plural cue words (except for *a* and *an*) may also serve as pronoun subjects. In this use, they are usually followed by a prepositional phrase beginning with *of.*

SINGULAR   *One* of the cars in the showroom *is* my favorite shade of blue.

PLURAL   *Few* of the children *are* aware of the accident.

In the first example, *One* is the singular subject, requiring the singular verb *is.* In the second, *Few* is the plural subject, requiring the plural verb *are.*

Most of the cue words listed in this section are indefinite pronouns. You will learn more about them in the next chapter.

Exercise 16.3   **Working with Singular Nouns Ending in -s and Collective Nouns**

Each sentence in the following passage is preceded by the infinitive form of a verb in parentheses. Underline the subject for each sentence and then write the correct present tense form of the verb on the line provided. Use the example as a guide.

EXAMPLE   (to stop) The <u>flock</u> of Canadian geese _*stops*_ traffic when it wanders

across the road.

(1) (to meet) The <u>faculty</u> at my college _____meets_____ regularly with the administration to discuss the curriculum and other matters affecting students on campus. (2) (to present) At every meeting, for example, the <u>committee</u> on standards ___presents___ a serious educational issue for discussion. (3) (to become) At least once a semester, <u>mathematics</u> ___becomes___ the focus. (4) (to have) At the most recent meeting, the director of admissions presented a study indicating that the incoming <u>class</u>

_____has_____ stronger math skills than previous classes. (5) (to be) In addition, the study shows that the group of students with advanced courses in math _____is____ the largest ever.

Exercise 16.4 **Working with Cue Words**

Complete the following sentences. For each sentence, first circle the verb and then supply an appropriate cue word from the words listed. Use the example to guide you.

many	several	all
one	each	few

EXAMPLE   ___Many___ adults (enjoy) theme parks as much as children do.

(1) ___Several___ students (have) recently (petitioned) the Student Senate for funding to support an Outdoors club. (2) ___Many___ colleges in the tri-state region (have set up) such clubs as a way for students to enjoy nature. (3) ___Each___ activity, from hiking to kayaking to rock-climbing, (will be made available) to the entire college community at a reduced rate. (4) ___Few___ outdoor enthusiasts (will be able) to resist the chance to enjoy these kinds of activities at a discount. (5) ___One___ trip (has) already (been planned) contingent on funding from the Student Senate.

Exercise 16.5 **Working with Collective Nouns and Cue Words**

Add present tense verbs to complete the following sentences. If applicable, use the collective noun or cue word to help you decide whether a singular or plural verb form is required. Use the example as a guide.

EXAMPLE   The swarm of bees ___is attacking the barking dog___ .

(Answers will vary but number of cue word is shown.)

1. Many cub scouts _____ (plural) _____ .

2. Back in the courtroom, the jury _____ (singular) _____ .

3. The class of second graders _____ (singular) _____ .

4. Many of the picnic areas in the park _____ (plural) _____ .

5. Every item in the freezer _____ (singular) _____ .

6. Several of the teachers _____ (plural) _____ .

7. The varsity basketball team _____ (singular) _____ .

8. Our volunteer committee _____ (singular) _____ .

Challenge 16.2 ▶ **Working with Subjects That End in -s**

Look at these nouns that end in *-s: economics, dilemmas, appartitions, mathematics, news, diagnoses, checkers.* Are they singular or plural? Working with a partner, write a sentence using each of these words.

Working with Nouns Checklist

☐ Have you rechecked the plural nouns you've used, especially those ending in *-ch, -sh, -x, -s, -y, -f,* or *-fe* to make sure you have formed the plural ending properly?

☐ Have you examined any plural forms of combined or hyphenated nouns and nouns requiring an internal change to ensure that you have changed the words appropriately?

☐ Have you made sure you have not added an *-s* or *-es* to any nouns that have the same singular and plural form?

☐ Have you used a singular verb form with any singular noun ending in *-s* used as a subject?

☐ Have you used a singular verb form with any collective noun used as a subject?

☐ Have you focused on any cue words to make sure that you have used the nouns they identify appropriately?

Exploring Ideas through Journal Writing

As this chapter indicates, nouns are words that name persons, places, things, and ideas. Common nouns name general things, but proper nouns name particular things. But what is it about those particular names? Consider your own first or last name, for example. Is there a story associated with it? Are you named after a family member? Was your name chosen because it has some meaning? If it was easy enough to do, would you change it? Why or why not? When it comes to products and services, do you always choose a particular brand name? What are your reasons? Think of some topic associated with formal names and explore it in your journal for 20 to 30 minutes.

Chapter Quick Check: Working with Nouns

Each sentence in the following passage contains an error in noun or cue word use, including problems with subject–verb agreement. First review the discussion of the number of nouns, collective nouns, and cue words. Then correct each error by crossing out the incorrect word and writing the correct form above it.

(1) The newest class of hand-held computers ~~represent~~ *represents* a huge breakthrough in technology. (2) By comparison, earlier versions were just ~~toyes~~ *toys,* simple devices for storing addresses and dates. (3) The news about these new powerful units ~~are~~ *is* that they have as much memory as many desktop computers. (4) More memory means these new hand-helds can perform a wide variety of ~~taskes~~ *tasks.* (5) The processors on these units are up to four times faster than those of the earlier ~~modeles,~~ *models,* increasing efficiency. (6) These hand-held units have some amazing ~~capabilitys~~ *capabilities.* (7) Users can receive and send ~~e-mailes~~ *e-mails* and download various documents and spreadsheets. (8) ~~Every~~ *All* data can then be easily transferred to their computers. (9) This group of hand-held computers also ~~enable~~ *enables* users to beam data to other hand-helds within a range of several yards. (10) The color ~~displayes~~ *displays* on almost all these units are far more vibrant than on earlier versions, making reading the screen even easier. (11) Even more remarkable, many hand-helds now include digital recorders, and ~~a~~ *many* models can even double as cell phones.

Discovering Connections 16.2

COLLABORATION

1. For Discovering Connections 16.1 on page 301, you began prewriting in response to an anonymous quotation or a photo. Now continue your prewriting on one of these options:
   a. Although the quote and the photo indicate that we should move on from the past, other people suggest the opposite: that we should learn from our past behavior. Which side of this debate are you on? Why?
   b. In your view, what is the best formula for success?
2. Evaluate your prewriting material, identify a focus, and create a draft of about 100 words.
3. Exchange your draft with a writing partner. Using the material in this chapter as a guide, evaluate the draft you receive, and note any problems with nouns and pronouns as well as any other weaknesses. Return the draft to the writer.
4. Revise your draft, eliminating any errors that your reader identified.

Summary Exercise: Working with Nouns

Each sentence in the following passage contains an error in noun or cue word use, including problems with subject–verb agreement. First review the discussion of the number of nouns, collective nouns, and cue words. Then correct each error by crossing out the incorrect word and writing the correct form above it.

(1) Many experts agree that sports ~~is~~ *are* beneficial for everyone. (2) Historically, ~~opportunitys~~ *opportunities* to participate in sports haven't always existed, especially for females. (3) Even 30 years ago, the typical high school team ~~were~~ *was* all boys. (4) Meanwhile, the crowd in the stands ~~were~~ *was* often composed of girls, relegated to watching rather than participating. (5) Today, though, things have changed, and athletics ~~are~~ *is* for everyone. (6) This shift to increased physical activity for all has many ~~benefites~~ *benefits.* (7) For one thing, anyone on a team develops physical ~~abilitys~~ *abilities,* including improved agility, stronger muscles, and increased stamina. (8) In many

cases, these ~~peoples~~ [people] have healthier hearts and lungs as a result of their participation. (9) Most also find that their ~~leveles~~ [levels] of energy and alertness increase dramatically.

(10) Another factor that can result from involvement in athletics is the increase in confidence ~~a~~ participants report. (11) Skill levels almost always improve over time, regardless of whether the ~~activitys~~ [activities] are individual sports like running or team sports like softball. (12) When people perform better, their ~~attitudees~~ [attitudes] about themselves begin to change. (13) They may therefore be better prepared to endure the frustrations that come with mastering new ~~taskes~~ [tasks] in school or on the job.

(14) Sports often bring ~~familys~~ [families] together, too. (15) In the case of youth sports ~~associationes~~ [associations,] for example, many parents are highly involved. (16) Some parents serve as ~~coachs~~ [coaches] and referees, while others operate the snack bar or organize fundraisers. (17) By becoming involved, this group of parents ~~enjoy~~ [enjoys] even more time with their children.

(18) Athletics should be about more than admiring sports ~~heros~~ [heroes] from afar. (19) The news ~~are~~ [is] filled with stories of how out-of-shape and overweight people in the United States are. (20) ~~Many~~ [One] simple step that the public could take to reverse this trend is to become involved in some athletic activity.

RECAP

WORKING WITH NOUNS

New terms in this chapter	Definitions
● **noun**	● a word that names a person, place, thing, or idea
● **common noun**	● a noun that names a nonspecific person or thing

New terms in this chapter	Definitions
● **proper noun**	● a noun introduced by a capital letter that names a specific person or thing
● **subject**	● a word that answers **Who or What?** is doing the action or is being discussed
● **predicate nominative**	● a word that answers **Who or What?** *after* a linking verb
● **direct object**	● a word that answers **Whom or What?** *after* an action verb
● **indirect object**	● a word that answers **To Whom or For Whom, To What or For What?** *after* an action verb
● **object of a preposition**	● a word that follows a preposition, completing a prepositional phrase
● **appositive**	● a word that helps to explain or illustrate another noun
● **collective noun**	● a noun that represents a group of individuals or items Collective nouns are singular, generally calling for a singular form of a verb. *Example* The *committee wants* to review the software before making a decision.
● **cue word**	● a word such as *an* or *several* that indicates whether a noun is singular or plural

Using Pronouns: Considering Case, Clear Pronoun–Antecedent Agreement, and Nonsexist Pronoun Usage

Getting Started... **Q:** I often use pronouns when I write, but sometimes I'm not sure I'm using the right ones for the right situations. The most trouble I have is choosing the correct pronoun when it is the subject or an object. I also find it hard figuring out whether I need a singular or plural pronoun. What can I do to make sure that I always use the proper pronoun?

A: Choosing the correct pronoun for a particular situation starts with an understanding of the characteristics of the different kinds of pronouns. For example, when you use a pronoun as a subject, you need only be concerned with the personal pronouns because they are the ones that have different forms for subject and object. *Number* isn't usually much of a problem with pronouns because whether the words you are referring to are singular or plural is pretty obvious. The exception is with *indefinite pronouns*. Understand these features and you'll find working with them far easier.

Overview: Choosing the Correct Pronoun

When you need a substitute for a noun, the words you use are **pronouns.** The best way to think of pronouns are as a kind of verbal shorthand. Rather than repeat a noun several times, you can use one of these recognizable alternatives, adding variety to your writing at the same time. Pronouns can be classified in several groups including *demonstrative pronouns, interrogative* *pronouns, relative pronouns, reflexive/intensive pronouns, personal pronouns,* and *indefinite pronouns.* To use pronouns effectively, you need to keep several things in mind. You must consider the specific form or *case* of personal pronouns. You must also consider the *number* and *gender* with indefinite pronouns. In addition, you need to make sure that the pronouns and the words they refer to, called *antecedents,* match or *agree.* Otherwise, the people and things you are referring to won't be clear for your reader.

> ### In this chapter, you will learn to
>
> - recognize the different types of pronouns
> - understand the different cases of personal pronouns
> - identify number and gender with indefinite pronouns
> - ensure that pronouns and antecedents agree in number and gender

Discovering Connections 17.1

Consider the following quotation:

Many of life's failures are people who did not realize how close they were to success when they gave up.

—*Thomas Edison*

Or consider this photo.

Now, using the technique you prefer, do some prewriting about your reaction to the quotation or the photo. Save your work.

Considering Pronoun Types

We use several types of pronouns to communicate in speech and writing. They can be grouped in several classes:

- **personal pronouns,** which refer to *specific* people, places, things, and ideas

  I, me, my, mine   we, us, our, ours
  you, your, yours   she, he, her, him, hers, his
  it, its, their, theirs

- **indefinite pronouns,** which refer to *general* persons and things

all	each	little	nobody	others
another	either	many	none	several
any	everybody	more	no one	some
anybody	everyone	most	nothing	somebody
anyone	everyone	much	one	someone
anything	few	neither	other	something
both				

- **demonstrative pronouns,** which point out *particular* people or things referred to

this	that
these	those

- **reflexive intensive pronouns,** which add emphasis to antecedents

myself	ourselves
yourself	yourselves
himself, herself, itself	themselves
oneself	

- **relative pronouns,** which introduce dependent clauses, called *relative clauses,* within a sentence

who	which
whom	that
whose	

- **interrogative pronouns,** which begin questions

Who ...?	Whom ...?	Whose ...?
Whoever ...?	Whomever ...?	Which ...
Whichever ...?	What ...?	Whatever ...?

Working with pronouns is fairly straightforward, except for two areas. The first is **case,** that is, which of three *forms* of a personal pronoun is called for in a specific situation. The second is the **number** of the *antecedent,* that is, whether the word the pronoun refers to is singular or plural.

Dealing with Pronoun Case

The pronouns that writers use most often are **personal pronouns.** These pronouns are used to point out *particular* people, places, things, and ideas. Take a look at this chart.

Personal Pronouns

	Subjective	Objective	Possessive
first person	I, we	me, us	my, mine, our, ours
second person	you	you	your, yours
third person	she, he, it, they	her, him, it, them	her, hers, his, its, their, theirs

As the chart shows, personal pronouns have three separate forms, or *cases: subjective, objective,* and *possessive*

Subjective forms are used as subjects of sentences:

EXAMPLE   *They* arrived five minutes before the movie began.

EXAMPLE   *She* suddenly felt dizzy and sick.

You use objective forms of these pronouns when the word serves as an object. For example, a *direct object* receives the action of the verb. It answers the questions, *what?* or *whom?* after the verb. An *indirect object* answers the questions *to whom, to what, for whom,* or *for what* the action of the verb is being done. The object of the preposition completes the meaning of the prepositional phrase. Look at these examples:

direct object

EXAMPLE   As Jerry crossed the icy street, a skidding car hit *him*.

indirect object

EXAMPLE   The boy's mother gave *him* the confidence to perform on stage.

preposition   object of the preposition

EXAMPLE   The buildings all *around us* are more than 100 years old.

To avoid problems with personal pronouns, keep several guidelines in mind.

- *Objective pronouns can never serve as subjects.*

The exceptions among the personal pronouns are *you* and *it*, which can serve as objects and subjects. Particularly confusing are situations when the pronoun is part of a compound subject. The solution is to check each word to make sure it could stand as a subject *by itself*.

EXAMPLE   Marta, Carla, and ~~me~~ I had planned to go to the beach.

- *Subjective pronouns can never serve as objects.*

Errors in the use of the objective case also occur when pronouns are used in a compound object. The solution to avoiding the problem is the same: Check each word alone to see if it can serve as an object by itself:

EXAMPLE

>   me
> Nobody was sure if the nurse called Karen or ~~I~~.

- *Possessive pronouns do not require an apostrophe.*

Unlike possessive *nouns*, which need an *apostrophe* (')—Gretchen's book, the boys' bikes—possessive pronouns don't. No apostrophe is needed because possessive pronouns are already possessive. Of all the possessive pronouns, *its* is most often a problem because the contraction for *it is* or it has—*it's*—sounds the same. To avoid choosing the wrong form, first try using *it is*. If *it is* fits, then *it's* is correct. If *it is* doesn't work, then you need the possessive form, *its*.

EXAMPLE

>   its
> The dog ate from ~~it's~~ bowl.

EXAMPLE

>   It's
> ~~Its~~ too early to go running.

With the first sentence, you would not say "The dog ate from *it is* bowl," so *it's* is incorrect. The proper choice is *its*. With the second sentence, *it is* does fit, so the proper choice would be *it's*.

Exercise 17.1   **Identifying Pronoun Case**

Underline all personal pronouns you find in the paragraph below. Then write an *S* above subjective pronouns, an *O* above objective pronouns, and a *P* above possessive pronouns. Review the chart on page 317, and use the example as a guide.

EXAMPLE

>   *S*   *O*   *S*   *P*
> <u>We</u> promised <u>him</u> that <u>we</u> would return <u>his</u> Dave Matthews CD.

                                                               S

(1) When the Beatles came to America in 1964, <u>they</u> were an enor-
                                                     O

mous success. (2) Huge crowds of fans greeted <u>them</u> at the airport. (3)
P   P

<u>My</u> Aunt Barbara was in the audience for <u>their</u> appearance on the *Ed*
                  S   O   P

Sullivan Show. (4) <u>She</u> has told <u>me</u> that the performance is one of <u>her</u> fa-
                                                   S

vorite teenage memories. (5) Soon after <u>they</u> returned to England, the
                                                   O

Beatles began work on a movie that many of <u>us</u> love, *A Hard Day's Night*.

Exercise 17.2   **Choosing the Appropriate Personal Pronoun**

Fill in the blanks by supplying an appropriate pronoun. Then identify its case. Write *S* above subjective pronouns, *O* above objective pronouns, and *P* above possessive pronouns. Use the example to guide you.

EXAMPLE

When people disagree with a law or government ruling, ___*they*___ often

find the official procedure complicated and expensive.

(1) Most cat owners take good care of their pets; ___they___ spend a
lifetime average of $8,665 on each of ___their___ cats. (2) Those of
___us___ who spoil our cats probably spend even more. (3) Cats can
live to be twenty years old, and it's not uncommon for ___them___ to survive to age twenty-five. (4) As ___they___ age, cats often get the same diseases as people, for example, arthritis or diabetes. (5) Besides these
human diseases, older cats are susceptible to ___their___ own ailments,
such as feline respiratory disease. (6) Most cat owners want to do everything ___they___ can to cure ___their___ pets. (7) However, the cost of
___their___ care can be very high. (8) How many of ___us___ could afford the $16,000 price tag for a feline kidney transplant?

Exercise 17.3   **Selecting the Correct Personal Pronoun**

Each sentence in the following paragraph contains a pair of personal pronouns. Circle the correct word to complete the sentences. Remember that
objective pronouns can't serve as subjects, that subjective pronouns can't
serve as objects, and that the possessive pronoun *its* does not have an apostrophe. Use the example as a guide.

EXAMPLE

After class, Jose and (I, me) usually stay on campus to work out in the

gym.

(1) Kevin and (I, me) enjoy bird-watching in our spare time. (2)
Because birds are everywhere, (we, us) can identify (they, them) and

enjoy this hobby everywhere. (3) (It's, Its) also an inexpensive hobby that encourages (us, we) to walk outside and get some exercise. (4) If Kevin spots a bird (he, him) hasn't identified before, he asks (I, me) to record it on a list that (he and I, him and me) keep. (5) (We, Us) have learned to identify each bird by (its, it's) song and appearance.

Challenge 17.1   **Evaluating the Use of Personal Pronouns in Your Writing**

How have you used personal pronouns in your own writing? Review several paragraphs that you have written, and find three examples of each case of the personal pronouns: subjective, objective, and possessive. Write these sentences on a separate piece of paper and exchange them with a classmate. In the sentences you receive, underline any pronoun errors you find, and then return the sentences. Using the material in the preceding section to guide you, make any necessary adjustments in your own sentences.

Avoiding Errors in Agreement in Number

One important area of agreement is matching singular antecedents with singular pronouns and plural antecedents with plural pronouns. As stated earlier, **antecedents** are the words a specific pronoun refers to. To make sure you have made the proper choice, first identify whether the antecedent is singular or plural. Then make sure the pronoun you have chosen matches.

Note the pronouns and their antecedents in the following sentences:

singular antecedent		singular pronoun	

EXAMPLE   The *singer* broke a string on *her* guitar.

plural antecedent		plural pronoun	

EXAMPLE   *Whales* are very protective of *their* young.

Collective nouns sometimes confuse writers. Common collective nouns include words like *class, herd, jury,* and *team*. As Chapter 16 showed (page 305), collective nouns represent *groups* of people or things. Nonetheless, the words themselves are generally considered *singular*, so they call for singular pronouns.

collective noun		singular pronoun	

EXAMPLE   The *flock* of geese flew gracefully toward *its* summer feeding grounds.

Exercise 17.4   **Maintaining Agreement with Antecedents**

Underline the antecedents in the following paragraph, and decide if they are singular or plural. Then circle the correct pronoun in parentheses to maintain agreement. Use the example as a guide.

EXAMPLE   The tourists lugged ((their) her) souvenirs through the airport.

(1) Children can learn at an early age how to manage ((their) his) money. (2) When kids learn to budget and save money, (he, (they)) usually manage ((it) them) better as adults. (3) Some parents give (her, (their)) children a weekly allowance to spend and save. (4) A family can discuss ((its) their) budget plan and savings goals together. (5) Teens can even learn about the stock market, if (she, (they)) have earned money to invest in ((it) them).

Exercise 17.5   **Creating Sentences with Correct Pronoun–Antecedent Agreement**

Below is a list of twelve nouns that you can use as antecedents. Several of them are collective. Working with a classmate, compose a short paragraph on a separate sheet of paper that includes five of these antecedents. For every antecedent you use, in the same sentence provide a pronoun that agrees with it. Use the example to guide you.

band	audience	singer	crowd
musicians	concert	stage crew	sound system
stage	technical staff	rock group	spotlights

EXAMPLE   The band always takes a five-minute break between its sets.

Challenge 17.2   **Adjusting Pronoun–Antecedent Agreement in a Paragraph**

1. In each of the sentences in Exercise 17.4, you selected the correct pronoun to agree with an antecedent. Now, working with a classmate, rewrite the paragraph, using the other pronoun in parentheses and then changing its antecedent. Keep in mind that you may also have to change some of the verbs to maintain subject–verb agreement.

2. Still working together, write a brief paragraph in which you explain which version is better and why.

Maintaining Agreement with Indefinite Pronouns

When writers want to refer to someone or something general, they use **indefinite pronouns.** Some indefinite pronouns are always singular:

Singular Indefinite Pronouns

another	each	everything	nobody	other
anybody	either	little	no one	somebody
anyone	everybody	much	nothing	someone
anything	everyone	neither	one	something

Singular indefinite pronouns call for singular verbs, and they must also be referred to by singular pronouns, as these examples show:

EXAMPLE   *Nobody* in the emergency room waiting area *was* talking.

EXAMPLE   *Everybody* exposed to the spilled chemicals must have *her or his* lungs checked.

Some indefinite pronouns are always plural:

Plural Indefinite Pronouns

both	others
few	several
many	

Plural indefinite pronouns call for plural verbs, and they must also be referred to by plural pronouns, as these examples show:

EXAMPLE   *Many* of the students *are* unable to pay the increase in tuition without taking out loans.

EXAMPLE   *Several* of the angry residents had *their* water service turned off by mistake.

Some indefinite pronouns can be either singular or plural, depending on the words to which they refer.

Indefinite Pronouns Affected by the Words That Follow Them

all	more	none
any	most	some

When you use one of these pronouns as a subject, find the word to which it refers, and check its number. If that word is singular, choose a singular form of the verb; if the word is plural, choose a plural form, as these examples show:

EXAMPLE   *All* of the **magazines** *focus* on style issues every month.

EXAMPLE   *All* of the frozen **food** *has* melted because of the power failure.

Indefinite pronouns can be especially tricky when they serve as antecedents for another pronoun. To avoid errors in pronoun–antecedent agreement when the antecedent is an indefinite pronoun, find *both* pronouns and see if they agree. If they don't agree, change one of the pronouns with a word—noun or pronoun—that does match, as these examples show:

SINGULAR ANTECEDENT   *Everyone* seeking a refund for the show must turn in ~~their~~ *his or her* tickets at the box office.

PLURAL ANTECEDENT   *People* ~~Everyone~~ seeking a refund for the show must turn in *their* tickets at the box office.

PLURAL ANTECEDENT   *All* of the students will be notified that the schedule to register for ~~his or her~~ *their* classes has changed.

SINGULAR ANTECEDENT   *Each* ~~All~~ of the students will be notified that the schedule to register for *his or her* classes has changed.

As the examples show, agreement can come about in one of two ways: (1) change the pronoun to make it agree with the antecedent or (2) replace the antecedent with a word or words that agree with the pronoun. In your writing, make the choice that sounds best and helps you communicate your meaning most clearly.

Exercise 17.6   **Choosing the Correct Verbs for Indefinite Pronouns**

Underline the indefinite pronouns in the sentences below. Decide if the pronoun is singular or plural and then circle the correct verb in parentheses. Use the example and the lists of singular and plural pronouns (pages 322–323) to guide you.

EXAMPLE   *Both* of my parents (is, **are**) retired.

(1) If <u>something</u> (**is**, are) not done about the traffic at the intersection near the industrial park, an accident will happen soon. (2) <u>All</u> of the residents of that area (**fear**, fears) driving home at rush hour. (3) This is not surprising, since <u>everybody</u> (seem, **seems**) to be converging at this intersection. (4) <u>Nobody</u> (want, **wants**) to ask the city council to study the problem because the city lacks funding. (5) <u>Many</u> of our residents (**think**, thinks) a recent change is the answer. (6) To increase revenue, <u>anyone</u> driving to the industrial park now (pay, **pays**) a toll to help fund new traffic lights.

Exercise 17.7   **Correcting Errors in Agreement with Indefinite Pronoun Antecedents**

Each sentence in the following passage contains an error in pronoun–antecedent agreement. First underline the pronouns, and then cross out each error and write the correct pronoun above it. Change the verb if necessary. More than one answer may be possible, as the following example shows:
(Answers may vary somewhat. Representative answers are shown.)

EXAMPLE   <u>Everybody</u> in the calculus class passed <u>their</u> final exam.

Everybody in the calculus class passed his or her final exam.

  or

All of the students in the calculus class passed their exam.

All people
(1) <s>Everybody</s> should have an opportunity to participate in a parenting class before <u>they</u> have children. (2) It's one of the best ways for

people
~~anybody~~ to learn the basic skills they will need to care for a new baby.

his or her
(3) At a typical class, one of the experienced parents shares ~~their~~ knowl-

edge and offers tips to expectant parents. (4) Few of the people in these

them
classes have ever cared for a baby, so the advice reassures ~~him or her~~.

(5) In most cases, when the classes are over, all of the mothers- and fa-

their
thers-to-be feel prepared for the day when ~~his or her~~ bundles of joy fi-

nally arrive.

Exercise 17.8   Working with Indefinite Pronoun Antecedents

Complete each of the following sentences in the space provided, making
sure to supply a pronoun for the italicized antecedent. Check to be certain
that the pronoun you provide agrees with the antecedent. Use the example
as a guide (Answers will vary. Representative answers are shown.)

EXAMPLE   Some of the animals _hunt by night to catch their prey off guard_

1. *Each* of the planets in our solar system ___gets its light from the sun___

_____ .

2. *Most* of the women at the meeting were happy to ___take their turns___

delivering food _____ .

3. *Nobody* likes harsh criticism, especially criticism of ___his or her taste___

in clothes _____ .

4. *Both* of the babies are ___wearing their first pair of shoes___

_____ .

5. Only a *few* of the survivors were able to ___talk about the disaster___

they had witnessed _____ .

6. The customers' food was undercooked, so *many* refused __to pay their checks__ .

7. *Anyone* who wants to play a sport well must __give up some__ __of his or her free time__ .

8. *All* of the passengers were bothered by the delay, but __they did__ __not complain__ .

Challenge 17.3 **Working with Indefinite Pronouns That Change Number**

COLLABORATION

As page 323 shows, six indefinite pronouns—all, any, more, most, none, and some—are either singular or plural depending on what they refer to. Working with a classmate, write two sentences for each of these pronouns, using each one first as a singular word and then as a plural word.

Understanding the Role of Demonstrative Pronouns and Adjectives

When writing longer passages, you must maintain pronoun–antecedent agreement as you move from sentence to sentence. The procedure is the same whether the writing is two sentences or several paragraphs long. Make sure that you use singular pronouns to refer to singular antecedents and plural pronouns to refer to plural antecedents.

Demonstrative pronouns point out a particular person or thing. They sometimes confuse writers who are trying to maintain consistency from sentence to sentence. This is because they are often used to begin a sentence that refers back to a word, phrase, or clause in the sentence before.

There are four demonstrative pronouns:

Demonstrative Pronouns

Singular	*Plural*
this	these
that	those

As you can see, *this* and *that* are always singular.

EXAMPLE   *This* is a true apple; *that* is an apple pear.

These and *those* are merely the plural forms of *this* and *that*.

Do the demonstrative pronouns agree with antecedents in the following sentences?

EXAMPLE   *This* is the perfect *apartment* for my grandmother.

EXAMPLE   *Those* are not good *reasons* to quit a job.

The first sentence includes the singular demonstrative pronoun *this*, which agrees with the singular noun *apartment*. The second includes the plural demonstrative pronoun *those,* which agrees with the plural noun *reasons.* Note that in both sentences, the pronoun comes *before* the antecedent. This is often the case for demonstrative pronoun–antecedent pairs.

Often demonstrative pronouns are placed next to nouns, where they answer the question *which person, place, or thing?* In effect, they function as adjectives. For this reason, they are called **demonstrative adjectives** in this position and usage.

EXAMPLE   *This* apartment will suit grandmother just fine.

In this usage, they agree with the noun beside which they are placed. *Apartment* is singular, so the singular demonstrative adjective *this* agrees. In this chapter, we will treat demonstrative pronouns and demonstrative adjectives together in discussions and exercises.

Exercise 17.9   **Identifying Demonstrative Pronouns and Adjectives**

Underline the demonstrative pronouns and adjectives in the following paragraph. Then write *S* above the demonstrative pronouns and adjectives that are singular and *P* above those that are plural, as the example shows.

EXAMPLE
S   P
That trip to the harbor changed my mind about those new water pollution laws.

(1) Each day I put off completing and filing my taxes, the more diffi-
                    S   S
cult that job gets. (2) I hate doing it, and this makes me delay even more.
        P
(3) All of those forms are piled on the desk ready to go, but I keep ignoring them. (4) I know I'll make mistakes in the math and be frustrated by
                                    P
the instructions, but those aren't good reasons to ignore the job. (5) I
                                    S
should get to work because this is the year I hope to get a refund.

Exercise 17.10   **Choosing the Correct Demonstrative Pronouns and Adjectives**

Circle the correct demonstrative pronouns and adjectives to complete the sentences. Study the example first.

EXAMPLE   The fruit was going to waste; (that, those) was the reason I gave it away.

1. (This, These) photograph is an example of creative photojournalism.

2. Let's clean together; I'll do (this, these) room, and you do (that, those) one.

3. Lesley lost her wallet; (that, those) was a serious loss.

4. These blue sandals match my purse better than (that, those) do.

5. This shirt is beautiful but too expensive; we will buy (that, those) one.

6. (This, These) park is so private and restful.

7. I enjoy most biographies, but I cannot seem to get into (this, these) one.

8. (This, These) was the reason he gave: Because I'm the Dad!

Challenge 17.4   **Using Demonstrative Pronouns and Adjectives Correctly**

1. The sentences below contain errors in pronoun–antecedent agreement. In each sentence, cross out the incorrect demonstrative pronoun or adjective. Above it, write one that matches the italicized antecedent. (Remember that the antecedent may be positioned before or after the demonstrative pronoun.) Also change the noun following the demonstrative adjective if necessary. Study the example first.

EXAMPLE   *Rabbits* used to be made into fur coats, but now it's unfashionable to use ~~this animal~~ these animals for clothing.

(1) Some *days* it doesn't pay to get out of bed; today was one of ~~that~~ those days. (2) In the morning, my car's *battery was dead*, but I solved ~~these~~ this problem by replacing it for fifty dollars. (3) On top of ~~these~~ this *expense,* I had to have a garage tow my car—another twenty-five dollars. (4) I finally

This
arrived at work, only to be told "~~These~~ will be your last *week*—you are

Those
being laid off." (5) ~~That~~ are just *three* of my disasters from a terrible day.

2. Now write a paragraph of about five sentences in which you describe a disastrous day of your own.

COLLABORATION

3. Exchange your work with a partner. On the paper you receive, underline any demonstrative pronouns and circle any errors in agreement. Then return the paper to its writer. Using the material in the preceding section to guide you, correct any errors identified in your paragraph.

Avoiding Errors in Agreement with Demonstrative Pronouns and Adjectives

When a demonstrative pronoun or adjective begins a sentence, the antecedent is often in the previous sentence. To make sure you've used the correct demonstrative pronoun or adjective, you must find the antecedent. If the antecedent is singular, use *this* or *that*. If the antecedent is plural, use *these* or *those*.

Compare the antecedents and the demonstrative pronouns in the following pairs of sentences.

FAULTY   There are five major road reconstruction *projects* in the city. *This* has caused long delays for people using public transportation.

FAULTY   Right now, the city has instituted a 10 P.M. *curfew* at all parks and playgrounds. *Those* should be changed to give kids places to go at night.

In the first example, the demonstrative pronoun *this* is singular. It does not agree with the plural antecedent *projects*. In the second example, the plural demonstrative pronoun *those* does not agree with the singular antecedent *curfew*.

To correct these errors, you could simply change the demonstrative pronouns (and the verb, as in the first example) so that they match their antecedents:

REVISED   There are five major road reconstruction *projects* in the city. *These* have caused long delays for people using public transportation.

REVISED

Right now, the city has instituted a 10 P.M. *curfew* at all parks and playgrounds. *This* should be changed to give kids places to go at night.

An even better strategy for eliminating these kinds of errors is to add a *clarifying word* to the pronoun. Either repeat the antecedent, or use another word with a similar meaning.

Look at these versions of the same pairs of sentences, this time with clarifying words:

REVISED

There are five major road reconstruction *projects* in the city. These *projects* have caused long delays for people using public transportation.

REVISED

Right now, the city has instituted a 10 P.M. *curfew* at all parks and playgrounds. This *rule* should be changed to give kids places to go at night.

In the first sentence, the antecedent *projects* appears again as a clarifying word. In the second sentence, the antecedent *curfew* is not used as a clarifying word. Instead, the clarifying word is a word with a similar meaning: *rule*.

Notice that the addition of the clarifying word, a noun, changes the role of the demonstrative pronoun. It now acts as an adjective, describing the noun next to it: *Which projects? These projects. Which rule? This rule.*

Another area of concern in maintaining pronoun–antecedent agreement involves the **reflexive or intensive pronouns:**

Reflexive or Intensive Pronouns

myself	oneself
yourself	ourselves
himself, herself	yourselves
itself	themselves

You use these pronouns to emphasize the words to which they refer. You should never use one unless you have also included the word to which it refers in the same sentence, as these examples show:

REFLEXIVE

Reaching across the table, Verna burned *herself* on the lit candle in the decorative lantern. *[To direct the verb's action back to the subject]*

INTENSIVE

The signal box *itself* is the cause of the many power outages. *[To emphasize a particular word]*

Keep in mind, however, that these pronouns can't serve as subjects. Should you find that you have made this error, simply replace the reflexive or intensive form with an appropriate personal pronoun, as this example shows:

EXAMPLE

Tim and ~~myself~~ played racquetball for two hours yesterday.
(I above myself)

Exercise 17.11   **Maintaining Agreement with Demonstrative Pronouns and Adjectives**

Each set of sentences below contains an error in agreement. Underline the antecedent and the demonstrative pronoun or adjective in each item. Then cross out the incorrect demonstrative pronoun or adjective and replace it with the correct one. Review text examples and the example below to see whether any other words in the sentences should also be changed.

EXAMPLE

There are six games left in the season. ~~This~~ *These* should all be exciting.

1 In 1891, Dr. James Naismith invented the game of basketball for a YMCA fitness program. ~~These~~ *This* game was not immediately popular, because some people felt it was too violent.

2. The first professional basketball game was played in 1896 between two teams in Trenton, New Jersey. ~~This~~ *These* teams were made up of men who held day jobs as factory workers, laborers, and small businessmen.

3. The Buffalo Germans were the first powerhouse team, having a record of 792 wins and only 86 losses. ~~These~~ *This* was the envy of many other teams.

4. In 1914, the New York Celtics were organized, playing a new style of basketball. ~~These~~ *This* used zone defense, the fast break, and a pivot man.

5. What began as a YMCA fitness program has expanded to 32 teams from all over North America. Dr. Naismith would have been proud of ~~those~~ *that*.

Exercise 17.12   **Using Demonstrative Pronouns and Adjectives That Agree with Antecedents**

Add a second sentence to each item below. In each, use a demonstrative pronoun or adjective that refers to the italicized antecedent in the first sentence. Use the example as a guide. (Answers will vary.)

| EXAMPLE | My sister was both *pretty and popular.* _Those qualities made me jealous._ |

1. When I was two, I was bitten by a *dog.*

_____

_____

2. I missed the *class* before the exam.

_____

_____

3. These running *shoes* are really sturdy.

_____

_____

4. I admired his hand-crafted toy *birdhouses.*

_____

_____

5. Here are the rules for entering the chess *tournament.*

_____

_____

Exercise 17.13   Working with Reflexive and Intensive Pronouns

Fill in the blanks in the following sentences with an appropriate reflexive or intensive pronoun from the list on page 330. Use the example as a guide.

| EXAMPLE | Ty finally decided to vacuum the house _himself_ . |

1. After a half hour, the tired puppy finally whimpered ____itself____ to sleep.

2. If they want reforms in insurance laws, then physicians ____themselves____

    need to make their case to Congress.

3. When you are tired, you may find motivating ____yourself____ to study

    even harder.

4. Even though she is the manager, tonight, Beverly ___herself___ will join

the rest of the workers in cleaning the shelves.

5. When my friends and I go out for a night, we spend as much time making

___ourselves___ laugh as we do dancing.

Challenge 17.5   **Using Clarifying Words with Demonstrative Pronouns**

Working with a classmate, add a clarifying word to the demonstrative pronouns in items 3–5 of Exercise 17.11. Then write a brief paragraph discussing how adding a clarifying word can help clarify meaning for writers and readers.

Maintaining Agreement in *That, Who,* and *Which* Clauses

As Chapter 8, "Subordination," explains, the pronouns *that, who,* and *which* may also introduce a subordinate clause that describes an antecedent. These pronouns are called **relative pronouns.** The verb in a *that, who,* or *which* clause must agree with the antecedent. If the antecedent is singular, then the verb in the *that, who,* or *which* clause must be singular. However, if the antecedent is plural, then the verb must also be plural:

> subordinate clause

EXAMPLE   The candidates *who run for President* spend too much time and

money on image.

The antecedent *candidates* is plural. The clause describing *candidates* is *who run for President.* The verb in the clause is *run,* the plural form.

Find the antecedents for the italicized clauses in the following sentences:

FAULTY   The rooms *that faces the beach* are all taken.

FAULTY   My favorite shirt, *which are made of silk,* is now almost ten years old.

In the first sentence, the antecedent for the *that* clause is the plural noun *rooms,* but the verb in the clause is *faces,* a singular form. There is a problem with agreement. In the second sentence, the antecedent for the *which* clause is the singular noun *shirt.* It does not agree with the plural verb *are* in the *which* clause.

To correct these kinds of errors in agreement, simply change the verbs in the subordinate clauses:

REVISED   The *rooms* that *face* the beach are all taken.

REVISED   My favorite *shirt,* which *is* made of silk, is now almost ten years old.

Exercise 17.14   **Maintaining Agreement with *That, Who,* and *Which* Clauses**

The italicized clauses in the following paragraph contain errors in agreement. Correct each error by underlining the antecedent and then changing the verb in the clause. Cross out the incorrect verb, and write the correct one above it. Use the example as a guide.

EXAMPLE
                            are
My teacher asks <u>students</u> who ~~is~~ *late for class* to enter the classroom as

quietly as possible.

(1) Television <u>programs</u> *that ~~has~~ adult content* should air after 10:00
             have

P.M. (2) <u>Children,</u> *who ~~is~~ awake earlier in the evening,* should not be ex-
            are
                                                                          studies
posed to violence, profanity, and adult situations. (3) <u>Research</u> *that ~~study~~*

the effects of these programs on children has given mixed results. (4)
            know
<u>Parents</u> *who ~~knows~~ their children best,* have their own opinions. (5) They
                                                              are
believe television <u>programs</u> *that ~~is~~ inappropriate for children* may harm

their development.

Exercise 17.15   **Identifying Agreement with *That, Who,* and *Which* Clauses**

Some of the sentences in the paragraph below contain errors in agreement in *that, which,* or *who* clauses.

1. Locate the subordinate clause in each sentence, and decide if there is an agreement error.

2. If there is an agreement error, change the verb form so that it agrees with the antecedent. Cross out the incorrect form, and write the correct one above it, as the example shows.

3. If a sentence is correct as written, mark it *OK*.

lies
One who ~~lie~~ cannot be trusted.

(1) Both men and women are impressed by partners who are con-
OK
siderate and polite. (2) A person who ~~disregard~~ a partner's comfort and
disregards
feelings won't get very far in a relationship. (3) Small things that ~~doesn't~~
don't
cost a lot of money can make a romantic partner happy. (4) After all, it's
the thought that ~~count~~. (5) For most people, a paperback book that ~~are~~
counts   *is*
given with feeling is just as good as a fancier gift. (6) In addition, most
people value a partner who ~~are~~ informal and spontaneous. (7) A man
is
or woman who ~~don't~~ adjust to new or surprising circumstances is not
doesn't
much fun to be with. (8) People of both sexes also want a partner who
~~are~~ supportive.
is

 Challenge 17.6   **Maintaining Subordinate Clause–Antecedent
Agreement in Your Writing**

COLLABORATION   Write three sentences, using a *that, which,* or *who* clause in each. Exchange
your sentences with a classmate, and review each other's work to make sure
you have maintained agreement.

Avoiding Problems with Gender
in Pronoun–Antecedent Agreement

Gender refers to whether a word is *feminine* or *masculine*. The gender of a
pronoun must agree with the gender of its antecedent. Feminine words call
for feminine pronouns, and masculine words require masculine pronouns.
Below is a list of masculine and feminine pronouns.

Masculine Pronouns	*Feminine Pronouns*
he	she
him	her
his	hers

In English, maintaining agreement in gender is fairly simple. Unlike many languages, English requires that you consider gender only when you are writing about people and animals. The pronoun *it* is used to refer to all other kinds of singular nouns.

In fact, you have to be concerned with gender when you are using pronouns that refer to singular nouns only. *They* is used to refer to all plural nouns.

Match the antecedents and the pronouns in these sentences:

FAULTY   Movie star *Denzel Washington* got *her* start on television in *St. Elsewhere*.

FAULTY   The *woman* left the house with no money in *his* purse.

In the first sentence, the antecedent is *Denzel Washington*, and its pronoun is *her*. However, Denzel Washington is a man, so the pronoun should be masculine. There is also an error in agreement in the second sentence. The antecedent (*woman*) is feminine, but the pronoun (*his*) is masculine.

To eliminate this type of error in agreement, simply change the pronoun so it matches the gender of its antecedent:

REVISED   Movie star *Denzel Washington* got *his* start on television in *St. Elsewhere*.

REVISED   The *woman* left the house with no money in *her* purse.

Avoiding Sexist Language When Choosing Pronouns

It is important to avoid sexist language when you are matching up antecedents and pronouns. **Sexist language** is any wording that inappropriately excludes one gender. A word like *foreman* is sexist because it excludes women. It suggests that only a man could perform such a job. A better choice would be the nonsexist word *supervisor*.

Problems with sexist language sometimes arise when writers try to match up antecedents like *each, everybody,* and *someone* with singular pronouns. For many years, it was acceptable to use *he, him,* or *his* as pronouns for these words, even though they represent *all* people.

FAULTY   *Everyone* should have *his* vision checked once a year.

Today, however, using only a masculine pronoun to refer to a word like *everyone* is considered sexist.

There are two main ways to avoid using sexist language in these instances. One option is to use *both* a feminine and a masculine pronoun connected by *or,* as shown below:

REVISED	*Everyone* should have *his or her* vision checked once a year.

The second option—and often the better choice—is to make both the pronoun and its antecedent plural. This may require replacing the antecedent with a different word or phrase. Look at this version of the sentence, with both pronoun and antecedent plural:

REVISED	*People* should have *their* vision checked once a year.

In this instance, the plural noun *people* is a better choice than the singular pronoun *everyone.* It allows the writer to avoid the issue of gender altogether.

Exercise 17.16   **Maintaining Agreement with Gender and Avoiding Sexist Language**

The sentences in the paragraph below contain errors in agreement or sexist language. Underline both the antecedents and their pronouns. Then rewrite each sentence on a separate sheet of paper, making any changes you need to correct the error. Use the example to guide you.

EXAMPLE	<u>Anybody</u> attending the dance had to have <u>his</u> hand stamped.
	Students attending the dance had to have their hands stamped.
	or
	Anybody attending the dance had to have his or her hand stamped.

(1) Ida Minerva Tarbell was a <u>newspaperman</u> who left <u>her</u> mark on the field of investigative journalism. (2) <u>Everyone</u> who studies the history of magazines should include Tarbell on <u>his</u> list of influential writers. (3) <u>Tarbell</u> reported for *McClure's Magazine* on <u>his</u> investigation of Standard Oil. (4) <u>Tarbell's articles</u> exposed the company's <u>corrupt</u> practices, and <u>it</u> helped break the Standard Oil Trust. (5) Any reporter today should be proud if <u>he</u> can follow in Ida Tarbell's footsteps.

Exercise 17.17 **Using Nonsexist Language**

On a separate piece of paper, rewrite the following sentences, correcting each gender error in two different ways. Be sure to avoid sexist language in your revisions. Use the example as a guide.

EXAMPLE

Everybody in the office will be asked to submit his vacation plans.

Everybody in the office will be asked to submit his or her vacation plans.

or

Employees will be asked to submit their vacation plans.

1. Every passenger must sit in his seat until the pilot shuts off the "fasten seat belt" sign.

2. Anyone who is late will have to pay extra for his ticket.

3. Nobody should be unprepared for his first day of class.

4. Each customer will be asked for his opinion.

5. Someone who works in sales should know his product well.

6. A police officer must be prepared to risk his life when on duty.

7. It makes sense for a doctor to know a little about his patients' lives.

8. Every one of the candidates must complete his nomination forms.

Exercise 17.18 **Avoiding Sexist Language**

Below is a list of eight sexist words. Write a neutral substitute next to each one, being careful not to use another equally sexist word in its place. (For example, don't replace *maid* with *butler*.) Next, on a separate sheet of paper, compose a sentence for each substitution.

(Answers may vary. Suitable responses are shown.)

- chairman _____ chairperson _____
- mailman _____ mail carrier _____
- manpower _____ people power _____
- master _____ head of household _____

- serviceman _____ service person _____

- maid _____ household help _____

- poetess _____ poet _____

- stewardess _____ flight attendant _____

Challenge 17.7   **Analyzing Sexist Language**

What nouns have you read or heard that you think are sexist? List at least five of them, along with replacement words that are nonsexist. Bring your list to class, and discuss it with your classmates. In your discussion, explore ways sexist language may affect people.

Using Pronouns Checklist

☐ Have you made sure that you have used subjective case personal pronouns only as subjects and objective case pronouns only as objects?

☐ Have you made sure that you have used possessive case personal pronouns without apostrophes, paying particular attention to the use of *its?*

☐ Have you checked the number of any personal and indefinite pronouns you have used to make sure they are the correct choice for the situation?

☐ Have you used singular pronouns as antecedents for any collective nouns?

Exploring Ideas through Journal Writing

When it comes to number, most pronouns can be easily identified as singular or plural. But as page 323 points out, six indefinite pronouns can be either singular or plural depending on what they refer to. What have you found in your experiences that changes dramatically depending on the circumstances? For example, do you project one image at school or work and another at home? Why? Do you have a friend who treats you differently from the way he or she treats other friends? How does that make you feel? Does your campus, city, or neighborhood take on a very different look or atmosphere after dark? What causes the change? Which do you like better? Why? Consider one of these topics or one related to them, and explore it in your journal for 20 to 30 minutes.

Chapter Quick Check: Using Pronouns

The following passage contains errors in pronoun–antecedent agreement and sexist language. Make corrections by crossing out the incorrect words and writing the correct versions above them.

(Answer may vary somewhat.)

(1) The planet Mars, which ~~are~~ *is* one of our closest neighbors in the solar system, remains an enticing enigma to scientists. (2) Many of ~~this~~ *these* scientists believe that Mars was once a warm planet like Earth, with water and an atmosphere. (3) Photographs and other evidence transmitted by unmanned probes to Mars show enormous canyons, and ~~it~~ *they* also ~~reveals~~ *reveal* areas that appear to be dried up lakes or river beds. (4) But ~~no one is~~ *none of the experts are* sure where the water went, nor can they tell for sure whether life existed or remains somewhere on the planet. (5) Of course, today ~~nobody~~ *no experts* who seriously ~~studies~~ *study* the issue ~~thinks~~ *think* that they are talking about life that remotely resembles human life forms. (6) Rather, for ~~they~~ *them* and others who share their view, the hope is to find some kind of bacterial organism. (7) ~~Those~~ *This* could be living in the frozen mixture of water, rock, and sand that these scientists believe lies beneath the surface of Mars. (8) More recently, a group of scientists has presented another theory, which ~~suggest~~ *suggests* that Mars has led a largely chilly existence. (9) According to this theory, Mars was hit by numerous enormous asteroids billions of years ago, and ~~it~~ *they* caused huge amounts of water within the planet and asteroids to vaporize. (10) The water that resulted when the vapor condensed and rained down created the physical characteristics that convinced early astronomers that ~~he was~~ *they were* looking at canals.

Discovering Connections 17.2

1. For Discovering Connections 17.1 on page 315, you began prewriting in response to a quotation by Thomas Edison or a photo. Now continue your prewriting on one of these options:
   a. What is it that keeps people who do succeed from giving up?
   b. Have you ever experienced or witnessed what Edison describes?
2. Evaluate your prewriting material, identify a focus, and create a draft of about 100 words.
3. Exchange your draft with a writing partner. Using the material in this chapter as a guide, evaluate the draft you receive, and note any problems with pronoun–antecedent agreement as well as any other weaknesses. Return the draft to the writer.
4. Revise your draft, eliminating any errors that your reader identified.

Summary Exercise: Using Pronouns

The following passage contains errors in pronoun–antecedent agreement and sexist language. Make corrections by crossing out the incorrect words and writing the correct versions above it. Put *OK* above any sentence without an error.

OK
(1) One of the most exciting technological developments of the past

This
twenty-five years is the Internet. (2) ~~These~~ is an expanding worldwide sys-

are
tem of computer networks. (3) The Internet lets people who ~~is~~ separated

by thousands of miles communicate easily and quickly. (4) Also, the

people
Internet gives ~~everyone~~ a chance to share and exchange their files and

businesspeople
programs. (5) More recently, ~~businessmen~~ using the Internet are finding

it
~~them~~ a new and growing marketplace.

they have
(6) People can communicate using the computer network if ~~he has~~

are
an Internet address. (7) Messages that ~~is~~ sent over the Internet are called

Those
electronic mail, or e-mail. (8) ~~This~~ messages are sent through the com-

is
puter world, which ~~are~~ called cyberspace. (9) The World Wide Web now

makes it very easy for many to publish ~~his~~ *their* own writing and even graphics for others to read.

(10) *OK* The government wants to regulate cyberspace. (11) ~~They are~~ *It is* concerned about issues such as consumer fraud and child pornography online. (12) Others, who ~~is~~ *are* also concerned about the rapid growth in Internet use, ∧ see regulation as a threat to ~~his~~ *their* free speech. (13) *OK* This debate about regulation will be interesting. (14) Some of ~~them~~ *it* will take place on the Internet.

(15) *OK* No one knows what the future will be like in cyberspace. (16) Internet users can already view video on ~~his~~ *their* screens. (17) Scientists of the future may sit at ~~his computer~~ *their computers* and perform an experiment with a researcher on the other side of the world. (18) *OK* We may order all our food and buy all our clothes online. (19) ~~A student~~ *Students* may sit at home and join their classmates online instead of in school. (20) *OK* Our children will certainly have a different way to communicate their ideas than we do.

USING PRONOUNS: CONSIDERING CASE, CLEAR PRONOUN–ANTECEDENT AGREEMENT, AND NONSEXIST PRONOUN USAGE

New terms in this chapter	Definitions
● **pronoun**	● a word used in place of a noun *Example* Larry picked up the *CD player* and shook *it*.
● **personal pronoun**	● a pronoun that specifies a particular person, place, thing, or idea Personal pronouns have three separate forms, or cases, to show person.

Personal Pronouns
Case

	Subjective	Objective	Possessive
First person	I, we	me, us	my, mine, our, ours
Second person	you	you	your, yours
Third person	she, he, it, they	her, him, it, them	her, hers, his, its, their, theirs

New terms in this chapter	Definitions
● **antecedent**	● the word or words to which a pronoun refers Singular antecedents call for singular pronouns; plural antecedents call for plural pronouns. *Example* The little *boy* dropped *his* hat. Indefinite pronoun antecedents must agree with their pronouns. *Example* *Everyone* who has a student ID will receive 25 percent off *her or his* purchase.
● **indefinite pronoun**	● a pronoun used to refer to someone or something in general

Singular Indefinite Pronouns

another	each	everything	nobody	other
anybody	either	little	no one	somebody
anyone	everybody	much	nothing	someone
anything	everyone	neither	one	something

Plural Indefinite Pronouns

both	others
few	several
many	

Indefinite Pronouns Affected by the Words That Follow Them

all	more	none
any	most	some

New terms in this chapter	Definitions
● **demonstrative pronoun / demonstrative adjective**	● singular: *this, that* ● plural: *these, those* If a demonstrative pronoun begins a sentence, find the antecedent in the preceding sentence. A demonstrative pronoun placed next to a noun is then called a *demonstrative adjective*. *Example* Some CDs in *that box* are damaged. *Those* should be discarded.

Continued

New terms in this chapter	Definitions
● **reflexive/intensive pronoun**	● a combination of a personal pronoun with *-self* or *-selves: myself, yourself, himself, herself, itself, ourselves, yourselves, themselves.* Reflexive or intensive pronouns are used for emphasis (Liz *herself* answered the question) or to direct the action of the verb back to the subject (Peter allowed *himself* a period of rest)
● **relative pronoun**	● *that, who, which, whom, whose* A relative pronoun introduces a clause that describes an antecedent; the verb in the clause must agree with the antecedent. *Example* The nurse who *is* addressing my class this morning graduated from this college.
● **interrogative pronoun**	● What . . . ? Whatever . . . ? Which . . . ? Whichever . . . ? Who . . . ? Whoever . . . ? Whom . . . ? Whomever . . . ? Whose . . . ? An interrogative pronoun introduces a question. *Example* *What* is the problem?
● **gender**	● refers to whether a word is masculine or feminine Pronouns must match the gender of their antecedents.
● **sexist language**	● language that inappropriately excludes one gender Try using plural antecedents and pronouns instead. *Example* *All bicyclists* using the municipal bike path must wear *their* helmets.

Pronoun Agreement Chart

Type	Gender	Number Singular	Number Plural
personal pronouns			
subject pronouns		I	we
		you	you
	masculine	he	
	feminine	she	
	neutral	it	they
object pronouns		me	us
		you	you
	masculine	him	
	feminine	her	
	neutral	it	them
possessive pronouns		my, mine	our, ours
		your, yours	your, yours
	masculine	his	
	feminine	her, hers	
	neutral	its	their, theirs

Type	Number Singular	Number Plural
indefinite pronouns	another much anybody neither anyone nobody anything no one each nothing either one everybody other everyone somebody everything someone little something Indefinite pronouns that can be either singular *or* plural: all, none, most, any, some, more	both few many others several
demonstrative pronouns	this that	these those
relative pronouns	who which that	who which that

Chapter 18

Working with Adjectives and Adverbs: Using Modifiers Effectively

Getting Started... **Q:** So that my ideas are as clear and specific as I can make them, I use plenty of words that describe and modify. The problem is that I'm not always sure that I've correctly used them. What's the best way to avoid making mistakes with modifying and describing words?

A: The words that you use to modify and describe—adjectives and adverbs—do help to make your writing clear and specific. That's because adjectives and adverbs bring what you are writing into sharper focus for your reader. The secret to making sure you don't make errors with their use is to concentrate on the most likely problem spots. Using the wrong form of a describing word to make comparisons is one, and so is using two negatives, words like *not* or *never,* in the same subject–verb unit is another. Putting a modifier in the wrong position in a sentence is also a concern.

Overview: Building Precise Detail with Modifiers

To make their ideas more precise and informative, writers use a group of tools called *modifiers.* Two kinds of modifiers are *adjectives,* which describe nouns and pronouns, and *adverbs,* which describe verbs, adjectives, and other adverbs. These modifiers paint a more vivid picture of a person, place, or thing, or they bring an action or event into sharper focus for the reader.

Adjectives and adverbs are also useful to pinpoint the degree to which a noun or verb possesses the quality described—that is, to make comparisons. They take different forms to allow these comparisons.

Adjectives and adverbs are among a writer's most powerful tools. These modifiers enable writers to create memorable images in their readers' minds. They can give your writing not only clarity, but also excitement. To use modifiers correctly, however, you first need to recognize the forms that modifiers take.

> ***This chapter will introduce you to these forms of modifiers and help you discover how to use them. You will learn about***
>
> - the roles of adjectives and adverbs as modifiers
> - the positive, comparative, and superlative forms of modifiers
> - the forms of common irregular modifiers
> - how to use *-ing* modifiers accurately
> - ways to avoid double negatives

Discovering Connections 18.1

Consider the following quotation:

Creativity is inventing, experimenting, growing, taking risks, breaking rules, making mistakes, and having fun.

—*Mary Lou Cook*

Or look at this photo.

Now, using the technique you prefer, do some prewriting about your reaction to the quotation or the photo. Save your work.

Using the Positive Form of Modifiers

Modifiers may be adjectives or adverbs. An **adjective** describes a noun or pronoun by telling *which one, how many,* or *what kind*:

which one?	what kind?	how many?

EXAMPLES   *the first* desk   *antique* desk   *one* desk

An **adverb** describes a verb, adjective, or other adverb by telling *how, when, where, to what extent,* or *how much:*

how?	when?	where?

EXAMPLES   He ran *quickly.*   He ran *daily.*   He ran *here.*

to what extent?	how much?

He ran *very* quickly.   He ran *enough.*

Both adjectives and adverbs have more than one form. The positive form is used to modify a single word. Look at these sentences:

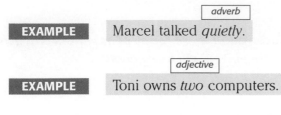

adverb

EXAMPLE   Marcel talked *quietly*.

adjective

EXAMPLE   Toni owns *two* computers.

In the first sentence, the adverb *quietly* modifies the verb *talked*. It explains how Marcel talked. In the second sentence, the adjective *two* modifies the noun *television*. It tells how many televisions.

With the positive form of modifiers, you use a special category of adjectives called *articles*. There are just three articles: *a, an,* and *the*. You use *a* before a word beginning with a consonant sound: *a television*. You use *an* before a word beginning with a vowel sound: *an apple*. These words help specify which noun or pronoun is being discussed. Often they appear in combination with other adjectives, in usages that call for an article.

article and adjective

EXAMPLE   Hermine washes *the blue* car every other Thursday.

Note that it would not be correct to say "Hermine washes blue car every other Thursday."

Exercise 18.1   **Identifying the Positive Form of Modifiers**

Circle the adjectives (including articles), and underline the adverbs that you identify in the sentences below. Use the example to guide you.

EXAMPLE   (One) program I <u>never</u> miss is (the evening) news.

(1) Gerbils make (great) pets for (young) children to raise. (2) (The small) animals thrive <u>efficiently</u> on (a small) amount of food and (clean) water <u>daily</u>. (3) Gerbils can live in (a simple) cage or (glass) aquarium. (4) For exercise they scurry <u>quickly</u> in (exercise) wheels, explore (plastic) tunnels, or chew up cardboard to make nests. (5) <u>Never</u> buy both a male and (a female) gerbil, however, or you will <u>inevitably</u> have (more) gerbils than you need.

Exercise 18.2   **Working with the Positive Form of Modifiers**

Write an adjective or adverb on each blank in the sentences below. Choose a modifier that will help create a picture about the topic in a reader's mind. Use the example as a guide. (Answers will vary.)

EXAMPLE

After the race, the _*exhausted*_ runners rested under the shade of the

*maple* tree.

(1) Renovating a(n) _____ room in a(n) _____ house is _____ work. (2) The _____ results, however, _____ justify all the effort. (3) For the _____ step, clean the space. (4) Then discard and replace _____ windows, scrape _____ paint, and patch _____ sections of plaster. (5) Choose your _____ paint to brighten the room. (6) Pick a(n) _____ yellow or _____ white to make the room look _____. (7) A(n) _____ floor improves _____ in appearance with a coat of _____ varnish and a(n) _____ rug. (8) You will feel _____ when you step back and admire your _____ room.

Exercise 18.3   **Using the Positive Form of Modifiers to Write a Paragraph**

Use at least ten of the modifiers in the list below to write a short paragraph. After you have finished your paragraph, circle the adjectives and articles, and underline the adverbs.

dark	slowly	the	chillingly	clammy
musty	dismal	carefully	mournfully	dark
anxiously	quiet	icy	dreadful	a

Challenge 18.1 **Using Modifiers to Improve Your Writing**

1. Read the paragraph you wrote for Exercise 18.3 aloud to a classmate. Then have your classmate read it to you, this time omitting the modifiers. How has the paragraph changed? Discuss with your class how the modifiers improve the writing.

2. Choose a paragraph you have written, and improve it by adding several modifiers.

Using the Comparative Form of Modifiers

Modifiers may be used to show the degree or extent to which the modified word possesses a certain quality. When modifiers are used to compare, their forms change. Both adjectives and adverbs have **comparative forms.** Writers use these to compare or contrast two things or actions. Look at these examples:

adjective

EXAMPLE   This movie starring Robin Williams is *more hilarious* than his last one.

adverb

EXAMPLE   At that restaurant, the dishwashers work *harder* than the waitresses.

In the first sentence, the modifier *more hilarious* indicates which one of two movies is funnier. In the second sentence, the modifier *harder* specifies how one type of employee works compared to another.

Forming the comparative of most modifiers is simple. Use one of these two methods, depending on the number of syllables in the modifier.

1. For words of *one syllable,* add *-er* to the positive form.

Positive	*Comparative*
clean	clean**er**
loud	loud**er**
fast	fast**er**

2. For modifiers of *more than two syllables,* put *more* before the modifier.

Positive	*Comparative*
extravagant	**more** extravagant
enjoyable	**more** enjoyable
awkwardly	**more** awkwardly

With modifiers of exactly *two* syllables, however, there is no automatic way to know whether to add *-er* or *more* to form the comparative. Some two-syllable modifiers form their comparative by dropping a *-y* from the end of the positive form, changing it to *-i,* and then adding *-er:*

Positive	Comparative
angry	angri**er**
hungry	hungri**er**
happy	happi**er**

Other two-syllable modifiers form their comparative by placing *more* before them:

Positive	Comparative
anxious	**more** anxious
helpful	**more** helpful
promptly	**more** promptly

If you are unsure, check in a dictionary. It often lists the correct way to form the comparative of two-syllable modifiers.

One point to remember. *Never* add both *-er* and *more* to the same modifier. It is never correct to write *more prouder* or *more humider. Always* use one method or the other.

Exercise 10.4   **Using the Comparative Form of Modifiers**

The positive form of a modifier is given in parentheses in each sentence below. Cross out the positive form, and write the correct comparative form above it. Study the example first.

EXAMPLE   The snowbanks are (~~high~~) *higher* in my neighborhood than in the city.

(1) Rollerblading, or in-line skating, is (~~enjoyable~~) *more enjoyable* than walking for exercise. (2) I can go (~~fast~~) *faster* when I rollerblade, and my heart pumps (~~hard~~) *harder* than when I walk. (3) At first, I found it (~~difficult~~) *more difficult* to rollerblade and (~~dangerous~~) *more dangerous*, too, but I kept practicing. (4) Now I can use the bike path (~~safely~~) *more safely* as a skater than as a walker. (5) A good pair of skates is (~~expensive~~) *more expensive* than similar quality walking shoes. (6) Nevertheless, I am (~~happy~~) *happier* now when I head out to exercise than I used to be because skating is so much (~~fun~~) *more fun*.

Exercise 18.5   **Working with the Comparative Form of Modifiers**

In the following paragraph, comparative forms of modifiers are italicized. Some are incorrect. Cross out each incorrect form, and write the correct form above it. If a sentence is correct as written, mark it *OK*. Use the example as a guide.

EXAMPLE   Some movie sequels follow the original ~~closer~~ *more closely* than others.

(1) Susan and Heather are twins, but they are not identical; for example, Susan is three inches *taller* than Heather. **OK** (2) Both have dark brown eyes, but Susan is definitely ~~*more blonder*~~ *blonder* than Heather. (3) Both girls can sing well, but Heather has a ~~*more low*~~ *lower* voice than Susan. (4) Whenever they sing together, Heather sings the low notes while Susan takes the ~~*more high*~~ *higher* notes. (5) Many people think that Heather is the ~~*more pretty*~~ *prettier* of the two. (6) Maybe that's why she is the *more outgoing* of the sisters. **OK** (7) Susan is usually ~~*more quieter*~~ *quieter*. (8) She is ~~*unlikelier*~~ *more unlikely* to strike up a conversation with someone she doesn't know.

Challenge 18.2   **Using the Comparative Form of Modifiers in Your Writing**

COLLABORATION

Make a list of at least ten modifiers. Exchange the list with a writing partner, and change the positive form of the modifier to the comparative form. Then, working with your partner, write sentences for five of the comparative form modifiers.

Using the Superlative Form of Modifiers

Writers use the **superlative form** of a modifier when they are comparing *more than two* things. As with the comparative, the superlative of most adjectives and adverbs is formed in one of two ways: (1) by adding an ending or (2) by placing a word in front of the modifier. Look at these examples:

adjective

EXAMPLE   Of all the new video releases, the one starring Tom Hanks was the *newest*.

> *adverb*

EXAMPLE   Kathryn was running the *most gracefully* of all the contestants.

In the first sentence, the superlative *newest* indicates which video was the most recent among many. In the second sentence, the superlative *most gracefully* explains how Kathryn's running style differed from that of other runners.

Form the superlative of any one-syllable modifier simply by adding *-est* to the positive form:

Positive	*Superlative*
bright	bright**est**
slow	slow**est**
young	young**est**

Form the superlative of words of *more than two syllables* by adding *most* before the modifier:

Positive	*Superlative*
considerate	**most** considerate
frightening	**most** frightening
unfortunately	**most** unfortunately

There is also no automatic way to tell whether to add *-est* or *most* to form the superlative of a two-syllable modifier. Some two-syllable modifiers form their superlatives by adding *-est*. Notice in the following examples that a modifier ending in a *consonant + y* requires a spelling change:

Positive	*Superlative*
heavy	heavi**est**
easy	easi**est**
simple	simpl**est**

Other two-syllable modifiers form their superlatives by the addition of *most:*

Positive	*Superlative*
eager	**most** eager
private	**most** private
famous	**most** famous

As with comparatives, remember you can use a dictionary to check for the correct way to form the superlatives of two-syllable modifiers.

As with comparative forms, *never* use both methods of forming the superlative with the same modifier. It is *never* correct to write *most smallest* or *most curiousest. Always* use one method or the other.

Using the Superlative Form of Modifiers

Revise the sentences below by changing the modifier in parentheses to the superlative form. Follow the guidelines in the section above. Cross out the positive form, and write the superlative form above it. Study the example first.

EXAMPLE
                                        most frightening
The dream I had last night was the (~~frightening~~) one I ever had.

                                                            fastest
(1) The way movies are shown has been one of the (~~fast~~) changing
                                          earliest
aspects of the film business. (2) One of the (~~early~~) ways individuals saw

movies was by looking in a peephole at film passing by a lightbulb. (3)

The kinetoscope, one of the first movie projectors, was developed by one
          most famous
of our (~~famous~~) inventors, Thomas Edison. (4) By the early 1900s, going
                                   most popular
to the local nickelodeon was the (~~popular~~) way to see movies. (5)
                                          newest
Edison had brought from France the (~~new~~) way to project movies: on a
                                                    most profitable
wall for many people to watch together. (6) Today, one of the (~~profitable~~)

trends is to show several movies in one building called a multiscreen

theater.

Working with the Superlative Form of Modifiers

In the following paragraph, superlative forms of modifiers are italicized. Some are incorrect. Cross out each incorrect form, and write the correct one above it. If a sentence is correct as written, mark it *OK*. Study the example first.

EXAMPLE
                          dullest
That has to be the ~~most dull~~ movie I've seen in a long time.

                                          OK
(1) A vacation in London can be the *best* experience if you know

what to expect and plan ahead. (2) London, known as the Gateway to
                              most international
Europe, is possibly the ~~internationalest~~ city in the world. (3) Unfortunately,
                    cheapest   most quickly
it is also not the ~~most cheap~~ city in the world. (4) The hotels fill ~~quickliest~~

in the summertime, when the rates are the ~~most highest.~~ (over: highest) (5) However, you can find affordable bed and breakfast inns in some of the ~~most nicest~~ (over: nicest) neighborhoods if you book far enough in advance. (6) The *greatest* (over: OK) deal in London is transportation. (7) The London underground, known as "the tube," is the *fastest*, (over: OK) ~~efficientest~~ (over: most efficient) urban transportation system in the world. (8) You can do your sightseeing and shopping *most easily* (over: OK) if you take the tube.

Challenge 18.3   Using the Superlative Form of Modifiers in Your Writing

A fun book to explore is the *Guinness Book of World Records*, a collection of astonishing records from around the world. Visit your local or college library, and leaf through the pages of this book or another book of records. Use superlative form modifiers to write some superlative facts that you find interesting. Bring them to class to share with your classmates. For example, what company has the greatest annual sales? What is the tallest building in the world? How long is the longest snake?

Using Irregular Modifiers

A few modifiers do not form their comparative and superlative forms in the standard ways described above. These modifiers are called *irregular modifiers*. Here is a list of common irregular modifiers:

Common Irregular Modifiers

Positive	Comparative	Superlative
bad (adjective)	worse	worst
badly (adverb)	worse	worst
good (adjective)	better	best
well (adverb)	better	best
little	less	least
much	more	most

As this list shows, the first two sets of modifiers form their comparatives and superlatives the same way. The adjectives *bad* and *good* are used to describe people and things; the adverbs *badly* and *well* are used to say how something was done. (The differences between *good* and *well* are discussed further on page 358.) However, in both cases, these pairs of words share the same comparative and superlative forms.

As you do with other modifiers, use the comparative form when you are talking about two and the superlative when you are discussing more than two. Look at the following examples:

EXAMPLE

adjective

That new nightclub has *less* room than the club across the street.

EXAMPLE

Of all the rides at that amusement park, I enjoyed the roller coaster the

adverb

most.

In the first sentence, the comparative form *less* sizes up two clubs. In the second, the superlative form *most* tells how much the roller coaster was enjoyed compared to at least two other rides.

Exercise 18.8 **Working with Irregular Modifiers**

Underline the correct form of the irregular modifier in parentheses in each sentence below. Use the example as a guide.

EXAMPLE

Cheryl was voted the (more, most) likely to succeed of all her classmates.

(1) One of my (least, less) favorite chores is doing laundry. (2) No matter how often I visit the laundromat, I find I should go (most, more) often to keep up with my family's dirty clothes. (3) The (worse, worst) part of the job is having to sit and wait for the washer and dryer to finish their cycles. (4) I have (less, least) patience than the majority of people do, I guess. (5) Maybe if I did the job (worse, worst) than I do, someone else in my family would take over at the laundromat.

Exercise 18.9 **Identifying Errors with Irregular Modifiers**

The following paragraph contains some errors in the use of irregular modifiers. Cross out each incorrect modifier, and write the correct form above it. If a sentence is correct as written, mark it *OK*. Use the example to guide you.

EXAMPLE

most

Of all of my professors, Dr. Han is the ~~more~~ helpful.

earliest

(1) The Mir Space Station was humankind's ~~more early~~ experiment on long-term life in space. (2) Living in space for no less than two

months at a time, Mir scientists spent ~~mucher~~ *most* of their time performing a variety of experiments. *OK* (3) The mission of most scientists on Mir was to study both the good and bad effects of long-term life in space. (4) Mir scientists also performed experiments on space technology, gravity, earth observation, and space sciences, but they spent ~~least~~ *less* of their time doing these kinds of experiments than on space life experiments. (5) Although the lessons learned on Mir were good ones, Mir can no longer provide the ~~bestest~~ *best* and ~~most safest~~ *safest* environment for the scientists to continue *OK* these experiments. (6) Mir floated above the Earth, more than 6 years longer than first expected. (7) After its 13 years in orbit, the space station was ~~worst~~ *worse* for the wear. *OK* (8) Several recent accidents showed that since Mir is badly damaged, it was no longer well suited to housing scientists in space.

Exercise 18.10   Using Comparative and Superlative Forms of Irregular Modifiers

1. Write topic sentences for three paragraphs of comparison. Include a comparative or superlative modifier in each topic sentence, as this example shows:

EXAMPLE   Those expensive shoes are the most uncomfortable ones I've ever worn.

2. List several details that you could use to develop each paragraph. Share these draft ideas with a writing partner. Together, choose one topic sentence and group of supporting ideas from the six you have, and write one paragraph. Be sure to include modifiers to help make your writing precise.

Challenge 18.4   Using Irregular Modifiers in Your Writing

1. To practice using the comparative and superlative forms of irregular modifiers, write a series of interview questions to ask a writing partner. Use the following words: *worse, worst, better, best, less, least, more, most.*

EXAMPLE   Do you like action movies *more* than comedies?

2. Interview your partner, taking notes on his or her responses. Then write a brief "Getting to Know ..." feature about your partner.

Dealing with Confusing Pairs of Modifiers

As a writer, you may find that you have trouble remembering which positive form of these irregular modifiers is an adjective and which is an adverb. To avoid confusion, it is helpful to remember how these different modifiers function: adjectives describe nouns and pronouns; adverbs modify verbs, adjectives, or other adverbs. Many people confuse *good*, which describes a person or thing, with *well*, which describes *how* something is done. *Good* is an adjective; *well* is an adverb. Look at how these words are used in these examples:

ADJECTIVE FORM   Karen is a *good* singer.

ADVERB FORM   Kevin sings *well*, too.

In the first sentence, *good* modifies the noun *singer*. It describes what kind of singer Karen is. In the second sentence, *well* modifies the verb *sings*. It explains how Kevin sings.

Learning the following chart of confusing pairs of modifiers will help you overcome confusion about them.

Adjective	*Adverb*
awful	awfully
bad	badly
good	well
poor	poorly
quick	quickly
quiet	quietly
real	really

Look at the modifiers in the following examples:

FAULTY   Matt is *real* unhappy with his new work–study assignment.

FAULTY   Caitlyn ran across the playground *quick*.

In the first sentence, an adverb is needed to indicate *to what extent* Matt is unhappy; the adjective *real* is used incorrectly. In the second, the adjective *quick* is used incorrectly to indicate *how* Caitlyn ran across the playground. When you need to indicate *to what extent* or *how*, always choose the adverb form:

| REVISED | Matt is *really* unhappy with his new work–study assignment. |

| REVISED | Caitlyn ran across the playground *quickly*. |

Another pair of modifiers that sometimes confuses writers is *worse* and *worst*. *Worse* is the comparative form, and *worst* is the superlative. The problem is that these two words sound much alike when spoken aloud. It's easy to use the wrong form. Look at these examples:

| FAULTY | At the beginning of the course, Oscar had *worst* typing skills than Flo. |

| FAULTY | The *worse* part of the evening was when my car was towed away. |

The first sentence incorrectly uses *worst* to compare the typing skills of *two* students. *Worst* should be used to compare *more than two* things. The second sentence uses *worse* to indicate the *least pleasant* part of a night that had many parts, but *worse* is the form for comparing only *two* things.

To eliminate these errors, simply change the form of the modifiers:

| REVISED | At the beginning of the course, Oscar had *worse* typing skills than Flo. |

| REVISED | The *worst* part of the evening was when my car was towed away. |

Exercise 18.11   **Choosing between Confusing Pairs of Modifiers**

Underline the correct modifier from the pair in parentheses in each of the sentences below. Remember—use the adjective forms to tell *which one, how many,* or *what kind;* use the adverb forms to tell *how* or *to what extent.* Use the example as a guide.

| EXAMPLE | Helen performed (poor, poorly) in the gymnastics meet. |

(1) Budgeting is a (good, well) skill to learn. (2) It is (real, really) important to keep track of personal expenses and income. (3) Several new computer programs can help people budget (quick, quickly) and (good, well). (4) Without a plan and (good, well) record keeping, it is (awful, awfully) difficult to save for a big item, such as a car or tuition. (5) However, the (worse, worst) budget situation is not knowing where your money has gone.

Exercise 18.12   **Identifying Errors with Confusing Pairs of Modifiers**

This short letter, written by a distressed young man to his girlfriend, contains some incorrect choices among frequently confused modifiers. Help him out by correcting his errors. Cross out each incorrect form, and write the correct one above it. Use the example to guide you.

EXAMPLE   Of all the runners in the race, he has the ~~baddest~~ *worst* lane position.

Dear Michelle,

(1) I'm ~~awful~~ *awfully* sorry about what happened last night. (2) I want you to know that it really wasn't my fault. (3) The ~~worse~~ *worst* part is that you won't believe me. (4) The whole thing happened so ~~quick~~ *quickly* that I didn't have time to react. (5) Afterward, you just sat there so ~~quiet~~ *quietly* in your ruined, punch-stained gown. (6) That was ~~worst~~ *worse* than if you had yelled and screamed at me. (7) It made me feel so bad. (8) I know that this whole thing has turned into a real mess, but if we talk about it, I think we can work it out.

Love, Dan

Challenge 18.5   **Using Specific Detail to Make Meaning Exact**

COLLABORATION   Sometimes writers use more exact ways to describe things or actions than simply adding an adjective or adverb. Working with a writing partner, revise the general sentences below to make their meaning more exact and to give them emphasis. Use the example as a guide.

EXAMPLE   It is really cold outside.

The temperature outside is ten degrees below freezing.

1. He sang poorly.

2. The apartment was messy.

3. The traffic was the worst I had ever seen.

4. The dessert was good.

5. The professor reviewed the lesson quickly.

Avoiding Double Negatives

Many writers have trouble expressing negatives correctly. *No, not,* and *never* are modifiers that express *negation*—the idea of *no.* Modifiers like *scarcely, hardly,* and *barely* also suggest negation because they imply that there is almost none. In addition, a few pronouns such as *nowhere, nothing, nobody, no one,* and *none* also add negative emphasis to a thought.

When you use two of these negative words together in the same phrase or sentence, you create an error called a **double negative.** Although double negatives can be heard in casual conversation and street talk, they aren't acceptable in college or professional writing.

Avoid errors by checking your sentences to make sure you have only one negative in each unit of ideas. Find the negatives in these examples:

FAULTY   My best friend has *not* had *no* luck in finding a good part-time job.

FAULTY   The factory workers *couldn't* do *nothing* to speed up production.

The first sentence contains two negatives: *not* and *no.* The second sentence also has two negatives: *couldn't* (could + *not*) and *nothing.* Often, contractions such as *couldn't* confuse writers. Because contractions combine words and omit letters, it's easy to forget that they can contain negatives.

Eliminating double negatives is easy. Simply delete one of the negatives or change it to a positive form.

REVISED   My best friend has had *no* luck in finding a good part-time job.

or

REVISED   My best friend has *not* had *any* luck in finding a good part-time job.

REVISED   The factory workers could do *nothing* to speed up production.

or

REVISED   The factory workers *couldn't* do *anything* to speed up production.

Each of these sentences expresses the writer's real point correctly, with a single negative. In each pair of sentences, notice how the writer eliminated one negative in the first sentence. In the second, one negative is changed to a positive form: *no* luck → *any* luck, and *nothing* → *anything.* Both strategies are equally correct and effective.

Exercise 18.13   **Avoiding Double Negatives**

Read the following paragraph, and underline any double negatives you find. If a sentence is correct as written, mark it *OK*. On a separate sheet of paper, revise each faulty sentence. Eliminate one of the negatives or change one to a positive. Use the example to guide you.

EXAMPLE

Tiffany <u>can't</u> do <u>nothing</u> except go home after the game.

Tiffany can't do anything except go home after the game.

or

Tiffany can do nothing except go home after the game.

           OK
(1) Alzheimer's disease is a tragic illness that affects about 10 percent
                                 OK
of people over sixty-five. (2) Doctors <u>don't</u> have <u>no</u> cure for it. (3) It is a very difficult disease to diagnose early because the symptoms are hard to identify. (4) Some elderly people <u>can't</u> seem to remember <u>nothing</u>, but their relatives think this is just a normal part of aging. (5) Eventually, the
                                OK
disease progresses, and the brain <u>doesn't</u> function well <u>no</u> more. (6) Some
                             OK
victims of Alzheimer's get worse very quickly. (7) Others can live for many years and remain active. (8) One case <u>isn't</u> like <u>no</u> other.

Exercise 18.14   **Eliminating Double Negatives**

Read the paragraph below, and underline any double negatives you find. If a sentence is correct as written, mark it *OK*. On a separate sheet of paper, revise the faulty sentences to eliminate the double negatives. Use the example as a guide.

EXAMPLE

I <u>wouldn't never</u> want to have to go through high school again.

I would never want to have to go through high school again.

or

I wouldn't want to have to go through high school again.

(1) Once alligators lived away from humans in Florida and avoided them—not <u>no</u> more! (2) In earlier years, people didn't have <u>no</u> reason to

OK

fear the gators. (3) They <u>never</u> saw <u>none</u>. (4) Now the creatures fre-

OK

quently find their way into people's yards, garages, pools, and even their

OK

houses. (5) Experts claim that some people are feeding the alligators. (6)

OK

Those people <u>don't</u> seem to know <u>no</u> better. (7) Feeding these reptiles is

illegal; but even worse, the feeding makes the gators link humans with

food. (8) When a hungry gator comes to call, there is <u>not</u> <u>no</u> choice but

to call a professional trapper.

Challenge 18.6 **Analyzing Problems Caused by Double Negatives**

Sometimes double negatives are accepted, for instance, in informal conversation or music. For a week (or for another time period your instructor assigns), write down examples of double negatives you hear or read. Bring your list to class and, with your classmates, discuss occasions when double negatives are used. Try to determine why they are not acceptable in college writing.

Using -*ing* Modifiers

Another kind of modifier that can be troublesome is the -*ing* word. As Chapter 14, "Using Passive Voice and Progressive Tenses, and Maintaining Consistency in Tense," showed, sometimes words that end in -*ing* function as verbs in a sentence:

EXAMPLE The toddler was *bouncing* around the room gleefully.

When an -*ing* word is used as a verb, it always needs a helping verb, such as *was* or *is*. Without the helping verb, the -*ing* word switches roles. It often functions as a modifier. Look at these examples:

EXAMPLE *Dancing* in the end zone, Shannon celebrated his game-winning play.

EXAMPLE The principal tried to calm the *crying* children.

In the first sentence, the -*ing* modifier *dancing* describes *Shannon*. In the second, the -*ing* modifier *crying* describes *children*.

Using *-ing* modifiers is one way to combine two brief sentences and avoid choppiness in your writing. Look at the pairs of sentences in these examples:

| -ing phrase |

CHOPPY *The workers were sitting* under the highway overpass. They were taking a break.

| -ing phrase |

CHOPPY *I was talking* quietly to the frightened kitten. I tried to get it down from the tree.

The two sentences in each example are correct, but they are choppy. To eliminate this choppiness, remove from one of the sentences all the words except the phrase that contains the *-ing* word. Next, change the other sentence to fill in any words that are needed, and then add the words from the *-ing* phrase as a modifier.

| modifier |

COMBINED *Sitting* under the highway overpass, the *workers* were taking a break.

| modifier |

COMBINED *Talking* quietly to the frightened kitten, *I* tried to get it down from the tree.

In the first example, *Sitting* is now a modifier describing the *workers*. In the second, *Talking* has become a modifier describing *I*.

Exercise 18.15 **Distinguishing between *-ing* Modifiers and *-ing* Verbs**

Write an *M* over the *-ing* words that are modifiers, and a *V* above the *-ing* words that are verbs in the paragraph below. Underline the *-ing* verbs and their helping verbs. Remember that an *-ing* word without a helping verb acts as a modifier. Use the example to guide you.

EXAMPLE
           V   M
Marla <u>was kicking</u> the ball when she heard a popping sound in her knee.

                  M   M
(1) The smell of frying burgers and steaming coffee beckoned me, so
               M   M
I entered the diner. (2) The waving hand of a smiling waitress led me to
      M
an empty table. (3) Looking at the menu, I couldn't decide which of my
                              V   V
favorite foods to order. (4) My mouth <u>was watering</u> as I <u>was deciding</u> be-
                                           V
tween fried chicken and beef stew. (5) The hardest part <u>was choosing</u>
      M
which tempting pie I would have for dessert.

Exercise 18.16   **Identifying and Using *-ing* Modifiers**

1. Decide whether the italicized *-ing* word in each sentence below functions as a verb or as a modifier. Label each *V* or *M*.

2. On the blank line below each sentence, compose a new sentence that transforms the *-ing* word. If it was used as a verb, make it a modifier in your sentence. If it was used as a modifier, then use it as a verb. Study the example first. (Sentences will vary.)

EXAMPLE

      M
Jim felt a *tearing* sensation in his shoulder.

    The dog was tearing around the kitchen.

      V
1. She was *ironing* all of her dresses and suits.

_____

        M
2. An action-packed, *exciting* movie is what most teens and preteens enjoy.

_____

       V
3. The Brauer family is *moving* to Arizona.

_____

     M
4. The *cleaning* lady was almost finished with her chores.

_____

   M
5. *Sobbing* as if her heart would break, the little girl followed her mother home.

_____

   M
6. *Resting* comfortably, the patient recuperated in the recovery room.

_____

    V
7. The man was *hoping* that his train had been delayed.

_____

M
8. *Reading* silently, the child seemed fascinated by his book.

Challenge 18.7   **Using Modifiers to Combine Sentences**

Working with a partner, combine the following pairs of simple sentences to eliminate choppiness. From the first sentence of each pair, remove all the words except the phrase that contains the *-ing* word. Then change words in the other sentence as necessary, and add the words from the *-ing* phrase. Use the *-ing* word as a modifier. Follow the guidelines on page 364.

1. The baby was sitting quietly in her highchair. The baby waited for her oatmeal.

2. The customers were waiting to get into the movie theater. The customers grew impatient.

3. Genia was skiing too fast. She hit a large bump and fell.

4. I was shopping for a new tape player. I saw my old friend Richard.

5. The sky was growing suddenly dark. It started to look threatening.

Avoiding Problems with *-ing* Modifiers

When you use an *-ing* modifier in a sentence, you must be careful to place it as close as you can to the word it is describing. Also, be sure you include the word you actually want to modify. Otherwise, the sentence will be awkward or confusing. Look at these examples:

CONFUSING   *Hanging* from the top of the building, Del saw the old flag.

CONFUSING   *Studying* for a test, Wayne's dog leaped on his lap.

The first sentence features the *-ing* modifier *hanging*. As the sentence now reads, it implies that *Del* was hanging from the top of the building. The second sentence includes the *-ing* modifier *studying*. As worded, the sentence suggests that the *dog* is studying for a test, not *Wayne*. These errors in placement are called *misplaced modifiers*.

To avoid this kind of error, check any sentence you write that contains an *-ing* modifier. Be sure you have clearly shown which word the *-ing* word is modifying. If there is a problem, you have two ways to eliminate it:

(1) Move the *-ing* modifier as close as possible to the word it describes, or (2) change the wording of the sentence:

| CLEAR | Del saw the old flag *hanging* from the top of the building. |

or

| CLEAR | *Hanging* from the top of the building, the old flag looked faded to Del. |

| CLEAR | *Studying* for a test, Wayne had to contend with his playful dog. |

or

| CLEAR | While Wayne was *studying* for a test, his dog jumped in his lap. |

Exercise 18.17 Identifying Problems with *-ing* Modifiers

To avoid errors when you use *-ing* modifiers, you need to identify both the *-ing* modifier and the word it modifies. In the sentences below, underline the *-ing* modifier, and draw an arrow from it to the word that it *appears* to modify. Use the example to guide you. Save this work to continue in Challenge 18.8.

| EXAMPLE | Putting the last dishes in place, the table was finally set. |

(1) Barking loudly, I couldn't catch my dog. (2) I saw my dog Max run down the beach dragging a leash. (3) Getting overexcited and playful, the trainer had told me Max didn't yet understand how to heel. (4) Sure enough, now here I was, chasing after a runaway dog. (5) Laughing, I turned away and hoped Max would follow. (6) Hearing the approach of running paws, Max started to run back at top speed. (7) I felt good, winning the game this time.

Exercise 18.18 Avoiding Problems with *-ing* Modifiers

Complete each sentence below with a thought of your own. Make sure you place the word being modified as close as possible to the *-ing* modifier. Study the example first. (Answers will vary.)

EXAMPLE   While sitting up late one night, *I noticed that the walls and floor of my room were starting to vibrate.*

1. Slipping out of the chair, _____

   _____ .

2. Realizing it was an earthquake, _____

   _____ .

3. Striking in the middle of the night, _____

   _____ .

4. Wondering how earthquakes are predicted, _____

   _____ .

5. Taking measurements during earthquakes, _____

   _____ .

Challenge 18.8   **Revising to Correct Problems with *-ing* Modifiers**

COLLABORATION

As you discovered, some sentences in Exercise 18.17 were confusing because the *-ing* modifier was dangling. Using a separate sheet of paper, rewrite the confusing sentences to clarify their meaning. Remember—you have two ways to eliminate the confusion. Then exchange your sentences with a writing partner, and compare how you each revised the sentences. Discuss which versions are most effective and why.

Working with Adjectives and Adverbs Checklist

- ☐ Have you chosen the comparative form for any modifiers used to compare *two* people or things?

- ☐ Have you chosen the superlative form of any modifiers used to *compare more than two* people or things?

- ☐ Have you double checked the forms of any irregular modifiers you have used?

- ☐ Have you chosen the proper form of any modifiers used from the list of commonly confused modifiers like *good/well?*

☐ Have you used only one negative word in each subject–verb unit?

☐ Have you placed *-ing* modifiers next to the words they modify?

Exploring Ideas through Journal Writing

As this chapter shows, adjectives and adverbs add clarity and specificity to your writing. When you include modifiers in your writing, you *enhance* it, turning something general into something distinct and particular. Now think in terms of your day-to-day life: What enhances it now? Is it a personal relationship of some kind? Or is it school, your job, or some hobby or other interest? What *could* enhance it if you had the opportunity? Why would it make a difference for you? Consider some aspect of this subject, and then explore it for 20 to 30 minutes in your journal.

Chapter Quick Check: Working with Adjectives and Adverbs

The following passage contains errors involving incorrect forms of adjectives and adverbs, double negatives, and misplaced modifiers. First, underline all the modifiers and articles in the sentences below. Then cross out each error and write the correct form above it. For misplaced modifiers, you may need to insert new words or cross out an entire clause and rewrite it. You may also be able to correct any double negatives in more than one way.

(1) For millions of people across the United States, the day ~~quick~~ quickly goes downhill as soon as they reach the traffic-clogged streets and highways that lead to work or school. (2) In order to alleviate these kinds of traffic problems, cities have adopted many strategies, the ~~popularest~~ most popular of which include subways and busing. (3) Unfortunately, these strategies generally haven't resulted in ~~no~~ any serious reduction of traffic. (4) Of all the solutions suggested, traveling high above the traffic by monorail seems to possess the ~~more~~ most potential to ease these traffic woes. (5) Monorail systems are ~~more quiet~~ quieter and better for the environment than any other

system. (6) Yet until now, no city has considered the monorail as a ~~really~~ real
solution to its transportation woes. (7) In fact, the ~~goodest~~ best known
monorail system in the United States isn't in a city at all. (8) Disney
World in Orlando, Florida, has a monorail system that is several miles
~~longest~~ longer than any existing U.S. monorail. (9) But Disney World is not
alone ~~no~~ any longer because Seattle, Washington, has begun work on a 14-
mile monorail system serving the city and surrounding suburbs. (10)
Costing almost $2 billion, ~~experts expect that~~ Seattle's monorail system
will be fully operational by 2009.

Discovering Connections 18.2

1. For Discovering Connections 18.1 on page 347, you began prewriting
   in response to a quotation by Mary Lou Cook or a photo. Now, continue your prewriting on one of these options:
   a. What part of Mary Lou Cook's definition of creativity surprises
      you the most? Why?
   b. What should parents and schools do to encourage students to be
      as creative as they can be?
2. Evaluate your prewriting material, identify a focus, and create a draft
   of about 100 words.
3. Exchange your draft with a writing partner. Using the material in this
   chapter as a guide, evaluate the draft you receive, and note any problems with modifiers or double negatives as well as any other weaknesses. Return the draft to the writer.
4. Revise your draft, eliminating any errors that your reader identified.

COLLABORATION

Summary Exercise: Working with Adjectives, Adverbs, and Other Modifiers

The following passage contains errors involving incorrect forms of adjectives and adverbs, double negatives, and misplaced modifiers. First, underline all the modifiers and articles in the sentences below. Then cross out

each error and write the correct form above it. For misplaced modifiers, you may need to insert new words or cross out an entire clause and rewrite it. You may also be able to correct any double negatives in more than one way.

(1) Anthropologist Maeve Leakey recently discovered the ~~most~~ oldest prehuman fossil to date. (2) The teeth and bones she found in Kenya belong to a being that lived 4.2 million years ago. (3) The fossil pieces show that the species walked upright. (4) ~~Having this ability, we~~ We know it is an not ~~no~~ ancestor of modern apes, , since it had this ability.

(5) Before Leakey's discovery, the oldest prehuman fossil on record was known as "Lucy." (6) Her skeleton dates back 3.6 million years. (7) ~~Looking something like a chimpanzee, the~~ The scientist who discovered her showed that Lucy, although she looked something like a chimpanzee, nevertheless walked upright.

(8) The presence of strong shinbones is one indication to scientists that the fossil is really a human ancestor. (9) Scientists also look at fossil teeth. (10) Big, broad molars and thick tooth enamel indicate a prehuman creature. (11) Ancestors of both apes and humans had little ears, big canine teeth, and small heads.

(12) Working carefully to uncover the fossils is an ~~awful~~ awfully tedious job. (13) The scientists must slowly unearth the ~~most small~~ smallest pieces of fossil. (14) Sometimes it takes them weeks, working ~~slow~~ slowly and ~~careful~~ carefully, to uncover a bone and remove it from the dry earth and rocks. (15) Although the climate isn't ~~hardly~~ the ~~worse~~ worst on earth, the hot, dry weather also makes the job more difficult.

(16) There are probably ~~not~~ no more famous anthropologists today than the scientists working on the team with Leakey. (17) Their efforts have produced good results. (18) They have found more and older fos-

sils than <u>any other</u> group. (19) Their discoveries help us understand our <u>common biological</u> roots <u>better</u>.

RECAP USING MODIFIERS

New terms in this chapter	Definitions
● **adjective**	● a word that describes a noun or pronoun ● tells *which one, how many, what kind*
● **adverb**	● a word that describes verbs, adjectives, and other adverbs ● tells *how, when, where, to what extent, how much*
● **comparative form**	● a modifier used to compare two things *Example* *more* handsome, hungr*ier*
● **superlative form**	● a modifier used to compare more than two things *Example* *most* considerate, slow*est*
● **double negative**	● incorrect use of two negative words in the same phrase or sentence Do not use two of these words in a single sentence: *not, no, never, nowhere, nobody, nothing, no one, none, scarcely, hardly, barely.* *Example* Nobody should bring nothing flammable. Revised Nobody should bring anything flammable.

Forming Modifiers

Positive form	Comparative form	Superlative form
one-syllable word *brave*	positive form + *-er* *braver*	positive form + *-est* *bravest*
words of three or more syllables *enjoyable*	*more* + positive form *more enjoyable*	*most* + positive form *most enjoyable*
some two-syllable words *funny*	change *-y* to *-i* + *-er* *funnier*	change *-y* to *-i* + *-est* *funniest*
other two-syllable words *famous*	*more* + positive form *more famous*	*most* + positive form *most famous*

Common Irregular Modifiers		
Positive form	**Comparative form**	**Superlative form**
bad (adjective)	worse	worst
badly (adverb)	worse	worst
good (adjective)	better	best
well (adverb)	better	best
little	less	least
much	more	most

Writers' Café

Will concentrating on the reading I do also help me as a writer?

It certainly will. When you read attentively, you also . . .

- broaden your breadth of knowledge
- strengthen your vocabulary
- increase your awareness of sentences and paragraphs
- see the strategies another writer uses to deal with a subject

In fact, increasing your reading may be the easiest way to improve your writing.

Is it really important to give my writing a good title?

Yes it is, for several reasons. An effective title can . . .

- encapsulate your main idea in a way that differs from your topic sentence or thesis
- entice your reader to read on
- offer an opinion about your topic

I do a better job writing on some subjects than on others. Is this normal?

Of course. In general, people write best about the things they know and care about. So what should you do when you face a topic that you don't necessarily know well or care about?

- Do some reading to learn more about it.
- Compare it to something that you do know well or that you are interested in.
- Examine the subject to find out why you don't like or understand it. The examination alone may give you something to write about.
- Write to explore the subject, which itself often results in a focus for writing.

How important are format and page layout in terms of creating an effective piece of writing?

More important than many people realize. The appropriate format and an effective page layout . . .

- present your ideas in an easy-to-read fashion
- encourage a reader to view your work favorably
- draw a reader into your discussion
- fulfill the special requirements of particular fields of study and work

Concentrating on format and page design helps to frame your ideas, setting them off in the best possible light. Therefore, make it a point to ask instructors and supervisors specific questions about these two elements.

Consistency Workshop: Aiming for Correctness

Chapter 19

Capitalizing Correctly

Getting Started... **Q:** I wish I could always be sure about capitalization. Sometimes I don't capitalize words that need it, and other times I capitalize words that don't need it. It all seems pretty confusing. What should I do to make sure I am capitalizing the right words?

A: Capitalization does seem confusing at first glance, but a couple of strategies can help you keep it straight. First, identify whether the word is common or proper. Common words generally don't call for capitalization, but proper nouns do. Next, consider the word's location. If it begins a sentence, it is always capitalized, regardless of its type or class.

Overview: Understanding Proper Capitalization

When you write, you emphasize certain words by beginning them with capital letters. This system of emphasis is called **capitalization.**

A capital letter announces, "Here is a particular person, place, or thing." It does not refer to a member of a general class of persons, places, or things. To use capitalization properly, you need to understand some broad guidelines about this system.

> *This chapter presents capitalization guidelines and shows you how to apply them. You will learn*
>
> ● when words should be capitalized
>
> ● when words should not be capitalized

Discovering Connections 19.1

Consider the following quotation:

Life's more amusing than we thought.

—*Andrew Lang*

Or consider this photo.

Now, using the prewriting technique you prefer, do some prewriting about your reaction to the quotation or photo. Save your work.

Understanding When Words Should Be Capitalized

Sometimes writers overuse capitalization and capitalize any words they think are important. This is not acceptable in formal, or *standard,* English usage. You should use capitalization according to the basic rules followed in standard usage.

A number of circumstances call for you to capitalize words. For example, always capitalize the first word in a sentence:

EXAMPLE   **T**he vacant lot was filled with piles of trash.

EXAMPLE   **W**hen will Nancy arrive?

Capitalize the proper names of people, things, and places as well. These names can be specific holidays, countries, states, cities, bodies of water, parks, historical periods or events, months, days of the week, planets, races, religions, and nationalities:

Michael **M**c**N**ulty	**H**ispanic	Vietnam **W**ar
Renaissance	**T**hursday	**I**rish
Uranus	**Y**ellowstone **N**ational **P**ark	Lake **H**uron
Asia	**B**uddhist	**M**ississippi
October	**F**ather's **D**ay	Los **A**ngeles

Months and days of the week are always capitalized. However, note that the four seasons are not capitalized:

EXAMPLE   I think **w**inter is a high price to pay for **f**all.

Note also that the *N* in McNulty is capitalized. The first letter after *Mc* in a surname is capitalized.

Whenever you use the personal pronoun *I,* capitalize it, too:

EXAMPLE   Donnie and **I** made plans to meet after class.

Capitalize a word that designates a family relationship when you use that word as part of, or as a substitute for, a specific name:

EXAMPLE   My family visits **U**ncle Joe and **A**unt Sara every summer.

EXAMPLE   Gregory loves his talks with **G**randma.

However, do not capitalize family relationship words that are not used as part of the name:

EXAMPLE   My **s**ister Jubilee has always wished we had lots of **c**ousins.

In addition, capitalize formal titles like *doctor, senator, mayor,* and so on when you use them in conjunction with a person's name:

EXAMPLE   After class, **P**rofessor Dion requested volunteers for his experiment.

EXAMPLE   At a fund-raiser, **R**epresentative Marshall promised to lower taxes.

However, if the title is not used with the individual's name, do not capitalize it:

EXAMPLE   Marcus was elected **p**resident of the club.

Capitalize words like *street, avenue,* and *boulevard* when they are part of a specific address:

    49 Richmond **S**treet
    5 Washington **C**ourt
    1450 South **S**treet East

Capitalize words like *south* and *west* when they designate specific sections of a country:

EXAMPLE   His girlfriend has lived in the **E**ast most of her life.

EXAMPLE   Once I graduate, I hope to live in the **N**orth.

However, do not capitalize these words when they designate a direction:

EXAMPLES   Travel two miles **s**outh on this road to Oblong. Much of the town was destroyed by a twister that blew in from the **w**est.

Capitalize all main words of the names of languages and specific course names.

Introduction to Computers   Writing 110
Spanish III   Italian

However, do not capitalize the names of school subjects or classes in general:

I took **h**istory, **a**lgebra, and **c**hemistry as a junior.

Also, capitalize the first word and all main words in the titles of books, poems, newspapers, magazines, television shows, movies, and so on:

Pride and Prejudice   *Los Angeles Times*   *Ebony*
The Matrix   "Ode on a Grecian Urn"   *Friends*

Capitalize brand names, companies, clubs, and associations:

Nike   Macintosh
New York Runners Club   National Organization for Women
Geo   Molten Metals Technology

In addition, capitalize all letters of abbreviations of proper names and acronyms:

NAACP (National Association for the Advancement of Colored People)
NBC (National Broadcasting Corporation)
IBM (International Business Machines)
NASA (National Aeronautics and Space Administration)
USC (University of Southern California)

Finally, capitalize the first letters of the beginning of a letter, called the *salutation*. Also capitalize the first word of the ending, called the *complimentary close*:

Common Salutations   *Common Complimentary Closings*

Dear **M**r. James: **S**incerely,
Dear Terry,   **Y**ours truly,
Gentlemen and **L**adies: **R**espectfully,

Exercise 19.1   **Working with Words Needing to Be Capitalized**

Decide which words in the following paragraph should be capitalized. Cross out each incorrect lowercase, or small, letter, and write a capital letter above it. Refer to the guidelines in this chapter and the following example to help you.

EXAMPLE

E   B   G   H

every morning the ~~boston~~ ~~globe~~ is delivered to my apartment on ~~hastings~~

S

~~street~~.

M   A   CBS

(1) ~~many~~ people in ~~america~~ panicked when they heard a ~~cbs~~ radio

W   W   H   O   W

broadcast of "~~war~~ of the ~~worlds~~" on ~~halloween~~ in 1938. (2) ~~orson~~ ~~welles~~

E

produced this radio play, based on the science fiction novel by ~~english~~-

H G W   I   M   E

man ~~h.g.~~ ~~wells~~. (3) ~~in~~ the story, aliens from ~~mars~~ attack ~~earth~~ by invading

N   E   S   N

~~new~~ ~~england~~. (4) ~~so~~ many radio listeners in the ~~northeast~~ believed the

fiction that they fled; traffic jams blocked highways out of major cities.

W

(5) ~~welles~~ did broadcast disclaimers during the show, but many people

E   B   C   M C

tuned in late—after listening to ~~edgar~~ ~~bergen~~ and ~~charlie~~ ~~mcearthy~~ on

A   FCC

another station. (6) ~~as~~ a result of the extreme reaction, the ~~fcc~~ revised its

C

broadcast rules. (7) ~~courses~~ in broadcasting and psychology still focus

M   T   N   Y   C

on this historic broadcast from the ~~mercury~~ ~~theater~~ in ~~new~~ ~~york~~ ~~city~~. (8)

I   I

~~it~~ made the young actor–director from ~~illinois~~ a household name and

C   K

paved the way for his masterpiece of film, ~~citizen~~ ~~kane~~.

Exercise 19.2   **Identifying Errors with Words Needing to Be Capitalized**

Capitalize letters where necessary in each sentence. Cross out the incorrect lowercase letter, and write the capital above it. Use the example to guide you.

EXAMPLE

N   F   U

From the forests of the ~~northwest~~ to the beaches of ~~florida~~, the ~~united~~

S

~~states~~ is overflowing with great vacation sites.

M   D   K   I   S

1. Last year ~~mom~~, ~~dad~~, ~~kevin~~, and ~~i~~ took a driving tour of the ~~southwest~~, in-

N   M   A   N

cluding ~~new~~ ~~mexico~~, ~~arizona~~, and ~~nevada~~.

2. Seeing the ~~grand~~ ~~canyon~~ was a highlight; between the hiking and photographing, ~~i~~ nearly wore out my ~~reebok~~ walking shoes and ~~kodak~~ camera.
   G   C   I   R   K

3. We celebrated my birthday and the ~~fourth~~ of ~~july~~ in ~~tucson~~, ~~arizona~~.
   F   J   T   A

4. Kevin sent ~~gramps~~ and ~~grannie~~ postcards at 1529 ~~whispering~~ ~~pines~~ ~~lane~~, ~~aurora~~, ~~illinois~~, even though they were staying at ~~green~~ ~~lake~~ in ~~wisconsin~~ that week.
   G   G   W   P   L   A   I   G   L   W

5. It rained on ~~tuesday~~, the day we had scheduled to see the ~~saguaro~~ ~~national~~ ~~monument~~.
   T   S   N   M

6. While our parents read *~~popular~~ ~~mechanics~~* and watched old ~~cary~~ ~~grant~~ films, ~~kevin~~ and ~~i~~ visited ~~el~~ ~~con~~ ~~regional~~ ~~mall~~.
   P   M   C   G   K   I   E   C   R   M

7. With my birthday money, ~~i~~ bought ~~italian~~ sandals and a game for my ~~macintosh~~ computer.
   I   I   M

8. Another day, we heard the ~~arizona~~ governor speak at a special event held at the ~~university~~ of ~~arizona~~.
   A   U   A

Exercise 19.3   Correcting Errors with Words Needing to Be Capitalized

Each of the following sentences contains an underlined word or words that do not need to be capitalized. Cross out the underlined words, and replace them with appropriate words that *do* need to be capitalized. Use the following example as a model. (Answers will vary.)

EXAMPLE   *The Sears Tower*
~~That building~~ is one of the tallest buildings in the world.

1. The <u>mayor</u> met with the striking city workers in the <u>municipal building</u>.

2. My uncle always carves the turkey at our <u>holiday</u> feast.

3. The <u>street</u> is a one-way street.

4. That <u>movie</u> is a very enjoyable romantic comedy.

5. The <u>leaf-raking</u> month has arrived at last.

6. She would be homesick if she moved away from <u>her hometown.</u>

7. They all speak <u>the same language.</u>

8. I earned an A in <u>that course</u> because my paper on <u>a major war</u> was so impressive.

Challenge 19.1   **Analyzing Capitalization in an Article**

Clip an article from the front page of a daily newspaper, and circle the words that are capitalized. Bring the article into class, and exchange it with a classmate. On a separate sheet of paper, write the capitalized words your classmate has circled. Beside each, explain why the word should be capitalized.

Challenge 19.2   **Using Capitalization in Your Writing**

Write a letter to a corporation or institution, praising the staff for their good work or complaining about a problem you have experienced. Exchange your letter with a writing partner. Check your partner's letter for correct use of capitals.

Capitalizing Correctly Checklist

- ☐ Have you capitalized the first word in each sentence and the pronoun *I?*
- ☐ Have you capitalized the proper names and titles of people and places, including countries, states, cities, bodies of water, parks, and planets?
- ☐ Have you capitalized the proper names of specific things and events, including days of the week, geographical areas, months, holidays, religions, races, historical periods or occurrences, and nationalities?
- ☐ Have you capitalized the titles of books, periodicals, movies, television shows, clubs, academic courses, languages, brand names, and abbreviations of the proper names of organizations and businesses?
- ☐ Have you used lowercase letters for the names of all nonspecific people, places, events, titles, compass directions, and academic subjects?

Exploring Ideas through Journal Writing

As this chapter illustrates, capitalizing a word distinguishes it, making it stand out from words naming someone or something general. But that doesn't mean that words that aren't capitalized aren't important. For instance, *grandparent* is a nonspecific word. So are words like *love, career, success, time, intelligence, talent, education,* and *vacation.* Choose one of these words or select some other, and then explore its importance or significance for 20 to 30 minutes in your journal.

Chapter Quick Check:
Capitalizing Correctly

The following sentences contain a number of capitalization errors. Cross out the capital letter of any incorrectly capitalized word, inserting the lower-case version above it. Cross out the lowercase letter of any word that should be capitalized, inserting the capital letter version above it.

(1) Whether it is called ~~h~~ighland ~~r~~oad ~~e~~states or ~~r~~iverview ~~g~~ardens, [H R E R G]

the name chosen for a housing development can play an important role

in Its success. (2) When ~~C~~onstruction ~~E~~xecutives consider what to call [c e]

their ~~D~~evelopments, they often try to capture some special quality of the [d]

surrounding area. (3) For example, if a ~~D~~eveloper is building an apart- [d]

ment complex on the shores of ~~l~~ake ~~s~~pringfield, calling the development [L S]

~~L~~akeview ~~a~~cres highlights the advantages of the location. (4) With ~~C~~ondo- [L A c]

miniums at the foot of a ~~M~~ountain in a ski area, a name like ~~b~~lack ~~d~~ia- [m B D]

mond ~~r~~un conjures up a vision of skiers racing down snow-covered [R]

slopes. (5) Calling a housing development near a ~~S~~tate ~~F~~orest ~~p~~ine ~~c~~one [s f P C]

~~p~~reserve underscores the beauty inherent in the ~~L~~ocale. (6) ~~d~~evelopers [P l D]

must also make sure that they don't choose a name of some well-known

~~C~~orporation or ~~P~~roduct. (7) Names like ~~g~~ateway ~~h~~eights or ~~r~~olex ~~v~~illas [c p G H R V]

would not be acceptable because they might infringe on corporate

~~T~~rademarks or ~~C~~opyrights. (8) Unfortunately, some ~~R~~eal ~~E~~state ~~C~~ompanies [t c r e c]

aren't always completely honest when they assign names to their

~~H~~ousing ~~U~~nits. (9) Not every ~~D~~evelopment named ~~o~~cean ~~e~~cho ~~c~~ottages [h u d O E C]

or ~~d~~esert ~~v~~iew ~~g~~ardens is within sight of the ~~O~~cean or ~~D~~esert. (10) ~~a~~s [D V G o d A]

with so many other C̶onsumer I̶ssues, a potential buyer must investigate
(c above C, i above I)

things fully before actually making such a significant F̶inancial
(f above F)

I̶nvestment.
(i above I)

Discovering Connections 19.2

COLLABORATION

1. For Discovering Connections 19.1 on page 379, you began prewriting in response to a quotation by Andrew Lang or a photo. Now, continue your prewriting on one of these options:
   a. What recommendation would you make to someone who needs to be amused?
   b. What is the single funniest incident you have ever witnessed or experienced? What made it so funny?
2. Evaluate your prewriting material, identify a focus, and create a draft of about 100 words.
3. Exchange your draft with a writing partner. Using the material in this chapter as a guide, evaluate the draft you receive, and note any errors in capitalization as well as any other weaknesses. Return the draft to the writer.
4. Revise your draft, eliminating any errors that your reader identified.

Summary Exercise: Capitalizing Correctly

The following sentences contain a number of capitalization errors. Cross out the capital letter of any incorrectly capitalized word, inserting the lowercase version above it. Cross out the lowercase letter of any word that should be capitalized, inserting the capital letter version above it.

(1) t̶he m̶arx brothers were S̶tars of b̶roadway theaters and h̶olly-
(T above t, M above m, s above S, B above b, H above h)
wood movies for three decades. (2) t̶heir names were l̶eonard, a̶dolph,
(T above t, L above l, A above a)
j̶ulius, m̶ilton, and h̶erbert, but we know them better by their S̶tage
(J above j, M above m, H above h, s above S)
N̶ames: c̶hico, h̶arpo, g̶roucho, g̶ummo, and z̶eppo. (3) t̶hey were E̶xperts
(n above N, C above c, H above h, G above g, G above g, Z above z, T above t, e above E)
at both physical and verbal comedy. (4) m̶ore than fifty years after the
(M above m)
b̶rothers made their first movies, their fans still laugh at g̶roucho's winks
(b above B, G above g)

and puns, harpo's crazy Slapstick, and chico's silly accent. (5) zeppo was the straight man; gummo left the Act after a few years.

(6) being stars on stage led to their Movie careers. (7) in the 1920s they were on broadway in two hit Plays with the funny names of coconuts and animal crackers. (8) next, the hollywood Studio, paramount, filmed both plays. (9) other Movies they made for paramount included monkey business, horse feathers, and duck soup.

(10) some famous writers, directors, and Producers contributed to the marx brothers' early success. (11) their Writers included george s. kaufman, morrie ryskind, and s. j. perelman. (12) the famous Directors leo mcarcy and norman z. mcleod let the comedy team strut their stuff without emphasizing plot. (13) their early movies were Satires of politics, Government, college, and other establishments. (14) when they were hired by mgm studios, production Chief irving thalberg produced two more famous movies: a night at the opera and a day at the races.

(15) groucho was the most successful after the marx brothers split up in the 1950s. (16) he hosted a very popular Show on tv and radio called you bet your life. (17) The ambitious brother also wrote and Published the marx brothers scrapbook in 1973. (18) hollywood gave the marx brothers an Honorary oscar in 1974. (19) groucho was still alive to accept it.

RECAP CAPITALIZING CORRECTLY

New term in this chapter	Definition
● capitalization	● the emphasis given to words by beginning them with a capital letter
● Do capitalize	● first word in a sentence
	Example **T**he accident created a traffic jam.

Continued

New term in this chapter	Definition
	● proper names of people, things, and places
	Example **S**usan and **I** leave on **T**uesday to visit **C**hicago.
	● words that designate family relationships when part of or a substitute for a specific name
	Example On my birthday, **A**unt Margaret sent me $10.
	● formal titles used in conjunction with a person's name
	Example Send a letter about the bridge repairs to **S**enator Dayton.
	● words that are part of a specific address or specific section of a country
	Example **K**ennedy **S**treet is a common street name in the **N**ortheast.
	● main words in specific academic subjects, languages, and titles
	Example I stopped studying for my **S**panish and **E**conomics 205 finals to watch a **S**einfeld rerun.
	● brand names, company and association names, and abbreviations for proper names
	Example Does **M**icrosoft make software for both **IBM** and **M**acintosh computers?
	● first letters of the salutation and complimentary closing of a letter
	Example **D**ear **S**ir, **S**incerely yours
● **Do not capitalize**	● words that designate a family relationship, unless they are part of or a substitute for a family name
	Example She vacations with her **m**om and **d**ad.
	● titles if they aren't used with a person's name
	Example Martina is **p**resident of the **s**tudent **g**overning **b**ody.
	● words that designate a direction
	Example Travel **s**outheast for five blocks.
	● general school subjects
	Example Most colleges require three years of **m**ath and **s**cience.
	● seasons of the year
	Example For once, **s**pring came early.

Chapter 20

Using Punctuation Properly

Getting Started... **Q:** Sometimes trying to figure out which mark of punctuation fits in a particular situation is frustrating. I would like to be more confident in this area. How can I develop greater skill with punctuation?

A: It's true that selecting the right mark of punctuation can occasionally be confusing. The secret is to think in terms of the *function* involved— ending, connecting, pausing, and so on. Once you identify the function, you can supply the mark of punctuation that supplies that function.

Overview: Understanding the Role of Punctuation

Listen to any conversation around you. You can hear the people start, pause, and change the tone and pitch of their voices as they tell their stories. In writing, **punctuation** is the system of symbols that guides your reader through all of these starts, stops, and changes. Punctuation makes it possible for readers to understand clearly the meaning of a piece of writing. Without punctuation, many sentences would be confusing or ambiguous.

> *This chapter helps you discover how to use punctuation effectively and correctly in your writing. You will learn how to use*
>
> ● periods, question marks, and exclamation points, which signal the end of a thought
>
> ● colons and semicolons, which indicate a pause within a thought
>
> ● quotation marks, which indicate a person's exact words
>
> ● apostrophes, which indicate ownership or take the place of letters left out in contractions

Discovering Connections 20.1

Consider the following quotation:

What I need is someone who will make me do what I can.

—*Ralph Waldo Emerson*

Or look at this photo.

Now, using the prewriting technique you prefer, do some prewriting about your reaction to the quotation or the photo. Save your work.

Using Periods, Question Marks, and Exclamation Points

Writers indicate the end of a thought by using one of three punctuation marks. When a sentence makes a statement (rather than asking a question or making an exclamation), writers use a **period** to indicate a stop in the flow of words. Most of the sentences you write call for a period. Look at these examples:

EXAMPLE   The audience at the theater laughed loudly at the movie**.**

EXAMPLE   Carole speaks three languages**.**

Periods also serve other purposes in writing. For example, a period is used between dollars and cents in monetary amounts: $79.56. A period is also used with many abbreviations and most initials:

Mr**.** (Mister)   D. H. Lawrence
Dr**.** (Doctor)   W. H. Auden
Lt**.** (Lieutenant)   P.M. (post meridian)
etc**.** (et cetera)   M.D.

When a sentence expresses a question directly, writers use a **question mark:**

EXAMPLE   When will the party start**?**

EXAMPLE   Why did Erick choose to major in accounting**?**

But if the question is *indirect,* no question mark is used. An indirect question is embedded within a statement and requires a period:

EXAMPLE   Doug asked when the party would start**.**

EXAMPLE   I wondered why Erick chose to major in accounting**.**

When a sentence expresses strong excitement or emotion, writers use an **exclamation point:**

EXAMPLE   Don't touch that wire**!**

EXAMPLE   The truck driver had just seriously injured another driver, and all he could think about was his insurance rates**!**

One danger with exclamation points is the temptation to overuse them. Don't rely on exclamation points to spice up your writing. Instead, reserve them for those few occasions when you need to demonstrate profound excitement or emotion.

Exercise 20.1   **Using End Punctuation**

Place the appropriate punctuation mark at the end of each of the following sentences. Use the example to guide you.

EXAMPLE   When are you going to the laundromat __?__

(1) Do you know that the tradition of sending manufactured Christmas cards is over 120 years old __?__ (2) Louis Prang, who had a business in Boston, printed cards from 1875 until 1890 __.__ (3) Early Christmas card decorations included flower designs and arrange-ments __.__ (4) Some of my friends wonder if sending cards is worth the time and trouble __.__ (5) However, I love sending and receiving holiday greetings __.__ (6) My answer is an enthusiastic "Yes__!__"

Exercise 20.2   **Identifying Errors in End Punctuation**

The following paragraph contains errors in the use of the period, question mark, and exclamation point. Cross out the incorrect punctuation marks, and write the correct ones in the space above. If a sentence is punctuated correctly, mark *OK* above its end mark. Use the example as a guide.

EXAMPLE   Where did the family move⸮

(1) Newborn babies require endless attention and lots of work. (2) For one thing, babies need to eat a lot more frequently than older children and adults. OK (3) You might ask why this is so. (4) The reason is that a baby's stomach can hold only small amounts of milk at a time. (5) Babies become hungry very quickly, and when they do, they let you know about it. OK (6) How is it possible for such a tiny person to make so much noise? (7) Coping becomes even more difficult if the baby gets sick. OK (8) You don't have to be an M.D. to figure out that something is wrong.

Challenge 20.1   **Revising for Correct End Punctuation**

COLLABORATION

Choose a paragraph from one of your textbooks or one of your own paragraphs. Copy these sentences on a separate sheet of paper, but omit the punctuation at the end of each sentence. Exchange sentences with a writing partner, and add the appropriate punctuation marks on the paper you receive. Return the paper, and correct your sentences, comparing your version to the original one.

Using Colons and Semicolons

Both colons and semicolons are types of pausing punctuation, used in specific cases to indicate a break *within* a sentence.

A **colon** is used to signal readers that the information following it is important. The material *before* the colon should be able to stand on its own as a sentence. This opening material prepares the reader for the material following the colon. Sometimes the material after the colon is an explanation or announcement; sometimes it's a list. Look at these examples:

EXAMPLE   The reason for Doreen's strange behavior was suddenly clear: she was using drugs again.

EXAMPLE   So far, I've chosen three courses for next semester: Writing 102, American Civilization, and Business Mathematics.

In the first example, the colon introduces an explanation. In the second example, the colon introduces a list.

As Chapter 9, "Coordination," and Chapter 10, "Comma Splices and Run-On Sentences," explained, a **semicolon** is used to connect closely related simple sentences. A semicolon has the same power to connect as a coordinating conjunction and a comma. The semicolon calls attention to the connection.

Look at these examples:

> **EXAMPLE**   The day had been long and hot; all I wanted to do was go for a swim.

> **EXAMPLE**   For months Peter had avoided speaking to Valerie; now he had no choice.

In the first example, the semicolon connects the two simple sentences closely, as the ideas they express are closely related. It emphasizes *why* taking a swim was so important. In the second example, the semicolon not only connects the related ideas but also adds drama to the description of Peter's situation.

Sometimes semicolons are used with *conjunctive adverbs*, such as *finally, however, then,* and *still.* (For a complete listing of common conjunctive adverbs, see page 183.) Conjunctive adverbs suggest a relationship or condition, so you can use them to relate two thoughts. But conjunctive adverbs are adverbs, not conjunctions, so they do not serve as connectors by themselves. You need to use a semicolon *before* the conjunctive adverb in order to connect the sentences.

Look at these examples:

> **EXAMPLE**   The manager was hoping to reopen the store today; *however,* carbon monoxide levels were still too high.

> **EXAMPLE**   The lifeguards continued to search in the water for the missing man; *meanwhile,* volunteers searched the grounds around the lake.

In the first example, the conjunctive adverb *however* indicates that something happened to disrupt the plans spelled out in the first part of the sentence. In the second example, the conjunctive adverb *meanwhile* specifies that something else was going on at the same time as the action described in the first part of the sentence.

Exercise 20.3   **Using Colons and Semicolons**

Decide which type of pausing punctuation is correct in the following sentences. Then insert either a colon or a semicolon where needed. Use the example as a guide.

> **EXAMPLE**   I have identified three steps in my writing process __:__ exploring, composing, and organizing.

(1) People who enroll in college usually look forward to their courses _:_ however, not every required subject is to everyone's liking. (2) For example, some college students don't like studying literature for several reasons _:_ difficulty of the words, relevance of the poems and plays, and the complex subject matter. (3) Math can also cause anxiety _;_ I get nervous just hearing the word *equations*. (4) Nevertheless, required courses are important _:_ a general education helps give students a new perspective on their career interests. (5) Core courses also build a college community in one way in particular _:_ students who share knowledge about a subject can share other ideas, too.

Exercise 20.4   **Correcting Errors in Colon and Semicolon Use**

In the following paragraph, correct the errors in the use of the colon and semicolon. Either cross out the incorrect punctuation mark and write the correct one in the space above, or insert the correct punctuation mark where it is missing. Use the example to guide you.

EXAMPLE   After two hours of work, we finally discovered the cause of the blackout: a frayed wire.

(1) For our Fourth of July picnic, every family brings a covered dish, and before you know it, the table is spread with all sorts of delicious foods: barbecued chicken, cold salads, hot-dogs and burgers, Jell-O molds, and home-baked pies. (2) Somebody always brings a tape deck and lots of tapes _:_ oldies, the latest Whitney Houston album, old-time folk tunes, and even some Disney sound tracks. (3) Our family is very musical; in addition, everyone loves to sing. (4) We love all kinds of music_:_ therefore, you hear a bit of just about everything at our Independence Day get-togethers. (5) Once all have eaten their fill, the best part of the party gets going _:_ some serious music-making and

dancing. (6) A space is cleared in the grass; then, the couples pair up. (7) The oldest folks prefer the swing sound of the 1940s big bands; Benny Goodman, Tommy Dorsey, and Artie Shaw. (8) Soon, however, that sound gives way to the music of classic rockers; the Rolling Stones, Chicago, Sting, and Bruce Springsteen.

Challenge 20.2   **Analyzing the Use of Colons and Semicolons**

COLLABORATION

Exchange your completed versions of Exercises 20.3 and 20.4 with a classmate. Compare the choices you each made. Answer these questions as you talk about the paragraphs. Are your choices similar? Where are they different? Why did you make the choices that you did?

Using Quotation Marks

Writers use **quotation marks** to enclose a direct quotation—someone's exact words. Look at the following examples:

> **EXAMPLE**   Robert asked, *"What time does the show start?"*

> **EXAMPLE**   *"You are responsible for the first $50 charged to a stolen credit card,"* said the customer service representative.

As you can see, the italicized sections are direct quotations, so they are enclosed in quotation marks. The first word of a direct quotation is always capitalized. If the quote ends the sentence, the end punctuation is placed within the closing quotation mark, and a comma is placed *before* the opening quotation mark. If the quote begins the sentence, then the ending period of the quote is replaced by a comma. The ending punctuation follows the "she said" portion. If the quote ends with a question mark or exclamation mark, a period is still required after the "she said" portion:

> **EXAMPLE**   "Did you pay your charge card bill this month**?"** asked Helen.

> **EXAMPLE**   "As a matter of fact, I did**,"** replied Scott.

Indirect quotations are the writer's *restatement* of someone else's words. Because this restatement *doesn't present the person's exact words*, no quotation marks are used. Look at the italicized sections in these versions of the example sentence at the beginning of the section:

<blockquote>

EXAMPLE   Robert asked *what time the show starts.*

</blockquote>

<blockquote>

EXAMPLE   The customer service representative said *that I was responsible for the first $50 charged to my stolen credit card.*

</blockquote>

The italicized sections in both sentences are restatements of the direct quotations. Therefore, no quotation marks are needed.

Exercise 20.5   **Working with Direct and Indirect Quotations**

Insert quotation marks in the following sentences if you think they are needed. Some sentences are indirect quotations and do not need quotation marks. Use the example as a guide.

<blockquote>

EXAMPLE   As she ran across the street, Alisse yelled, "I'll see you next week!"

</blockquote>

(1) "I can't believe how rude the salesperson in that jewelry store was!" Dawn exclaimed. (2) I was about to ask her to tell me what happened, but she kept on talking. (3) "First she looked at me as if I was going to steal something," Dawn continued, "and then she didn't come to the counter to help me."

(4) "I've had that happen to me, too," I replied. (5) We compared notes, and we said that some clerks assume we can't afford to buy anything because of our age and the way we dress.

Exercise 20.6   **Evaluating Direct and Indirect Quotations**

Some of the following sentences are direct quotations, while others are indirect quotations. If the sentence is a direct quotation, rewrite it on a separate piece of paper, adding the needed quotation marks. If the sentence is an indirect quotation, rewrite it on a separate sheet of paper, changing it into a direct quotation. Use the example as a guide.

<blockquote>

EXAMPLE   As the defendant emerged from the courthouse, the reporters hurried after him to ask whether he was ready to give a statement.

As the defendant emerged from the courthouse, the reporters hurried after him. They asked, "Are you ready to give a statement, sir?"

</blockquote>

1. Confucius, a philosopher who lived in ancient China, is famous for saying that it is only the wisest and the stupidest who cannot change.
2. Once, a boy asked Confucius what the definition of wisdom is.

3. Confucius answered him, Devotion to one's duties as a subject and re-spect for the spirits while keeping them at a distance. This may be called wisdom.

4. As a sign of respect for Confucius' own wisdom and insight, the ancient Chinese did not address Confucious by his name. Instead they would say Greetings, Grand Master K'ung.

5. Because the teachings of Confucius are more practical and ethical than religious, followers of Confucianism refer to the teachings as, The way of the sages, or, The way of the ancients.

Challenge 20.3   **Formatting and Punctuating Dialogue**

When your writing includes a conversation, or dialogue, you have to start a new paragraph each time you switch speakers. This way readers can clearly and easily follow the flow of words between two or more speakers. Revise the sentences in Exercise 20.5 into normal paragraph form. Start a new line and indent every time a different person speaks.

Using Apostrophes

One of the most useful—and most often used—marks of punctuation is the **apostrophe.** Apostrophes show ownership, or possession, in nouns. The noun form they make is called the *possessive* form.

To change a *singular* noun into a possessive form, add an apostrophe and -s.

a boy**'s** shoe   an actor**'s** costume   a giraffe**'s** neck

Add an apostrophe and an -s even for singular words that already end in -s:

Jacques**'s** problem   boss**'s** concerns   witness**'s** response

If the resulting possessive form is awkward, you have another option. Use a prepositional phrase to replace it. In other words, instead of writing *Moses's teachings,* write *the teachings of Moses.*

To make most plural nouns possessive, simply add an apostrophe:

those boys**'** shoes   several actors**'** costumes   all giraffes**'** necks

Some plural words don't end in -s. Make these words possessive by adding an apostrophe and -s to the plural noun:

people**'s** lives   children**'s** toys   women**'s** issues

Apostrophes are also used to signify letters left out in a *contraction,* a word created by combining two words. They may also replace numbers omitted in dates. Look at these sentences, with the contractions italicized:

EXAMPLE   The new key *wouldn't* open the lock.

EXAMPLE   *We'll* never forget the blizzard of '78.

In the first example, the contraction *wouldn't* is used instead of *would not*. In the second, the contraction *we'll* is used in place of *we will; '03* represents 2003.

Here is a list of other common contractions:

Common Contractions

are**n't** (are not)	he**'d** (he would)	should**'ve** (should have)
ca**n't** (cannot)	I**'m** (I am)	should**n't** (should not)
could**n't** (could not)	I**'ll** (I will)	that**'s** (that is)
did**n't** (did not)	I**'d** (I would)	they**'re** (they are)
do**n't** (do not)	is**n't** (is not)	they**'ll** (they will)
does**n't** (does not)	it**'s** (it has)	who**'s** (who has)
had**n't** (had not)	it**'s** (it is)	who**'s** (who is)
has**n't** (has not)	it**'ll** (it will)	wo**n't** (will not)
have**n't** (have not)	she**'s** (she has)	you**'re** (you are)
he**'s** (he has)	she**'s** (she is)	you**'ll** (you will)
he**'s** (he is)	she**'ll** (she will)	you**'d** (you would)
he**'ll** (he will)	she**'d** (she would)	

In every case except one, the letters in a contraction follow the same order as the original two words. The exception is the contraction for *will not: won't*.

Exercise 20.7   **Using Apostrophes**

Correct each italicized noun below that is meant to show ownership or possession. Cross out the unpunctuated form and write the correctly punctuated possessive form above it. For each italicized pair of words, create a contraction. Cross out the word pairs, and write the contraction above them. Use the example to guide you.

EXAMPLE   *I'm*
~~*I am*~~ planning to join my friends to play cards at ~~*Chriss*~~ *Chris's* apartment on Saturday.

(1) My ~~*mothers*~~ *mother's* stories about shopping for ~~*childrens*~~ *children's* shoes make her laugh now, but that ~~*was not*~~ *wasn't* always the case. (2) ~~*She would*~~ *She'd* put off the expensive trip to the shoe store as long as possible, but then ~~*we would*~~ *we'd* all

outgrow our shoes at the same time. (3) Mom says She ~~will not~~ ever [won't]
forget the expressions on *sales* ~~*representatives*~~ faces when all five of us [representatives']
would troop into the store. (4) ~~*Moms*~~ biggest challenge was buying ~~*girls*~~ [Mom's] [girl's]
shoes; ~~*boys*~~ shoes were easier to find because my brothers just wanted [boy's]
sneakers. (5) Mom thinks ~~*it is*~~ odd that I like to hear stories about these [it's]
stressful moments in our ~~*familys*~~ past. [family's]

<hr>

Exercise 20.8   **Correcting Errors with Apostrophes**

The following paragraph contains some words that need an apostrophe, either because they are contractions or because they show ownership. Cross out any words that need an apostrophe. Write them correctly in the space above. Use the example as a guide.

EXAMPLE

If ~~theres~~ one thing I ~~cant~~ stand, ~~its~~ noisy, undisciplined children. [there's] [can't] [it's]

(1) Children who ~~havent~~ been taught how to behave in a restaurant [haven't]
try ~~everyones~~ patience. (2) Of course, ~~its~~ not the ~~childrens~~ fault, but [everyone's] [it's] [children's]
rather their ~~parents~~ fault. (3) Children, even very small children, can be- [parent's]
have very well if ~~theyve~~ been shown how. (4) The most inconsiderate [they've]
parents allow their kids to roam around the restaurant, bother other people, and get in the ~~servers~~ way. (5) ~~Im~~ always amazed by parents who pay [servers'] [I'm]
so little attention to their children. (6) Slightly better are the parents who
manage to keep children in their seats, but who seem unable to keep the
~~childrens~~ noise level within reasonable limits. (7) ~~Ive~~ left many restau- [children's] [I've]
rants without even taking a seat if the place seemed too noisy. (8) ~~Its~~ not [It's]
that I dislike children; ~~its~~ simply the fact that I ~~cant~~ eat in a very noisy en- [it's] [can't]
vironment.

Exercise 20.9   **Using Apostrophes to Form Contractions and Possessives**

The italicized phrases in the following sentences can be simplified using apostrophes. Cross out each of these phrases. Above the crossed out phrase write a new version, using an apostrophe to create a possessive noun or a contraction. Use the example to guide you.

EXAMPLE

The bus ~~does not~~ *doesn't* stop at ~~the child care center of my daughter~~ *my daughter's child care center*.

(1) Parents often complain about ~~the teen fashion of today.~~ *today's teen fashions* (2) Those parents must have forgotten ~~the criticism of their own parents~~ *their own parents' criticism* about styles of earlier decades. (3) ~~The clothes of teens~~ *Teens' clothes* in the 1960s included wildly colored hip-hugging, bell-bottomed pants. (4) ~~The favorite outfit that belonged to my aunt~~ *My aunt's favorite outfit* was a beaded, fringed vest that she wore over a pair of ripped jeans. (5) My uncle says ~~he will~~ *he'll* never be allowed to forget his purple tie-dyed bell-bottoms. (6) ~~The hairstyles of yesterday could not~~ *Yesterday's hairstyles couldn't* have pleased many parents, either. (7) ~~The hair of many young men~~ *Many young men's hair* reached almost to their waists, for example. (8) Generations ~~are not~~ *aren't* all that different after all; ~~the individuality of young people~~ *young people's individuality* will always be expressed through fashion.

Challenge 20.4   **Using *Its* and *It's* in Your Writing**

As you can see from the list of common contractions on page 398, contractions of *it has* and *it is* are written as *it's*. Therefore, to eliminate confusion, *its* is used to show ownership. This possessive form uses no apostrophe: a picture and *its* frame.

COLLABORATION

Write five sentences using *its* and *it's*, but omit apostrophes. Exchange your sentences with a classmate. Add apostrophes where needed in the paper you received, and then return it.

Punctuation Checklist

- [ ] Have you examined each sentence to see whether it makes a statement, asks a question, or shows great excitement or emotion and then chosen the appropriate mark of end punctuation?

- [ ] Have you rechecked to ensure that no question marks have been used with *indirect* questions?

- [ ] Have you used a colon when you had to signal that significant information follows in a sentence?

☐ Have you used a semicolon, with or without a conjunctive adverb, to connect related simple sentences?

☐ Have you used quotation marks with direct quotations only?

☐ Have you checked the apostrophes used to signal ownership and to form contractions, paying particular attention to *it's?*

Exploring Ideas through Journal Writing

Punctuation, as this chapter illustrates, is the system of marks that signal stops, pauses, direct address, announcements, combinations, and ownership. Of course, if punctuation as we know it didn't exist, all these concepts would still exist in life. We start and stop activities, relationships, and behaviors. We pause to consider things or take a break from activities. We have conversations, we talk with others and listen to what they have to say, and we announce important events. We provide connections between people and between things, and we assert custody or ownership of other elements in our lives. Focus on one of these aspects, and then take 20 to 30 minutes to explore it in your journal.

Chapter Quick Check: Using Punctuation Properly

In the following passage, many necessary punctuation marks are missing. Supply an appropriate mark of end punctuation—period, question mark, or exclamation point—for each sentence. You may also need to add a colon or semicolon, quotation marks, or apostrophes within a sentence. With any incorrect use of *its* or *it's*, cross out the word and write the correct version above it.

(1) When I think back to my childhood, I have one serious regret : my failure to take advantage of free guitar lessons offered in the sixth grade . (2) I can still remember when the school's music teacher, Ms . Souza, asked, "Is there anyone here who would like to learn to play the guitar ?" (3) After a few moments of silence, one of the girls raised her hand and asked what the charge would be . (4) Ms . Souza's answer was astonishing : a superintendent's grant would pay for the lessons and pay to rent the

instrument. (5) I'd always wanted to learn to play the guitar; still, I was afraid of what my friends might think. (6) What would my friends' attitude about me be if I didn't just stare at Ms. Souza as we all usually did? (7) When nobody spoke up, Ms. Souza said, "If nobody here wants to do this, I'll offer the chance to my other students." (8) It's funny, but even then I knew that I shouldn't have rejected her generous offer. (9) She was offering me the chance I'd always hoped for; however, I didn't want friends to think I was a nerd. (10) If I could go back in time, I'd kick myself for living my life in such a ridiculous way!

Discovering Connections 20.2

COLLABORATION

1. For Discovering Connections 20.1 on page 390, you began prewriting in response to a quotation by Ralph Waldo Emerson or a photo. Now, continue your prewriting on one of these options:
   a. What is the best way to motivate people?
   b. Emerson says that he needs someone to make him do what he can do, but is it truly possible for anyone to *make* anyone else do anything of significance?
2. Evaluate your prewriting material, identify a focus, and create a draft of about 100 words.
3. Exchange your draft with a writing partner. Using the material in this chapter as a guide, evaluate the draft you receive, and note any problems with punctuation as well as any other weaknesses. Return the draft to the writer.
4. Revise your draft, eliminating any errors that your reader identified.

Summary Exercise: Using Punctuation Properly

In the following passage, many necessary punctuation marks are missing. Supply an appropriate mark of end punctuation—period, question mark, or exclamation point—for each sentence. You may also need to add a colon or semicolon, quotation marks, or apostrophes within a sentence. With any incorrect use of *its* or *it's,* cross out the word and write the correct version above it.

(1) One of these days, I'm going to get organized. (2) Maybe I'll make these New Year's resolutions: clean my desk, buy a pocket calendar, and make a to-do list. (3) I hope I can keep these resolutions.

(4) My desk looks as if someone emptied a wastebasket on it. (5) "How can you live with this mess?" my husband asks me at least once a week. (6) I don't know where to start. (7) The piles of paper and books will fall over if I touch them; nevertheless, I intend to try someday. (8) The problem is, I spend so much time looking for homework, appointment cards, letters, and phone numbers that I've lost on my desk, there's no time left to get organized.

(9) One easy thing I can do is buy a pocket calendar to keep track of what I have to do. (10) It's not an expensive item, and I can carry it with me. (11) When I get my assignments, I'll write them down. (12) My sister's friend has a leather one that cost $11.95. (13) I'll have to ask her where she bought it.

(14) What else can I do? (15) That's right: I can make a list of things to do. (16) I will have to find the time to sit and write the list; meanwhile, the number of things I have to do will keep growing. (17) Here's my promise to myself: I will take care of one item on my list every day. (18) It's no one else's fault but my own that I'm so unorganized. (19) It's up to me to get started. (20) "Never put off until tomorrow what you can do today," says a wise old adage.

RECAP USING PUNCTUATION PROPERLY

New terms in this chapter	Definitions
● **punctuation**	● the system of symbols that signal starts, stops, and pauses in writing
● **period**	● used to indicate a stop at the end of a sentence, to separate dollars and cents in monetary amounts, and to show abbreviations and initials *Example* The pharmacy bill was $129**.**42**.**
● **question mark**	● used at the end of a sentence to indicate a direct question *Example* Did the baseball game go into extra innings**?**
● **exclamation point**	● used at the end of a sentence to express strong emotion *Example* That fire is hot**!**
● **colon**	● marks a pause within a sentence and prepares for following words that explain, announce, or list *Example* After the storm, the town was devastated**:** windows broke, roads flooded, wires fell.
● **semicolon**	● connects simple sentences and calls attention to the connection *Example* The boys were fighting again**;** one of them got hurt.
● **quotation marks**	● used to set off someone's exact words ● *not used with indirect quotations,* a restatement of someone else's words *Example* **"**Who is your favorite movie star?**"** Whitney asked, after I told her that I loved watching movies.
● **apostrophe**	● used to show ownership or possession in nouns and to signify letters left out in a contraction *Example* I haven**'**t seen Brian**'**s new car yet.

To Form the Possessive

add **'s** to singular nouns	the bike of the boy → the boy**'s** bike
add **'** to plural nouns	the bikes of the two boys → the two boys**'** bikes
add **'s** to irregular plural nouns	the issues of women → women**'s** issues

Chapter 21

Using Commas

Getting Started... **Q:** Of all the marks of punctuation, the comma is the one I feel the least confident about using. Sometimes I think I am using too many, and other times I don't know if I've included enough. What can I do to make sure I put commas only where they are supposed to be?

A: When it comes to being unsure about commas, you have lots of company. Even people with plenty of writing experience have difficulties with comma use. The good news is that comma use falls into seven main categories. Write seven brief sentences, one for each of the seven comma functions, and keep them in your notebook or next to your computer. Then when you have a question, you have the answer right at your fingertips. If the comma you're contemplating doesn't fit into one of the seven categories, you probably don't need it.

Overview: Understanding When Commas Are Needed

When you speak, you include brief natural pauses within your sentences to make your meaning clear. In writing, you use punctuation to indicate those pauses. Of the three pausing punctuation marks, the **comma** is the one you'll use most frequently. It is also the most troublesome one because it serves so many different purposes. Writers sometimes have difficulty determining when and where to use commas.

> *In this chapter you will learn*
> - seven functions of commas
> - guidelines to determine when a comma is needed
> - guidelines to help you decide where to place commas

Consider the following quotation:

Life's greatest happiness is to be convinced we are loved.

—*Victor Hugo*

Or consider this photo.

Now, using the technique you prefer, do some prewriting about your reaction to the quotation or photo. Save your work.

Comma Function 1

To indicate a pause between two simple sentences connected by a coordinating conjunction

Chapter 9, "Coordination," discussed sentence combining. Remember that one way to combine two simple sentences is by linking them with a coordinating conjunction such as *and* or *but,* and then placing a comma before the conjunction. The comma indicates a pause. Look at these examples, and say them out loud:

> **EXAMPLE**   Those sunglasses are attractive**,** but they are too expensive.

> **EXAMPLE**   The back door flew open**,** and four huskies raced out.

In the first sentence, the comma is used to indicate a pause between the independent clauses connected by the conjunction *but.* In the second sentence, the comma is used to indicate a pause between the clauses connected by *and.*

Exercise 21.1   **Working with Commas and Coordinating Conjunctions**

Read the following sentences, and place a comma where needed to indicate a pause between clauses joined by a coordinating conjunction. Use the example to guide you.

> **EXAMPLE**   Michael and his twin sister both took the class**,** but she was the only one
>
> who passed.

(1) Experts are studying the effects of media violence⌄and they are concentrating on children. (2) Many studies have been done in the past few decades⌄but few of the scientists agree about what the results mean. (3) One theory says media violence acts as a catharsis⌄for it allows us to release our emotions harmlessly. (4) Another theory says that watching violence leads to violence⌄and there is a direct cause-and-effect link between what we see and what we do. (5) The truth probably falls in the middle of these two extremes⌄but more studies will need to be completed and evaluated.

Exercise 21. 2   Working with Commas and Coordinating Conjunctions

Complete the following compound sentences by adding a comma, a coordinating conjunction (*and, but, yet, nor, so, or*), and an independent clause. Remember that the clause you add must be a complete thought with a subject and verb. Use the example as a guide. (Answers will vary.)

EXAMPLE   After the holidays, I discovered to my regret that I had gained a few

pounds *, so I had to put myself on a diet.*

1. Many people feel that there is too much violence in the media these

   days _____ .

2. Violence in the media is often blamed for violent crimes that people

   commit _____ .

3. Sociologists and psychologists are studying the effects of violent media

   on the human brain _____ .

4. An increasing number of these studies are focused on the way that violent programming affects children _____ .

5. Since violent crimes committed by children are on the rise, violent TV

    shows, movies, and video games have often been blamed _____

    _____ .

6. Some children who have committed violent crimes have said that they

    were affected by exposure to violence in the media _____

    _____ .

7. Recent attention to this link between violent media and violent crime

    has inspired laws designed to limit violence in the media _____

    _____ .

8. Some people say that all violence should be banned from the media

    _____ .

Comma Function 2

To separate items in a series

Commas are also used to indicate the natural pauses in your speech when you are listing more than two items. The series of items may consist of words, phrases, or even clauses. Look at these examples, and say them out loud:

> **EXAMPLE**   Georgie bought paint, tape, rollers, and brushes.

> **EXAMPLE**   Jack's eighty-year-old grandfather still drives his truck, plays the piano, and walks five miles every day.

Now try saying these sentences out loud without any pauses between the items in the series. Do you feel confused? In the first sentence, the commas are needed to separate the various one-word items Georgie purchased. In the second, the commas separate phrases that describe the activities of Jack's elderly grandfather. Again, the sentence would not be understandable without the commas.

If you have only two items in a series, don't use a comma. Just use the conjunctions *and* or *or* to connect the items.

> **EXAMPLE**   Liz enjoys dancing *and* singing.

EXAMPLE Please bring canned goods *or* cleaning supplies to the food bank.

Exercise 21.3 **Using Commas in a Series**

Place commas where they are needed in this paragraph to separate items in a series. If a sentence is correct as written, write *OK* in the space above it. Use the example to guide you.

EXAMPLE Let's pick up some pizza, soda, and ice cream at the store.

OK
(1) Even though families and friends miss them, hospital patients need rest and quiet. (2) Visitors who stay for hours, talk loudly, and struggle to be cheerful can tire the recovering patient. (3) Visitors should follow hospital rules, observe visiting hours, and keep visits short. (4) Many patients enjoy receiving cards, flowers, and reading materials as much as visits. (5) When the patient goes home, visitors could bring a home-cooked meal, help with housework, or take care of young children.

Exercise 21.4 **Working with Commas in a Series**

In the following sentences, supply the items in the series. If you see only two blanks, provide only two items. If you see three blanks, provide three items and the commas needed to separate them. Your items may consist of more than one word. Use the example as a guide. (Answers will vary.)

EXAMPLE Before leaving on vacation, we have a lot to do: *cancel the newspaper,* *put a hold on our mail delivery,* and *make arrangements for the care of* *our dog.*

1. If it's a summer vacation, we pack _____

_____ and _____ .

2. The two youngest kids always insist on bringing along more than they need, including _____ and

    _____ .

3. My wife gathers her supply of maps of _____

    _____ and _____ .

4. I take charge of buying the traveler's checks; I get them in denominations of _____ _____ and _____ .

5. Of course, the car's stockpile of junk has to be cleaned out; we always find _____ _____ and

    _____ .

6. Our teenage daughter insists on packing all of her beauty products, such as _____ _____ and

    _____ .

7. Our twelve-year-old son, on the other hand, has to be pushed to pack some bare essentials like _____ and

    _____ .

8. Winter vacations can be even more complicated, especially around the holidays, because we have to pack gifts for _____

    _____ and _____ .

Comma Function 3

To separate an introductory phrase from the rest of the sentence

Sometimes you will begin a sentence with an introductory phrase that describes a time, place, or condition. If that phrase is four or more words long, then you should separate it from the rest of the sentence with a comma. Look at these examples, and say them out loud:

EXAMPLE   *At the entrance to the mall,* several people were handing out Earth Day flyers.

EXAMPLE

Within the shelter of the old barn, two bike riders waited for the storm to end.

The introductory phrase in both sentences is long enough that a comma is helpful.

For introductory phrases of three words or less, you *may not* need to include a comma. Look at the sentence, and ask yourself this question: *Is the meaning of my sentence clearer with the comma?* If the answer is yes, always include the comma. Look at the two sentences below, and read them out loud. Do they need commas?

CLEAR

After supper Kathy and John dropped by.

CONFUSING

Overall workers at the factory performed better in the redesigned production area.

The first sentence is clear without any comma between the introductory phrase *After supper* and the rest of the sentence. On the other hand, the second sentence is confusing because the word *overall* has two possible meanings. It can mean "taken as a whole," or "covering all jobs within the workplace." A comma makes it clear that *overall* here means "taken as a whole."

CLEAR

Overall, workers at the factory performed better in the redesigned production area.

Exercise 21.5   Using Commas after Introductory Phrases

Place commas where they are needed in the following sentences to separate introductory phrases from the rest of the sentence. If a sentence is correct, write *OK* above it. Use the example as a guide.

EXAMPLE

In our city, block parties are common.
        ∧

1. Month after month and year after year, my city keeps growing.
                                              ∧

2. For most of the city's population, that increasing size means a faster pace
                                        ∧

    of life and more stress.

    OK

3. By evening most city dwellers are more than ready to enter the familiar

    cocoon of their neighborhoods.

4. Offering a stable and welcoming environment, your own block gives you a place to belong and to be safe.

5. With the huge buildup of industry, some neighborhoods in my city are becoming less desirable.

    OK

6. In some places the streets are growing noisier and dirtier.

7. Without motivation to stay, many families are moving to the quieter and cleaner suburbs.

8. Called urban flight, this phenomenon has contributed to an economic decline in my city.

Exercise 21.6   **Working with Commas after Introductory Phrases**

In the following sentences, some commas have been left out, and others have been unnecessarily added. If an introductory phrase should be set off by a comma, add it. If a comma appears where it is not necessary, cross it out. If a sentence is correctly punctuated, write *OK* above it. Use the example to guide you.

EXAMPLE   For months, I have anticipated the coming of spring.

1. In our region, winter comes early and stays late.

2. Having lost their brilliant fall plumage, the trees stand stark as skeletons.

3. Before the end of November, you can count on at least one snowfall.

4. By Christmas, it seems winter has been a fact of life for a long time.

5. Waiting eagerly with their skis in hand, ski enthusiasts applaud the first snowfalls.

    OK

6. Before long they also tire of the fierce windchill and colorless landscape.

OK
7. Seeking warmth and bright colors, many escape to a sunny resort.

8. With the coming of April, wan northerners emerge like groundhogs to test the air.

Comma Function 4

To set off an introductory subordinate clause

As Chapter 8, "Subordination," showed, a subordinate clause may be joined to a main clause to indicate the relationship between the two thoughts. If the subordinate clause comes *first* in the sentence, it must be set off by a comma. Look at these examples, and say them aloud:

EXAMPLE   Until I actually saw Mount Rushmore, I couldn't understand what all the fuss was about.

The subordinate clause *Until I actually saw Mount Rushmore* introduces the sentence and leads up to the main clause, or independent thought. The comma indicates the pause before the main clause. Note that when the subordinate clause follows the main clause, no comma is needed:

EXAMPLE   We didn't mention the lost necklace *until we found it again.*

Exercise 21.7   **Using Commas after Introductory Subordinate Clauses**

Add commas where they are needed to set off subordinate clauses. If a sentence is correct as punctuated, write *OK* above it. Use the example as a guide.

EXAMPLE   Before you walk on the carpet, please take off your muddy boots.

1. Although I live far from Cajun country, I love to hear zydeco bands.
   OK
2. I never miss them when they come to my area.

3. Because my friends like rap music, they can't understand my interest.
   OK
4. While my favorite zydeco musician was in the area, I took them to a dance.

5. By the time the band took a break¸we were all tired from dancing.

Working with Commas with Introductory Subordinate Clauses

In the following paragraph, find the subordinate clauses. Set off each introductory subordinate clause with a comma. If a sentence needs no comma added, write *OK* above it. Use the example to guide you.

EXAMPLE

When people have limited financial resources¸they have to make

sacrifices.

(1) As community colleges have caught on and grown¸they have begun to serve many functions. (2) Because so many communities now have these colleges¸underprivileged students now have a much less ex-
pensive alternative to a university education. (OK) (3) Community colleges also address the needs of students who are academically unprepared. (4) While they pursue courses in their major¸students can also take basic courses to bring them up to speed in math and composition. (5) Although community colleges are lenient about admissions standards¸they are not so easygoing about performance once a student has en-
rolled. (OK) (6) Students are still required to do the work to rigorous stan-
dards. (7) If students expect to get an education¸they must be diligent and committed. (8) Even though the instructors at community colleges are rarely famous¸they are usually dedicated and demanding teachers.

Comma Function 5

To set off word groups that would otherwise interrupt the flow of a sentence

Sometimes you use a word, phrase, or clause within a sentence that describes something you have just named or that emphasizes a thought or action. When these additions interrupt the main flow of the action in the sentence, they require pauses. You should use commas *before* and *after* these interrupters to set them off from the rest of the sentence. Look at these examples, and say them out loud:

EXAMPLE

The L.A. Shuffle, which is the fifth action film of the summer, has already made $30 million.

EXAMPLE

The biggest reason to promote sex education, *however,* is the AIDS epidemic.

EXAMPLE

The utility shed, *a rickety building behind our apartment complex,* is infested with rats.

EXAMPLE

I called to tell you, *Andrea,* that your dress is ready.

In the first sentence, the clause *which is the fifth action film of the summer* describes the subject of the sentence: *The L.A. Shuffle.* At the same time, this clause separates the subject from the verb phrase that shows what the subject did. Because it interrupts the flow of the action in the sentence, the words are set off by commas before and after.

In the second example, the word *however* interrupts the main thought of the sentence to emphasize its importance, so it needs to be set off by commas as well. It falls into a category called parenthetical expressions, or side remarks, that are injected into a sentence to quality the idea. Other examples include *nevertheless, in my opinion, by the way, in fact,* and *as a matter of fact.*

In the third example sentence, an appositive phrase that describes the word *shed* interrupts the flow of the sentence. An appositive phrase renames a noun or pronoun in a sentence and should almost always be set off by commas. (See Chapter 7, "Sentence Fragments," for a more complete discussion of appositives.)

The fourth example illustrates a kind of interrupter called a *noun of direct address.* The person who is addressed directly in the sentence is named, and that name is set off by commas. In this example, *Andrea* is set off in this way.

Any of these types of interrupters may also be placed at the beginning or end of a sentence. Place a comma after an interrupter that begins a sentence. Place a comma before one that ends a sentence.

EXAMPLE

In my opinion, the food processor is a great invention.

EXAMPLE

My in-laws won a cruise, *a dream vacation in the Caribbean.*

Exercise 21.9   **Using Commas to Set Off Words, Phrases, or Clauses That Interrupt Sentence Flow**

Place commas where they are needed to set off words from the rest of the sentence. Use the example as a guide.

EXAMPLE   Calculus which is a required math course in my program is offered only once this school year.

(1) I think the autumn months in New England which is where I live are the prettiest months. (2) The colorful foliage with leaves changing to orange, yellow, and red can take your breath away. (3) Those aren't the only colors to see however on a fall day. (4) The sky a brilliant blue envelope on a crisp October day adds to the beauty. (5) Even farm stands which dot the country roads are filled with color—orange pumpkins, red apples, and green and yellow squash.

Exercise 21.10   **Working with Commas to Set Off Words, Phrases, or Clauses That Interrupt Sentence Flow**

In the sentences below, insert commas where they are necessary. If a sentence is punctuated correctly, write *OK* above it. Use the example as a guide.

EXAMPLE   The weather over the last month rain almost every day has hurt the tourist industry badly.

(1) A stand-up comedian someone who voluntarily tries to make a bunch of strangers laugh has one of the most stressful jobs in the world. (2) Even airline pilots though they bear a heavy responsibility do get some "down time" while they work. (3) The comedian however has to be OK "on" every second. (4) He or she has to have perfect timing, that instinc-

tive sense of when to throw in the punch line, in order to succeed. (5) Fortunately, club audiences who are usually already in a good mood are not hard to please. (6) Every now and then, the comedian our brave pioneer in humor, has to deal with a hostile audience. (7) Hecklers who seem to get nastier as the evening progresses are enough to drive a newcomer out of the business. (8) However, the survivors, those who hang in there and profit from their mistakes, often become sought-after headliners.

Comma Function 6

To set off a direct quotation from the rest of a sentence

Writers use quotation marks to show when they are using someone else's exact words. The quote, and therefore the quotation marks, can appear at the beginning, at the end, or in the middle of a sentence. It all depends on where you place the *attribution*, the part that identifies the speaker. Look at these three versions of the same sentence:

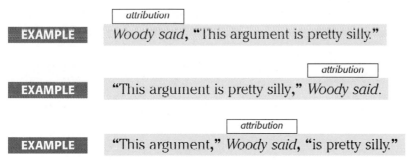

EXAMPLE   *Woody said,* "This argument is pretty silly."

EXAMPLE   "This argument is pretty silly," *Woody said.*

EXAMPLE   "This argument," *Woody said,* "is pretty silly."

Note that in all three locations, the quotation begins with a capital letter and is surrounded by quotation marks. Also note that commas are necessary to set off the quote from the attribution.

- Place a comma *after* the attribution if it comes at the beginning of the sentence.
- Place the comma *at the end of the quotation,* within the closing quotation mark if the attribution comes at the end.
- If the attribution appears in the middle of the quotation, place one comma *within the first closing quotation mark* and a second comma *after the attribution*.

See pages 395–396 for further discussion about quotations.

Exercise 21.11   **Using Commas with Quotation Marks**

In each sentence below, underline the attribution. Place commas where they are needed to help separate the attribution from the exact words of the speaker. Use the example to guide you.

EXAMPLE   "I have a terrible headache," *I complained*.

(1) "I'm going to quit smoking this year," Joe said. (2) He looked serious as he declared, "I'll take one day at a time, but I'm determined to succeed this time."

(3) "The nicotine patch has helped other smokers," I told him. (4) "Maybe using that would help you, too," I said, "or chewing nicotine gum."

(5) Joe smiled and said, "Thanks for the suggestions."

Exercise 21.12   **Working with Commas and Quotation Marks**

Write two alternative sentences for each quotation below by moving the attribution to other locations in the sentence. Be careful to punctuate your sentences correctly. Use the example as a guide.

EXAMPLE   The little girl sobbed, "I lost it, but I don't know where."

a. "I lost it," the little girl sobbed, "but I don't know where."

b. "I lost it, but I don't know where," the little girl sobbed.

1. "You do that one more time," the mother warned, "and you'll be sent to your room."

   The mother warned, "You do that one more time, and you'll be sent to your room."

   "You do that one more time, and you'll be sent to your room," the mother warned.

2. "I hate it when I can't find my keys," she said irritably.

She said irritably, "I hate it when I can't find my keys."

"I hate it," she said irritably, "when I can't find my keys."

_____

_____

3. He shouted above the clamor, "Ladies and gentlemen, please remain calm."

"Ladies and gentlemen, please remain calm," he shouted above the clamor.

"Ladies and gentlemen," he shouted above the clamor, "please remain calm."

_____

_____

4 "You can do it if you just try a little harder," she encouraged.

She encouraged, "You can do it if you just try a little harder."

"You can do it," she encouraged, "if you just try a little harder."

_____

_____

5. "There are no seats left for this showing," the manager explained, "but we can sell you advance tickets for the 9 o'clock show."

The manager explained, "There are no seats left for this showing, but we can sell

you advance tickets for the 9 o'clock show."

"There are no seats left for this showing, but we can sell you advance tickets for the

9 o'clock show," the manager explained.

Challenge 21.1   **Analyzing Comma Functions in a Paragraph by a Professional Writer**

COLLABORATION

Choose a three- or four-paragraph passage from one of your textbooks or a magazine article and copy it. Make a second copy and exchange it with a classmate. Read the passage you receive and analyze the function of each comma. When you are finished, discuss what you have found with your classmate.

Comma Function 7

To punctuate dates and addresses

Commas are used to separate items in dates and addresses. In the example below, note that not only do commas separate each part of the date, but a comma also follows the last item in the date.

> **EXAMPLE**   On Friday, June 30, 1915, my great-grandfather arrived in America.

Usually, a comma follows the last item in an address or multiple-part place name. However, no comma is placed before the zip code in an address.

Moreover, if a date or address is one word and is preceded by a preposition, then no comma is needed:

> **EXAMPLE**   Our address has changed from 11 Sylvan Lane, DeKalb, Illinois, to Route 79, Thaxton, Virginia 24174.

> **EXAMPLE**   The sales manager drives to Fort Wayne on Wednesday.

Exercise 21.13   **Using Commas in Dates and Addresses**

Insert commas where they are needed to set off dates and addresses in the following sentences. Use the example to guide you.

> **EXAMPLE**   Our first date was on March 13, 2003, in Elberton, Georgia.

1. We would like to invite you to our parents' 50th wedding anniversary on Saturday, June 14, 2001, at 2 P.M.

2. A celebration mass will be held at Sacred Heart Cathedral, 2575 South Wells Avenue, St. Paul, Minnesota.

3. You are cordially invited to a party to be held afterward at the home of Sharon and Keith Balster, 1977 Tallchief Drive, Shakopee, Minnesota.

4. The favor of a reply is requested by June 1 to Rebecca Brauer, P. O. Box 550, Deerfield, Massachusetts 01342.

5. In place of gifts, we ask that you write a memory of your friendship with Edith and Roy during their years in Tempe_, Arizona_, and Minneapolis_, Minnesota.

Exercise 21.14   **Working with Commas in Dates and Addresses**

Correct the punctuation in the following sentences. If commas are needed, insert them. If commas are used incorrectly, cross them out. Use the example as a guide.

EXAMPLE   My roommate moved sometime in July~~,~~ or early August~~,~~ to St. Louis, Missouri.

1. While my best friend was spending his summer hauling boxes for his father's moving company, I was biking through the Midwestern~~,~~ states, marveling at the sights.

2. I suppose he never got the postcards I sent him at 405A~~,~~ Ninth Street, Ada, Ohio 45810.

3. It amazed me how many Midwestern towns borrowed their names from glamorous cities—Geneva, Illinois, and Paris, Missouri, for example.

4. River towns along the Mississippi, like Camanche, Iowa, and Prairie du Chien, Wisconsin, have a quaint, old-fashioned feel.

5. By Wednesday, August 10, I had covered 500 miles of my 650-mile journey.

Using Comma Checklist

☐ Have you used a comma following the conjunction joining two simple sentences to indicate the needed pause?

☐ Have you used a comma to separate items in a series and to set off an introductory passage of four or more words at the beginning of a sentence?

☐ Have you used a comma to set off an introductory subordinate clause introduced by a subordinating conjunction?

☐ Have you used a comma *before* and *after* any word or group of words interrupting the flow of a sentence?

(continued)

☐ Have you used a comma to set off a direct quotation from the rest of a sentence?

☐ Have you used commas to separate the elements in dates and addresses appearing in the middle of a sentence, including one after the last element?

Exploring Ideas through Journal Writing

As the various examples in this chapter illustrate, commas perform several functions. If you reduce them to one primary purpose, you could say that they keep things *separated* within a sentence. In terms of life in general, *separated* doesn't carry much of a positive connotation. It suggests people or things kept apart or divided in some way. However, the word doesn't necessarily mean something negative. For example, some synonyms for *separate* are *independent, distinct,* or *individual.* Consider one meaning for *separate*—positive or negative—and think of it in terms of something you have read about, experienced or witnessed. Then explore it for 20 to 30 minutes in your journal.

Chapter Quick Check: Using Commas

The following passage is missing a number of commas. Review the seven functions of commas, and then proofread the passage and add the necessary commas.

(1) Except for a select group of scholars most people have never had the chance to examine the priceless illustrated manuscripts that date back to before the invention of the printing press. (2) Only a relatively small number of these manuscripts exist, and age makes them highly fragile so most are kept locked away often under climate-controlled conditions. (3) In fact most people have only seen illustrations or copies of these beautiful documents in textbooks museums or specialized journals. (4) A software system owned by the British Library *Turning the Pages* is changing this however. (5) Although users don't actually touch or turn these electronic pages they can virtually touch and turn them by running a finger across the page pictured on the screen causing

the page to flip to the next page. (6) As with a real page, the virtual page reacts if the user stops short of the end of the page, slipping back to the original position. (7) The image on the screen is an exact digital image of the original page, so it includes colorful paintings of birds, biblical scenes, and everyday medieval life. (8) The software has some features, including audio clips, that the creators of the original manuscript could never possibly have imagined. (9) For example, because the entire page has been digitized, a touch of the screen at any point enlarges words, icons, or images so the viewer can study them in close detail as well. (10) So far, eight texts have been recorded in this way, including a fifth-century Buddhist work, a collection of Leonardo da Vinci's drawings, and a book about medicinal herbs and plants.

Discovering Connections 21.2

1. For Discovering Connections 21.1 on page 406, you began prewriting in response to a quotation by Victor Hugo or to a picture. Now, continue your prewriting on one of these options:
   a. Why does knowing that we are loved make such a difference in our lives?
   b. In your view, what is the best way to ensure that the people who are important to us know that they are loved?
   c. After conferring with your instructor, write on some other aspect associated with the quotation.
2. Evaluate your prewriting material, identify a focus, and create a draft of about 100 words.
3. Exchange your draft with a writing partner. Using the material in this chapter as a guide, evaluate the draft you receive, and note any mistakes in comma use as well as any other weaknesses. Return the draft to the writer.
4. Revise your draft, eliminating any errors that your reader identified.

COLLABORATION

Summary Exercise: Using Commas

The following passage is missing a number of commas. Review the seven functions of commas, and then proofread the passage and add the necessary commas. Some of the sentences are correct as written. Write *OK* above them.

OK

(1) In my neighborhood we have both helpful and annoying neighbors. (2) Everyone gets along well ^,^ however ^,^ because we all have learned to accept each other as we are.

(3) Lionel ^,^ Marilyn ^,^ and their two sons are kind and helpful neighbors. (4) When it snows ^,^ for example ^,^ Lionel and his boys are the first ones outside shoveling out everyone's cars and parking spaces. (5) This kindness is much appreciated by neighbors who are elderly ^,^ sick ^,^ or dis-
OK ^ ^
abled ^,^ and therefore unable to shovel heavy snow. (6) Once Marilyn brought me homemade vegetable soup when I had the flu. (7) She invites neighbors for dinner ^,^ and she always brings us extra tomatoes and peppers from her garden. (8) The boys ^,^ who are named Joe and Sam ^,^ love to play street hockey. (9) They broke my car window ^,^ but they told me and paid for it themselves.

OK

(10) We have other neighbors across the street who can be annoying. (11) Each morning before 7 ^,^ I wake up hearing the father, Eric, yelling and whistling for his dog to come in. (12) When I asked him why he had to make so much noise so early ^,^ he just said ^,^ "Because I have to go to
OK
work ^,^ Freda ^,^ and get the dog in before I leave." (13) I put up with this
OK
early alarm clock. (14) At least I can sleep on weekends and on Eric's vacation. (15) Sometimes late at night ^,^ Eric's daughter plays her guitar ^,^ an electric one with an amplifier ^,^ very loudly. (16) I can't fall asleep listening to her try to imitate Jimi Hendrix ^,^ Eric Clapton ^,^ or Dave Matthews. (17) I don't complain too much ^,^ though ^,^ because Rose entertains us with her music at our summer block parties.

(18) From time to time ⟨,⟩ I probably annoy my neighbors as much as they annoy me. OK (19) My family also makes noise and breaks things at times. (20) Neighbors have to look for the best in each other ⟨,⟩ or they won't get along at all.

RECAP   USING COMMAS

New term in this chapter	Definition
● **comma**	● a punctuation mark that indicates a pause within a sentence

Seven Comma Functions

● to indicate a pause between two simple sentences connected by a coordinating conjunction

> *Example*   I bought new shoes, but they don't fit.

● to separate the items in a series

> *Example*   Math, chemistry, and anatomy are required courses in my major field.

● to separate an introductory phrase from the rest of the sentence

> *Example*   In almost every North American home, a TV blares for hours a day.

● to set off an introductory subordinate clause

> *Example*   Before I pay this bill, I want an itemized list of expenses.

● to set off word groups that would otherwise interrupt the flow of a sentence

> *Example*   These shoes, which I bought on sale, don't fit.

● to set off a direct quotation from the rest of a sentence

> *Example*   "That book," said Luis, "was made into a movie."

● to punctuate dates and addresses

> *Example*   The wedding will be held on Saturday, August 10, in Kansas City, Missouri.

Chapter 22

Mastering Spelling

Getting Started... **Q:** I've really tried to improve my spelling and learn all the rules, but I still have so much trouble with it. Why is spelling in English so complicated? More important, how can I become a better speller?

A: Spelling in English is difficult for many good reasons. To begin, English has been drawn from a number of other languages. That's why no set of rules can cover every word. Most rules have exceptions, and these exceptions are the words that often cause difficulties. Probably the best strategy, then, is to prepare a list of the words that you personally have misspelled. Keep this list available when you write, and use it to check each draft you write. After a while, you will notice errors more quickly and find that you are becoming a better speller overall.

Overview: Understanding the Importance of Correct Spelling

If you have difficulty with spelling, you can point to a number of reasons for your errors. English words don't follow consistent spelling patterns. Many words, such as *pneumonia* and *though,* are not spelled the way they sound. Some words, such as *there, their,* and *they're,* sound the same but are spelled differently and have different meanings.

Nonetheless, you must spell correctly if you want your papers to communicate as you intend. Mistakes in spelling are among the first things a reader notices. They definitely make your writing less effective.

> *In this chapter you'll discover strategies to help you ensure that you spell words correctly. You will learn*
>
> ● some basic spelling rules
>
> ● different meanings and spellings of commonly confused words

Discovering Connections 22.1

Consider the following quotation:

Common sense is perhaps the most equally divided, but surely the most underemployed talent in the world.

—*Christiane Collange*

Or look at this photo.

Now, using the technique you prefer, do some prewriting about your reaction to the quotation or photo. Save your work.

Forming Plurals

As Chapter 16, "Working with Nouns," showed, you can form the plural of most nouns by adding -s to the singular form:

helicopter   helicopter**s**   cat   cat**s**   television   television**s**

Nouns That End in -ch, -sh, -x, and -s   For nouns ending in -ch, -sh, -x, and s, form the plural by adding -es.

church   church**es**   bush   bush**es**   box   box**es**

Nouns That End in -y   For nouns ending in -y preceded by a *vowel* (a, e, i, o, u), form the plural by adding -s:

toy   toy**s**   play   play**s**   key   key**s**

For nouns ending in -y preceded by a *consonant* (any of the rest of the letters in the alphabet), form the plural by changing the -y to -i and adding -es:

story   stor**ies**   baby   bab**ies**   butterfly   butterfl**ies**

Compound Nouns   Most combined or compound nouns form the plural by adding -s to the *main* word:

runner up   runner**s** up   maid of honor   maid**s** of honor
brother-in-law   brother**s**-in-law

Foreign Words   With some words from foreign languages, you form the plural in keeping with the original language. The following Latin words form the plural by changing the final -i to -e.

analysis   analys**es**   crisis   cris**es**   thesis   thes**es**

Nouns That End in -o   Some nouns share the same ending but form their plurals differently. For nouns that end in -o, for instance, the plural form depends on one of three things:

- If the noun ends in a vowel plus -o, add -s to form the plural:

  patio   patio**s**   radio   radio**s**

- If the noun ends in a consonant plus -o, add -es to form the plural:

  tomato   tomato**es**   hero   hero**es**   veto   veto**es**

- Nouns ending in -o that refer to music are an exception. They form the plural by adding -s:

  piano   piano**s**   soprano   soprano**s**   solo   solo**s**

Nouns That End in -f and -fe   Nouns that share the -f or -fe ending also may have different plural forms. For most of these nouns, you form the plural by simply adding -s:

belief   belief**s**   chief   chief**s**   roof   roof**s**

However, some nouns with this same ending form the plural by changing the -f or -fe to -v and adding -es:

half   hal**ves**   wife   wi**ves**   leaf   lea**ves**

Irregular Nouns   For some common irregular nouns, you form the plural by changing letters within the word:

woman   wom**e**n   tooth   t**ee**th   mouse   m**ice**

Nouns That Have the Same Singular and Plural Forms   Finally, a few nouns have the same singular and plural forms:

sheep   sheep   deer   deer   antelope   antelope

If you are not sure how a noun forms the plural, consult a dictionary. The dictionary lists the plural ending for words that do not form plurals simply by adding -s.

Exercise 22.1   **Forming Plurals**

Using the guidelines in the preceding section or a dictionary, change the italicized singular words in the paragraph below to their correct plural forms. Write your answers above the italicized words. Use the example to guide you.

tomatoes
EXAMPLE   We'll raise *tomato* in the garden.

Families   options
(1) *Family* have to consider all the *option* when they decide which
        systems   megabytes
computer to buy. (2) Efficient computer *system* need several *megabyte* of
  processors   modems   monitors   lots
RAM, powerful *processor,* fast *modem,* quality *monitor,* and *lot* of storage
    graphics   capabilities
space. (3) CD-ROM, *graphic,* and sound *capability* are also important for
   programs   issues
running multimedia *program.* (4) Other *issue* to consider include ease of
    components   boxes
setting up the computer *component* once they come out of their *box*
        prices   analyses
and degree of "user-friendliness." (5) Computer *price* are high; *analysis* of
  brands   consumers   decisions
competing *brand* will help *consumer* make informed *decision.*

Exercise 22.2   Correcting Improper Plurals

Using a dictionary, correct all of the italicized words that are spelled incorrectly. Cross out the incorrect spelling, and write the correct one above it. If a word is correct as written, mark it *OK*. Use the example as a guide.

EXAMPLE
                   artisans
In today's world there are still ~~artisanes~~ dedicated to keeping ancient
OK
crafts alive.

       OK
(1) For centuries, American *Indians* living in what is now the northeastern United States used birch bark *canos.* (2) These *boates* were built
out of cedarwood and the bark of *birchs.* (3) The *roots* of black *sprues*
were used to sew together different *sections* of the canoe. (4) Crooked
knifes were used to shape the *planks* of the canoe. (5) The Indians used
wooden *paddls* to steer their *craftes* through *riveres* and other
waterwayes. (6) Today, a man named Henri Vaillancourt is still pursuing
the art of the old Indian boat *builderes.* (7) He has sold his *canos* to
collectors, museums, and *universitys.* (8) *Storyes* of their beauty have
spread. (9) In the cold weather, he makes *snowshos.* (10) Vaillancourt
loves the idea of keeping alive craft *traditiones* practiced *agees* ago.

Challenge 22.1   **Analyzing Plural Noun Forms**

Working with a partner, choose a reading you would both like to explore from the selections in Part Six, "Discovering Connections through Reading." On a separate sheet of paper, list ten singular nouns that you identify in the reading. Then change these nouns to their plural forms.

Adding Prefixes and Suffixes

Prefixes and suffixes are units of one or more letters that you add to nouns, verbs, adjectives, and adverbs to change their meaning. A **prefix** is a unit such as *un-*, *dis-*, or *semi-* that you add to the *beginning* of a word. A **suffix** is a unit such as *-ness*, *-able*, and *-ous* that you add at the *end* of a word.

When you add a prefix to a word, you *don't* change the spelling of the word:

necessary	**un**necessary	agree	**dis**agree
spell	**mis**spell	conscious	**semi**conscious

Suffixes *-ly* and *-ness* When you add the suffixes *-ly* and *-ness* to a word, you *usually* don't change the spelling of the word:

usual	usual**ly**	rare	rare**ly**	mean	mean**ness**

However, for words of more than one syllable that end in *-y*, you change the *-y* to *-i* before adding the *-ly* or *-ness:*

happy	happ**iness**	easy	eas**ily**	crazy	craz**iness**

Exception   One exception to this rule is the word *true.* When you add *-ly* to *true*, you drop the *-e:* tru**ly.**

For other suffixes, however, you may have to change the spelling of the word itself.

Words That End in *-y*   For words ending in *-y*, change the *-y* to *-i* before adding a suffix:

worry	worr**ied**	modify	modif**ied**	identify	identif**ied**

However, if the suffix begins with *-i*, keep the *-y:*

worry	worry**ing**	modify	modify**ing**	identify	identif**ing**

Words That End in *-e*   When the word ends in *-e* and the suffix begins with a *vowel*, drop the final *-e* before adding the suffix:

hope	hop**ing**	approve	approv**al**	fame	fam**ous**

If the suffix begins with a *consonant,* keep the final *-e:*

care   care**less**   safe   safe**ty**   arrange   arrange**ment**

Exceptions   Here are several exceptions to these guidelines. You will need to memorize them.

notice   notice**able**   mile   mile**age**   peace   peace**able**
argue   argu**ment**   whole   whol**ly**   judge   judg**ment**

Adding Prefixes and Suffixes

Add the prefix or suffix in parentheses to each italicized word in the paragraph below. Write the new word in the space above. Check the guidelines in the section above for help. Use the example as a guide.

EXAMPLE
hoping
We are *hope* (ing) for warm weather during our vacation.

leaving   *happiness*
(1) Some women are *leave* (ing) their careers to find *happy* (ness) at
raising   *guilty*
home *raise* (ing) their children. (2) These women say they felt *guilt* (y)
disappointed   *missing*
and (dis) *appoint* (ed) about *miss* (ing) their children's first years of life.
worried   *making*
(3) Now, however, the full-time moms are often *worry* ('ed') about *make*
Unless
(ing) ends meet. (4) (Un) *less* their spouses or partners can support the
comfortably   *probably*
family *comfort* (able) (ly), many of these women will *probable* (ly) either

return to work part-time or find work to do at home. (5) Many people
disagree   *arrangement*
may (dis) *agree* with the *arrange* (ment) they have made. (6) Neverthe-
devoting   *fulfilling*
less, these women find that *devote* (ing) time to childrearing is *fulfill* (ing).

Checking for Misspellings Involving Prefixes and Suffixes

Check the italicized words in the paragraph below to see if they are spelled correctly. Cross out any misspellings and write the correctly spelled version above it. If an italicized word is correct as written, mark it *OK.* Use the example to guide you.

inquiring
EXAMPLE   She has a very ~~inquireing~~ mind.

OK
(1) My son had a terrible time *learning* how to swim. (2) During the
breaking   suffering
summer, my heart would be *~~breakking~~* as I'd watch him *~~suffereing~~* at the
happily paddling
neighborhood pool. (3) All of the other kids would be *~~happyly paddeling~~*
OK   OK
or *courageously diving*, and there he'd be, huddled at the shallow end
enviously   OK   rarely   OK
~~envioussly~~ watching them. (4) He would *~~rarly~~* venture into the *deeper*
desperately   finally
water. (5) If he did, he'd cling *~~desperatly~~* to the rim of the pool. (6) I *~~finaly~~*
urging   OK
decided that *~~urgeing~~* him to try just wasn't *going* to work. (7) I could not
OK   disadvantage
let him continue with this *dangerous ~~dissadvantage~~*. (8) I signed him up
lessons
for swimming *~~lessones~~* at the YMCA.

Exercise 22.5   **Adding Suffixes**

On a separate piece of paper, add the suffixes in parentheses to the following ten words. Make any spelling changes necessary. Then write a sentence
using each of the words. Exchange your work with a classmate, and underline any misspelled words you find in your classmate's sentences. Return
the sentences to the writer.

1. finish (ed)   5. refer (ed)

2. occur (ed)   6. judge (ment)

3. snowy (est)   7. create (ed)

4. hammer (ed)   8. notice (able)

Challenge 22.2   **Analyzing Meaning with and without Prefixes and Suffixes**

Adding a prefix or suffix changes the meaning of a word. To help you discover how the meaning can change, choose five words from among those
used as examples on pages 430–431. On a separate sheet of paper, write
them both with and without the suffix or prefix. Then write what you think
the words mean, with and without their suffixes or prefixes. For example,
conscious means "alert and awake"; *semiconscious* means "partially alert
and awake." Use a dictionary if you are not sure how the meaning changes.

Doubling the Final Consonant

When you add a suffix that begins with a vowel to a word that ends in a consonant, do you double that final consonant? The answer depends on the word itself.

One-Syllable Words If the word has one syllable, and the letter before the final consonant is a *single vowel*, double that consonant before adding a suffix beginning with a vowel:

stop   stop**ping**   plan   plan**ned**   fat   fat**test**

However, if the final consonant is preceded by a consonant (as in wa**r**n) or more than one vowel (as in **ea**t), just add the suffix beginning with a vowel:

warn   warn**ed**   eat   eat**er**   sail   sail**ing**

Words of Two or More Syllables What do you do if a word ends in a single consonant preceded by a single vowel, but the word has *more than one syllable?* If the *accent,* or emphasis, is on the *last syllable,* double the final consonant before adding the suffix. (Say the word out loud to identify which syllable is *accented.*)

begin   begin**ning**   admit   admit**ted**   occur   occur**rences**

If the accent is *not* on the last syllable, simply add the suffix:

travel   travel**ed**   suffer   suffer**ed**   abandon   abandon**ing**

Exercise 22.6   **Deciding Whether to Double the Final Consonant**

In each sentence below, add the suffixes in parentheses to the italicized words. Write the new word above the italicized word. Refer to the rules in the section above to help you decide whether to double the final consonant of the original word. Use the example as a guide.

EXAMPLE   Aunt Sophie always picks out the *fat* (est) turkey for Thanksgiving dinner. → *fattest*

(1) "*Stop* (ing) by Woods on a Snowy Evening," by Robert Frost, is one → Stopping
of my favorite poems. (2) I had *plan* (ed) to read it at the *begin* (ing) of → planned, beginning
the poetry *read* (ing) my class was *sponsor* (ing). (3) However, because a → reading, sponsoring
huge snowstorm *occur* (ed) on that day, the event was *cancel* (ed). → occurred, canceled

The poem is about a man who paused as he *travel* (ed) [traveled] on a *winter* (y) [wintery]

night to his destination miles away. (5) Like the speaker in the poem, I

too have *talk* (ed) [talked] myself into going on, even when I would have liked to

stop and enjoy where I am.

Exercise 22.7   **Considering Whether to Double the Final Consonant**

Check the italicized words in the paragraph below to see if they are spelled correctly. Cross out any incorrectly spelled word, and write the correctly spelled form above it. If the word is correct as written, mark it *OK*. Use the example to guide you.

EXAMPLE   This meat looks ~~leanner~~. [*leaner*]

(1) Years ago, before the age of ~~motorrization~~, [motorization] winter weather in some ways ~~actualy~~ [actually] made ~~travelling~~ [traveling] easier. (2) For example, the blades on a sleigh ~~glidded~~ [glided] easily over a frozen river. (3) That meant *going* [OK] miles out of your way to find a bridge was unnecessary. (4) Back then you could make your own road through the woods, ~~slidding~~ [sliding] along on ~~runers~~ [runners] instead of ~~roling~~ [rolling] along on wheels. (5) There was no such thing as ~~snowplowwing~~, [snowplowing] nor was there any need for it. (6) Instead, the snow was *packed* [OK] down firmly by huge rollers ~~draged~~ [dragged] by horsepower. (7) Everyone was in favor of *stretching* [OK] out the sleigh season as long as possible. (8) Once the spring thaw set in, however, the roads ~~turnned~~ [turned] into rivers of mud.

Challenge 22.3   **Analyzing Accented Syllables**

It can be a challenge to decide which syllable of a word is accented. Bring a portion of a song lyric, a favorite poem, or even a nursery rhyme to class, and exchange it with a classmate. On the paper you receive, put a / above the syllable of each multisyllable word that you think should be accented the most. Read the piece aloud. Do the words have a beat or a rhythm? Is it regular?

Words with *ie* or *ei* Combinations

Another challenge for writers is to spell words with *ie* or *ei* combinations correctly. The basic rule, taught to millions of school children each year, is this:

> *I* before *e*
> Except after *c*
> And when sounded like *a*
> As in *neighbor* or *weigh*.

You can depend on this simple rule for spelling many words with *ie* or *ei* combinations. Words with *ie* combinations have the long *e* sound:

bel**ie**ve   n**ie**ce   f**ie**ld   ach**ie**ve

Words with *ei* combinations either follow a *c* or have an *a* sound:

rec**ei**ve   conc**ei**ve   **ei**ght   v**ei**n

Receive and *conceive* are spelled with *ei* combinations because the letters follow *c*. *Eight* and *vein* are spelled with *ei* combinations because the combination is pronounced as *a*.

Exceptions   There are a number of exceptions to this rule. *Either, neither, leisure, seize,* and *weird* feature *ei* combinations even though these letters *don't* follow *c*. Also, *species, ancient,* and *science* contain an *ie* combination even though these letters *do* follow *c*.

Exercise 22.8   **Working with Words with *ie* or *ei* Combinations**

Decide if the italicized words are spelled correctly, and make any necessary corrections. Cross out the incorrect version, and write the correct word above it. If the word is correct as written, write *OK* above it. Use the example as a guide.

EXAMPLE   When Lee caught the huge fish, he had it ~~wieghed~~ *weighed* at the *pier*. *OK*

(1) Are you one of the millions of people who ~~recieve~~ *receive* an unending supply of catalogs in the mail? (2) My ~~nieghbor~~ *neighbor* got *eighteen* catalogs *OK* in one week last fall, just in time for Christmas shopping. (3) She ~~beleives~~ *believes* that shopping by mail helps her save money and allows her to shop at her ~~liesure~~ *leisure*. (4) Catalog shopping is convenient, too, because companies

OK
accept *either* mail or telephone orders twenty-four hours a day. (5) It is a

relief   OK
great *releif* to busy workers because *their* time is precious.

Using Words with *ie* or *ei* Combinations in Your Writing

Below is a list of *ie* and *ei* words. If the word is misspelled, write it correctly next to the incorrect version. If the word is spelled correctly, write *OK* next to it. Then choose any five words from the list, and, or a separate piece of paper use them in five sentences of your own. Use the example to guide you.

EXAMPLE   seige _____*siege*_____

When fresh troops arrived, the city was still under siege by the enemy.

acheive ____achieve____   reciept ____receipt____

neither ____OK____   brief ____OK____

beige ____OK____   frieght ____freight____

foriegn ____foreign____   seize ____OK____

Correcting and Using Words with *ie* or *ei* in Your Writing

Here are some more *ie* or *ei* combinations in words. On the line beside each, write the correct spelling for any misspelled word, or write *OK* if the word is correct. Then exchange your list with a classmate, and compare to make sure your lists are correct. Finally, with your partner, write five sentences on a separate sheet of paper, using five of these words.

piece ____OK____   vein ____OK____

cheif ____chief____   cieling ____ceiling____

protien ____protein____   yeild ____yield____

height ____OK____   peirce ____pierce____

Dealing with Confusing Endings and Incorrect Forms

-ceed, -cede, -sede *Proceed*, *concede*, and *supersede* are examples of words with endings that sound the same but that are spelled differently. It is easy to keep straight the words that end in this sound. Only one word in English ends in *-sede: super***sede.*** Only three words in English end in *-ceed:*

pro**ceed**   ex**ceed**   suc**ceed**

Spell all other words ending in this sound with *-cede:*

pre**cede**   con**cede**   re**cede**   inter**cede**

Contractions That Confuse   A word's sound may cause difficulty with spelling. The contractions for *would have, could have,* and *should have* are good examples. *Would've, could've,* and *should've* sound like the incorrect forms *would of, could of,* and *should of.* Rather than risk making a mistake, avoid these contractions as you draft your paper.

Also, don't trust your ear when it comes to the common expressions *use**d** to* and *suppose**d** to.* In both cases, the final *-d* is almost silent, so it's easy to write the forms incorrectly: *use to* and *suppose to.* Therefore, even though you might not hear the *-d,* always add it when you write these expressions.

Exercise 22.10   **Dealing with Confusing Endings and Incorrect Forms**

Correct the spelling errors in the following sentences. Cross out the incorrect word, and write the correct spelling above it. If a sentence contains no error, write *OK* above it. Use the example as a guide.

EXAMPLE   To arrive on time, I ~~would of~~ *would have* had to ~~excede~~ *exceed* the speed limit.

(1) "~~Procede~~ *Proceed* with caution" has always been my motto. (2) I ~~use~~ *used* to think that people who jumped into situations couldn't possibly ~~succede~~ *succeed*. (3) I should ~~of~~ *have* known better; I do now. (4) I'll ~~conceed~~ *concede* that enthusiasm and spontaneity can make life fun. (5) I just make sure I don't exceed *OK* any reasonable limits.

Exercise 22.11   **Working with Words with Confusing Endings and Incorrect Forms**

Correct any incorrect forms or words with incorrect endings in the paragraph below. Cross out the incorrect word, and write the correct one above it. If a sentence contains no error, write *OK* above it. Use the example to guide you.

recede

EXAMPLE I sat on the sand and watched the tide ~~receed~~.

used
(1) Not so long ago, a lot of people ~~use~~ to smoke. (2) Now that people
supposed
know that they're not ~~suppose~~ to smoke, fewer people do. (3) Many peo-
have
ple would ~~of~~ quit much earlier if they had realized the dangers. (4) By
have
doing so, they could ~~of~~ added years to their lives. (5) The risks of smoking
have
should ~~of~~ been emphasized in the 1960s, once it was clear that smoking
_OK_
was a definite health hazard. (6) Of course, some people procede to
have
smoke even though they know it's bad for them. (7) My uncle should ~~of~~
quit when the doctor said he was developing a heart problem. (8) He
_OK_
tried a few times, but he never could succeed in kicking the habit.

Challenge 22.5 **Understanding and Using Words with Confusing Endings**

COLLABORATION Using a dictionary, look up the definitions of these words. On a separate sheet of paper, write each word and its definition(s). Then use each in a sentence. Working with a writing partner, proofread and compare one another's work.

intercede	precede	concede
supersede	exceed	recede

Dealing with Commonly Confused Words

Another way that our ears can mislead us is with homonyms. _Homonyms_ are words that sound alike but that have different spellings and different meanings, like _threw_ and _through_. On the following pages is a list of some homonyms and other commonly confused word pairs and trios.

Commonly Confused Words

Words	Definitions	Examples
accept	to take or receive	The patient refused to *accept* any visitors.
except	to leave out; excluding, but	No visitors are allowed *except* family.
advice	opinions, suggestions (a noun)	The lawyer gave me sound *advice*.
advise	to give suggestions, guide (a verb)	I asked her to *advise* me of my rights.
affect	to influence, stir the emotions (a verb)	Any amount of stress *affects* Paul.
effect	a result, something brought about by a cause (a noun)	The most noticeable *effect* is irritability.
brake	a device for stopping forward motion; to come to a halt	I jammed on the *brake* when the light changed.
break	to shatter; pause	I hit the windshield, but it didn't *break*.
buy	to purchase	Tim tried to *buy* a ticket to the concert.
by	near; no later than; through	Tickets must be ordered *by* mail.
choose	to decide or select (present tense)	I will *choose* my classes more carefully next time.
chose	decided or selected (past tense)	Last semester, I *chose* my classes without enough thought.
conscience	inner sense of right and wrong	My *conscience* still bothers me.
conscious	aware, awake	I'm especially *conscious* of the way I treated my younger brother.
desert	(1) to abandon (2) a dry, arid, sandy place	People began to *desert* the picnic. The park was as hot as a *desert*.
dessert	final part of a meal	The picnic *dessert* was untouched.
fine	(1) excellent, very good (2) money paid as a penalty	Last night, Jarod had a *fine* game. Maura received a *fine* for speeding.
find	(1) to discover, come upon (2) something found or discovered	He managed to *find* the basket. The antique vase was a great *find*.
hear	to take in sounds by ear	Can you *hear* that noise?
here	in this place, at this point	I think it's coming from right *here*.
hole	an empty spot	A spark burned a *hole* in the carpet.
whole	complete	The *whole* carpet has to be replaced.

(continued)

Commonly Confused Words (*continued*)

Words	Definitions	Examples
its	possessive form of *it*	The mustang broke free from *its* handlers.
it's	contraction for *it is* or *it has*	*It's* dangerous to handle wild animals.
knew	understood (past tense)	I *knew* what that noise meant.
new	recent, not old	I'd have to buy a *new* muffler.
know	to understand (present tense)	Most people *know* how to exercise.
no	negative, the opposite of *yes*	The problem is they have *no* discipline.
lead	(1) to go first, direct (present tense, rhymes with *bead*)	The manager told Brian to *lead* the team to victory.
	(2) soft metal, graphite (rhymes with *bed*)	Brian took the *lead* warm-up ring off his bat.
led	went first, directed (past tense)	He swung and *led* off the inning with a double to center field.
loose	not tight	During the warmer months, I wear *loose* clothing.
lose	misplace; fail, not win	I still sweat and *lose* weight.
mine	belonging to me	That old shirt is *mine*.
mind	(1) intellect	(1) Happy memories come to *mind* whenever wear it.
	(2) to object to, be careful of	(2) *Mind* your manners when you eat.
of	stemming from; connected with or to	The best day *of* the vacation was our day at Wet 'n' Wild.
off	away from; no longer on	Riding the biggest water slide felt like dropping *off* a cliff.
passed	went beyond or by (past tense)	The speeding car *passed* a police car.
past	time gone by, former time	*Past* experience may not teach speeders to slow down.
precede	to come before	An overture will *precede* the first act.
proceed	to go on	After the play, *proceed* to the cast party.
quiet	not noisy; solitude	The room was completely *quiet*.
quite	very; really	We were *quite* surprised by the party.
than	used in comparisons	Bill can run faster *than* Jimmy.
then	next; at that time	First, they warm up; *then* they practice.

Commonly Confused Words (*concluded*)

Words	Definitions	Examples
their	possessive form of *they*	The protesters are devoted to *their* cause.
there	that place or position; function word introducing a sentence	*There* were twenty police officers watching from over *there*.
they're	contraction for *they are*	*They're* staying on the picket line all night.
though	despite; however	*Though* they all may fail, they all will try.
thought	idea; process of reasoning	I *thought* hard about his meaning.
threw	tossed, hurled (past tense)	A child *threw* a rock at the passing car.
through	in one side and out the other; from beginning to end	The rock went *through* the driver's window.
to	(1) in the direction of, toward (2) used to form infinitives	She handed the receipt *to* the clerk. The clerk refused *to* give a refund.
too	also; excessively	The receipt was *too* illegible.
two	the whole number between one and three	The warranty had expired *two* months ago.
weak	not strong, feeble	The muscles of the broken leg are *weak*.
week	seven days	Even after a *week* of exercise, I can lift very little.
weather	atmospheric conditions	The *weather* this past summer was unusually hot.
whether	indicating alternatives	Winter will come *whether* we like it or not.
were	past tense of *are*	Last week we *were* unable to go see the movie.
we're	contraction for *we are*	*We're* finally going to go tonight, however.
where	indicates or raises a question about a specific direction or location	The theater is in the mall *where* we met.
wear	have on (clothing)	We *wear* casual clothes to shop.
who's	contraction for *who is* or *who has*	*Who's* supposed to drive the carpool?
whose	possessive form of *who*	I can never remember *whose* turn it is.
your	possessive form of *you*	I left *your* gift in the living room.
you're	contraction for *you are*	I think *you're* really going to like it.

Exercise 22.12   **Making Correct Choices with Commonly Confused Words**

Circle the correct word from the pair in parentheses. Refer to the preceding list of commonly confused words, and use the meaning of the sentence to guide you. Use the example as a guide.

EXAMPLE   The taxi driver had to (brake, break) suddenly.

(1) (You're, Your) ready to leave the house (except, accept) you can't find (you're, your) car keys. (2) (Its, It's) in (your, you're) (mine, mind) that you (through, threw) them over (their, there) on the kitchen counter last night. (3) (Whether, Weather) you find them or not is important because (of, off) the job interview you have in an hour. (4) You (no, know) you don't want to (here, hear) any (advise, advice) about how not to (loose, lose) things at this point. (5) This scene is a good example (of, off) how everyday situations can (lead, led) to (quite, quiet) a lot of stress.

Exercise 22.13   **Dealing with Commonly Confused Words**

The paragraph below contains a number of commonly confused words used incorrectly. Using the list in this chapter and the meaning of the sentence itself, decide which words are wrong. Cross out the incorrect words, and write correct ones above them. Use the example to guide you.

EXAMPLE   Cigarette smoking is a hard habit to ~~brake.~~ *break*

(1) ~~Weather your~~ *Whether you're* a golf fan or not, you have probably heard of Tiger Woods. (2) The popularity of this young golfer has a widespread ~~affect~~ *effect* on the sport of golf, attracting new fans from all walks of life. (3) Tiger, ~~who's~~ *whose* real name is Eldrick Woods, ~~choose~~ *chose* to become a professional golfer in the late summer of 1996 after considering the ~~advise~~ *advice* of many

coaches and family members. (4) Since ~~than,~~ *then* he has gone on ~~too~~ *to* win

many professional tournaments, including the Masters Championship

and the PGA Championship. (5) Tiger grew up in California, in a town sit-

uated between the ~~dessert~~ *desert* and Los Angeles. (6) He was only six months

old when he made his first ~~brake~~ *break* into the sport of golf by watching his

father hit golf balls into a net. (7) Even though he was not yet one year

old, Tiger showed early talent ~~buy~~ *by* imitating his father's swing. (8) By age

five, Tiger had hit his first ~~whole~~ *hole* in one. (9) It was not long until Tiger

was widely ~~excepted~~ *accepted* as a golf prodigy. (10) These days, Tiger is known

worldwide as one ~~off~~ *of* professional golf's top players.

Exercise 22.14   **Using Commonly Confused Words Correctly**

On a separate sheet of paper, write ten sentences using each of the following commonly confused words once. Be sure to use each word correctly for
the meaning of the sentence.

1. affect	6. then
2. effect	7. knew
3. your	8. new
4. you're	9. who's
5. than	10. whose

Maintaining a Personal Spelling Dictionary

If you write with a word processor, you may think that your program can
check your spelling for you. That is not entirely true. The spell check feature
can find *some* spelling mistakes. However, it cannot tell if you are using the
wrong homonym or a word that is only similar to the one you want. It is still
important for you to learn and remember correct spelling on your own.

One of the best ways to help yourself spell accurately is to maintain
your own spelling dictionary. Make a list of the words that you have trouble

spelling. Keep the list in alphabetical order, and leave two or three lines between each word. Whenever you discover that you have misspelled a word in your notes or on a paper you have written, add that word on a blank line according to alphabetical order. If you keep your dictionary on a computer, simply insert the new words, and then print out a new list. Review the list frequently, especially as you are completing drafts of a paper, so that you can master the spelling of these words.

In addition to the commonly confused words presented earlier, many—if not most—of the words you have trouble with are probably on the following list of frequently misspelled words. To make this list work for you, read through it, marking the ones that you misspell. Then add them to the list you have already started, and you will be well on your way to having your own complete personal spelling dictionary.

Commonly Misspelled Words

A

absence	acquired	all right	answer	assented
academic	acre	although	antarctic	association
acceptance	across	aluminum	anxious	athlete
accident	actual	always	apologize	attacked
accidentally	actually	amateur	apparatus	attempt
accommodate	address	among	apparent	attendance
accompany	administration	amount	appreciate	attorney
accomplish	advertise	analysis	approach	authority
accumulate	again	analyze	approval	auxiliary
accurate	agreeable	angel	argument	available
accustom	aisle	angle	arrival	awful
ache	alcohol	angry	article	awkward
achieve	a lot	anonymous	ascended	
acquaintance				

B

bachelor	bathe	believe	boundaries	bureau
balance	beautiful	benefit	breath	bury
bargain	because	biscuits	breathe	business
basically	beginning	bookkeeping	brilliant	
bath	belief	bottom	Britain	

C

cafeteria	cemetery	cigarette	comfortable	condition
calendar	cereal	circuit	commitment	consistent
campaign	certain	cocoa	committed	continuous
cannot	change	collect	committee	convenience
careful	characteristic	colonel	company	cooperate
careless	cheap	color	comparative	cooperation
catastrophe	chief	colossal	competent	corporation
category	children	column	competitive	correspondence
ceiling	church	comedy	conceivable	courteous

Commonly Misspelled Words (*continued*)

C (*continued*)

courtesy	criticize	curriculum

D

daily	definitely	diameter	discuss	dominate
daughter	definition	diary	disease	doubt
dealt	dependent	different	disgust	dozen
debt	describe	direction	distance	drowned
deceased	description	disappointment	distinction	duplicate
decision	despair	disastrous	distinguish	
defense	despise	discipline	dominant	

E

earliest	emergency	environment	essential	exhausted
efficiency	emphasis	equip	exaggerated	existence
efficient	emphasize	equipment	excellent	experience
eligible	employee	equipped	excessive	extraordinary
embarrass	envelop	especially	excitable	extremely
embarrassment	envelope			

F

fallacy	February	fiery	fourth	fulfill
familiar	feminine	foreign	freight	further
fascinate	fictitious	forty	frequent	futile
fatigue				

G

garden	genuine	gracious	guarantee	guest
gauge	ghost	grammar	guardian	guidance
general	government	grateful	guess	gymnasium
generally				

H

handicapped	height	humor	hygiene	hypocrite
handkerchief	hoping	humorous	hypocrisy	

I

illiterate	incidentally	inevitable	intelligence	irresistible
imaginative	incredible	infinite	interest	irreverent
immediately	independent	inquiry	interfere	island
immigrant	indictment	instead	interpret	isle
important				

J

jealousy	jewelry	judgment

K

kitchen	knowledge	knuckles	(*continued*)

Commonly Misspelled Words (*continued*)

L

language	leave	lengthen	library	literature
later	legitimate	lesson	license	livelihood
latter	leisure	letter	lieutenant	lounge
laugh	length	liable	lightning	luxury

M

machinery	mathematics	miniature	missile	mortgage
maintain	measure	minimum	misspell	mountain
maintenance	mechanical	minute	mistake	muscle
marriage	medicine	miscellaneous	moderate	mustache
marry	medieval	mischief	month	mutual
marvelous	merchandise	mischievous	morning	mysterious

N

naturally	necessity	nickel	noticeable	nuisance
necessary	negotiate	niece		

O

obedience	occurrence	omit	opportunity	organization
obstacle	official	opinion	oppose	original
occasion	often	opponent	optimism	ought
occurred				

P

pamphlet	perceive	phase	practically	probably
parallel	percentage	phenomenon	precisely	procedure
paralyze	perform	physical	preferred	professor
parentheses	performance	physician	prejudice	protein
participant	permanent	picnic	preparation	psychology
particularly	permitted	piece	presence	publicity
pastime	perseverance	pleasant	pressure	pursuing
patience	personality	politics	primitive	pursuit
peasant	perspiration	possess	priority	
peculiar	persuade	possibility	privilege	

Q

qualified	quantity	quarter	question	questionnaire
quality				

R

readily	recipient	reign	removal	residence
realize	recognize	relevant	renewal	resistance
really	recommendation	relieve	repeat	responsibility
reasonably	reference	remember	repetition	restaurant
receipt	referring	remembrance	requirement	rhythm
receive	regretting	reminisce	reservoir	ridiculous

Commonly Misspelled Words (*concluded*)

S

salary	sergeant	specimen	strategy	sufficient
sandwich	severely	statistics	strength	summarize
scenery	similar	statue	stretch	superior
schedule	solemn	stature	subsidize	surprise
scissors	sophisticated	statute	substantial	surprising
secretary	sophomore	stomach	substitute	susceptible
sensible	souvenir	straight	subtle	suspicion
separate				

T

technique	thorough	tournament	transferring	tremendous
temperament	thoroughly	tragedy	travel	truly
temperature	through	traitor	traveled	Tuesday
tendency	tomorrow	transfer	treasure	typical
theory	tongue			

U

unanimous	urgent	useful	utensil

V

vacancy	valuable	vein	villain	visibility
vacuum	vane	vicinity	violence	visitor
vain	vegetable			

W

warrant	Wednesday	weird	writing	written

Y

yesterday

Z

zealous

Exercise 22.15   **Maintaining a Personal Spelling Dictionary**

Reread a short story or essay that you read for one of your courses. Underline all the words that were unfamiliar to you. Jot them down, and look up their definitions in a dictionary. Then add them to your personal spelling list. This activity will improve not only your spelling but also your vocabulary.

Exercise 22.16   **Recognizing and Using Commonly Misspelled Words Correctly**

Here is a list of some commonly misspelled words. Some are spelled correctly, and some are not. Working with a partner, correct the misspelled words, or write *OK* if the word is correct. Cross out the incorrect version, and write the correctly spelled word next to it. After completing this step, use the list of commonly misspelled words to check your corrections. For each word, write a sentence on a separate sheet of paper, using the word with its correct meaning.

abcense _____ absence _____   although _____ OK _____

cafateria _____ cafeteria _____   differant _____ different _____

corespondence _____ correspondence _____   disipline _____ discipline _____

commitee _____ committee _____   seperate _____ separate _____

exxagerate _____ exaggerate _____   Febuary _____ February _____

independant _____ independent _____   responsability _____ responsibility _____

scissors _____ OK _____   salery _____ salary _____

schedule _____ OK _____   imediately _____ immediately _____

Wenesday _____ Wednesday _____   requirement _____ OK _____

Challenge 22.6 **Analyzing Your Methods of Checking for Spelling Errors**

COLLABORATION

How have you proofread for possible spelling errors in writing you have completed up to this point? Write a paragraph in which you explain the methods, rules, guidelines, or helpful hints you have followed. Share these procedures in a discussion with your classmates. You may help a peer, or discover some new ways to deal with your own spelling challenges.

Spelling Checklist

☐ Have you checked the endings of the plurals you have used, especially those ending in *-ch*, *-sh*, *-x*, *-s*, *-y*, *-o*, and *-f* or *-fe?*

☐ Have you checked the plural forms of compound nouns, foreign words, irregular nouns, and words that have only one form?

☐ Have you checked the spelling of any words to which a prefix or suffix has been added, especially those that are exceptions to the rules?

☐ Have you evaluated the spelling of words that end in a single consonant preceded by a single vowel to determine whether the final letter should be doubled before adding an ending?

☐ Have you checked the spelling of words with *-ie* combinations, especially the exceptions, with confusing endings, and with confusing contractions?

☐ Have you checked the spelling of any words from the list of commonly confused words to ensure that you've made the correct choice and from the list of commonly misspelled words to make sure you've avoided error?

Exploring Ideas through Journal Writing

Spelling a word correctly, as this chapter shows, is a matter of using the correct combination of letters in the proper order. Change the combination or adjust the order, and the spelling is no longer correct. Combination and order play important roles in other aspects of life. For example, the right combination of players or workers makes a winning team. Change this combination, and suddenly everything can change. Try to play a song without seeing the music ahead of time, and you'll find it a very different experience than if you did so after studying and practicing the piece. Consider some aspect of combination or order, and then explore it for 20 to 30 minutes in your journal.

Chapter Quick Check: Mastering Spelling

The following passage contains a number of misspelled words and incorrect word choices. Using the guidelines and examples in the chapter and your personal spelling dictionary as a guide, find and cross out the errors. Write the correct version above the incorrect one.

(1) Experts continue to discuss the possible ~~affects~~ [effects] that television advertising for alcoholic beverages can have on the ~~veiwing~~ [viewing] public, especially on impressionable teenagers. (2) The ads in question are ~~largly~~ [largely] for beer, although ~~companys~~ [companies] that market wine and, more recently, hard liquor also advertise on television. (3) Those interested in ~~stoping~~ [stopping] this kind of advertising have raised a number of objections, including the ~~beleif~~ [belief] that the ads don't show drinking in a realistic light. (4) For example, the characters in the ads ~~by~~ [buy] beer or some other alcoholic beverage and happily socialize but never ~~excede~~ [exceed] their limits or show any signs of intoxication. (5) Opponents also raise the ~~arguement~~ [argument] that these commercials air more heavily during sporting events ~~then~~ [than] during any other type of programming. (6) The opponents assert that by linking sports and drinking, manufacturers are ~~consciencely~~ [consciously] emphasizing that sports fans, especially young people, are ~~suppose~~ [supposed] to see drinking as an extension of

sports. (7) More recently, opponents have also complained about the

sheer volume of advertisements, ~~accept~~ [except] on shows geared primarily ~~too~~ [to]

children. (8) Predictably, manufacturers of alcoholic beverages ~~dissagree~~ [disagree]

strongly, claiming its not their intent to mislead or influence anyone. (9)

They argue that ~~weather~~ [whether] television advertising ~~effects~~ [affects] anyone's behavior

has never been positively proven. (10) In addition, they argue that they

have a legal right to ~~advertize~~ [advertise] on television, regardless of what ~~there~~ [their] op-

ponents might feel about them.

Discovering Connections 22.2

COLLABORATION

1. For Discovering Connections 22.1 on page 427, you began prewriting in response to a quotation by Christiane Collange or to a photo. Now, continue your prewriting on one of these options:
   a. How would you define common sense?
   b. Why do you think common sense is so uncommon?
2. Evaluate your prewriting material, identify a focus, and create a draft of about 100 words.
3. Exchange your draft with a writing partner. Using the material in this chapter as a guide, evaluate the draft you receive, and note any spelling errors as well as any other weaknesses. Return the draft to the writer.
4. Revise your draft, eliminating any errors that your reader identified.

Summary Exercise: Mastering Spelling

The following passage contains a number of misspelled words and incorrect word choices. Using the guidelines and examples in the chapter and your personal spelling dictionary as a guide, find and cross out the errors. Write the correct version above the incorrect one.

(1) Children can sometimes ~~by~~ [be] cruel when they refuse to ~~except~~ [accept]

other children who are different from them. (2) ~~Their~~ [There] are many people

who now have bad memories of how they were treated at school.

(3) Children need to have ~~freinds~~ [friends] and to ~~beleive~~ [believe] that ~~their~~ [they're] liked. (4) When they are first ~~admited~~ [admitted] to school, many children are afraid to leave home and may even feel ~~abandonned~~ [abandoned] when a parent leaves them at the door. (5) Their self-confidence can ~~brake~~ [break] even more if they aren't happy in their ~~knew~~ [new] surroundings. (6) One ~~freindly~~ [friendly] face can ~~positivly effect~~ [positively affect] a child's ~~hole~~ [whole] day.

(7) ~~Weather~~ [Whether] a child is accepted may depend on his or her looks or mannerisms. (8) Some children are ~~chubbyer~~ [chubbier] or ~~thiner~~ [thinner] or taller than others. (9) For others, stuttering or poor hearing may be a problem, and so they seem ~~to quiet~~ [too quiet] or shy. (10) Children who are ~~learnning~~ [learning] English often hesitate to speak out. (11) They are afraid if they ~~chose~~ [choose] the wrong word, others will make fun of them. (12) The problem for some kids is the ~~cloths~~ [clothes] they ~~where~~ [wear]. (13) ~~There familys~~ [Their families] are ~~to~~ [too] poor for them to keep up with fads and styles.

(14) Some school children, of ~~coarse~~ [course], ~~succede~~ [succeed] in spite of these painful experiences. (15) They still ~~reech~~ [reach] out to others, and they are rarely mean or ~~disagreable~~ [disagreeable]. (16) Sometimes ~~their~~ [they're] lucky enough to ~~fine~~ [find] other children who are good at ~~identifing~~ [identifying] the best in everyone and ~~noticeing~~ [noticing] children who feel left out. (17) I was ~~quiet~~ [quite] lucky myself when I ~~movd~~ [moved] to a new city. (18) ~~Too~~ [Two] children reached out to me, and ~~their~~ [they're] still my friends. (19) As time ~~gos buy~~ [goes by], just the ~~though~~ [thought] of my school ~~buddys~~ [buddies] makes ~~my~~ [me] smile. (20) I am ~~hopeing~~ [hoping] that my own children will also reach out to others when they start school.

RECAP

MASTERING SPELLING

New terms in this chapter	Definitions
● prefix	● the letter or letters added to the beginning of a word that change its meaning: *un-, dis-, semi-, re-, il-, ex-* *Example* **un**able, **re**run
● suffix	● the letter or letters added to the end of a word that change its meaning: *-ness, -able, -ous, -ly, -er, -ed, -ing* *Example* sad**ness**, danger**ous**

Spelling Guidelines for Adding Prefixes and Suffixes	
Check the dictionary for exceptions to these general guidelines	
● **To add a prefix**	prefix + word (no spelling change) dis + agree = **dis**agree
● **To add -*ly* or -*ness***	word + *-ly* or *-ness* (usually no spelling change) mean + ness = mean**ness** change *-y* to *-i* before adding *-ly* or *-ness* happy + ness = happ**iness**
● **To add -*ed***	change *-y* to *-i* before adding *-ed* worry + ed = worr**ied**
● **To add a suffix that begins with a vowel**	drop *-e* at the end of a word before adding the suffix hope + ing = hop**ing** double the final consonant if ● the word has one syllable plan + ed = plan**ned** ● the accent is on the last syllable of a word with two or more syllables begin + ing = begin**ning** ● the final consonant is preceded by a single vowel fat + est = fat**test**
● **To add a suffix that begins with a consonant**	keep *-e* at the end of the word safe + ty = safe**ty**

Chapter 23

Maintaining Parallelism

Getting Started... **Q:** Sometimes when I write about related ideas in pairs or in a series, it doesn't always sound right: The items or ideas don't seem to *match* each other in meaning. How can I make sure that sentences with these kinds of pairs or series sound correct and *are* correct?

A: What you are talking about is parallelism, and it may be less complicated than you think. Because parallelism becomes an issue when you combine things, focus on any words connected by conjunctions, especially *and, or,* and *but.* Identify the first word in the combination or series and then make any other item in the series match it in form. The result will *be* correct and *sound* correct.

Overview: Learning to Create Balance in Writing

When you write, you frequently need to discuss similar or related ideas in the same sentence. When you do, you must make sure that the ideas are expressed in a *parallel,* or similar, form.

The easiest way to think about **parallelism** is to picture a seesaw or an old-fashioned scale. To keep everything balanced, you need to place objects of similar weight at each end. When you write, you balance out pairs or groups of connected ideas by presenting them in a similar form.

If your connected items don't match, your reader can become distracted from the point you are trying to make in the sentence. Maintaining parallelism in your writing, therefore, is an important strategy for expressing yourself clearly.

In this chapter you will learn ways to balance

- individual words in a series

- phrases in a series

- words linked by pairs of connecting words

Discovering Connections 23.1

Consider the following quotation:

Ability is useless unless it's used.

—*Robert Half*

Or look at this photo.

Now, using the technique you prefer, do some prewriting about your reaction to the quotation or photo. Save your work.

Keeping Individual Words in a Series Parallel

Whenever you connect individual words in a series, make sure that the words are similar parts of speech. For example, it's correct to connect nouns and pronouns to other nouns and pronouns, verbs to other verbs, adjectives to other adjectives, and adverbs to other adverbs. But it's *incorrect* to connect *different* types of words. You can't connect nouns to adverbs, for example, or verbs to adjectives.

In English, *conjunctions* are the words we use to connect other words. *And* and *or* are the most common conjunctions. Therefore, one way to make sure that you have maintained parallelism is to look at every sentence that contains one of these two words. Then double-check the words they connect to make sure they are similar parts of speech.

Look at the examples below. What words are being connected?

EXAMPLE   Her favorite jeans were *old* **and** *torn*.

EXAMPLE   To keep fit, you should *walk, run,* **or** *swim* three times a week.

In the first sentence, the conjunction *and* is connecting two *adjectives: old* and *torn*. In the second, the conjunction *or* connects three *verbs: walk, run,* and *swim*. The structure of each series of words is therefore *parallel*.

Now look at these examples:

FAULTY   Lauren didn't take an art course because she wasn't interested in *sketching* **or** *to create paintings*.

FAULTY   Shark attacks can be *quick, unexpected,* **and** *they are deadly*.

In the first sentence, the conjunction *or* is connecting *sketching*, a gerund (an *-ing* verb form used as a noun), and *to create paintings*, an infinitive phrase. These different types of verbals don't match. In addition, the one-word and three-word units are not balanced in length. The structure of the sentence is not parallel. In the second sentence, the conjunction *and* connects *quick* and *unexpected*, two adjectives, to *they are deadly*, a clause. Only the adjectives match, so this sentence also lacks a parallel structure.

It is easy to give sentences like these parallel structure. Simply change the parts of speech that do not match, as these versions show:

REVISED   Lauren didn't take an art course because she wasn't interested in *sketching* **or** *painting*.

REVISED   Shark attacks can be *quick, unexpected,* **and** *deadly*.

In the first sentence, the infinitive phrase *to create paintings* is changed to *painting*, a gerund, so that it matches *sketching*. In the second example, the clause *they can be deadly* is shortened to a single adjective, *deadly*, which matches the adjectives *quick* and *unexpected*.

Exercise 23.1   **Maintaining Parallel Structure**

Check the following sentences to make sure they are parallel. First, circle the conjunctions in the sentences. Then underline the items that are connected. Finally, make any changes necessary to maintain parallelism. Cross out the incorrect item, and write a correct version above it. Use the example as a guide.

EXAMPLE   After work I usually exercise, shop, or ~~to take a~~ *nap* ~~nap~~.

(1) A trip to the grocery store can be fun and ~~a good education~~ *educational* for children. (2) For safety, children should ride in a shopping carriage or ~~walking~~ *walk* along with an adult. (3) Preschool kids can name the colors, shapes, and ~~look for different~~ sizes of items on the shelves. (4) Older children can practice math skills by comparing prices or ~~to weigh~~ *weighing* fruit. (5) At the checkout line and the cash register, children can learn ~~to be patient~~ *patience* and the value of money.

Exercise 23.2 **Keeping Individual Words Parallel**

Complete each of the following sentences by adding a word that completes the thought and maintains parallel structure. Use the example to guide you. (Answers will vary.)

EXAMPLE   Men and _____*women*_____ have significantly different life spans.

1. The impulse to shoplift hits both wealthy and _____ people.

2. Certain adults may shoplift not because they are greedy but because they are angry, anxious, or _____ .

3. For them, shoplifting is a kind of protest against the expensive and _____ task that shopping often becomes.

4. Customers become irritated because they must depend on poorly paid salesclerks and cashiers who have no loyalty or _____ in their jobs.

5. Perhaps shoplifters are taking their revenge on merchants whom they feel overcharge or _____ their customers.

6. Experienced shoplifters move quickly and _____ .

7. Once they have stolen the merchandise, they quickly conceal it in their pocket or _____ .

8. Despite the presence of store detectives and _____ , they often succeed in sneaking the item out of the store.

Challenge 23.1 **Analyzing Use of Parallel Structure**

The paragraph below, from an article by Kenneth Woodward and Patrice Johnson, originally appeared in *Newsweek*. The authors are writing about the commercialization of Kwanzaa, an African American "festival of family, roots, and community." As you read the paragraph, underline any parts of sentences that have parallel items. For each group of parallel items, name the part of speech that describes it (nouns, verbs, adjectives, etc.) and write the name in the space above the grouped items. Compare your analysis with those of your classmates.

Although the festival doesn't begin until December 26, about 300 vendors in New York City will open a four-day Kwanzaa holiday expo at the huge Jacob Javits Convention Center next week. There, shoppers will be able to purchase the <u>candelabras, straw mats, and libation cups</u> [nouns] used to celebrate the holiday—plus a growing list of Afrocentric <u>crafts, clothes, books, and dolls</u> [nouns] for after-Christmas Kwanzaa-giving. The expo will also feature black <u>entertainers and politicians</u> [nouns] in an effort to get customers into the Kwanzaa spirit before Christmas shopping leaves them financially tapped out.

Keeping Phrases in a Series Parallel

In the examples on pages 454–455, some of the items changed to correct the sentences were *phrases,* or *groups of words.* Instead of shortening these phrases to match the single words, the single words might have been expanded into matching phrases. Whenever you connect two phrases with a conjunction, the phrases must also be parallel. In other words, they must contain the same word forms. For example, it's correct to connect *prepositional phrases* with other *prepositional phrases.* It's also correct to connect *-ing verbal phrases* to other *-ing verbal phrases,* and *infinitive phrases* (*to eat, to dream*) to other *infinitive phrases.*

To check parallelism for phrases, follow the same process you use for individual words. First find every *and* or *or* in your sentences. Then, if you've used these conjunctions to connect phrases, make sure the phrases match.

Find the connected phrases in these examples:

EXAMPLE   Steve knew his missing hamster was in the closet, under the couch, **or** behind the bookcase.

EXAMPLE   Roberta wants to major in accounting **and** to take as many Spanish courses as possible.

In the first sentence, *or* is connecting two prepositional phrases—*in the closet* and *under the couch*—with a third one: *behind the bookcase*. In the second sentence, *and* is connecting two infinitive phrases: *to major in accounting* and *to take as many Spanish courses as possible*. The structure of each sentence is therefore *parallel*.

Now consider these examples:

FAULTY The greatest challenges for me in school are *keeping up with my homework* **and** *to study for exams.*

FAULTY I get parts for my old motorcycle *through catalogs, calling junk dealers,* **or** *at flea markets.*

In the first sentence, *and* connects a gerund phrase, *keeping up with my homework*, to an infinitive phrase, *to study for exams*. These phrases don't match, so they are not parallel. In the second sentence, *or* connects two prepositional phrases, *through catalogs* and *at flea markets* to an *-ing* phrase, *calling junk dealers*. The *-ing* phrase does not match the other two.

To make both of these sentences parallel, you would need to change one of the elements in each sentence so that it matches the word or words to which it is connected. Look at these two corrected versions of the sentence concerning school difficulties:

REVISED The greatest challenges for me in school are *keeping* up with my homework **and** *studying* for exams.

or

REVISED The greatest challenges for me in school are *to keep* up with my homework **and** *to study* for exams.

In the first of these sentences, *and* is now connecting two *-ing* phrases. In the second version, *and* is now connecting two infinitive phrases. Now both phrases match, so each of these sentences is now parallel.

The sentence about the old motorcycle can also be revised in more than one way to make its phrases parallel:

REVISED I get parts for my old motorcycle *through* catalogs, *from* junk dealers, **or** *at* flea markets.

or

REVISED I get parts for my old motorcycle by *checking* through catalogs, *calling* junk dealers, **or** *going* to flea markets.

In the first of these sentences, *or* is now connecting three prepositional phrases. In the second version, *or* is connecting three *-ing* phrases. Each group of phrases now matches, so the structure of each sentence is parallel. As these examples show, there is often more than one way to make a sentence parallel.

Exercise 23.3   Keeping Phrases Parallel

Circle the conjunctions in each sentence below. Then underline the items that each conjunction connects. If the items are not parallel, change one so that the connected phrases match in form. There may be more than one way to correct each sentence, as this example shows. (Answers may vary.)

EXAMPLE

The shoppers rushed through the door, hurried across the lobby, (and) they
                    ran
~~went running~~ for the sale.

or

                    went rushing   *hurrying*
The shoppers ~~rushed~~ through the door, ~~hurried~~ across the lobby, (and) ~~they~~

~~went~~ running for the sale.

(1) Last week I attended a program about sex discrimination (and)
                    sexual harassment
about ~~harassing people sexually.~~ (2) The speaker began by showing a
                    leading
movie (and) ~~she led~~ a discussion about what we had seen. (3) I learned
                    how to get information about it,
that many people don't know what harassment is, ~~getting information~~

~~about it is difficult,~~ (or) where to go for help. (4) We discovered that solu-
                    admitting
tions for discrimination at work (and) school include ~~to admit~~ discrimina-
                    keeping
tion exists, attending educational programs, (and) ~~to keep~~ the lines of

communication open. (5) At the end of the program, the audience ~~was~~
applauded
~~applauding~~ the speaker (and) asked the sponsors to have her return.

Exercise 23.4   Maintaining Parallelism with Phrases

Complete the following sentences by adding phrases that complete the thought and maintain sentence parallelism. Use the sample as a guide. (Answers will vary.)

EXAMPLE	My best friend enjoys running, hiking, and _____ *swimming.* _____

_____

1. My husband's cooking pleasures include shopping for the freshest ingredients, hunting down hard-to-find spices, and _____

   _____ .

2. Unfortunately, some of his other activities include messing up the kitchen

   and _____

   _____ .

3. During the holiday season, he bakes dozens of cookies, arranges them

   on gift platters, and _____

   _____ .

4. The cookies are perfectly baked, beautifully decorated, and _____

   _____ .

5. Afterwards, however, I'm the one who has to scrub the bowls and pots,

   put away all of the ingredients, and _____

   _____ .

6. According to him, a master chef shouldn't have to be bothered with

   mopping up the floor or _____

   _____ .

7. Once, when I insisted that he clean up after himself, I found the sugar in

   the refrigerator, the mixer in the attic, and _____

   _____ .

8. Another consequence of his baking is that I always eat too many cookies, gain too many pounds, and _____

   _____ .

Evaluating Use of Parallel Structure

Exchange the work you did for Exercise 23.3 with a classmate, and discuss the revisions you each made. Did you use the same option to make the sentences parallel? If you chose different options, read the two versions aloud and decide which version sounds better to you.

Dealing with Other Parallel Structure Challenges

Certain pairs of connecting words also call for parallel structure:

either + or   both + and   whether + or
neither + nor   not only + but also

These pairs are especially useful to you as a writer because they enable you to focus on two ideas in the same sentence. Take a look at these examples:

EXAMPLE I enjoy **both** *mountain biking* **and** *in-line skating*.

EXAMPLE The problem with that printer is **either** *a paper jam* **or** *a short circuit*.

The first example uses a *both–and* pair of connectors. Each word in the pair is followed by a participle and its modifier: *mountain bik**ing*** and *in-line skat**ing.*** Therefore, the sentence structure is parallel. The second example uses an *either–or* pair. Each of these words is followed by a noun plus its modifiers: *a paper jam* and *a short circuit*. These word groups follow the same pattern; this sentence also illustrates parallel structure.

Now look at these examples:

FAULTY The salesclerk was **not only** *rude* **but also** *her work was completed slowly*.

FAULTY The security guard had **neither** *a flashlight* **nor** *did he have a two-way radio*.

The first sentence uses the *not only–but also* pair. However, the ideas that follow these words aren't parallel. *Rude* is an adjective, but *her work was completed slowly* is a clause that could stand on its own as a sentence. The second sentence uses a *neither–nor* pair. The ideas that follow these words aren't expressed in parallel fashion either. *A flashlight* is a single noun plus an article, but *did he have a two-way radio* is a clause.

Eliminating this faulty parallelism is easy. Simply change the form of the more awkwardly expressed item to match the more concise one.

REVISED	The salesclerk was **not only** *rude* **but also** *slow*.

REVISED	The security guard had **neither** *a flashlight* **nor** *a two-way radio*.

In the first example, the clause is reduced to a single adjective, *slow*, which matches the adjective *rude*. In the second example, the clause is reduced to a noun and its modifiers, *a two-way radio*, which matches the unit *a flashlight*. The ideas in both sentences are now balanced.

Exercise 23.5   **Correcting Errors with Special Parallel Structure Challenges**

Circle the pair of connecting words in each sentence, and underline the words that they connect. Then, on a separate piece of paper, rewrite the sentences to make them parallel. Remember—there may be more than one correct version, as the example shows. (Answers will vary.)

| EXAMPLE | To our surprise, (neither) the falling snow (nor) the wind that was howling caused the ski lift to close.

To our surprise, neither the falling snow nor the howling wind caused the ski lift to close.

or

To our surprise, neither the snow that was falling nor the wind that was howling caused the ski lift to close. |
|---|---|

(1) (Both) knitting (and) to sew are my favorite hobbies. (2) These activities occupy (not only) my hands (but also) I have to think about them. (3) Besides, they are good hobbies because (neither) is expensive to maintain (nor) did I have a hard time learning them. (4) I can knit or sew when I am (either) watching TV (or) I can also visit with friends. (5) The best benefit of these activities is that I (not only) have fun (but also) creating something beautiful to wear.

Exercise 23.6 **Solving Problems with Special Parallel Structure Challenges**

Complete the following sentences by adding an appropriate connecting word or phrase. Use the example to guide you. (Answers may vary.)

EXAMPLE _____*Not only*_____ is drag racing dangerous, _____*but*_____ it is _____*also*_____ illegal.

1. Oprah Winfrey, host of the award-winning daytime program called *The Oprah Winfrey Show*, is ____*not only*____ famous ____*but also*____ loved by millions of fans all over the world.

2. When Winfrey began her radio broadcasting career at age nineteen in Nashville, Tennessee, she had ____*neither*____ experience ____*nor*____ any formal education in journalism.

3. She decided to enroll at Tennessee State University, where she studied ____*both*____ speech ____*and*____ the performance arts.

4. In her sophomore year at Tennessee State, Winfrey switched broadcast mediums and became the first African American news anchor at Nashville's WTVF-TV. Now she had ____*both*____ radio experience ____*and*____ broadcast television work under her belt.

5. It was not long before Winfrey had to make a choice: ____*either*____ stick with television ____*or*____ return to radio.

6. Winfry chose television, and this proved to be the right choice. After making the decision to remain a television journalist, Winfrey was offered ____*not only*____ her own local talk show, called *People Are Talking,* ____*but also*____ an opportunity for great success.

7. Because she wanted her talk show to be less formal than other talk shows, Winfrey used ____*neither*____ polished interview techniques ____*nor*____ high-profile guest lists.

8. Although she valued her career as a talk show host, Winfrey had always dreamed of becoming an actress. When she won an Oscar nomination for her role in the film *The Color Purple*, Winfrey again had to choose. _____Either_____ she should continue as a successful talk show host, _____or_____ she should try to develop her acting career.

Exercise 23.7   **Correcting Errors with Parallelism**

One element in each of the following series is not parallel. Cross it out, and write a new, parallel version in the space above. Then choose five of the parallel series, and, on a separate piece of paper, write sentences using them.

1. painting, ~~put up wallpaper~~ wallpapering, sanding, and scraping

2. heavy metal, light classical, or ~~music by~~ 1950s rock 'n' roll ~~stars~~

3. punt, pass, and ~~kicking~~ kick

4. flying, ~~to go by car,~~ driving and boating

5. slow, painful, and ~~it is~~ unexpected

6. behind the desk, ~~rolling~~ near the door, and under the table

7. both children and ~~when people get older~~ adults

8. either come on time or ~~to be early~~ come early

Challenge 23.3   **Analyzing Parallel Structure**

Read the following passages from Abraham Lincoln's "Gettysburg Address," given at the consecration of the Gettysburg National Cemetery. Discuss with your classmates the questions that follow.

Four score and seven years ago our fathers brought forth upon this continent, a new nation, conceived in Liberty, and dedicated to the proposition that all men are created equal.…

But, in a larger sense, we cannot dedicate—we cannot consecrate—we cannot hallow this ground. The brave men, living and dead, who struggled here, have consecrated it, far above our poor power to add or detract. The world will little note, nor long remember, what we say here, but it can never forget what they did here.... we here highly resolve that these dead shall not have died in vain; that this nation, under God, shall have a new birth of freedom, and that government of the people, by the people, for the people, shall not perish from the earth.

1. What parallel elements can you find in these passages? Underline them.

2. On a separate piece of paper, explain how the parallel structure helps you understand Lincoln's ideas.

Maintaining Parallelism Checklist

- ☐ Have you checked any individual words connected by the conjunctions *and, or,* or *but* to make sure they match in form?

- ☐ Have you checked any prepositional phrases connected by the conjunctions *and, or,* or *but* to make sure they match in form?

- ☐ Have you checked any *-ing* verbal phrases connected by the conjunctions *and, or,* or *but* to make sure they match in form?

- ☐ Have you checked any infinitive phrases connected by the conjunctions *and, or,* or *but* to make sure they match in form?

- ☐ Have you checked any units connected by pairs of correlative conjunctions *such as not only–but also* and *either–or* to make sure they match in form?

Exploring Ideas through Journal Writing

As this chapter indicates, maintaining correct parallelism involves making sure that related elements match in form. When things match in a sentence—or in life—it's easy to recognize. Do you know twins, for instance, or people who look enough alike to be twins? Are their actions as similar as their appearance? Or have you been to two places that look quite different on the surface but are actually very similar? Think of one of these subjects or some other aspect related to similarities, and then explore it for 20 to 30 minutes in your journal.

Chapter Quick Check: Maintaining Parallelism

Revise the following sentences, making sure that similar or related ideas are expressed in parallel form. Cross out words, phrases, or clauses that aren't parallel, and write your revisions above them.

(1) Americans have a big thirst, and today they have a wide variety of beverages, both hot and ~~some of them are~~ cold, available to help them quench it. (2) If consumers want something hot to drink, they can often find the coffee they are looking for at a convenience store, ~~they~~ ~~can go to~~ [at] a small neighborhood bistro, or at a kiosk within a mall or shopping center. (3) Major chains like Starbucks, Dunkin' Donuts, and ~~then there is~~ Seattle's Best have franchises spread across the country. (4) Here, consumers can enjoy not only a wide variety of regular and flavored coffee but also ~~they can enjoy~~ specialty coffee, including café au lait, latte, and espresso. (5) Visitors can see customers savoring rich coffees, enjoying various hot and cold whipped coffee drinks, and [drinking] ~~to drink~~ fruit-flavored frozen drinks. (6) Carbonated soft drinks have traditionally made up a large share of the soft-drink market, both caffeinated colas like Coke and Pepsi and citrus-flavored sodas like Sprite and Seven-up ^ ~~make up a good portion, too~~. (7) Today, sports drinks have become increasingly popular for active people, whether they are competing in some athletic activity or [doing] ^ yard work is ~~being completed by them~~ ^. (8) These kinds of drinks are designed to restore some of the minerals, ~~they~~ ~~restore~~ electrolytes, and other nutrients lost during physical activities. (9) But the beverage that increasing numbers of people are using to slake their thirst, either while exercising or ~~when they are~~ relaxing, is also the most basic drink: water. (10) Clear plastic bottles of water are now commonplace in homes, ~~they are~~ in offices, and in classrooms across the country, something that few people would have imagined ten years ago.

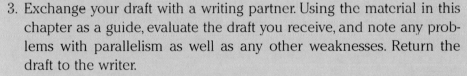

Discovering Connections 23.2

COLLABORATION

1. For Discovering Connections 23.1 on page 454, you began prewriting in response to a quotation by Robert Half or a photo. Now, continue your prewriting on one of these options:
   a. What keeps some people from fulfilling their potential?
   b. What can people do to make sure they recognize their special abilities?
2. Evaluate your prewriting material, identify a focus, and create a draft of about 100 words.
3. Exchange your draft with a writing partner. Using the material in this chapter as a guide, evaluate the draft you receive, and note any problems with parallelism as well as any other weaknesses. Return the draft to the writer.
4. Revise your draft, eliminating any errors that your reader identified.

Summary Exercise: Maintaining Parallelism

Revise the following sentences, making sure that similar or related ideas are expressed in parallel form. Cross out words, phrases, or clauses that aren't parallel, and write your revisions above them. If a sentence is correct as written, write *OK* above it.

(1) I had to decide last summer whether to look for another job or

~~going~~ [go] back to school. [OK] (2) I think I made the best decision for both me

and my family.

(3) After I was laid off in June, I tried to find either a job ~~where I~~

[full-time]
^

~~could work full-time~~ or two part-time jobs. (4) Employers kept telling me

I needed new computer skills, more experience, or ~~having a college de-~~

[a college degree.]

~~gree would help~~. (5) A lot of the jobs were either temporary ones or ~~had~~

~~only a few hours a week open to me~~. [part-time positions.] (6) Whether I took this job or that [OK]

job, I could see I was going nowhere. (7) The jobs I could get had low

pay and ~~benefits didn't exist~~. [no benefits.]

(8) I decided that if I went back to school, I could get a better job

and ~~I also wanted some things for my children~~. [some things for my children.] (9) I also felt it would be good for them to see me ~~striving~~ *strive* for a better life and succeed. (10) With a better education, I could feel proud of myself and ~~I would also improve our standard of living~~ *improve our standard of living.* (11) Still, I wasn't sure I could apply for school, ~~finding a part-time job would be hard~~ *find a part-time job,* arrange for child-care, and keep my sanity.

(12) My thoughts of going to college were not only exciting but also † ~~was scared~~ *scary.* †OK (13) At home we would have to tighten our belts even more and to make time in our hectic schedule for my studying. (14) I worried about my kids, who would miss me in the evening and ~~weekends would be lonely, too~~ *on weekends.* (15) The kids would have to either do their own laundry or ~~their clothes would be worn dirty~~ *wear dirty clothes.* (16) They might come home after school to find dirty dishes, ~~dust on the floors~~, *dusty floors,* and unmade beds.

(17) Once I made the decision, I felt hopeful and ~~happiness~~ *happy.* (18) Tough times and ~~when I felt bad about myself now~~ *bad feelings* will end. (19) Going to college will give me a better future and my kids ~~might have a better outlook~~ *a better outlook.*

MAINTAINING PARALLELISM

New term in this chapter	Definition
● parallelism	● a balanced structure in writing, achieved by expressing similar or related ideas in the same grammatical form Individual words that are connected by a conjunction should be parallel. *Example* My office is *messy* **and** *dusty*.

New term in this chapter	Definition
	• Phrases that are connected by a conjunction should be parallel. *Example* I like to *bake pies* **and** *decorate cakes*. • Words that follow pairs of connecting words should be parallel. *Example* The forecast was for **either** *heavy snow* **or** *freezing rain*.

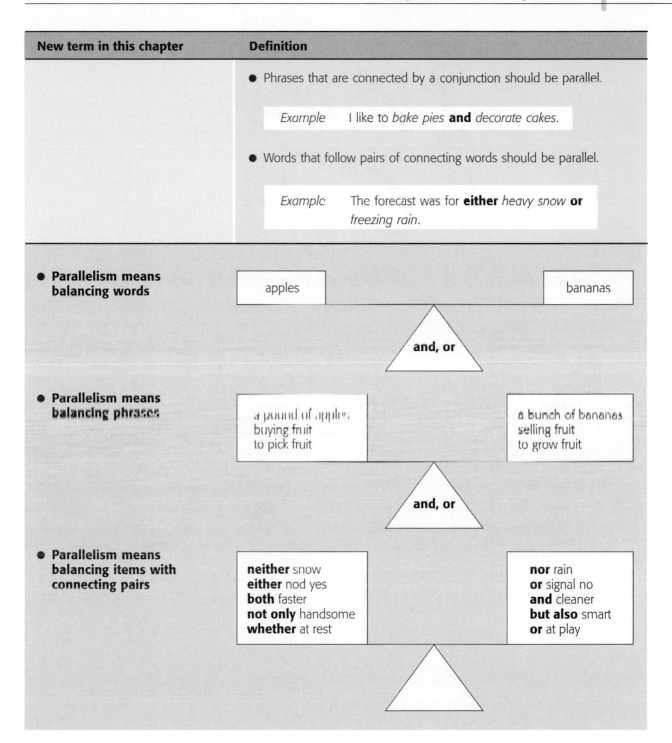

• **Parallelism means balancing words**

apples   bananas

and, or

• **Parallelism means balancing phrases**

a pound of apples   a bunch of bananas
buying fruit   selling fruit
to pick fruit   to grow fruit

and, or

• **Parallelism means balancing items with connecting pairs**

neither snow   **nor** rain
either nod yes   **or** signal no
both faster   **and** cleaner
not only handsome   **but also** smart
whether at rest   **or** at play

Writers' Café

Is it important to continue to develop my style in writing?

Absolutely. Think of style as the *voice* and overall presentation—the mark of individuality you put on a piece of writing. In life, not every situation calls for the same style and presentation, and the same is true for writing. Each type of document calls for a unique approach and an adjustment in style. For instance,

- a personal essay
- a letter of application
- a research paper
- a newspaper article
- a script for a radio or television advertisement

All call for different styles.

One way you can develop your style is to examine the work of writers you like, paying attention to their key stylistic features, including

- choice and level of vocabulary
- sentence length
- tone—the writer's attitude toward the subject

Then experiment a bit with these same features, especially in your journal writing.

Does the amount of time I have available really make a difference in my writing?

Without a doubt. Time is one of those *make it* or *break it* ingredients in writing. When you have only a little time, as with an in-class assignment, or when you allow yourself only a little time, odds are you won't be able to cover every point as carefully and thoroughly as you should. Allowing yourself sufficient time to do your writing enables you to

- discuss a subject in greater detail
- create a distance so that you can view what you wrote more objectively
- find gaps in content and errors in form that you might have otherwise missed because of fatigue

When I'm stuck, I try to figure out how to spell a word by how it sounds. Is that such a bad idea?

In theory, this strategy sounds good. The reality, however, is that it doesn't work because

- people speak English in slightly different ways in various regions of the country, in some cases mispronouncing words—*ideaR* instead of *idea* or *aX* instead of *ask*
- many words in English have silent letters (*pneumonia, restaurant, know*)
- many words with different meanings sound the same or close to the same (*your/you're, affect/effect, conscience/conscious*)

When you are stuck

- use a word you *do* know how to spell
- wait until you have a dictionary at hand

Is there any perfect length for a paragraph?

No. The length of a paragraph depends on several factors, including the type of document.

- Newspaper articles often have one-sentence paragraphs to allow frequent visual breaks for readers.
- Scholarly articles often have paragraphs that cover nearly an entire page because the readers are generally specialists in the field under discussion.

For the writing you will do as a college student, consider the following guidelines:

- If you are asked to write a single paragraph, assume that you are expected to write 75 to 100 words—five to ten sentences, depending on sentence length.
- If you are asked to write an essay, the individual paragraphs making up the essay will vary in length. Set a minimum of three sentences per paragraph.

Discovering Connections through Reading

Overview: Using Active Reading Strategies

Actively reading what other authors have written can help improve your own writing. Active reading requires that you get involved with the words on the page. Writers read actively to respond to the ideas other authors have developed and to discover the strategies they have used to express those ideas.

This part of the text includes writings by students and professional authors. After each selection, you will find questions to help you respond to and think about the ideas in the readings. You will also find questions that help you discover the connections between those ideas and your own experiences, and they will lead you to try various techniques in your own writing.

> **This section of the text will help you discover**
>
> ● active reading strategies
>
> ● some additional subjects for writing
>
> ● some new writing techniques

Taking Notes

Learning to write well involves experience and practice. In the same way, the more you practice reading actively, the more skilled you will become. One important learning strategy is to record your responses, questions, and comments about what you read. Your instructor may ask you to record in a journal what you discover by reading. Some readers make notes in the margins of the pages they are reading or highlight sections for later reference. Still others keep responses in a computer file or on an audio cassette tape. Whatever method or methods you use, cultivate the habit of taking notes. Your notes will help you prepare for discussions with your classmates and explore ideas for your own writing assignments.

Active Reading Strategies

The five reading strategies below will help you decide what questions to ask and what notes to take as you read. These guidelines will provide some direction and help you focus your responses to the readings.

Review these five tips before you read each selection. Be sure to record your responses to these questions as you read.

1. **Establish the context**

   What's going on? Who is involved? When did it happen? Where? How? Why? These are the questions that news stories generally answer in their opening sentences. As you read, use these kinds of questions to identify those details that establish the *context* of the reading.

2. **Discover the organization**

   How many paragraphs are in the writing? Does the selection have a beginning, a middle, and an end? How does the author connect these sections? As you read, note where one section begins and the next ends. Usually, you will find the author's main idea in the beginning of the writing, or *introduction*. The middle often develops the main idea through supporting examples or details. Writers call this section the *body*. At the end, the author usually restates the main point and explains the significance of the piece in the *conclusion*.

   As you read, highlight or record in your journal

   - parts of the reading that state the author's main idea
   - evidence that supports that idea
   - the author's conclusions about the subject

3. **Explore the main ideas**

   Try to identify the main idea or topic sentence of each paragraph. Are there sentences or paragraphs that confuse you or sections that you don't understand? Make note of these to discuss with your classmates. Active reading does not mean you have to find all the answers, but it does require that you ask questions. Next, take special note of supporting information that helps you understand the writer's points. What details catch your eye? Why are these effective?

4. **Respond to the ideas**

   What do you think of the selection? Why do you think the way you do? Do you agree with the ideas the author has expressed? Are you familiar with the context or the ideas in the reading? Does the author present an experience or a view of the world that is new to you? Your answers to these questions will help you greatly in understanding the writing. As you talk or write about the piece, you will also be making sense of it.

   Remember as you read that a good piece of writing touches the reader. When you read, identify what the writer has done to make this happen. The better able you are to find out how a writer has reached you, the better prepared you'll be to reach your own reader.

5. **Read again**

   As you can see, active reading is both challenging and rewarding. It also usually requires that you read a piece of writing more than once. You'll no doubt discover some elements or aspects in a second reading that you missed in the first. Regardless of what they are, those elements or aspects help to make the writing successful. Therefore, they are worth exploring so that you will be able to use similar elements in your own writing.

Active Reading Illustrated

Here is a brief excerpt from David Feldman's book *Do Penguins Have Knees? An Imponderables Book*. This book provides answers to questions about both unusual and mundane matters related to the world around us. The following passage discusses the economic purposes of and strategies behind mail-in refunds and coupons. The annotations that accompany the excerpt illustrate how active reading can help you. Through active reading, you can discover the meaning of the reading as well as the techniques the writer has used to express that meaning:

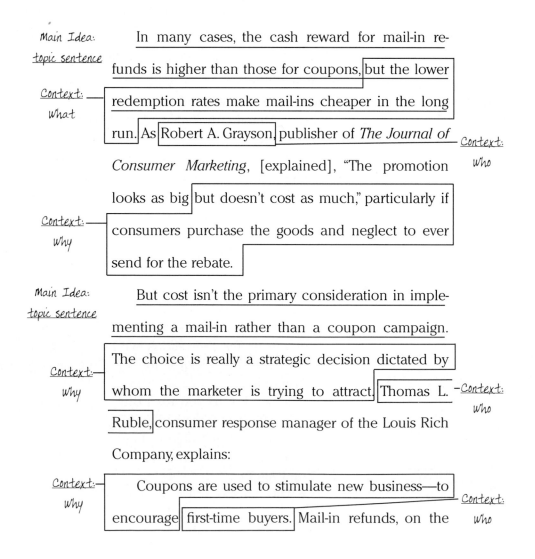

Main Idea: topic sentence

In many cases, the cash reward for mail-in refunds is higher than those for coupons, but the lower redemption rates make mail-ins cheaper in the long run.

Context: What

As Robert A. Grayson, publisher of *The Journal of Consumer Marketing*, [explained], "The promotion looks as big but doesn't cost as much," particularly if consumers purchase the goods and neglect to ever send for the rebate.

Context: who

Context: why

Main Idea: topic sentence

But cost isn't the primary consideration in implementing a mail-in rather than a coupon campaign.

Context: why

The choice is really a strategic decision dictated by whom the marketer is trying to attract. Thomas L. Ruble, consumer response manager of the Louis Rich Company, explains:

Context: who

Context: why

Coupons are used to stimulate new business—to encourage first-time buyers. Mail-in refunds, on the

Context: who

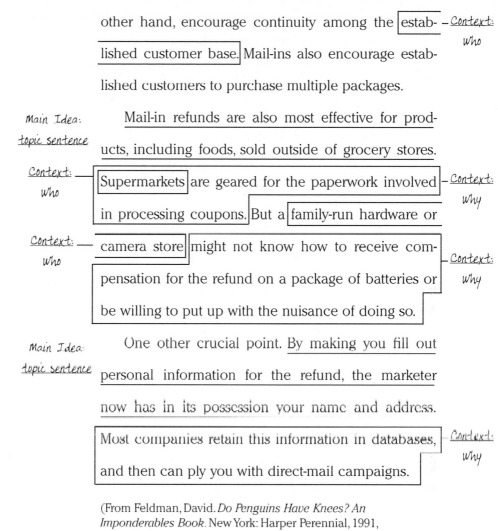

other hand, encourage continuity among the estab- — *Context:*
who

lished customer base. Mail-ins also encourage estab-

lished customers to purchase multiple packages.

Main Idea: Mail-in refunds are also most effective for prod-

topic sentence   ucts, including foods, sold outside of grocery stores.

Context: —   Supermarkets are geared for the paperwork involved — *Context:*
who   *why*

in processing coupons. But a family-run hardware or

Context: —   camera store might not know how to receive com- — *Context:*
who   *why*

pensation for the refund on a package of batteries or

be willing to put up with the nuisance of doing so.

Main Idea: One other crucial point. By making you fill out

topic sentence   personal information for the refund, the marketer

now has in its possession your name and address.

Most companies retain this information in databases, — *Context:*
why

and then can ply you with direct-mail campaigns.

(From Feldman, David. *Do Penguins Have Knees? An
Imponderables Book.* New York: Harper Perennial, 1991,
page 188.)

*So that's why some companies choose coupons and
some select rebates. Both strategies make us
buy more! Therefore, it's about $$$!*

As the annotations show, active reading enables you to identify a number of elements in the writing. Through active reading, you can specify the *context.* For example, it shows *who* would adopt a coupon campaign (a supermarket) and *who* would follow a mail-in refund strategy (a company pushing products not sold in supermarkets). At the same time, it shows *who* among consumers would be the targets of such campaigns. It also indicates *what* motivates manufacturers to choose one of the options (attracting new customers versus holding on to longtime buyers). In addition, it spells out *why* one method is generally cheaper than the other (people often redeem coupons but don't always mail away for rebates).

Besides helping you to establish the context, active reading enables you to highlight the main ideas as expressed in the *topic sentences* and the *supporting sentences.* Furthermore, when you *respond* to the reading, you focus more completely on the significance or meaning of the passage. Understanding how a writer communicates ideas to a reader enables you to communicate your own ideas more effectively to your reader.

To Be an All-American Girl

Elizabeth Wong

The author, Elizabeth Wong, is the daughter of immigrant parents. This essay, first printed in the Los Angeles Times *in 1989, explores her memories about learning the "language of [her] heritage." As you read, see what you discover about what it means "[t]o Be an All-American Girl."*

It's still there, the Chinese school on Yale Street where my brother and I used to go. Despite the new coat of paint and the high wire fence, the school I knew 10 years ago remains remarkably, stoically the same.

Every day at 5 P.M., instead of playing with our fourth- and fifth-grade friends or sneaking out to the empty lot to hunt ghosts and animal bones, my brother and I had to go to Chinese school. No amount of kicking, screaming, or pleading could dissuade my mother, who was solidly determined to have us learn the language of our heritage.

Forcibly, she walked us the seven long, hilly blocks from our home to school, depositing our defiant tearful faces before the stern principal. My only memory of him is that he swayed on his heels like a palm tree, and he always clasped his impatient twitching hands behind his back. I recognized him as a repressed maniacal child killer, and knew that if we ever saw his hands we'd be in big trouble.

We all sat in little chairs in an empty auditorium. The room smelled like Chinese medicine, an imported faraway mustiness. Like ancient mothballs or dirty closets. I hated that smell. I favored crisp new scents. Like the soft French perfume that my American teacher wore in public school.

There was a stage far to the right, flanked by an American flag and the flag of the Nationalist Republic of China, which was also red, white and blue but not as pretty.

Although the emphasis at the school was mainly language—speaking, reading, writing—the lessons always began with an exercise in politeness. With the entrance of the teacher, the best student would tap a bell and everyone would get up, kowtow, and chant, "Sing san ho," the phonetic for "How are you, teacher?"

Being ten years old, I had better things to learn than ideographs copied painstakingly in lines that ran right to left from the tip of a *moc but,* a real ink pen that had to be held in an awkward way if blotches were to be avoided. After all, I could do the multiplication tables, name the satellites of Mars, and write reports on "Little Women" and "Black Beauty." Nancy Drew, my favorite book heroine, never spoke Chinese.

The language was a source of embarrassment. More times than not, I had tried to disassociate myself from the nagging loud voice that followed me wherever I wandered in the nearby American supermarket outside Chinatown. The voice belonged to my grandmother, a fragile woman in her seventies who could outshout the best of the street vendors. Her humor was raunchy, her Chinese rhythmless, patternless. It was quick, it was loud, it was unbeautiful. It was not like the quiet, lilting romance of French or the gentle refinement of the American South. Chinese sounded pedestrian. Public.

In Chinatown, the comings and goings of hundreds of Chinese on their daily tasks sounded chaotic and frenzied. I did not want to be thought of as mad, as talking gibberish. When I spoke English, people nodded at me, smiled sweetly, said encouraging words. Even the people in my culture would cluck and say that I'd do well in life. "My, doesn't she move her lips fast," they would say, meaning that I'd be able to keep up with the world outside Chinatown.

My brother was even more fanatical than I about speaking English. He was especially hard on my mother, criticizing her, often cruelly, for her pidgin speech—smatterings of Chinese scattered like chop suey in her conversation. "It's not 'What it is' Mom," he'd say in exasperation. "It's 'What *is* it, what *is* it, what *is* it!' " Sometimes Mom might leave out an occasional "the" or "a," or perhaps a verb of being. He would stop her in midsentence: "Say it again, Mom. Say it right." When he tripped over his own tongue, he'd blame it on her: "See, Mom, it's all your fault. You set a bad example."

What infuriated my mother most was when my brother cornered her on her consonants, especially "r." My father had played a cruel joke on Mom by assigning her an American name that her tongue wouldn't allow her to say. No matter how hard she tried, "Ruth" always ended up "Luth" or "Roof."

After two years of writing with a *moc but* and reciting words with multiples of meanings, I finally was granted a cultural divorce. I was permitted to stop Chinese school.

I thought of myself as multicultural. I preferred tacos to egg rolls; I enjoyed Cinco de Mayo more than Chinese New Year.

At last, I was one of you; I wasn't one of them.

Sadly, I still am.

Exploring the Reading through Discussion

1. Where did the author and her brother have to go every day after school? Why?

2. Why is the Chinese language a "source of embarrassment" to Wong?

3. What does Wong mean by a "cultural divorce," granted to her after two years of Chinese school?

4. Who are the people Wong refers to as *you* and *them* at the end of her essay? Why is she sad to be "one of you"? Did she always feel this way?

5. Wong writes about the sights, sounds, and smells she remembers from her childhood. Find as many of these sensory descriptions as you can in the writing, and underline or highlight them. Why are these effective?

Developing Vocabulary

List at least three words in this selection that are new to you. Looking for clues in the context, the sentences surrounding the words you have chosen, write what you think is a good definition for each word. Then look up each word in the dictionary, and write the correct dictionary definition next to your original definition.

Discovering Connections through Writing

1. Have you or someone you know well had to learn English as a second language? Write about that experience. Here are some questions to help you explore the topic: What was difficult about learning a new language? Have you ever felt embarrassed or frustrated when trying to speak or write? How do you react when someone trips over his or her own tongue?

2. Most children are sometimes embarrassed by parents and family members. What are some causes? Can you recall a time when a family member embarrassed you? Or when you embarrassed your child? Tell the story in writing.

3. Who are Americans? How would you recognize an American? Here's what Michael Dorris, a Native American, wrote about these questions:

> The answer is clear: to be Americans means to be not the clone of the people next door. I fly back from any homogeneous country, from a place where every person I see is blond, or black, or belongs to only one religion, and then disembark at JFK. I revel in the cadence of many accents, catch a ride to the city with a Nigerian–American or Russian–American cab driver. Eat Thai food at a Greek restaurant next to a table of Chinese–American conventioneers from Alabama. Get directions from an Iranian–American cop and drink a cup of Turkish coffee served by a Navajo student at Fordham who's majoring in Japanese literature. Argue with everybody about everything. I'm home.

What does Michael Dorris love about America? Do you think Elizabeth Wong would agree with him? Do you agree with him? Write about your response to one or more of these questions.

Education

Malcolm X

In this selection from The Autobiography of Malcolm X, *coauthored by Alex Haley, Malcolm X explores how his studies during his time in prison affected him. As a result of reading about his experience, what do you discover about the power of writing?*

It was because of my letters that I happened to stumble upon starting to acquire some kind of a homemade education.

I became increasingly frustrated at not being able to express what I wanted to convey in letters that I wrote, especially those to Mr. Elijah Muhammad. In the street, I had been the most articulate hustler out there—I had commanded attention when I said something. But now, trying to write simple English, I not only wasn't articulate, I wasn't even functional. How would I sound writing in slang, the way I would *say* it, something such as, "Look, daddy, let me pull your coat about a cat, Elijah Muhammad—"

Many who today hear me somewhere in person, or on television, or those who read something I've said, will think I went to school far beyond the eighth grade. This impression is due entirely to my prison studies.

It had really begun back in the Charlestown Prison, when Bimbi first made me feel envy of his stock of knowledge. Bimbi had always taken charge of any conversations he was in, and I had tried to emulate him. But every book I picked up had few sentences which didn't contain anywhere from one to nearly all of the words that might as well have been in Chinese. When I just skipped those words, of course, I really ended up with little idea of what the book said. So I had come to the Norfolk Prison Colony still going through only book-reading motions. Pretty soon, I would have quit even these motions, unless I had received the motivation that I did.

I saw that the best thing I could do was get hold of a dictionary—to study, to learn some words. I was lucky enough to reason also that I should try to improve my penmanship. It was sad. I couldn't even write in a straight line. It was both ideas together that moved me to request a dictionary along with some tablets and pencils from the Norfolk Prison Colony school.

I spent two days just riffling uncertainly through the dictionary's pages. I'd never realized so many words existed! I didn't know *which* words I needed to learn. Finally, just to start some kind of action, I began copying.

In my slow, painstaking, ragged handwriting, I copied into my tablet everything printed on that first page, down to the punctuation marks.

I believe it took me a day. Then, aloud, I read back, to myself, everything I'd written on the tablet. Over and over, aloud, to myself, I read my own handwriting.

I woke up the next morning, thinking about those words—immensely proud to realize that not only had I written so much at one time, but I'd written words that I never knew were in the world. Moreover, with a little effort, I also could remember what many of these words meant. I reviewed the words whose meanings I didn't remember. Funny thing, from the dictionary first page right now, that "aardvark" springs to my mind. The dictionary had a picture of it, a long-tailed, long-eared, burrowing African mammal, which lives off termites caught by sticking out its tongue as an anteater does for ants.

I was so fascinated that I went on—I copied the dictionary's next page. And the same experience came when I studied that. With every succeeding page, I also learned of people and places and events from history. Actually the dictionary is like a miniature encyclopedia. Finally the dictionary's A section had filled a whole tablet—and I went on into the B's. That was the way I started copying what eventually became the entire dictionary. It went a lot faster after so much practice helped me to pick up handwriting speed. Between what I wrote in my tablet, and writing letters, during the rest of my time in prison I would guess I wrote a million words.

I suppose it was inevitable that as my word-base broadened, I could for the first time pick up a book and read and now begin to understand what the book was saying. Anyone who has read a great deal can imagine the new world that opened. Let me tell you something: from then until I left that prison, in every free moment I had, if I was not reading in the library, I was reading on my bunk. You couldn't have gotten me out of books with a wedge. Between Mr. Muhammad's teachings, my correspondence, my visitors—usually Ella and Reginald—and my reading of books, months passed without my even thinking about being imprisoned. In fact, up to then, I never had been so truly free in my life.

Exploring the Reading through Discussion

1. Malcolm X writes about being articulate when speaking and being articulate when writing. What is the difference? Why do you think there is a difference?

2. Why would someone think Malcolm X went to school beyond the eighth grade after hearing him speak?

3. Malcolm X copied the entire dictionary when he was in prison. Why did he do that, and what did he learn as a result?

4. Explain your understanding of the last sentence of this selection.

5. What is a synonym? Look up the word in the dictionary to find the definition if you are not sure. Then find synonyms for these words that are in the reading: *convey, functional, emulate, inevitable, correspondence.* Why do you think the author used these particular words?

Developing Vocabulary

List at least three words in this selection that are new to you. Looking for clues in the context, the sentences surrounding the words you have chosen, write what you think is a good definition for each word. Then look up each word in the dictionary, and write the correct dictionary definition next to your original definition.

Discovering Connections through Writing

1. Malcolm X writes later in his book that he "preferred to read in the total isolation of [his] own room," and that he'd read after "lights out" by the light from the prison corridor "until three or four every morning." Describe your own reading habits. Use these questions to help you explore this topic: Do you like to read? Why? Where is your favorite place to read? What do you like to read? Or do you dislike reading? Why?

2. What do you remember about learning to read and write? Explore your memories, and write about what you recall. Here are some questions to help you remember: Were you in school? Did someone in your family or a friend help you? Did you want to learn? Why? What was difficult about learning to read? Do you remember a favorite book that you read or that was read to you? Did you visit a library?

3. Was Malcolm X an educated person? What motivated him to get an education? What motivates you? Write about what you think an educated person should know, or explain what you think are the benefits of education.

Suicide Solution

Anna Quindlen

In this selection, written when she was a New York Times *columnist, Anna Quindlen writes about a 1990 lawsuit against the heavy metal group Judas Priest. The band was accused of influencing the suicide of two young men with their lyrics and hidden, or subliminal, messages. No charges against the band were upheld by the trial, which was widely covered by the media. As you read, try to explore your attitudes about the issue of media influence.*

It was two days before Christmas when Jay Vance blew off the bottom of his face with a shotgun still slippery with his best friend's blood. He went second. Ray Belknap went first. Ray died and Jay lived, and people said that when you looked at Jay's face afterward it was hard to tell which of them got the worst of the deal. "He just had no luck," Ray's mother would later say of her son to a writer from *Rolling Stone*, which was a considerable understatement.

Jay and Ray are both dead now. They might be only two of an endless number of American teenagers in concert T-shirts who drop out of school and live from album to album and beer to beer, except for two things. The first was that they decided to kill themselves as 1985 drew to a close.

The second is that their parents decided to blame it on rock 'n' roll.

When it was first filed in Nevada, the lawsuit brought by the families of Jay Vance and Ray Belknap against the members of the English band Judas Priest and their record company was said to be heavy metal on trial. I would love to convict heavy metal of almost anything—I would rather be locked in a room with one hundred accordion players than listen to Metallica—but music has little to do with this litigation. It is a sad attempt by grieving grown-ups to say, in a public forum, what their boys had been saying privately for years: "Someone's to blame for my failures, but it can't be me."

The product liability suit, which sought $6.2 million in damages, contended that the boys were "mesmerized" by subliminal suicide messages on a Judas Priest album. The most famous subliminal before this case came to trial was the section of a Beatles song that fans believed hinted at the death of Paul McCartney. The enormous interest that surrounded this seems terribly silly now, when Paul McCartney, far from being dead, has become the oldest living cute boy in the world.

There is nothing silly about the Judas Priest case—only something infinitely sad. Ray Belknap was eighteen. His parents split up before he was born. His mother has been married four times. Her last husband beat Ray with a belt, and, according to police, once threatened her with a gun while Ray watched. Like Jay Vance, Ray had a police record and had quit high school after two years. Like Jay, he liked guns and beer and used marijuana, hallucinogens, and cocaine.

Jay Vance, who died three years after the suicide attempt, his face a reconstructed Halloween mask, had a comparable coming of age. His mother was seventeen when he was born. When he was a child, she beat him often. As he got older, he beat her back. Once, checking himself into a detox center, he was asked, "What is your favorite leisure-time activity?" He answered, "Doing drugs." Jay is said to have consumed two six-packs of beer a day. There's a suicide note if I ever heard one.

It is difficult to understand how anyone could blame covert musical mumbling for what happened to these boys. On paper they had little to live for. But the truth is that their lives were not unlike the lives of many kids who live for their stereos and their beer buzz, who open the door to the corridor of the next forty years and see a future as empty and truncated as a closet. "Get a life," they say to one another. In the responsibility department, no one is home.

They are legion. Young men kill someone for a handful of coins, then are remorseless, even casual: Hey, man, things happen. And their parents nab the culprit: it was the city, the cops, the system, the crowd, the music. Anyone but him. Anyone but me. There's a new product on the market I call Parent in a Can. You can wipe a piece of paper on something in your kid's room and then spray the paper with this chemical. Cocaine traces, and the paper will turn turquoise. Marijuana, reddish brown. So easy to use—and no messy heart-to-heart talks, no constant parental presence. Only $44.95 plus $5 shipping and handling to do in a minute what you should have been doing for years.

In the Judas Priest lawsuit, it's easy to see how kids get the idea that they are not responsible for their actions. They inherit it. Heavy metal music is filled with violence, but Jay and Ray got plenty of that even with the stereo unplugged. The trial judge ruled that the band was not responsible for the suicides, but the families are pressing ahead with an appeal, looking for absolution for the horrible deaths of their sons. Heavy metal made them do it—not the revolving fathers, the beatings, the alcohol, the drugs, a failure of will or of nurturing. Someone's to blame. Someone else. Always someone else.

Exploring the Reading through Discussion

1. Why did the families of Jay Vance and Ray Belknap sue the rock band Judas Priest?

2. Is Anna Quindlen writing about any other young men besides Vance and Belknap in her essay? How do you know?

3. Do you think Quindlen approves of a product she calls "Parent in a Can"? What does she suggest are parents' responsibilities? Do you agree?

4. Who or what do you think was responsible for the deaths of Jay Vance and Ray Belknap?

5. Quindlen writes in the conclusion that, "Heavy metal music is filled with violence, but Jay and Ray got plenty of that even with the stereo unplugged." What examples in earlier paragraphs about the boys' lives does she give to support her statement?

Developing Vocabulary

List at least three words in this selection that are new to you. Looking for clues in the context, the sentences surrounding the words you have chosen, write what you think is a good definition for each word. Then look up each word in the dictionary, and write the correct dictionary definition next to your original definition.

Discovering Connections through Writing

1. Do you think music lyrics influence listeners' attitudes or behavior? If so, is the influence positive or negative? Provide examples of lyrics you know to explain your answer.

2. Some recorded music is labeled with a parental advisory warning. Do you think it should be? Explain your reasons so that a reader will understand why you think the way you do.

3. What can parents do to influence positively their children's behavior? Write about actions you think responsible parents should take. Include specific examples, as Quindlen does, to support your general ideas.

Complaining

Maya Angelou

In her book Wouldn't Take Nothing for My Journey Now, *Maya Angelou explores her life and what her experiences, friendships, and relationships have taught her. As you read this chapter from the book, see what useful advice you can discover.*

When my grandmother was raising me in Stamps, Arkansas, she had a particular routine when people who were known to be whiners entered her store. Whenever she saw a known complainer coming, she would call me from whatever I was doing and say conspiratorially, "Sister, come inside. Come." Of course I would obey.

My grandmother would ask the customer, "How are you doing today, Brother Thomas?" And the person would reply, "Not so good." There would be a distinct whine in the voice. "Not so good today, Sister Henderson. You see, it's this summer. It's this summer heat. I just hate it. Oh, I hate it so much. It just frazzles me up and frazzles me down. I just hate the heat. It's almost killing me." Then my grandmother would stand stoically, her arms folded, and mumble, "Uh-huh, uh-huh." And she would cut her eyes at me to make certain that I had heard the lamentation.

At another time a whiner would mewl, "I hate plowing. That packed-down dirt ain't got no reasoning, and mules ain't got good sense. . . . Sure ain't. It's killing me. I can't ever seem to get done. My feet and my hands stay sore, and I get dirt in my eyes and up my nose. I just can't stand it." And my grandmother, again stoically with her arms folded, would say, "Uh-huh, uh-huh," and then look at me and nod.

As soon as the complainer was out of the store, my grandmother would call me to stand in front of her. And then she would say the same thing she had said at least a thousand times, it seemed to me. "Sister, did you hear what Brother So-and-So or Sister Much to Do complained about? You heard that?" And I would nod. Mamma would continue, "Sister, there are people who went to sleep all over the world last night, poor and rich and white and black, but they will never wake again. Sister, those who expected to rise did not, their beds became their cooling boards, and their blankets became their winding sheets. And those dead folks would give anything, anything at all for just five minutes of this weather or ten minutes of that plowing that person was grumbling about. So you watch yourself about complaining, Sister. What you're supposed to do when you don't like a thing is change it. If you can't change it, change the way you think about it. Don't complain."

It is said that persons have few teachable moments in their lives. Mamma seemed to have caught me at each one I had between the age of three and thirteen. Whining is not only graceless, but can be dangerous. It can alert a brute that a victim is in the neighborhood.

Exploring the Reading through Discussion

1. What was Mamma's routine when whiners entered her store?

2. Instead of complaining, what did Mamma suggest people do? Do you agree with her advice?

3. According to Angelou, why is whining dangerous?

4. Read the whiners' words out loud. What tone of voice do you use? Does written language have a tone as spoken words do? Explain.

5. Find and underline or highlight the transition words Angelou uses in this essay. How do they help her readers understand her experience and the lesson it taught her?

Developing Vocabulary

List at least three words in this selection that are new to you. Looking for clues in the context, the sentences surrounding the words you have chosen, write what you think is a good definition for each word. Then look up each word in the dictionary, and write the correct dictionary definition next to your original definition.

Discovering Connections through Writing

1. What is one change you would like to make in your job, or in a personal relationship, or in another aspect of your life? Write a plan for making that change.

2. What is a "teachable moment"? Write about a time you learned something at a teachable moment in your own life.

3. Besides whining, what other bad habits do people have that annoy you? Do you live with a sloppy person? Do you know someone who is always borrowing money or someone who is habitually late? Describe a person or a situation that helps your reader understand what annoys you and why.

The Plot against People

Russell Baker

A syndicated columnist, Pulitzer Prize–winning journalist, and humorist, Russell Baker has been writing professionally for about fifty years. This essay was published in The New York Times *in 1968. Think about the impact of technology on your life as you read about the conflict between humans and inanimate objects.*

Inanimate objects are classified scientifically into three major categories—those that break down, those that get lost, and those that don't work.

The goal of all inanimate objects is to resist man and ultimately to defeat him, and the three major classifications are based on the method each object uses to achieve its purpose. As a general rule, any object capable of breaking down at the moment when it is most needed will do so. The automobile is typical of the category.

With the cunning peculiar to its breed, the automobile never breaks down while entering a filling station which has a large staff of idle mechanics. It waits until it reaches a downtown intersection in the middle of the rush hour, or until it is fully loaded with family and luggage on the Ohio Turnpike. Thus it creates maximum inconvenience, frustration, and irritability, thereby reducing its owner's lifespan.

Washing machines, garbage disposals, lawn mowers, furnaces, TV sets, tape recorders, slide projectors—all are in league with the automobile to take their turn at breaking down whenever life threatens to flow smoothly for their enemies.

Many inanimate objects, of course, find it extremely difficult to break down. Pliers, for example, and gloves and keys are almost totally incapable of breaking down. Therefore, they have had to evolve a different technique for resisting man.

They get lost. Science has still not solved the mystery of how they do it, and no man has ever caught one of them in the act. The most plausible theory is that they have developed a secret method of locomotion which they are able to conceal from human eyes.

It is not uncommon for a pair of pliers to climb all the way from the cellar to the attic in its single-minded determination to raise its owner's blood pressure. Keys have been known to burrow three feet under mattresses. Women's purses, despite their great weight, frequently travel through six or seven rooms to find hiding space under a couch.

Scientists have been struck by the fact that things that break down virtually never get lost, while things that get lost hardly ever break down. A furnace, for example, will invariably break down at the depth of the first winter cold wave, but it will never get lost. A woman's purse hardly ever breaks down; it almost invariably chooses to get lost.

Some persons believe this constitutes evidence that inanimate objects are not entirely hostile to man. After all, they point out, a furnace could infuriate a man even more thoroughly by getting lost than by breaking down, just as a glove could upset him far more by breaking down than by getting lost.

Not everyone agrees, however, that this indicates a conciliatory attitude. Many say it merely proves that furnaces, gloves and pliers are incredibly stupid.

The third class of objects—those that don't work—is the most curious of all. These include such objects as barometers, car clocks, cigarette lighters, flashlights and toy-train locomotives. It is inaccurate, of course, to say that they *never* work. They work once, usually for the first few hours after being brought home, and then quit. Thereafter, they never work again.

In fact, it is widely assumed that they are built for the purpose of not working. Some people have reached advanced ages without ever seeing some of these objects—barometers, for example—in working order.

Science is utterly baffled by the entire category. There are many theories about it. The most interesting holds that the things that don't work have attained the highest state possible for an inanimate object, the state to which things that break down and things that get lost can still only aspire.

They have truly defeated man by conditioning him never to expect anything of them. When his cigarette lighter won't light or his flashlight fails to illuminate, it does not raise his blood pressure. Objects that don't work have given man the only peace he receives from inanimate society.

Exploring the Reading through Discussion

1. Baker writes about objects as if they were alive with minds of their own. Find as many examples of this as you can. What is the effect of this technique?

2. What does the title, "The Plot against People," add to the essay? Are titles important in your own writing? Why?

3. Describe Baker's tone, or attitude. Is he being funny, sarcastic, serious, silly, angry, or a combination of these? Point out sentences that support your answer.

4. What sentences are transitions that help Baker to connect the parts of his essay?

5. Find examples of effective use of parallelism in the essay.

Developing Vocabulary

List at least three words in this selection that are new to you. Looking for clues in the context, the sentences surrounding the words you have chosen, write what you think is a good definition for each word. Then look up each word in the dictionary, and write the correct dictionary definition next to your original definition.

Discovering Connections through Writing

1. "Any object capable of breaking down at the moment when it is most needed will do so." Using several examples, or one developed story, write about your experiences that prove this "general rule."

2. Do you disagree with Baker's thesis? Using plenty of examples as he does, write about objects and machines that improve the quality of human life.

3. Who is in charge: technology or us? Do computers, e-mail, cell phones, and beepers help us to work more efficiently or make us work more? Does technology ease or increase the stress in our lives? Explore these ideas in a writing of your own.

The House on Mango Street

Sandra Cisneros

This reading is the first chapter of a novel called The House on Mango Street, *which explores the life of a young girl growing up in the Latino section of Chicago. As you read, see what you discover about how homes and neighborhoods can affect people's feelings.*

We didn't always live on Mango Street. Before that we lived on Loomis on the third floor, and before that we lived on Keeler. Before Keeler it was Paulina, and before that I can't remember. But what I remember most is moving a lot. Each time it seemed there'd be one more of us. By the time we got to Mango Street we were six—Mama, Papa, Carlos, Kiki, my sister Nenny and me.

The house on Mango Street is ours, and we don't have to pay rent to anybody, or share the yard with the people downstairs, or be careful not to make too much noise, and there isn't a landlord banging on the ceiling with a broom. But even so, it's not the house we'd thought we'd get.

We had to leave the flat on Loomis quick. The water pipes broke and the landlord wouldn't fix them because the house was too old. We had to leave fast. We were using the washroom next door and carrying water over in empty milk gallons. That's why Mama and Papa looked for a house, and that's why we moved into the house on Mango Street, far away, on the other side of town.

They always told us that one day we would move into a house, a real house that would be ours for always so we wouldn't have to move each year. And our house would have running water and pipes that worked. And inside it would have real stairs, not hallway stairs, but stairs inside like the houses on TV. And we'd have a basement and at least three washrooms so when we took a bath we wouldn't have to tell everybody. Our house would be white with trees around it, a great big yard and grass growing without a fence. This was the house Papa talked about when he held a lottery ticket and this was the house Mama dreamed up in the stories she told us before we went to bed.

But the house on Mango Street is not the way they told it at all. It's small and red with tight steps in front and windows so small you'd think they were holding their breath. Bricks are crumbling in places, and the front door is so swollen you have to push hard to get in. There is no front yard, only four little elms the city planted by the curb. Out back is a small garage for the car we don't own yet and a small yard that looks smaller between the two buildings on either side. There are stairs in our house, but they're ordinary hallway stairs, and the house has only one washroom. Everybody has to share a bedroom—Mama and Papa, Carlos and Kiki, me and Nenny.

Once when we were living on Loomis, a nun from my school passed by and saw me playing out front. The laundromat downstairs had been boarded up because it had been robbed two days before and the owner had painted on the wood YES WE'RE OPEN so as not to lose business.

Where do you live? she asked.

There, I said pointing up to the third floor.

You live *there*?

There. I had to look to where she pointed—the third floor, the paint peeling, wooden bars Papa had nailed on the windows so we wouldn't fall out. You live *there*? The way she said it made me feel like nothing. *There.* I lived *there.* I nodded.

I knew then I had to have a house. A real house. One I could point to. But this isn't it. The house on Mango Street isn't it. For the time being, Mama says. Temporary, says Papa. But I know how those things go.

Exploring the Reading through Discussion

1. What do you like about this selection? Why?

2. The house on Mango Street is not the kind of house the little girl in the story (her name is Esperanza) "could point to." How did the places where she lived affect her feelings about herself?

3. What do you think Esperanza means when she says "I know how those things go," at the end of this piece?

4. What did you learn about Esperanza from reading this short piece? What clues about her does the writing give?

5. Find the two paragraphs about Esperanza's dream house and the house on Mango Street. Do the paragraphs have topic sentences? Underline or highlight them. Make two lists about the characteristics of each house. How does the author help you understand the differences between the two houses?

Developing Vocabulary

List at least three words in this selection that are new to you. Looking for clues in the context, the sentences surrounding the words you have chosen, write what you think is a good definition for each word. Then look up each word in the dictionary, and write the correct dictionary definition next to your original definition.

Discovering Connections through Writing

1. If you have a concept for a dream house of your own, what do you picture in your mind? Describe that picture in words. Think about the color and size and sounds and smells in your dream home, and take your reader on a tour.

2. Esperanza hopes for a house "like the houses on TV." What kind of house is that? Watch a television show that is about a family, and describe the house that you see. Is the house like the houses you know and have been in? How is it the same? How is it different?

3. Esperanza wants something she probably won't get. Have you ever had a similar experience? What did you want? Why was it important for you to have it?

You Can Call Me the Silver-Tongued Frog

Jason Shen

This essay appeared in a Newsweek *column called "My Turn" in July 2002. The author, who lives in Irvine, California, placed first in the Kaplan/*Newsweek *My Turn competition. As you read, consider what Shen discovered about himself and what led to his success.*

I can't remember the first time the bullies called me **Kermit.** Or Froggy. Or Toad. It has become such an integral part of me that I can't imagine myself without the nicknames.

It's not easy being ugly. OK, not ugly. That's too harsh. Not facially endowed. What else can you call a guy who resembles an amphibian? People say you shouldn't judge a book by its cover, but among teenagers, the cover is what sells the book. I watched from the sidelines as my more attractive friends matched up and broke up without a care. For me, one glance from a girl was enough to feed my heart, which was shrunken from deprivation like a hunger-stricken stomach. I'd lie in my room, listen to Sister Hazel's "Change Your Mind" and swear it was about me: "If you wanna be somebody else . . ."

At the beginning of my senior year of high school, I joined the mock-trial team. I needed a better way to spend my time than idling in front of my computer trying not to think of what my best friend was doing on his date with his girlfriend.

At the tryouts, in order to gauge my speaking skills, one of the lawyers who would coach the team looked me in the face and asked, "What do you think of the HIV epidemic in Africa?" Somehow I stammered out a comprehensible answer. Surprisingly, I was awarded one of the six coveted attorney positions, while the rest of my 19 teammates were relegated to witness or clerk roles.

It was clear from the start that our training would be intense. One of the lawyer-coaches put it bluntly: "At work we charge 500 bucks an hour. We're with you guys at least 10 hours a week. You do the math. Now you want to shut up and listen?"

At every practice, the coaches would cruelly criticize our every mistake and call us everything short of complete idiots. Our opening statements were too short, our direct examinations were too long and our cross-examinations just plain stank. Then, just before we'd break down, they'd build us back up by showing us how much we had improved. Before long, we were flexing our mental muscle like true lawyers.

After our two months of training, the first competition rolled around. Before we entered the county courtroom, one of our coaches offered us some not-so-gentle encouragement: "Winning's not everything. It's the only thing."

When I walked to the podium in my suit to stand before the real-life superior-court judge and examine the "witness," a new sensation grabbed hold of me. It took me a minute to realize that it was confidence, a feeling I had never fully experienced, definitely not while conversing with a girl or sitting alone at a party. At the end of the trial, I gave my closing argument. I forget exactly what I said that made the audience, and even the other team, stand up and applaud. I just remember smiling so much that it hurt, especially as the judge singled me out as a "silver-tongued devil."

The next month seemed the shortest of my life, as my team turned in a whirlwind of amazing performances. Before we knew it, we were in the sweet 16, the elite group that remained from the original 64 teams. Three rounds later, we advanced to the final match to determine who would go on to the state championships.

The opposing team was as polished and impressive as a real dream team of lawyers. They countered all of our normally impressive arguments with even more impressive arguments of their own. As I got up to give what I thought would be my last closing statement of the year, I told myself to relish every second of it. After this, it was back to the real world, where my speaking skills were of little value to my superficial peers. I practically cried during the best closing I ever gave.

I actually did cry when, after I finished, the judge announced that my team had won and the room exploded in a roar of celebration. I hugged my co-counsels to the brink of suffocation, then rushed around congratulating the rest of my teammates. One of my coaches heartily shook my hand and admitted with a grin, "Even I was impressed."

Then I heard it. ***"Kermit!"*** I whipped around to see who had teased me. My best friend stood in front of me, beaming. To my surprise, he had come to watch me compete. "Jason," he said, "I've never heard such an articulate ***frog.***"

The team began to chant, "Silver-tongued ***frog!*** Silver-tongued ***frog!***" In that moment I realized that I was no different from teenagers everywhere who struggle to be accepted; I won the struggle because I learned to accept myself. In that moment I was actually proud to be an amphibian. That moment was beautiful.

Exploring the Reading through Discussion

1. After reading the essay, how would you define a "mock-trial team"? What information does the author provide to help readers understand this type of competition?

2. Why did Jason Shen join the mock-trial team?

3. In both the introduction and conclusion of the essay, Shen writes about being called a "frog." Does he react the same way each time? Why?

4. What do you think is the most important lesson that the author learned through his experience on the mock-trial team?

5. What words are used to connect the paragraphs in this essay and to show the passage of time?

Developing Vocabulary

List any words in this selection that are new to you. Write your understanding of each word from the context. Then look up each word in the dictionary, and write the definition that you think best fits the meaning in this writing.

Discovering Connections through Writing

1. The author writes that "People say you shouldn't judge a book by its cover, but among teenagers, the cover is what sells the book." Do you agree? Be sure to include specific examples to support your point in your response.

2. Have you ever had the experience of speaking in front of a group? Did you feel confident or nervous? How did your audience react? Write about your public speaking experience. Be sure to include details that help readers understand both the situation and how you felt.

3. Shen writes about several aspects of team competition. If you have a similar experience, explore one or more aspects of team competition in

an essay of your own. Why did you join the team? What process did you follow to train and get into condition? How did the training affect or even change you? How important was winning?

Popularity

Marta Melendez (student)

Marta Melendez writes about changes she has noticed among teenagers since she was in high school in Puerto Rico. As you read, think about people you admire and why they are popular.

The meaning of popularity has changed during the last 30 years. When I was young, popularity came with special talents. Today popularity seems to be based on imitation of others.

When I was in high school in Puerto Rico, during the 1970s, anyone who was popular was seen as having some special talent. For example, one of the things that made me popular was being a singer in a band. Others would make friends with me just to say they knew me, and this would make them feel "cool." I also remember having a friend who was very popular because he designed clothes. Girls always surrounded him. If I wanted to have a private conversation with him, I would have to make an appointment about two or three days in advance. Once it took me a week to give him a message. His talent of designing clothes was a special talent that made him very popular.

In my days, being an athlete was also considered a special talent. For example, not everybody who wanted to be an athlete could be one. To be an athlete, you had to be good in some kind of sport and show you had talent. Athletes always had nice built-up bodies and looked so fine in their uniforms, all the girls wanted to have one as a boyfriend. My best friend had a boyfriend who was an athlete, and she said being with him made her feel like a queen.

As the years went by the concept of popularity changed. To be popular today, a person must dress like everyone else. Someone is popular if he or she wears brand-name clothes and shoes, such as Nike or Reebok. My son, like many adolescents, won't wear just any kind of shoes. When I go shopping for him, his clothes and shoes have to be name-brand. The most common shoe brands are Nike, Reebok, Adidas, and Fila, just to mention a few. His clothes have to be name-brand also, like Fubu, Paco, Mecca, South Pole, Tommy Hilfiger, and so many more. I once bought him a pair of Spalding shoes, which was like throwing money in the garbage because he never wore them. He said wearing them would make him feel stupid because he was the only one who was different. In my years of high school, we had to wear what our parents bought us and we didn't mind because popularity wasn't based on material possessions.

Another way to be popular today is by following the fad of body piercing and getting tattoos. In my neighborhood, my best friend's son came home with an earring and a tattoo. When she asked him the reason why he did it, the answer he gave her was that he wanted to be in style like all his friends. A few days ago, my son asked me for money as a Christmas gift because he wants to have a tattoo done. I certainly don't agree, but he says all his friends have one, and so he wants one, too. In my days, only girls had their ears pierced and mostly guys in jail had tattoos.

Nowadays the latest way of being popular for adolescents is carrying a gun. This has turned schools into a nightmare, as was witnessed with the shootings at Columbine High School, where many students died. Having a gun has become for many adolescents a way of being popular because they feel in control. I once asked a prisoner why having a gun was so important to him, and he said a gun made him feel he had power and control over everybody, and this made him feel "powerful." Although intimidating others with a gun doesn't make you popular with everybody, it does make you popular with your friends, who also want to feel powerful.

It makes me sad to see how people misunderstand popularity today. Today people think it's easy to be popular just by using the right clothes and shoes, piercing the right body parts, or having a gun. It makes me wish to be back in those days when popularity was based on special talent.

Exploring the Reading through Discussion

1. Do you agree that popularity today is based on imitating others and not on having special talents?

2. Discuss your response to the paragraph about guns and popularity.

3. Do you think that material possessions are more important to today's generations than they were to previous ones? What evidence do you have to support your answer?

4. In what ways are teenagers the same as they were twenty-five years ago? In what ways are they different?

5. Identify the topic sentences in this essay. Are they effective? Do they all connect to or support the author's thesis?

Developing Vocabulary

List at least three words in this selection that are new to you. Looking for clues in the context, the sentences surrounding the words you have chosen, write what you think is a good definition for each word. Then look up each word in the dictionary, and write the correct dictionary definition next to your original definition.

Discovering Connections through Writing

1. What do you think makes someone popular? How do you define popularity? Is this definition the same for everyone? Explore the term "popular" in a writing of your own.

2. Who are the people with special talents you admire today? Are any of them entertainers or athletes? Why do you admire them? Because of their popularity and influence, do they have any responsibilities to their fans? Explain your response to one or more of these questions.

3. Should tragic incidents of violence in schools be reported as much and as graphically as they are? Explain your position on this controversy, and be sure to include specific examples in your writing.

My Childhood Hobby

Daniel Hickok (student)

A hobby can help pass the time, but a hobby can also help children learn and discover new talents. Daniel Hickok writes about a unique leisure activity that fascinated him when he was growing up. How does this student author help readers understand what drew him to magic?

As a child, I was fascinated with magic. I used to watch magicians on television, and I would tape them. I would watch the tapes over and over again. Then, I'd try to figure out how it was done.

At that time I was working on my first job: a paperboy for the *New Bedford Standard Times*. I made about forty to fifty dollars a week. At the end of every week, I would buy a magic trick. Everyday I would browse through the Hank Lee's Magic Factory catalog over and over again and circle everything I wanted. There were over 600 pages in that catalog, and I would look through them all as often as a politician reads the newspaper. I collected so many tricks: the devil's canister, the flaming wallet, the floating match, and even mouth coils. I would practice these tricks all the time, carefully watching myself in the mirror. I constantly bothered my older sister and her friends every time I felt I had mastered a trick.

After lots of practice, I started to have magic shows at my dad's house. He told me he had been interested in magic, too, when he was my age. He even had magic books in his office. Anyway, I would set up a table outside in his backyard with some flashy tablecloth. My tricks would be set up under the table waiting to be performed. I would even have a list of the tricks in the order they would be performed. I knew tons of card tricks, and I would always pick my dad as the volunteer because if I screwed up the trick, he'd still pretend to be impressed. "Wow, that's my card!" he'd say, when it wasn't even the right card.

Soon, I felt I needed to upgrade my tricks. I would watch all those magicians on stage, and there was one thing they all had in common that I didn't have: doves! I opened the Yellow Pages and called every pet store. "Oh, we have a sale—only $120," they'd say. Then one day my grandmother called me. She has a farm and said she knew a breeder. As a result, I got two beautiful white doves for four dollars a piece! They were just like the ones I had seen on television.

The next week I bought a new trick: the Dove Pan! It was a shiny aluminum pan with a cover. A magician would show the audience the empty pan, but when he put the lid on and then took it off, a dove would come flying out. I used to pretend to crack eggs in the pan before I made the dove appear. I was so amazed at the tricks in Hank Lee's catalog. Finally, I could impress my sister and her friends, because girls love animals. No longer was I a little kid with a plastic toy magic kit; I felt like a real magician.

This was just the beginning of my magic career. When my next check arrived, I decided to take a trip to Hank Lee's Magic Factory in Boston. I wanted to meet the man himself.

I arrived at Hank Lee's the next morning; it was like a trip to Disney World for me. I saw huge illusions spread out all over the place with $1000 price tags on them. I think I started to drool. I watched as the employees performed tricks for me. Each tried to get his piece of the commission. They were good, though, obviously magicians themselves. I told one man that I wanted a dove trick, and his face lit up with joy. He rushed to the back of the store. I waited in suspense, wondering what he'd take out of the back room: a flaming birdcage?

Then, my face filled with disappointment as the man walked back with a small black tray. However, I had no idea what this tray was capable of doing. I watched as the employee blew up a balloon and placed it on the tray. I waited anxiously for something to happen. He told me how the trick was brand new and that he had just opened it today. "Get on with the damn trick," I thought to myself. Suddenly it happened; I could barely believe my eyes. "Is that even possible?" I had thought to myself. "Does this very trick defy science completely?" I had been staring at that black tray with that balloon taped to it, when the balloon suddenly popped, confetti flew everywhere, and a gorgeous white dove appeared. I was so happy until I thought to myself, "How much could this incredible trick actually cost?" All I had was one week's paperboy money in my pocket, a mere forty-five dollars. Surprisingly, the magician clerk said, "Forty dollars—it's yours." I wanted to leap with joy. When I got home, everyone was amazed with my new trick. I eventually did a few birthday parties for some relatives, and I even made some money.

Finally, I became tired of magic and I put all my tricks away. Sometimes I still go down to the basement and play with my old tricks. I still use the flaming wallet in restaurants, and everyone is always impressed.

Exploring the Reading through Discussion

1. What activities did Daniel Hickok undertake to become a magician? What did he know when he began his hobby? What had he learned when he put his tricks away?

2. How important were Hickok's family and friends as he learned and practiced magic?

3. When did Hickok say that he "felt like a real magician"? Why do you think this was a turning point?

4. Find colons and semicolons that are used in this essay. Why did the author choose to use these punctuation marks?

Developing Vocabulary

List any words in this selection that are new to you. Write your understanding of each word from the context. Then look up each word in the dictionary, and write the definition that you think best fits the meaning in this writing.

Discovering Connections through Writing

1. If you enjoy magic, describe one of the best tricks or illusions that you have seen performed. Provide details so that readers will be able to view the trick as you did.

2. Have you performed on stage or in front of an audience? Did you follow and learn from any experts? How much time did you devote to practice? Write to explain how you prepared for your performance.

3. Tell readers about your hobby: one that you enjoy now, one that you enjoyed in the past, or one that you have always wanted to explore. As you write, be sure to be consistent with verb tenses.

Remembering India

Elsa "Chachi" Maldonado (student)

In this essay, Elsa Maldonado remembers and honors her sister, India. Although some subjects can be difficult to write about, see whether you can discover as you read how writing can help to bring order to strong thoughts and feelings.

My sister, Carmen, and I were very close. We were inseparable until her untimely death. I can remember thinking at the time of her death that someone made a mistake. That was not my sister they found lying on the eighteenth floor of the Ringe Tower Projects in Cambridge, Massachusetts. Clearly, it had to be someone else's sister. My sister, Carmen, better known as India, was an outgoing, loving person who had no known enemy. I could not understand why anyone would want to take her away from us.

I can remember when I was about eight years old, my mother, Lucy, had to work two jobs in order to provide food, clothing, and shelter for my brothers, sister, and me. It wasn't easy for her, but she did her best to keep us all together as a family. The oldest child was India, and at the age of fourteen, she was the primary caregiver while Mom was away at work. Although I didn't understand at the time, I now realize how difficult it must have been for India to stay at home when she really wanted to be out with her friends. Sometimes her friends used to come over to our house and ask if she wanted to go hang out with them at the park. India would look over her shoulder only to find my brothers and me staring at her. She would then look back at her friends and tell them she was sorry, but she had to baby-sit. I can remember my brothers and me letting out a sigh of relief, knowing that she was not going to leave us alone—not that she ever did.

My sister never let the "I'm in charge" status go to her head. Whenever she wanted us to pick up our toys or put the dishes away, she would say to us, "O.K. guys, it's time to pick up after ourselves." She would even pick up our mess, even if she didn't join us in making the mess. One time, during one of our usual cleaning routines, I asked my sister how it felt to be the boss in charge of all of us. She replied by saying, "I don't know. I'm only your big sister looking out for you guys." Afterwards, my brothers and I decided to go play in our room. As I was leaving the living room, I looked back at my sister, who had decided to watch television. I noticed she had a big smile on her face as she turned to look back at me, saying, "I'll tell you what, though—it feels great to be a big sister." I smiled back and left the room to join my brothers.

India made sure that our days were not boring while in her care. Every day she would bring home a bag of penny candies that she picked up on her way home from school. When she walked in the door, we would greet her, and she would tell us in a low tone of voice who the birthday person was for the day. My brothers and I knew that India would have a small paper bag full of candy stashed away somewhere in the house, so we tried to be on our best behavior. We loved our mother, but sometimes we couldn't wait for Mom to go to work so we could spread the candy on top of the kitchen table and sing "Happy Birthday" to the birthday person. The candy was saved until our school work was completed and the dishes were cleaned and put away. With a birthday candle melting over the cream of a cupcake, we sang "Happy Birthday" off key. These parties were kept secret from my mother because she would never have allowed us to eat so much candy. After the party, my sister would impose her golden rules, which were that we had to brush our teeth and give each other a hug and a kiss. Of course, we gave her an extra kiss and hug, so she could pass it on to Mom when she got home.

When India was around sixteen, Mom started working one full-time job, so India's baby-sitting services were no longer needed. However, I believe that the time she spent baby-sitting us brought us all closer to each other. Even when she wasn't baby-sitting me, India and I spent a great deal of time together. We shared each other's secrets. She taught me how to play handball, how to keep up-to-date with dances, how to put on makeup and how to keep a diary, among other things. I even used her baby-sitting techniques when I started baby-sitting.

India's death left us all in disbelief, horror, and sadness. Although my sister is no longer with us physically, the love, laughter, caring, and joy that she inspired within our hearts will last a lifetime. Nothing, not even her untimely death, can destroy that.

Exploring the Reading through Discussion

1. Readers don't learn about the specific circumstances of India's death. Should the author have included that information? Explain?

2. Was India a good "primary caregiver" of her brothers and sisters? What evidence does the author provide?

3. How did India feel about caring for her siblings? How do you know?

4. What did the author learn from her sister?

5. Essays should have effective introduction and conclusion paragraphs. Do you think these paragraphs in this essay are effective? Why?

Developing Vocabulary

List at least three words in this selection that are new to you. Looking for clues in the context, the sentences surrounding the words you have chosen, write what you think is a good definition for each word. Then look up each word in the dictionary, and write the correct dictionary definition next to your original definition.

Discovering Connections through Writing

1. Write a memoir of someone you know and love. Be sure to identify a focus for your writing. Begin by exploring your memories through prewriting.

2. Write a guide for baby-sitters. Include as many specific tips and ideas as you can.

3. India was given a lot of responsibility as a young teenager. What should children be asked to do to help at home? What do they gain from the experience? Refer to this essay or your own experiences to support your ideas.

"Forget the past. No one becomes successful in the past."

Peter LeComte (student)

In this essay, the student author uses examples from his life to help explain his understanding of a quotation. As you read, what examples from your own experience can you discover that support or conflict with Peter LeComte's conclusions?

If we examine the grammar within this quotation, we can attempt to grasp the meaning of the words. No one *becomes* successful in the past; this is not saying that no one *became* successful in the past, but that the past is *our* past, and people become successful in *their* present. So what this statement has at its core is that you can never go back and alter what you believe to be past mistakes. We cannot undo what has already been done. If we wish to live a full life, we have to do it now. There is no use wallowing in our past mistakes.

Many people berate themselves over mistakes they have made in the past. Unfortunately, too many people never get past the anger stage. Of course, I am not exempt from this. As recently as this past Saturday, I found it difficult to forget the past. When I went to bed on Friday night, I set the alarm for 8:20. It should have given me plenty of time to get to work. Unbeknownst to me, I had inadvertently set it on P.M. rather than A.M. Needless to say, when I awoke at twenty-five past nine, I realized the error I had made the night before. When I arrived at work, I was nearly forty-five minutes late. Throughout the work day, the fact that I was late festered in the back of my mind. I was unable to put aside my anger and simply do my job. Thus, my work suffered.

I find this to be a perfect example, at least in my life, of being unable to free oneself from the past. In retrospect, I realize that had I just accepted the fact that I was late, I could have had a much more productive and enjoyable day. If we are able to grasp this linear concept of the past being the past while we are still in the situation, we can do our best to forgive ourselves and simply get on with our lives.

In this quotation, success does not necessarily pertain to finances. Success is something you achieve when you live your life the way you truly want to. I'll be honest. I do not want to continue to deny myself happiness right now because I never went to a high school prom, or because I quit playing hockey. These things just don't make sense. If I am upset that I don't play hockey, I could go get my stick and my skates and go and play. Sitting around being angry about not playing won't get me out on the ice.

When we make mistakes, and believe me, we all have regrets, we are powerless to rectify these past events. If we caused harm to another person, we cannot undo the pain we have caused; we can only ask for forgiveness from those we have hurt. The people we have hurt might include ourselves.

By letting go of the past, we become free from it, and we can live in the present, where we belong. I know we belong here because this is where we are. If we don't choose to let go of the past, we will continue to harbor resentment toward the present. We will continue to remember the pain we have lived, and our future will be filled with pain as well.

Exploring the Reading through Discussion

1. Peter LeComte writes, "We cannot undo what has already been done." Do you agree with him? Why or why not?

2. According to the author, how can anger about our own mistakes affect our lives?

3. How do you react when you realize that you have made a mistake? How does your reaction compare with the author's?

4. Can you think of other sayings that express the same idea as the quotation that begins this essay?

5. Identify the life mistakes the author writes about in his essay. How do these examples support the thesis of the essay?

Developing Vocabulary

List any words in this selection that are new to you. Write your understanding of each word from the context. Then look up each word in the dictionary, and write the definition that you think best fits the meaning in this writing.

Discovering Connections through Writing

1. Choose a quotation, as LeComte did, and explain what the words mean to you. Be sure to let readers know why the quotation is important to you.

2. The author defines success as "Something you achieve when you live your life the way you truly want to." Write your own definition of success. Include examples of success to help readers understand your definition.

3. Write about a time when you were able to let go of the past and live in the present.

Volunteering: More Rewarding Than Cash

Elizabeth Soares (student)

Elizabeth Soares's subject in this essay is one she cares about very much. She is writing to inform her audience, but as you read, try to discover another purpose for her writing.

Hey, do you want to make a difference in your community? Why not try volunteer work? It gives you the opportunity to make a change for the better not only in someone else's life, but also in your own. If you're saying to yourself, "Well, I don't have any time, plus I won't get paid for it," that's nonsense. Actually, it doesn't take that much time, and believe me, cash is not the only reward out there.

The first time I volunteered was when I was in third grade at John J. Doran Elementary School. The principal announced that there was going to be a huge clothing drive for the needy people in the community. When my mom heard about this, she insisted the whole family clean out their closets and donate as many clothes as possible. I gave away a black and fuchsia colored shirt. At the time, I thought, "Yeah, right, who would even think about wearing this ugly shirt with a funny looking kitten on it." I gladly donated it. My mom and I went to the school and helped out with organizing this successful event. The next day when I went to school, I noticed a girl with a bright smile on her face. She was wearing a black and fuchsia colored shirt with a funny kitten on it. It was then that I realized, "Wow! It doesn't take much work or sacrifice to make a difference."

Another volunteer experience I will never forget was at St. Anne's Hospital. I was a junior volunteer for two years doing simple tasks such as making beds, picking up trays, and changing the patients' water. There was one patient who truly had an impact on me. The other girls and I would try to avoid going into her room because her odor made our stomachs turn. It was the Saturday before Christmas and I couldn't wait to go home and finish wrapping the rest of my Christmas gifts. As I held my breath while walking by the room, I heard her call out, "Miss, miss, can you come in here please?" I could have gone home and let the nurse worry about her, but a little voice inside me said, "Liz, where's your Christmas spirit?" When I entered her room, she had a huge smile on her face. All I had to do was sit there and listen to her talk about how much she loved Christmas trees and how she wished she were home decorating her own tree. I enjoyed taking a few minutes out of my busy schedule to listen to her. She felt better, and that made me feel better.

Helping out at soup kitchens is something I have done in the past and would like to do again. My youth group got me involved with it. What we had to do was make food for about 100 people, set up tables, and clean up afterward. I admit I was a bit apprehensive about making food for people, since I am a terrible cook. It was O.K. though; no one cared if my potatoes were not perfectly cut or that the soup need a little extra salt. In addition to making the food, we also served it to hungry folks, and if they wanted to have a conversation with me, I was more than willing. One of the people who came in to receive a meal appeared to be mentally ill. All he needed was someone to listen to him. With him, he had a painting. It was a beautiful painting of a serene countryside. He claimed he painted it, but I knew he didn't because the Sears price tag was still on the back. I didn't mock, nor did I argue. I just sat back and listened. By the glow on his face and the tone of his voice, I knew that he was pleased that I was there.

In conclusion, all I want to say is that through the years of volunteering I've learned to appreciate things more and learn more about people and their situations. If you're interested in volunteering, contact your school, church, or just about anywhere in your community. Believe me, whomever you help out, I'm sure they will appreciate all you have to offer. Knowing that I helped make a difference in people's lives is more than any paycheck has ever brought me. So why not try it? You have nothing to lose and a whole lot to gain.

Exploring the Reading through Discussion

1. What are the rewards Soares gained from volunteering? Can you think of other rewards?

2. What services did the author perform "to make a change for the better not only in someone else's life, but also in [her] own"? Which actions do you think were the most important to others? Were these the most difficult to do?

3. Did Soares achieve her purpose (or purposes) for writing?

4. Identify the topic sentences of the body paragraphs. Are they effective? What does the last sentence of each of these paragraphs contribute to the essay?

5. How is the essay organized? Is this method effective? Why?

Developing Vocabulary

List at least three words in this selection that are new to you. Looking for clues in the context, the sentences surrounding the words you have chosen, write what you think would be a good definition for each word. Then look up each word in the dictionary and write the correct dictionary definition next to your original definition.

Discovering Connections through Writing

1. As Elizabeth Soares did, write about a volunteer experience or experiences of your own. What were the challenges and rewards?

2. Does your college or university have a service learning program or provide other opportunities for volunteer work? Discover what you can about the policies, procedures, and benefits of the program, and write to share your information with other students.

3. Should community service be a required component of high school education? Write to explain your reasons.

Differences in Child Rearing in Russia and the United States

Svetlana Melamedman (student)

Writers can help readers understand something new by comparing it to something familiar. As you read this essay by a student author, you will discover how children are raised in Russia. Consider how the Russian approach is similar to or different from the way you were brought up.

Sometimes I ask myself, "Am I ready to face the responsibility of raising a child?" Right now, my answer is no. It's not just because I am young but also because I have not decided which way I should raise my baby: American or Russian. Every country has a different system for the upbringing and education of young children. I know two ways, the Russian and American, but I'm not sure which one I prefer. They are so different in terms of attitudes about childbirth, education, and relationships with extended family.

One major difference between life in Russia and the United States is what happens before babies are born. In Russia, before women give birth, people don't talk about the babies or speculate about their future or sex. Also, nobody buys presents before babies are born. It is considered bad luck, and everyone believes in it. In my country, instead of trying to help women who are giving birth, men go shopping for baby clothes and other things. In addition, women and their babies are kept in a hospital for about a week while the new mothers are taught how to take care of their babies.

On the other hand, in the United States, before women give birth, people freely discuss the babies that are coming. Often, mothers are given baby showers. There are no restrictions on who can come to the parties, and when they are over, both mother and babies have received presents before the birth. Here, it is not considered to be bad luck if you want to know the gender of the baby. Also, in the U.S., moms and sometimes dads take classes in how to have and care for a baby. In addition, women and their babies are sent home within a day of birth.

Another important difference to me is the way children are educated in the two countries. In Russia, after spending their first three years home with their mothers, children begin formal schooling. They leave their parents and go to full-time day care, and then to kindergarten, and after that to elementary school, all usually run by the government. Every class has between twenty and twenty-five people. When kids turn seven years old, they go to a school that is located right near their house. Parents accompany their kids on the way to school for just a half year. After that, they go by themselves. Children attend five or six classes every day and study six days a week. They do their homework by themselves while their parents are at work. At night, parents will often check their work. Children stay in this system for ten years. After completing the last grade, they can choose a university or institute.

The American system is somewhat different. Before many children in the U.S. begin school, they have spent time with babysitters or day care providers. Pre-school is not a requirement for U.S. students as it is in Russia. When they start school in kindergarten, children often have to travel to and from the school by bus. After school, they do their homework with babysitters or parents. Schools in the U.S. have three levels, elementary, middle, and high school, and it takes twelve years to complete them. Then, if they want and have done well in school, they can go on to college or a technical school of some kind.

Another major difference for kids in Russia and those in the U.S. is the relationships children have with their extended families. In Russia, not many children spend time with family members other than their siblings and parents. Sometimes children don't even know about aunts or uncles or cousins until later in their lives. Houses and apartments are often arranged so that they share a big playground. Neighborhoods aren't private places, and kids from the houses nearby gather in the playground to play together. In the summer months, almost all kids go to camps or small villages to visit grandparents. Children therefore have many friends because they spend a lot of time separate from their families. This independence helps to make them more confident.

In my opinion, America is perfect in terms of family relationships. From the time most babies are born, their relationships with their extended families are usually closer than they are in Russia. U.S. children are more likely to know and spend time with cousins and other members of their extended families than kids in Russia do. Spending time at a summer camp isn't as common here as it is in Russia, so children spend their summers with family members, too.

As you can see, there are serious differences in the way things are done in the two countries, and they leave me with many questions. What is the right way for me to raise my child? I hope in the future that I am able figure out whether the Russian system or the U.S. system will be right for my baby and me.

Exploring the Reading through Discussion

1. Svetlana Melamedman writes about three important aspects of raising a child. What are they? What do you think are the most important aspects of child rearing?

2. What, if any, ideas about child rearing in Russia do you find surprising?

3. Are there any Russian practices that you think you might prefer to those you are more familiar with in the United States? Why? Do you have experience with other practices not mentioned in the essay?

4. Does the author present a balanced view of both country's practices? Explain your answer.

5. An essay should include both an introduction and a conclusion. What are the purposes of these paragraphs? Does Melamedman succeed in writing an effective introduction and conclusion? Explain.

Developing Vocabulary

List any words in this selection that are new to you. Write your understanding of each word from the context. Then look up each word in the dictionary, and write the definition that you think best fits the meaning in this writing.

Discovering Connections through Writing

1. The author asks herself an important question in the beginning of her essay, and her answer is "no." When do you think a person is "ready to face the responsibility of raising a child"? In your answer, write about at least three reasons why you think someone could answer "yes."

2. If you could do so, how would you change the education requirements for children? For example, should children begin their formal education earlier or spend more hours in school each week? As you write, consider the reasons you would propose the changes and what positive effects the changes would create.

3. How did you spend your summers as a child? Did you attend camp or spend time with your relatives? Did you have a summer job or help with family responsibilities? Write about your summer activities or tell the story of your happiest summer memory.

Talk Show Trash

Joy Saucier (student)

This author has strong feelings about a popular form of television programming. She doesn't regularly watch talk shows, and in this writing she explores the reasons why she doesn't. As you read, see if you discover statements you agree or disagree with.

I must be the only one in the entire universe who doesn't watch talk shows. In my opinion, talk shows are a total waste of air time! Talk shows promote dysfunctional behavior and attitudes. They encourage violence and disrespect. Instead of being an impartial forum for people to air their differences with mediation, they become a wrestling match complete with insults and put-downs! I cannot comprehend how anyone of moderate intelligence could enjoy such programs.

I detest talk shows because every aspect of them is in poor taste. The topics are offensive, the guests and audience members unruly, and the hosts argumentative. An excellent example of this poor taste happened just the other day. As I was aimlessly channel surfing, I happened to pause upon the popular talk show "Ricki Lake." The topic of her show was "Surprise, I'm pregnant by your husband!" The title shocked me enough to watch the show. I couldn't believe what I saw! Unsuspecting wives were being confronted by their husbands' pregnant mistresses. The total shock and pain was unbelievably apparent. Everyone on the stage was hurling insults, and the nastier the fighting got, the more the audience, and to my horror, my family, enjoyed it! Even the audience members got in on the act, until the show became a verbal free-for-all. The host added to the chaos by deliberately asking argumentative questions to further perpetuate the fighting. She even went a step further to throw in her own opinions, therefore aligning herself with one side. In summary, the wives crying, the mistresses glib, the audience fighting with the guests, and even among themselves, and the host ineffectively trying to keep the show under control all contributed to the craziness. This episode left me questioning why this dysfunctional show is so popular. What kind of people actually enjoy watching such total hysteria? Needless to say, this show left a bad taste in my mouth.

Also, these talk shows are an insult to the intelligence of viewers. How many people are interested in such frivolous topics as "I went into labor and didn't even know I was pregnant" or "I was abducted by space aliens"? These are two actual topics of two very popular talk shows which aired last week.

Who is interested in this junk? Upon doing research for this essay. I've learned that half to two-thirds of talk show viewers are teenagers. Knowing this, I would propose that the shows format some of their episodes to feature issues that are of importance to teenagers, such as STDs, underage drinking, and eating disorders. The talk shows could use their air time to inform and educate their viewers. Having shock value topics once in a while is fun, but if they never have shows with substance, then I do feel that my intelligence is being insulted.

Another concern that I have is how these shows can solve the guests' problems in sixty minutes, not including commercials. It *cannot* be done! The counselors they bring on the show are only present for the last ten minutes of the show. How can such a short time for therapy help? The guests don't even receive follow-up sessions in their hometowns! I ask you once again, how can this help? The guests leave with as much, if not more, emotional damage than they had before. Talk shows do not care about truly helping their guests. The only thing they care about is whether the guests' problems are interesting enough to boost the show's ratings.

The most compelling reason why I hate talk shows is because they exploit the guests and their problems. First of all, they lead some of the guests onto the show under false pretenses. The format of the most popular shows is confrontational. In order to get the guest who is to be confronted onto the show, they must lie to the guest with a false show topic. When this guest comes onto the stage, he or she is confronted by the other guest, and the true nature of the topic comes out.

An example of this would be the tragic case of Jonathan Schmitz, who was led onto "The Jenny Jones Show" believing that he was about to meet the woman of his dreams. However, the real reason was to confront Scott Amedure, who lived near him and who had a crush on him. The talk show host proceeded to shock Schmitz by bringing out the gay man, who told him that he had a crush on him. Schmitz's face registered total shock. After the show was taped (it was never actually aired), someone left an unsigned, suggestive note outside Schmitz's apartment. The humiliation, combined with a history of mental illness, was too much for Schmitz, who bought a gun and killed the gay man. The end of the story for both men was tragic: one was dead and the other was facing life in prison. The parents of both people sued "The Jenny Jones Show" for this. The publicist for the show said that Jones had nothing to do with what happened, and they would accept none of the blame. As you can see, these shows don't care about their guests or the consequences of using the "surprise" tactic.

In closing, having to watch talk shows is torture for me. I find them extremely insulting and rude. I don't understand why America is so hooked. From my research for this project, I've learned that talk shows won't be going away soon, either. They are the fastest growing type of television show. At last check, I counted nineteen shows! Wake up, America! Talk shows are trash!

Exploring the Reading through Discussion

1. Why does the author think talk shows are "a total waste of air time"? Do you agree with her?

2. How might someone who regularly watches talk shows respond to the author's statements?

3. Which example about talk shows do you think is the most convincing? Why is this example effective?

4. Of all the reasons Saucier dislikes talk shows, which one is the most important to her? Which reason is the most important one to you? Why?

5. Find and underline the topic sentences of all the paragraphs in this writing. Are these effective topic sentences? Why?

Developing Vocabulary

List at least three words in this selection that are new to you. Looking for clues in the context, the sentences surrounding the words you have chosen, write what you think is a good definition for each word. Then look up each word in the dictionary, and write the correct dictionary definition next to your original definition.

Discovering Connections through Writing

1. Saucier suggests that one way to improve talk shows would be to feature issues that would educate teen viewers. How would you improve talk shows? Describe your ideal talk show. Who would be the host? What would the format be? What topics would you raise?

2. Should the content of television talk shows be regulated? Why or why not? Help a reader understand your opinion by providing specific information to support your reasons.

3. What type of television program do you enjoy watching? Why do you like this type of program? Be sure to include enough specific details and examples in your writing to help readers understand your reasons.

What the Halloween Man Brought

Susan Messer

Susan Messer's selection is part of a longer piece exploring the nature of charitable giving. Her writing first appeared in the Chicago Reader, *a weekly newspaper. An important aspect of any giving, writes Messer, "is [to recognize] the humanity of the person who is asking." As you read, try to discover your own feelings about giving to others.*

It's Halloween, a balmy, magical night for children. My husband took our daughter out trick or treating. And I'm home alone—a nice two story stucco house in an old tree-lined suburb, right on the edge of Chicago's troubled west side.

I started the evening with four big bags of candy, but with about half an hour of official trick-or-treat time left, I'm down to my last few Tootsie Rolls. I switch to spare change—nickels, pennies, a few dimes I find lying around. I've got them in a ceramic bowl near the door.

Whenever the bell rings, I peek out first, then open the door. I pick up a few coins, drop them in the waiting bags. The kids look in, try to see what landed there. But each bag has so much candy, and I do the drop fast, so they can't see the thin disks as they slip into the cracks and crevices of all that loot. I hear one little boy say, "Hey, that lady's giving out quarters." I wonder, Doesn't he know what a quarter looks like?

I'm not enjoying myself. I recognize few kids from the neighborhood, can't tell what any of the costumes are, and I hate to guess, since I'm usually wrong. Also, vans park on my street and unload bunches of kids. Some don't have costumes at all, just a mask, or a smudge of makeup on their little faces. They carry huge dingy pillowcases of candy.

Some seem awfully big for trick or treating, and they arrive on my porch in large groups, nine, ten at a time, faces shadowed by their jacket hoods, real-life wraiths of the night who make me feel afraid to open my door. I don't open my door to strangers on any other night, and I start to wonder why I do on Halloween.

The bell rings again. I look out. It's a man. No kids. I wonder why he's there, whether I should open the door, but the spirit of Halloween presses me on.

"I don't mean any disrespect, ma'am," he says. He holds a mask in one hand, as some kind of evidence, a credential. He stretches the other hand toward me, empty, palm up, making a soft brown bowl.

"I heard you were giving out quarters," he says. We both look at my bowl. "My wife and I, we wanted to take the children out for hot dogs after trick or treating."

The bright ceiling light in my front hall shines like a spotlight on my six pennies and two nickels. I slide them around with the tip of my finger. I want this man to go away. I tip the bowl toward him, so he can see its contents.

The simple Halloween script no longer applies, and I'm trapped in a blur of logistics, mathematics, all flowing from mistrust. If I want to give him money, should I close the door while I get my purse? It's in the other room, and I don't want to walk away, leave the door open to him. But I don't want to open my wallet in front of him either. And if I do get my purse—door open or closed—how much do I give him? How much are hot dogs? How many kids?

"Sorry," I say to him, "that's not what Halloween's about. It's for the children, a few coins, a few pieces of candy." I shut the door, hands trembling, real-life haunted.

* * *

It's a few weeks after Halloween. I've been brooding about the man at the door. I tell my Halloween story to a friend named Bruce, and he responds with his own story—about a guy who came to his church, said he was in need, would pay them back if they helped him out. In the end, the stranger didn't do what he'd promised, and it left my friend with a sour, distrustful feeling about giving to strangers.

Another friend, Nancy, listens to the story, shakes her head, and says, "When someone asks me for money, I just send them to the food pantry, or tell them about the homeless shelter." She's fed up with being asked, prefers to maintain distance between herself and the needy.

When I tell a third friend, Deborah, she says, "I have a hard time saying no to people who ask for money."

Because I feel stingy by comparison, I don't pursue the subject. Still, I wonder about the logistics of this—though again, it feels like stingy thinking. Does she carry a few dollars in a coat pocket so she's ready to pull it out when asked? Does she open her wallet, sort through what's there, select the amount she wants to give?

She's kind to me, I feel, because she says, "Not everyone sees it the way I do. Tom and his wife don't give money to people who ask on the street because it might be for drugs. They'll give food, or help in some other way, but not money." But this doesn't make me feel any less stingy because I hadn't even thought of offering some alternative to money. I wonder how it's happened that I don't have a policy on giving to strangers.

Exploring the Reading through Discussion

1. As Halloween evening goes on, the author tells readers, "I'm not enjoying myself." What are the reasons?

2. In two sections of the essay, Susan Messer writes about the "logistics" of giving. Find the references in the essay and explain what this means.

3. Why doesn't she give the man at the door any money? Consider both what she says and what she thinks.

4. Do you agree with her decision? Why or why not?

5. What do you think the title of this essay means? What did the Halloween man bring?

Developing Vocabulary

List any words in this selection that are new to you. Write your understanding of each word from the context. Then look up each word in the dictionary, and write the definition that you think best fits the meaning in this writing.

Discovering Connections through Writing

1. Do you have a "policy on giving to strangers," as some of Messer's friends do? Do you think differently about giving to charities than giving to individuals? Explain your policy and the reasons you have it.

2. Tell the story of a memorable Halloween of your own experience. You can write about a childhood experience or a more recent adult occasion.

3. Do you think that there should be more government aid or more private fund-raising and giving to help support citizens in need?

Appendix
Tips for ESL Writers

When you write in English, you must consider many possible problems. For example, if you write a sentence with an unusual word order you will confuse your readers, so keep in mind the ways your language and English differ in sentence structure and word order. You must also learn the rules of English grammar so that you communicate clearly. Learning correct capitalization, articles, spelling, and punctuation can be confusing. However, correct, standard English is more easily understood. Most important of all, you must think about the logic of paragraphs and essays written in English, which might be very different from the logical forms of composition in your language group and culture. Sometimes even the logic of an argument will be different. If your goal is communication, you must learn to use the patterns that English speakers use.

Sentence Basics

- Make sure each sentence has a subject and a verb. If a group of words does not have both, it does not express a complete idea. *See Chapter 6, "Subjects and Verbs," Chapter 7, "Sentence Fragments," and Chapter 11, "Maintaining Subject–Verb Agreement."*

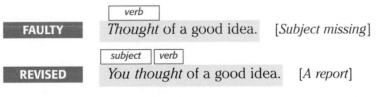

FAULTY   *Thought* of a good idea.   [*Subject missing*]

REVISED   *You thought* of a good idea.   [*A report*]

In writing, the subject can be an implied *you* only if you are making a command.

EXAMPLE   [*You*] *Think* of a good idea!   [*A command*]

- Make sure that your *is* and *are* verbs are linked to a subject. The words *there* and *here* and words describing a location can sometimes *substitute* in the normal location of a subject at the beginning of a sentence. In such cases, the actual subject is then found after the verb. (Usually, in English, the subject comes before the verb.) *See the section "Working with Forms of* to Be*" on page 595 in Chapter 15,*

"Dealing with Additional Elements of Verb Use," and the section "Correcting Errors in Sentences Beginning with There *and* Here" *on page 432 in Chapter 11, "Maintaining Subject–Verb Agreement."*

FAULTY | verb |
Is a good place to eat near here.   [*Subject missing*]

REVISED | substitute | verb | | subject |
There is a good *place* to eat near here.   [There *signals subject after verb*]

or

| location | verb | | subject |
Near here is a good *place* to eat.

- In English sentences, the word *there* with some form of the verb *to be* is commonly followed by a noun. The noun may have modifiers, or it may be followed by a word or phrases that specify a place.

EXAMPLES | noun | | modifier |
There will be a new *student entering class today.*

| noun | place |
There is *no one here.*

| noun | place |
There are three *cars in the lot.*

- The word *it* with the verb *to be* is frequently followed by an adjective, an adjective with a modifier, an identification, or an expression of time, weather, or distance.

EXAMPLES | adjective |
It is *hot.*

| adjective | modifier |
It is *hot outside and inside.*

| identification |
What is this? It is *my English book.*

| time |
It is *eleven o'clock on Wednesday morning.*

| weather |
It is *cold and rainy.*

| distance |
It is *twenty miles from school to home.*

The word *there* should not be used in these expressions.

FAULTY	There is long. There has been a long time.

REVISED	*It* is long. *It* has been a long time.

Word Order

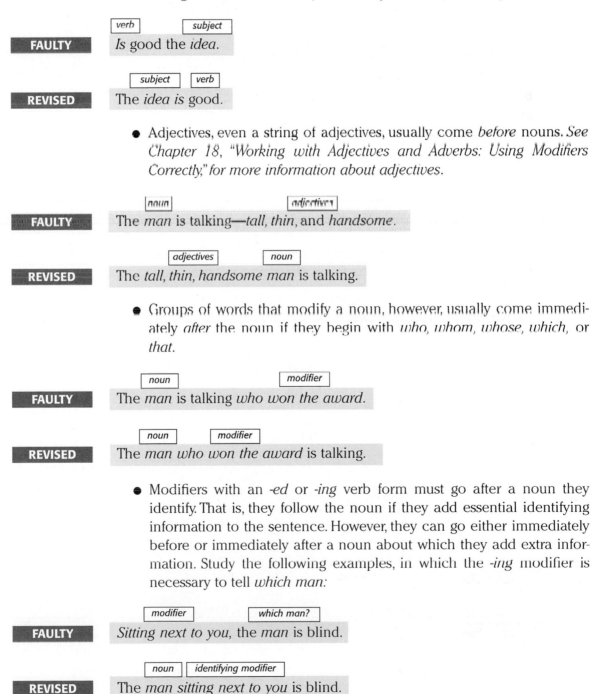

- In English most sentences *put the subject first, followed by the verb.*

	verb — subject
FAULTY	*Is* good the *idea*.

	subject — verb
REVISED	The *idea is* good.

- Adjectives, even a string of adjectives, usually come *before* nouns. *See Chapter 18, "Working with Adjectives and Adverbs: Using Modifiers Correctly," for more information about adjectives.*

	noun — adjective
FAULTY	The *man* is talking—*tall, thin*, and *handsome*.

	adjectives — noun
REVISED	The *tall, thin, handsome man* is talking.

- Groups of words that modify a noun, however, usually come immediately *after* the noun if they begin with *who, whom, whose, which,* or *that.*

	noun — modifier
FAULTY	The *man* is talking *who won the award.*

	noun — modifier
REVISED	The *man who won the award* is talking.

- Modifiers with an *-ed* or *-ing* verb form must go after a noun they identify. That is, they follow the noun if they add essential identifying information to the sentence. However, they can go either immediately before or immediately after a noun about which they add extra information. Study the following examples, in which the *-ing* modifier is necessary to tell *which man:*

	modifier — which man?
FAULTY	*Sitting next to you,* the *man* is blind.

	noun — identifying modifier
REVISED	The *man sitting next to you* is blind.

- Now compare this revised sentence with the example below, in which the modifier adds extra information.

<code>modifier</code>   <code>noun</code>

EXAMPLE *Forgetting his promise, John* is talking instead of listening.

- If the modifier is necessary to identify the noun, you don't use commas to separate it from the noun. If the modifier adds information about the noun, but the sentence makes sense without it, then set the modifier off with commas. *See the section "Comma Function 5" on page 414 in Chapter 21, "Using Commas."*

<code>noun</code>   <code>modifier</code>

EXAMPLE My *friend named Frank* works hard.

The modifier is needed to identify which friend, *my friend Frank,* not *my friend Tom,* so no commas are needed.

<code>noun</code>   <code>modifier</code>

EXAMPLE *Frank, who lives next door,* works hard.

The modifier provides extra information, so it needs commas.

- Adverbs are usually placed *after to be* verbs (is/are/was/were) but *before* other one-word verbs. *See the section "Using the Positive Form of Modifiers" on page 347 in Chapter 18, "Working with Adjectives and Adverbs: Using Modifiers Effectively."*

<code>verb</code> <code>adverb</code>

EXAMPLES They *are often* late.

<code>adverb</code>   <code>verb</code>

Birds *usually arrive* in the spring.

- Adverbs often go *between* verbs that have two parts (verb phrases).

<code>helping verb</code> <code>adverb</code> <code>verb</code>

EXAMPLE They *have often arrived* late.

- Pronouns that rename the subject in the same sentence are unnecessary and confusing—even when a long modifier separates the subject from the verb. The word order makes the idea clear.

<code>subject</code>   <code>modifier</code>   <code>subject</code> <code>verb</code>

FAULTY The *place* where they studied *it was* old.

<code>subject</code>   <code>modifier</code>   <code>verb</code>

REVISED The *place* where they studied *was* old.

Agreement

- Make the *subject and verb agree* in number. Be especially careful about collective nouns, such as *family* and *class,* and words that specify uncountable things, such as *sugar* and *water. See the section "Reviewing the Function and Form of Nouns" on page 305 in Chapter 16, "Working with Nouns," and Chapter 11, "Maintaining Subject–Verb Agreement."*

- You can count *fingers, books,* or *students,* so they are called *count* words. You cannot count *freedom, advice,* or *machinery,* so they are called *noncount.* Noncount words *always* take a *singular verb* and *a singular pronoun reference.*

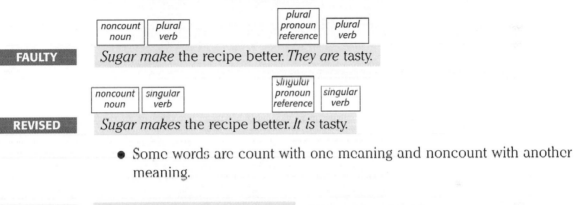

FAULTY   *Sugar make* the recipe better. *They are* tasty.

REVISED   *Sugar makes* the recipe better. *It is* tasty.

- Some words are count with one meaning and noncount with another meaning.

EXAMPLES   Three *chickens are* in the yard.   [*Countable animals*]

Chicken is good with white wine.   [*Noncountable meat*]

Three pieces of *chicken is* enough.   [*Quantity of noncountable meat*]

- As the last example shows, some aspects of noncount words can be measured. You can count the number of *lumps* of sugar, *cups* of milk, *tablespoons* of flour, or *gallons* of water, but you cannot say *ten sugars, three milks, two flours,* and *four waters* as a complete grammatical form. Even though you can number *quantities* like *two pounds, six quarts, three minutes, five dollars,* and *ten gallons,* the *of* phrase with the noncount word indicates a singular subject, which makes the verb singular (*two pounds of* butter is). You must use the *singular verb* with *any* quantity of noncount items. *See the section "Making Nouns Plural" on page 301 in Chapter 16, "Working with Nouns."*

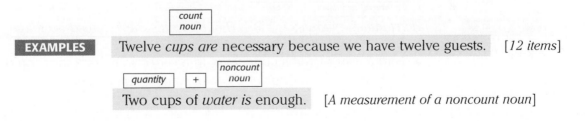

EXAMPLES   Twelve *cups are* necessary because we have twelve guests.   [*12 items*]

Two cups of *water is* enough.   [*A measurement of a noncount noun*]

EXAMPLES

noncount noun

Ten *dollars is* enough.   *[Amount]*

count noun

Ten dollar *bills are* enough.   *[Number]*

noncount noun

My *luggage is* heavy.   *[Amount]*

count noun

My two *bags are* heavy.   *[Number]*

FAULTY

quantity + *noncount noun*

Ten gallons of *gasoline are* all I need.

REVISED

quantity + *noncount noun*

Ten gallons of *gasoline is* all I need.

- Adjectives are *always* singular.

FAULTY

the *talls* men; the *six-year-olds* children

REVISED

the *tall* men; the six-year-*old* children

- Adjectives that end in *-ing* are active, while adjectives that end in *-ed* are passive. *See the section "Using the Passive Voice" on page 268 in Chapter 14, "Using Passive Voice and Progressive Tenses, and Maintaining Consistency in Tenses," and the section "Using -ing Modifiers" on page 363 in Chapter 18, "Working with Adjectives and Adverbs: Using Modifiers Effectively."*

EXAMPLE

I am *boring*.

This adjective is formed from the active verb. It shows the effect that I have on others—I make them feel bored.

EXAMPLE

I am *bored*.

This adjective is derived from the passive verb. It shows the effect something has on me—something makes me feel bored.

- A single phrase or clause subject takes a singular verb.

FAULTY

phrase as subject   *verb*   *clause as subject*   *verb*

Understanding the rules are hard. That they must be followed are clear.

REVISED

phrase as subject   *verb*   *clause as subject*   *verb*

Understanding the rules is hard. That they must be followed is clear.

- *Verb tenses* of verbs connected in a series with commas should agree in their form. *See Chapter 23, "Maintaining Parallelism."*

| FAULTY | The child *was running, jumped,* and *has skipped*.   [*Mixed tense forms*] |

| REVISED | The child *ran, jumped,* and *skipped*.   [*All past tense forms*] |

- Use the present or present perfect tense, not the future tense, in a subordinate clause whose main clause is future tense. *See the section "Maintaining Consistency in Tense" on page 274 in Chapter 14, "Using Passive Voice and Progressive Tenses, and Maintaining Consistency in Tense," for more information on keeping the voice of tense consistent.*

| | subordinate clause   main clause |
| FAULTY | After I will do my homework, I will go out. |

| | subordinate clause   main clause |
| REVISED | After I have done my homework, I will go out. |

Confusing Verb Forms

- Don't omit the *s* in third person singular present tense verb forms. *See the section "Using the Present Tense" on page 238 in Chapter 12, "Forming Basic Tenses for Regular Verbs"*

| FAULTY | He *come* here every day. |

| REVISED | He *comes* here every day. |

- Memorize the irregular verbs. *See Chapter 13, "Using Irregular Verbs Correctly."* Some verb pairs like the following can be confusing, but remembering which takes an object and which does not will help you tell the difference. The verbs *shine/shone, lie, sit,* and *rise* never have an object; the verbs *shine/shined, lay, set,* and *raise* always have an object:

No Object	Object
His shoes shone.	He shined *his shoes*.
She lay in the sun.	She laid *her books* on the floor.
She sat in the chair.	She set *the table* for four.
The sun rises every morning.	They raised *the flag*.

- Use *complete* passive verb forms; combine a form of *to be* with the past participle of another verb. *See the section "Using the Passive Voice" on page 268 in Chapter 14, "Using Passive Voice and Progressive Tenses, and Maintaining Consistency in Tense."*

FAULTY	His work finished.

REVISED	His work *was* finished. *[Add form of* to be*]*

or

He finished his work.   *[Transform to active voice]*

- Use *-'s* to make contractions using *is* and *has,* but shorten *has* only when it is a helping verb. To sound more formal, avoid contractions like *she's.* Write *she is* instead.

FAULTY	She's some money.

REVISED	She has some money.

INFORMAL	She's ready to help.

FORMAL	She is ready to help.

- Verbs describing a completed mental process (*believe, consider, forget, know, remember, think, understand*), a consistent preference (*drink, swim, eat*), a state of being (*am, appear, have, seem, remember, forget, love*), or perceptions (*feel, hear, see, taste*) can *never* be progressive. If the verb refers to an incomplete process, it can be progressive. *See the section "Using Progressive Tenses" on page 271 in Chapter 14, "Using Passive Voice and Progressive Tenses, and Maintaining Consistency in Tense."*

EXAMPLES	I *consider* my choice good. *[An already completed decision]*

I *am considering* going.   *[A decision-making process not yet complete]*

I *think* he should be president.   *[A completed intellectual position]*

I *am thinking* about what to do this summer.   *[An incomplete thought process]*

I *drink* coffee.   *[A consistent preference]*

I *am drinking* coffee.   *[An incomplete action]*

FAULTY   I *am seeing* you. I *am liking* you, but I *am loving* cheeseburgers.

REVISED   I *see* you. I *like* you, but I *love* cheeseburgers.

- *Do* and *make* do *not* mean the same thing in English. *Do* often refers to action that is mechanical or specific. *Make* often refers to action that is creative or general: the teacher *makes* up the exercise (creative), but the student *does* the exercise (mechanical). However, there is no clear rule explaining the difference. You will just have to memorize usage.

Mostly Mechanical or Specific	*Mostly Creative or General*
do the dishes	make the bed
do the homework	make an impression
do the laundry	make progress
do your hair	make up your mind
do (brush) your teeth	make (cook) a meal
do (write) a paper	make (build) a house
do the right thing	make mistakes
do someone a favor	make a speech
do good deeds	make a living
do away with	make arrangements

FAULTY   I have to *make the homework* before I can *do a speech*.

REVISED   I have to *do the homework* before I can *make a speech*.

- *Tell* and *say* do *not* mean the same thing in English:

tell time	say a prayer
tell a story or a joke	say hello
tell me	say that we should go
tell the difference	say, "Let's go!"

FAULTY   say me; tell hello; say a joke

REVISED   tell me; say hello; tell a joke

Articles

Articles (*a*, *an*, and *the*) are very confusing in English, so you must pay special attention to them.

- Use *a* before words that begin with consonant sounds and *an* before words that begin with vowels.
  1. *A* and *an* mean the same as *one* or *each:* I want *an* ice cream cone. *[Just one]*
  2. *A* and *an* go with an unidentified member of a class: *A* small dog came toward her, *a* bone in its mouth. *[Some unknown dog, some unknown bone]*
  3. *A* and *an* go with a representative member of a class: You can tell by the way he talks that he is *a* politician.
  4. *A* and *an* go with a noun that places an idea in a larger class: The car is *a* four-wheeled vehicle.
     See the section "Recognize Cue Words That Identify Number" on page 306 in Chapter 16, "Working with Nouns."

- *The* serves many functions:
  1. *The* modifies known people, objects, or ideas: *the* mother of *the* bride, *the* head of *the* household in which he stayed, *the* Copernican theory
  2. *The* goes with superlatives: *the* best, *the* least
  3. *The* goes with rank: *the* first book, *the* third child with this problem
  4. *The* goes with *of* phrases: the way *of the* world
  5. *The* goes with adjective phrases or clauses that limit or identify the noun: *the* topic being discussed
  6. *The* refers to a class as a whole: *The* giraffe is an African animal.
  7. *The* goes with the names of familiar objects (*the* store) and the names of newspapers (*The Wall Street Journal*), but not with the names of most magazines (*Time*).
  8. *The* goes with the names of historical periods (*the* French Revolution), of legislative acts (*the* Missouri Compromise), political parties (*the* Democratic Party), the branches of government (*the* executive branch), official titles (*the* President), government bodies (*the* Navy), and organizations (*the* Girl Scouts).
  9. *The* goes with rivers (but not lakes), canals, oceans, channels, gulfs, peninsulas, swamps, groups of islands, mountain ranges, hotels, libraries, museums, and geographic regions: *the* Panama Canal, *the* Mississippi River, Lake Superior, *the* Okefenokee Swamp, *the* Hilton, *the* Smithsonian, *the* South.

FAULTY According to *New York Times*, the Lake Victoria is one of most beautiful lakes in world.

REVISED According to *The New York Times*, Lake Victoria is one of *the* most beautiful lakes in *the* world.

Spelling

- Watch for these common spelling errors:

  1. Leaving *h* out of *wh* words: *which*, not *wich*
  2. Adding an *e* to words that start with *s: stupid*, not *estupid*
  3. Confusing words that sound alike in English but have different meanings and different spellings:

his/he's (he is)	which/witch	there/their
whether/weather	here/hear	through/threw
advice/advise (noun/verb)	too/to/two	though/thought

  4. Confusing grammatical functions because of familiar sound combinations: *whose* or *who's (who is)*, not *who his*
  5. Confusing words that sound similar using your native language's pronunciation patterns but have different meanings and different sounds in English:

this (singular)/these (plural)	chair/share
read/lead	boat/vote
heat/hit	

  See Chapter 22, "Mastering Spelling."

Other Common Grammar Problems

Double Negatives

- Never use a double negative; it is not acceptable in English. As in mathematics, two negatives equal a positive. *See the section "Avoiding Double Negatives" on page 361 in Chapter 18, "Working with Adjectives and Adverbs: Using Modifiers Effectively."*

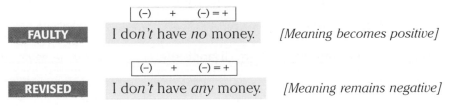

FAULTY I do*n't* have *no* money. *[Meaning becomes positive]*

REVISED I do*n't* have *any* money. *[Meaning remains negative]*

Confusing Words

Some key words are confusing:

- *Too* does not have the same meaning as *very*. *Very* is an intensifier; it emphasizes quantity. *Too* is often negative and critical. It is sometimes attached to a word that goes with an infinitive (*to* + verb) to emphasize negative effects.

EXAMPLES   It is *very* cold, but we can walk to the restaurant.   *[Very = intensely]*

It is *too* cold to walk, so we should take a taxi.   *[Too = negative]*

FAULTY   He is *very* fat to play on the soccer team.

REVISED   He is *too* fat to play on the soccer team.   *[He cannot play soccer because of so much fat.]*

- *Hard* can be an adjective or an adverb, but *hardly* is generally an adverb meaning *barely, almost none,* or *almost not at all.*

EXAMPLES

   adjective   noun
He learned a *hard* lesson.   *[A difficult lesson]*

   verb   adverb
He worked *hard*.   *[With great effort]*

   adverb   verb
He *hardly* worked.   *[Barely, almost not at all]*

   adverb   pronoun
Hardly anyone watches black-and-white television.   *[Almost no one]*

- A *few* (count) and *a little* (noncount) mean *some*, while *few* and *little* mean *almost none*. The difference is between a positive attitude and a negative attitude.

EXAMPLES   I have *a little* money, so I can lend you some.   *[Some, so positive]*

I have *little* money, so I can't lend you any.   *[Almost none, so negative]*

A few students came, so we were pleased.   *[Some, so positive]*

Few students came, so we were disappointed.   *[Almost none, so negative]*

- *Some* and *any* both mean an indefinite amount. However, *some* is used in positive statements while *any* is used in negative statements.

EXAMPLES   I have *some* money.   *[Positive]*

I don't have *any* money.   *[Negative]*

- Usually, *well* is an adverb, whereas *good* is an adjective. However, *well* can sometimes be an adjective referring to health.

| noun | | adjective |

EXAMPLES   The *boy* is *good*.   *[Well-behaved]*

| verb | | adverb |

He doesn't feel *well*.   *[Poor health]*

| noun | | adjective |

The *boy* is *well*.   *[Healthy, not sick]*

See the section "Dealing with Confusing Pairs of Modifiers" on page 358 in Chapter 18, "Working with Adjectives and Adverbs: Using Modifiers Effectively."

Prepositions

Prepositions can be very confusing.

- Use *on* when one thing touches the surface of another and *in* when one thing encloses another: *on* the desk (on top), *in* the desk (inside a drawer). Also, use *on* if you must step up to board (get *on* a motorcycle/bus/train/large ship) but *in* if you must step down (get *in* a small boat/car).

- *Since* goes with a specific initial time (*since* 3 P.M.; *since* July 3); *for* goes with duration, a length or period of time (*for* two hours; *for* ten days).

Punctuation and Capitalization

English rules for punctuation differ greatly from those in other languages.

- All sentences have an ending punctuation mark. Statements end with a period (**.**). Exclamations end with an exclamation mark (**!**). Questions end with a question mark (**?**). Statements, exclamations, and questions end with *only* one mark. Avoid multiple punctuation marks at the end of sentences. *See the section "Using Periods, Question Marks, and Exclamation Points" on page 390 in Chapter 20, "Using Punctuation Properly."*

- Do not use commas to connect complete ideas or statements that can stand alone. Instead, use a period and a capital letter, a semicolon, or a comma and a coordinating conjunction. *See Chapter 10, "Comma Splices and Run-On Sentences."*

FAULTY   We finished class, then we got a pizza, later we went to a movie.
[Comma splice]

REVISED   We finished class. Then we got a pizza. Later we went to a movie.
[Separate sentences]

or

We finished class; then we got a pizza; later we went to a movie.
[Clauses joined with semicolon]

or

We finished class, then got a pizza, and later went to a movie.
[Simple sentence with compound verb]

- Commas go before and after a modifying word, phrase, or clause that adds extra information. This means that the sentence can stand alone without the added information. Modifying words, phrases, or clauses that are necessary for identification take no commas. In other words, if the material is crucial to the meaning of the sentence, then do not use commas. *See the section "Comma Function 5" on page 414 in Chapter 21, "Using Commas."*

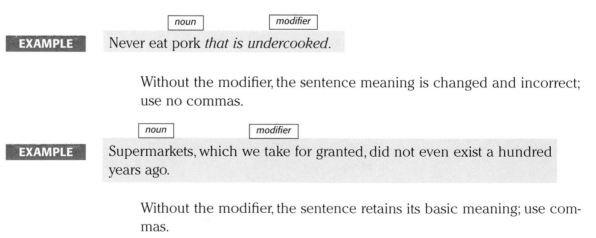

EXAMPLE   Never eat pork *that is undercooked*.

Without the modifier, the sentence meaning is changed and incorrect; use no commas.

EXAMPLE   Supermarkets, which we take for granted, did not even exist a hundred years ago.

Without the modifier, the sentence retains its basic meaning; use commas.

- Semicolons separate independent clauses. They may also be used to separate longer groups of words or lists that already contain commas.

EXAMPLES   Cats are lazy; dogs jump around.

Turn in your uniforms on Friday, May 24; Monday, May 27; or Wednesday, May 29.

- English rules for capitalization differ greatly from those in other languages. *See Chapter 19, "Capitalizing Correctly," for the English rules.*

Writing Paragraphs

Indentation

Don't use a dash (—) to signal the beginning of a new paragraph. Instead, indent the first line of the paragraph to identify your change of subject or focus. *See the section "Defining the Paragraph" on page 35 in Chapter 3, "Composing: Topic Sentences and Supporting Sentences."*

Unity

Every sentence in a paragraph should be connected to the same topic, or main idea. In other words, the material should be unified. *See the section "Coherence" on page 64 in Chapter 4, "Revising: Refining Your Draft," for more on unity.* If you change direction in the middle of the paragraph to talk about another idea, even if it is related, your teachers may call it a *digression.* Digressions are allowed in some languages but *not* in English. One way to avoid digression is to have a plan for organizing your examples. For example, move from most common to least common, or from the familiar to the unfamiliar, or from the least important to the most important.

EXAMPLES   most common traveler's problem in airports

next most common problem

not usual, but still a problem

or

an important study habit for final exams

a more important study habit for final exams

the most important study habit for final exams

Finally, avoid digression by keeping sentences short and tightly connected. Don't try to put too many unrelated ideas in one sentence or paragraph.

> **FAULTY**
>
> The writer warned us about the problem, he said it was very dangerous, he gave us convincing statistics.

[Three separate ideas; comma splice]

> **REVISED**
>
> The writer used convincing statistics to warn about the dangerous problem.

[Ideas are combined and connected]

Clarity

American readers like everything important to be explained; they don't like to guess. Keep your writing clear. Don't just write in generalities. American readers like specific information. Give them facts; give them details; give them examples. Choose the best examples to prove your point.

Keep your writing simple. Don't try to be too formal, but avoid the pronoun *you*. Say *who* you mean: the student, the tourist, the opposition. When you revise your sentences, eliminate extra words and imprecise expressions.

> **FAULTY**
>
> the group of people who lead the university and decide on policy

> **REVISED**
>
> the board of governors

Revise to Correct Errors

Proofread before you turn in an assignment. When you proofread, watch for the common mistakes discussed in this appendix. If possible, have a native speaker in a writing lab look at your assignment before you turn it in. *See Chapters 2 to 4 ("Prewriting," "Composing," "Revising") for guidelines on how to write a composition.*

Credits

Text Credits

Langston Hughes, "The Dream Deferred" ("Harlem") from *The Collected Poems of Langston Hughes* by Langston Hughes, copyright © 1994 by The estate of Langston Hughes. Used by permission of Alfred A. Knopf, a division of Random House, Inc.

Kenneth Woodward and Patrice Johnson, excerpt from "The Advent of Kwanzaa," from *Newsweek*, December 11, 1995 © 1995 Newsweek, Inc. All rights reserved. Reprinted by permission.

Elizabeth Wong, "To Be an All-American Girl." Copyright © 1989 by Elizabeth Wong. Reprinted by permission of Elizabeth Wong.

Michael Dorris, excerpt from "Americans All," *Paper Trail*, 1994, p. 321. Copyright © 1994 by Michael Dorris, HarperCollins Publishers, Inc.

"Saved," from *The Autobiography of Malcolm X* by Malcolm X and Alex Haley, copyright © 1964 by Alex Haley and Malcolm X. Copyright © 1965 by Alex Haley and Betty Shabazz. Used by permission of Random House, Inc.

"Suicide Solutions" by Anna Quindlen, copyright © 1993 by Anna Quindlen, from *Thinking Out Loud* by Anna Quindlen. Used by permission of Random House, Inc.

"Complaining," from *Wouldn't Take Nothing for My Journey* by Maya Angelou, copyright © 1993 by Maya Angelou. Used by permission of Random House, Inc.

Russell Baker, "The Plot Against People," Copyright © 1968 by The New York Times Co. Reprinted with permission.

Sandra Cisneros, excerpt from *The House on Mango Street*. Copyright © 1984 by Sandra Cisneros. Published by Vintage Books, a division of Random House, Inc., and in hardcover by Alfred A. Knopf in 1994. Reprinted by permission of Susan Bergholz Literary Services, New York. All rights reserved.

Jason Shen, "You Can Call Me the Silver-Tongued Frog." From *Newsweek*, July 8, 2002. All rights reserved. Reprinted by permission.

Marta Melendez, "Popularity." Used by permission of the author.

Daniel Hickok, "My Childhood Hobby." Used by permission of the author.

Elsa "Chachi" Maldonado, "Remembering India." Used by permission of the author.

Peter LeComte, "Forget the Past. No One Becomes Successful in the Past." Used by permission of the author.

Svetlana Melamedman, "Russia and the U.S. and Differences in Child Rearing." Used by permission of the author.

Elizabeth Soares, "Volunteering: More Rewarding than Cash." Used by permission of the author.

Joy Saucier, "Talk Show Trash." Used by permission of the author.

Susan Messer, excerpt from "What You Give and What You Get." From *Chicago Reader*, October 15, 1999, copyright © 1999 by Susan Messer. All rights reserved. Reprinted by permission of Susan Messer.

Photo Credits

Page 13 Javier Dauden/CORBIS; **32** Tony Freeman/Photo Edit; **59** Elena Segatini Bloom/CORBIS; **94** Mark C. Burnett/Stock, Boston, LLC; **114** Len Holsborg/Photonica; **116** Bottom Johner/Photonica; **116 Top** Bob Rowan, Progressive Image/CORBIS; **117** Verve Photographics, Inc./Photonica; **121** Jonathan Nourok /Photo Edit; **141** L. Migdale/Stock, Boston, LLC; **160** Felicia Martinez/Photo Edit; **177** Mary Kate Denny/Photo Edit; **192** Courtesy, Fair Street Pictures; **210** Robert Farber/CORBIS; **211** Bottom Jon Feingersh/CORBIS; **211** Top Randi Aglin/Syracuse Newspapers/The Image Works; **215** Ariel Skelley/CORBIS; **238** David Madison/Stone/Getty Images; **256** Elyse Lewin/The Image Bank/Getty Images; **268** Andy Johnstone/Panos Pictures; **284** Rhoda Sidney/The Image Works; **296 Bottom** Gary Conner/Photo Edit; **296 Top** Bob Daemmrich/Stock, Boston, LLC; **297** Fujiwara Ko/Photonica; **301** Simon Watson/The Imagebank Films/Getty Images; **315** Charly Franklin/Taxi/Getty Images; **347** Syracuse Newspapers/John Berry/The Image Works; **374 Bottom** Greg Ceo/Getty Images; **374 Top** Justin Hutchinson/Photonica; **375** Michael Newman/Photo Edit; **379** David Weintraub/Stock, Boston, LLC; **390** Sevans/AP/Wide World Photos; **406** Claudia Kunin/CORBIS; **427** Joe Sohm/The Image Works; **454** Reuters NewMedia Inc./CORBIS; **470** TinRoof/Photonica; **471 Bottom** Mark Adams/Taxi/Getty Images; **471 Top** Richard Cummins/CORBIS; **Parts 1–6** © 2003 Lazslo Kubinyi c/o theispot.com (detail).

Index